INTERNATIONAL LAW AND THE EUROPEAN UNION

The European Union plays a significant role in international affairs. *International Law and the European Union* examines the impact this has had on public international law by integrating perspectives from both EU law and international law. Its analysis focuses on fields of public international law where the EU has had an influence, including customary international law, the law of treaties, international organizations, international dispute settlement, and international responsibility. *International Law and the European Union* shows how the EU has had a subtle but significant impact on the development of international law and how the international legal order has developed and adjusted to accommodate the EU as a distinct legal actor. In doing so, it contributes to our understanding of how international law addresses legal subjects other than States.

Jed Odermatt is a Lecturer at City Law School, City, University of London.

International Law and the European Union

JED ODERMATT

City, University of London

CAMBRIDGE
UNIVERSITY PRESS

CAMBRIDGE
UNIVERSITY PRESS

University Printing House, Cambridge CB2 8BS, United Kingdom

One Liberty Plaza, 20th Floor, New York, NY 10006, USA

477 Williamstown Road, Port Melbourne, VIC 3207, Australia

314-321, 3rd Floor, Plot 3, Splendor Forum, Jasola District Centre, New Delhi - 110025, India

103 Penang Road, #05-06/07, Visioncrest Commercial, Singapore 238467

Cambridge University Press is part of the University of Cambridge.

It furthers the University's mission by disseminating knowledge in the pursuit of education, learning and research at the highest international levels of excellence.

www.cambridge.org
Information on this title: www.cambridge.org/9781108816052
DOI: 10.1017/9781108895705

First published 2021
First paperback edition 2022

A catalogue record for this publication is available from the British Library

ISBN 978-1-108-84199-3 Hardback
ISBN 978-1-108-81605-2 Paperback

Cambridge University Press has no responsibility for the persistence or accuracy of URLs for external or third-party internet websites referred to in this publication, and does not guarantee that any content on such websites is, or will remain, accurate or appropriate.

For mum and dad

Contents

List of Tables   *page* viii

    Introduction   1

1   The European Union in International Law   9

2   Customary International Law   33

3   The Law of Treaties   59

4   International Organizations   131

5   International Dispute Settlement   169

6   International Responsibility   196

    Concluding Remarks   246

Index   254

Tables

1.1   Models of the European Union in International Law   *page* 21

Introduction

The European Communities were first established and built using public
international law instruments. Since its establishment, there has been debate
about whether, and to which extent, the Community (now Union) transformed into something else – from an organization established under public
international law into a new legal order that has since escaped these international law origins. Early debates about the EU and international law dealt
with this question of whether the Union can still be understood as a 'creature
of international law'. Later debates focused on the question of how international law applies and is given effect within the EU legal order.[1] These
debates were less concerned with the international law origins of the EU, but
with whether the EU legal order was 'open' or friendly towards international
law.[2] This was influenced by the case law of the European Court of Justice, in
which the Union gave internal effect to obligations arising from international
law. Klabbers' study on *The European Union in International Law*, for
example, looks inwards to 'investigate how the European Union treats international law'.[3] Wouters et al., describe the Europeanization of international

---

[1]   See K. Lenaerts & E. De Smijter, 'The European Union as an Actor under International Law'
      (1999) 19 *Yearbook of European Law* 95–138.
[2]   See, e.g., M. Mendez, 'The Legal Effect of Community Agreements: Maximalist Treaty
      Enforcement and Judicial Avoidance Techniques' (2010) 21 *European Journal of International
      Law* 83, 88; P.-J. Kuijper, 'Customary International Law, Decisions of International
      Organisations and Other Techniques for Ensuring Respect for International Legal Rules in
      European Community Law' in J. Wouters, A. Nollkaemper & E. de Wet (eds), *The
      Europeanisation of International Law: The Status of International Law in the EU and its
      Member States* (The Hague: TMC Asser Press, 2008) 29; J. Klabbers, 'Völkerrechtsfreundlich?
      International Law and the Union Legal Order' in P. Koutrakos (ed), *European Foreign Policy:
      Legal and Political Aspects* (Cheltenham: Edward Elgar, 2011) 95.
[3]   J. Klabbers, *The European Union in International Law* (Paris: Pedone, 2012).

law as a process 'through which an ever increasing body of international law becomes binding on the EU and through which distinct qualities and features are given to such international law within the EU'.[4] A third phase of scholarship focused on the *interaction* between the EU and international law as two separate legal orders.[5] Inspired by high profile cases such as *Kadi*[6] this scholarship often examines 'clashes' between legal orders, and questions the narrative of the EU being friendly towards international law. More recently, there has been focus on clashes in other fields, such as between the EU courts and international investment tribunals. Each of these phases has coincided with the development of the EU as an international actor. In these debates, international law has moved from being a tool that was used to construct the EU legal order, to being considered a threat to the integrity and autonomy of that legal order.

The aim of this book is to examine whether and to what extent international law and the international legal order have had to change and adapt to accommodate the EU as a distinctive actor. The EU either demands, or the international legal order offers, a particular kind of accommodation for the EU's distinctive composite character. It examines various ways in which the EU engages with international law, focusing on the ways in which the international legal order has adapted to accommodate the unique character and practice of the EU. It builds on the work of scholars such as Hoffmeister[7] and Ličková[8], which has integrated insights from public international law and EU law to understand this complex dynamic. It takes as a starting point the fact that the EU is different from a state, being a composite legal entity composed of many states, all of which remain fully sovereign subjects of international law. This distinctiveness does not require international law to develop specialized rules, however, since the international legal order has relatively flexible ways of adapting to the EU's character and structure. It shows how the Union's contribution to public international law has not always

---

[4]   J. Wouters, A. Nollkaemper & E. d Wet, 'Introduction' in J. Wouters, A. Nollkaemper & E. de Wet (eds), *The Europeanization of International Law: The Status of International Law in the EU and its Member States* (The Hague: TMC Asser Press, 2008) 3.

[5]   I. Govaere & S. Garben (eds), *The Interface between EU and International Law* (Oxford: Hart, 2019) 2: 'Currently, the key question has rather become how the EU legal order should integrate and interact with international law . . . '

[6]   Judgment in *Kadi and Al Barakaat International Foundation* v. *Council and Commission*, Joined Cases C-402/05 P & C-415/05 P, EU:C:2008:461.

[7]   F. Hoffmeister, 'The Contribution of EU Practice to International Law' in M. Cremona (ed), *Developments in EU External Relations Law* (Oxford: Oxford University Press, 2008) 38.

[8]   M. Ličková, 'European Exceptionalism in International Law' (2008) 19 *European Journal of International Law* 463.

been a positive development, acting in a self-interested fashion, asserting the distinctiveness, autonomy and even primacy of EU law.

The EU now plays a significant role in international affairs. This phenomenon of the EU as a 'global actor' has been addressed in legal literature, particularly in the field of EU external relations law. International law scholarship has paid less attention to this phenomenon, and to the consequences this might have on international law generally.[9] Yet in various debates about public international law issues, there has been discussion about the impact and relevance of the EU and its practice. In debates about the formation and identification of customary international law; the law of treaties; in international organizations and institutions; before international dispute settlement bodies; and discussions on the responsibility of international organizations; international law has responded to claims based on the distinctiveness of the EU and its legal order.

These debates should not only be of interest to EU law experts, but also to those interested in international law. Examining the EU's practice in the international legal order not only tells us something about the EU, but also about international law. As Cannizzaro argues ' . . . to give a positive definition of the legal nature of the EU, and to explain the uniqueness of its features in the framework of the existing conceptual categories of international law, constitute formidable challenges for legal research and could ultimately lead to a renewal of our traditional conceptions of statehood and sovereignty'.[10] Studying the EU and how it is dealt with in international law tells us something about how *international law* deals with legal subjects other than states. Is international law rigidly 'state-centric' or is it sufficiently flexible to take into account organizations such as the EU acting on the international plane? Has international law adapted to the role of the EU as an international actor?

The book does not examine the EU's action in a particular policy field. One could focus on the EU's impact on the development of international human rights law, trade and investment law, or environmental law. The aim, however, is not to examine the EU's contribution to a particular area of law, but in a more fundamental way to certain international law principles. Chapter 2 introduces the idea that EU practice can contribute to the formation of

---

[9] This issue was addressed by Klabbers, who argues 'the more the EU matures, the more it acts as a global power, the more fundamental issues concerning its position in international law will be raised'. J. Klabbers, 'The EU and International Law', IVR Encyclopaedia of Jurisprudence, Legal Theory and Philosophy of Law, http://ivr-enc.info/index.php?title=The_EU_and_International_Law.

[10] E. Cannizzaro (ed), *The European Union as an Actor in International Relations* (The Hague: Kluwer Law International, 2002) xiii.

customary international law. Later chapters then provide examples of EU
practice in the fields of the law of treaties, international organizations, international dispute settlement and international responsibility. The book focuses
mainly on the EU's relationships with third states and international organizations, where the EU's position international law comes into focus. This
includes instances where the EU enters into treaties or joins international
organizations in its own right, when it participates in international dispute
settlement, or when issues arise regarding its international responsibility.
Much of the book is focused on the EU's action in the former so-called first
pillar and does not focus on the international law issues related to the EU's
Common Foreign and Security Policy. It does not give an exhaustive picture
of the EU's influence on the international legal order. The EU has also had an
impact, for instance, on the development of diplomatic and consular law.[11]
Rather, the book has been structured in a way to view the EU's impact on some
of the more fundamental concepts of public international law.

INFLUENCE AND SHAPING

Article 3(5) of the Treaty on European Union (TEU) sets out that the EU shall
contribute to the 'development of international law'.[12] There has been discussion about how the EU 'observes' international law,[13] for instance, when it
implements international legal norms within the EU legal order. What does it
mean for the EU to contribute to the development of international law? It
implies that the EU is more than a passive recipient of international norms,
but is also as an actor that can contribute to the shaping of developments.
Legal literature examining the EU's influence on international law almost

---

[11]   See J. Wouters & S. Duquet, 'The EU and International Diplomatic Law: New Horizons?'
       (2012) 7 *The Hague Journal of Diplomacy* 31; J. Wouters & S. Duquet, 'Unus inter plures? The
       EEAS, the Vienna Convention and International Diplomatic Practice' in D. Spence &
       J. Bátora (eds), *The European External Action Service: European Diplomacy Post-
       Westphalia*, (London: Palgrave Macmillan, 2015) 159–174.
[12]   Treaty on European Union (as amended by the Treaty of Lisbon) (13 December 2007) Official
       Journal C 326 (26 October 2012), entered into force 1 December 2009.
[13]   The CJEU has interpreted this to mean that 'when [the Union] adopts an act, it is bound to
       observe international law in its entirety, including customary international law, which is
       binding upon the institutions of the European Union'. Judgment in *Air Transport
       Association of America and Others v. Secretary of State for Energy and Climate Change*,
       C-366/10, EU:C:2011:864, para. 101. See P.-J. Kuijper, '"It Shall Contribute to ... the Strict
       Observance and Development of International Law" The Role of the Court of Justice' in
       A. Rosas, E. Levits & Y. Bot (eds), *The Court of Justice and the Construction of Europe:
       Analyses and Perspectives on Sixty Years of Case-law* (The Hague: TMC Asser Press, 2013)
       589–612.

entirely presents a positive story.[14] For instance, Hoffmeister describes the number of ways in which the EU 'contributes' to international law, presenting the EU's promotion of the Kyoto Protocol or the International Criminal Court as examples of such practice.[15] There is no doubt that the EU has influenced international law in certain fields of law, such as the law of the sea.[16] In these areas, the EU seeks to influence international developments so that international law aligns with its own policies, values and interests. The EU seeks to influence developments in global trade governance, data protection, environmental policy, financial governance or human rights in ways that align with its objectives. It is this type of 'shaping' of international law that has been discussed in the legal literature.[17] Kochenov and Amtenbrink identified how the EU 'co-shapes' international law through the EU's mere existence, meaning that simply by existing as a form of international cooperation between states, the EU stimulates and encourages similar steps by other regional bodies and international organizations.[18] There has been less focus, however, on how the EU contributes, not only to the development of particular rules or policies,

---

[14] See C. Timmermans, 'The EU and Public International Law' (1999) 4 *European Foreign Affairs Review* 181, 193: 'it could be argued – not over-optimistically – that the European Community more generally exercises a positive influence on the development and strengthening of international law'. J. A. Frowein, 'The Contribution of the European Union to Public International Law' in A. Von Bogdandy, P. C. Mavroidis, & Y. Mény (eds), *European Integration and International Co-Ordination: Studies in Transnational Economic Law in Honour of Claus-Dieter Ehlermann* (The Hague: Kluwer Law International, 2002) 171–179; D. Kochenov & F. Amtenbrink (eds), *The European Union's Shaping of the International Legal Order* (Cambridge: Cambridge University Press, 2014).

[15] F. Hoffmeister, 'The Contribution of EU Practice under International Law' in M. Cremona (ed), *Developments in EU External Relations Law* (Oxford: Oxford University Press, 2008) 37.

[16] See R. R. Churchill, 'The European Union as an Actor in the Law of the Sea, with Particular Reference to the Arctic' (2018) 33 *International Journal of Marine and Coastal Law* 290; E. Paasivirta, 'Four Contributions of the European Union to the Law of the Sea' in J. Czuczai & F. Naert (eds), *The EU as a Global Actor – Bridging Legal Theory and Practice. Liber Amicorum in Honour of Ricardo Gosalbo Bono* (Leiden Brill, 2016); S. Boelaert-Suominen, 'The European Community, the European Court of Justice and the Law of the Sea' (2008) 23 *International Journal of Marine and Coastal Law* 643.

[17] K. S. Ziegler, 'International Law and EU Law: Between Asymmetric Constitutionalization and Fragmentation' in A. Orakhelashvili (ed), *Research Handbook on the Theory of International Law* (Cheltenham: Edward Elgar, 2011) 268, 310. 'The large topic of Europeanisation of international law or the impact of EU law on international law merits a survey on its own . . . . It has several dimensions: export of European rules, enforcement of international norms through the EU, and influence over the enforcement and creation of international law more generally as an actor on the international plane'.

[18] The EU provides 'a model way of thinking about an alternative approach to the prevalent practice of framing international relations'. D. Kochenov & F. Amtenbrink, 'Introduction' in D. Kochenov & F. Amtenbrink (eds), *The European Union's Shaping of the International Legal Order* (Cambridge: Cambridge University Press, 2014) 2.

but also in a more fundamental way to the international legal order. For example, the phenomenon of 'European exceptionalism', which refers to when 'the EU members ask for and receive a growing number of EU-friendly exceptions from their international partners',[19] may have a negative effect on international law. The aim is to understand some of the more subtle and indirect ways that international law has been influenced by the Union and its practice.

Indirect shaping occurs when the international legal order adapts rules to accommodate the EU acting on the international stage. This is more subtle, but it is one that is beginning to be noticed by international lawyers.[20] The two modes are of course closely linked. In order for the EU to have an impact on the international legal order (active shaping) it finds itself needing to play a greater role as an international actor in its own right. This includes negotiating and entering into international agreements, joining and partici-pating in international organizations and treaty bodies, commenting on inter-national legal developments at the International Law Commission and Sixth Committee, participating in international dispute settlement mechanisms and so on. As the EU seeks to become a more active international actor, this in turn has an impact on the rules of public international law, which must react to the EU's greater international role (indirect shaping). The following chapters focus on different areas of EU interaction with the international legal order, focusing on customary international law, the law of treaties, inter-national organizations, international dispute settlement and international responsibility. In doing so, the study broadens the range of sources in its analysis. It not only examines the provisions of the EU Treaties and judgments of the EU Court of Justice, but also analyses these instances where the EU is dealt with 'externally'. The book is structured in a way that illustrates these interactions in different fields of public international law.

OUTLINE AND STRUCTURE

Chapter 1 analyses how the EU has been conceptualized in international law and EU law literature and practice. It shows how there are diverging views

---

[19] Ličková (n8) 465.

[20] M. Fitzmaurice & O. Elias, *Contemporary Issues in the Law of Treaties* (Utrecht: Eleven International Publishing, 2005) 107: 'The EU may present itself as a legal or a political entity. In both these forms, it may exert a direct or an indirect influence on the treaty-making process. For example, as a legal entity, the EU is a party . . . to international agreements such as those on fisheries or on environmental protection. The EU's dual character presents considerable difficulties in comprehending the legal aspects of its nature and activities'.

about the very nature of the EU and its legal order. The 'EU law view' is influenced by the Union's self-perception as a new legal order. The 'international law view', on the other hand, tends to view the EU as a type of international organization, albeit with certain unique features. The EU law view is often concerned with the autonomy of the EU legal order vis-à-vis international law, and tends to require rules to be adapted or developed to take into account the unique nature of the EU and its legal order. The international law view, on the other hand, tends to downplay these unique features, or argues that they are not legally relevant when analysing how international law applies to the Union. The international law view tends to be more concerned with the unity of the international legal order. These conceptualizations are not only found in legal literature, however. As discussed in the following chapters, we see how these various conceptualizations shape legal discussions and debates in various international law forums, such as within international organizations or in international dispute settlement bodies.

Chapter 2 focuses on customary international law, and the extent to which the EU might be capable of contributing to relevant practice in its own right. It does not focus on how customary international law is given effect internally for the EU. Rather, it argues that the EU's action on the plane of international law can, in certain circumstances, contribute to the formation and identification of customary international law. The central argument is that 'EU practice' could contribute to the formation of rules that apply in the relations between the EU and third states and organizations.

Chapter 3 turns to another key source of public international law: treaties. The EU has entered into hundreds of treaties in its own right and alongside its Member States, not only in the field of trade, but also in a wide range of new fields, including human rights and public health. The chapter discusses how the EU's well-developed treaty practice has contributed to the development of the law of treaties. It analyses the practice of 'EU-specific' clauses being used in agreements to which the EU is a party, and the effect of EU practice in relation to the conclusion of international agreements. Over time, this treaty practice has also contributed to rules regarding the conclusion of treaties by composite legal subjects like the EU.

Another way the EU engages with international law is through its role in international organizations. While the EU has been accepted as a treaty actor in many fields, the EU still faces legal and political hurdles when it seeks to join or upgrade its position within international institutions. This chapter challenges the claim that this is due to the state-centric nature of international law and international institutions. It argues that the challenges facing the EU when seeking to join or upgrade its status in international organizations stem mainly from political resistance, both in international organizations and from within the EU (institutions and Member States). The chapter investigates the way in which international organizations and international bodies have had to adapt to the membership or participation of the EU, thereby influencing international institutional law.

In recent years, the EU and its Member States have appeared before international dispute settlement bodies. The EU has also promoted the inclusion of dispute settlement clauses in international agreements. However, the EU and its Court of Justice have also emphasized the importance of safeguarding the autonomy of the EU and its legal order. This has meant that the EU Court of Justice has shown resistance to international dispute settlement bodies. Moreover, in some international dispute settlement bodies, especially investment tribunals, arguments based on the primacy of EU law have often been disregarded. The chapter shows the influence of the EU on the design and functioning of dispute settlement bodies.

Chapter 6 turns to the question of the international responsibility of the EU and its Member States. It discusses how the field of international responsibility has been influenced by arguments based on the unique nature of the EU. In this regard, it focuses on the International Law Commission's (ILC) project on developing Articles on the Responsibility of International Organizations. During this project, the ILC examined the EU practice, and the European Commission argued in favour of developing specialized rules to account for the unique nature of the Union and its system. This is an example of how the ILC sought to balance two often competing objectives: it sought to develop rules of a general character, that can apply to the broad range of international organizations that exist, but at the same time sought to recognize the special character of certain types of organizations, including the Union. The debates on this subject that played out in the ILC and in the academic community also reflect the deeper disagreements about the nature of the EU and its place in the international legal order.

1

The European Union in International Law

1.1 INTRODUCTION

How is the European Union (EU) understood from the perspective of international law? Much of the discussion about the EU in international law scholarship has dealt with questions such as whether the EU can still be considered a 'creature of international law',[1] and whether EU law should be considered international law.[2] The question addressed here is different. It focuses on how the EU fits within the wider system of international law. The way that the EU is perceived and dealt with from the perspective of international law is legally relevant when the EU acts on the plane of international law. The issues addressed in the following chapters regarding the EU's international responsibility, the application of the law of treaties, and the EU's reception in international organizations all touch upon this deeper question about how the EU fits within a state-centric international legal order.

This chapter first shows the different ways in which the EU is perceived in legal scholarship. It illustrates how there are diverging views about how to understand the EU and its place in the international legal order. It explores some of the reasons that these diverging views emerged, including academic and professional specialization, the state-centric nature of public international

[1] T. Schilling, 'The Autonomy of the Community Legal Order: An Analysis of Possible Foundations' (1996) 37 *Harvard International Law Journal* 389, 403–404: 'At least at its inception, the European Community was clearly a creature of international law. As there are no indications that a revolution in its legal sense has subsequently occurred ... the European Treaties are still creatures of international law'.

[2] See D. Wyatt, 'New Legal Order, or Old?' (1982) 7 *European Law Review* 147; B. de Witte, 'Sources and the Subjects of International Law: The European Union's Semi-Autonomous System of Sources' in S. Besson & J. d'Aspremont (eds), *The Oxford Handbook on the Sources of International Law* (Oxford: Oxford University Press, 2017) 769; O. Spiermann, 'The Other Side of the Story: An Unpopular Essay on the Making of the European Community Legal Order' (1999) 10 *European Journal of International Law* 763, 770.

law, and the underlying interests that lie beneath each of these emerging conceptions. The chapter also addresses some of the ways that EU and international law scholars have sought to address these diverging views. Much of the focus has been on the issue of normative conflict between these legal orders. The focus on conflict, however, obscures the many other ways in which the EU interacts with the international legal order.

1.2 THE INTERNAL VIEW: AN EU LAW PERSPECTIVE

The EU has developed its own self-understanding about the type of entity it is, and its relationship with international law. This internal or 'EU law view' tends to present the EU as a unique, or sui generis, international actor. This view tends to be accepted, not only by EU judges and officials but also within the scholarly community working on EU law. This view accepts the EU's self-perception as a 'new legal order', one that is now analytically distinct from international law. Such 'self-perception' was developed largely by the Court of Justice of the European Union (CJEU), which in *van Gend en Loos* held that Treaty establishing the European Economic Community was 'more than an agreement which merely creates mutual obligations between the contracting states'.[3] The CJEU continues to employ the logic of the 'new legal order' in its legal reasoning.[4]

The new legal order narrative was one of the foundational myths used to construct the elements of the EU legal order.[5] Like national myths, it is immaterial whether the 'new legal order' story is technically or historically correct – rather, the account provides a useful symbolic narrative of the polity's

---

[3] Judgment of 5 February 1963, *van Gend & Loos*, 26/62, EU:C:1963:1, 12.

[4] *Opinion 2/13*, 18 December 2014, EU:C:2014:2454, para. 157. Judgment in *Commission v. Council*, 28 April 2015, Case C-28/12, EU:C:2015:282, para. 39. T. Isikiel, 'European Exceptionalism and the EU's Accession to the ECHR' (2016) 27 *European Journal of International Law* 565, 566.

[5] '[I]l n'est nul besoin de se raccrocher au mythe de la rupture totale du droit communautaire par rapport au droit international général pour rendre compte de sa spécificité, qui est réelle et profonde. En réalité, l'ordre juridique communautaire, ancré dans le droit international, y trouve l'essentiel de sa force et de ses caractéristiques.' A. Pellet, 'Les fondements juridiques internationaux du droit communautaire' (1997) 5(2) *Collected Courses of the Academy of European Law* 268. '[O]ne of the greatest received truisms, or myths, of the European Union legal order is its alleged rupture with, or mutation from, public international law and its transformation into a constitutional legal order'. J. H. H. Weiler & U. R. Haltern, 'The Autonomy of the Community Legal Order – Through the Looking Glass' (1996) 37 *Harvard International Law Journal* 411, 420. See A. Cohen & A. Vauchez, 'The Social Construction of Law: The European Court of Justice and Its Legal Revolution Revisited' (2011) 7 *Annual Review of Law & Social Science* 417, 426.

construction and self-identity. The CJEU continued to put in place the cornerstones of EU law, including the notions of direct effect and primacy, in part, by building upon the new legal order narrative, which tends to set EU law apart from 'ordinary' international law.[6] The Court could have conceivably derived EU law principles such as direct effect and primacy by referring to existing public international law principles, such as customary rules of treaty interpretation.[7] Concepts such as supremacy and primacy predate the Union and its Court, and have been described as an 'appropriate synonym of *pacta sunt servanda*',[8] a fundamental principle of the law of treaties.[9] The EU is distinct from other polities, not because of these distinct features, but the *degree* to which the EU possesses and exercises them.[10] The

---

[6]   As Lowe points out, the CJEU 'imagined into existence an entire new, legal order, hammering into place the other great beams of that legal order, such as the supremacy of Community law … ' V. Lowe, 'The Law of Treaties; or Should this Book Exist?' in C. J. Tams, A. Tzanakopoulos & A. Zimmermann (eds), *Research Handbook on the Law of Treaties* (Cheltenham: Edward Elgar, 2014) 3, 6.

[7]   E. Denza, 'The Relationship between International Law and National Law' in M. D. Evans (ed), *International Law*, 4th edn (Oxford: Oxford University Press, 2014) 412, 416: 'This formulation of the supremacy of Community law – not self-evident on the face of the European Community Treaties – is among the features distinguishing European Community law from international law'. See B. de Witte, 'Retour à "Costa" La primauté du droit communautaire à la lumière du droit international' (1984) 20 *Revue trimestrielle de droit européen* 425.

[8]   O. Spiermann, 'The Other Side of the Story: An Unpopular Essay on the Making of the European Community Legal Order' (1999) 10 *European Journal of International Law* 766, 785. Spiermann argues that 'compared to other parts of the international law of cooperation, there is nothing new about direct effect and nothing innovative about precedence', 787.

[9]   Denza (n7) 428. Denza points out that 'Contrary to what is sometimes suggested, the ECJ did not invent the doctrine of direct effect, which can be traced back to rulings of the Permanent Court of International Justice and to cases in European jurisdictions, but it did lay down criteria to be uniformly applied throughout the European Community. It is this uniformity which is one of the most striking features distinguishing European Community from public international law'. De Baere and Roes argue that they are founded on the duty of loyalty. G. De Baere & T. Roes, 'EU Loyalty as Good Faith' (2015) 64 *International and Comparative Law Quarterly* 829, 840.

[10] B. de Witte, 'The European Union as an International Legal Experiment' in G. de Búrca & J. Weiler (eds), *The Worlds of European Constitutionalism* (Cambridge: Cambridge University Press, 2011) 20–21: '[T]he effort to sharply separate the EU from the field of international law might be misguided for two complementary reasons: because it overestimates the novelty of EU law, and because it underestimates the capacity of international law to develop innovative features in other contexts than that of European integration'. T. C. Hartley, *European Union Law in a Global Context: Text, Cases and Materials* (Cambridge: Cambridge University Press, 2004) xv. 'Some people say that the EU is unique – that it resembles no other entity and, in its concept and design, owes nothing to anything found anywhere else. That is not true. Although the breadth and depth of its powers put the EU in a special position, this is merely a matter of degree. The EU is simply the foremost among a whole pack of international bodies that have the power to control what countries do'.

position of individuals in the EU legal order; the exercise of governmental powers by EU institutions; the role of the Court of Justice in interpreting and applying EU law; and the inability of Member States to enforce EU law through traditional countermeasures[11] are put forward as features that set the EU apart from other forms of international legal cooperation. International law was presented as relatively weak and unenforceable, whereas EU law could be held up as superior to national law, and capable of direct effect, because the Member States had created something different – a new legal order.[12]

The view of the EU as a 'new legal order' is now largely accepted, not only by the CJEU but also by those who deal with EU law in practice. Few EU lawyers would conceive of themselves as working with a 'creature of international law'. Even if the EU has international law origins and its constitution is an international legal instrument,[13] treating the EU as a form of specialized international law is not useful for those who deal with EU law in everyday practice.

This conception of the EU works when applied to the 'internal sphere', that is, in the relations between the EU and its Member States, and relations between EU Member States. The new legal order narrative encounters opposition, however, when the EU seeks to apply this to the relationship between the EU and third states and organizations. As discussed subsequently and in the following chapters, the EU's self-perception remains contested at the international level.

1.2.1 *Sui Generis*

Closely associated with the new legal order narrative is the description of the EU as a sui generis legal and constitutional entity.[14] This accepts that the EU is

---

[11]   See J. H. H. Weiler, 'The Transformation of Europe' (1991) 100 *The Yale Law Journal* 2403, 2422.

[12]   'Par ses faiblesses intrinsèques, le droit international public diffère profondément du droit communautaire. Plusieurs traits du droit international sont ainsi devenus, par contraste, d'utiles repères pour apprécier la spécificité du droit communautaire et, par là même, pour mesurer l'écart qui s'est creusé entre les deux ordres juridiques'. O. Jacot-Guillarmod, *Droit communautaire et droit international public* (Genève: Librairie de l'université Georg, 1979) 258.

[13]   Barents argues that '[a]lthough the EC is based on a document which bears the name "treaty", this has but a formal meaning. In a material sense the EC Treaty has the character of an autonomous constitution and, as a result, it constitutes the exclusive source of Community law'. R. Barents, *The Autonomy of Community Law* (The Hague: Kluwer Law International, 2004) 112.

[14]   B. de Witte, 'The Emergence of a European System of Public International Law: The EU and its Member States as Strange Subjects' in J. Wouters, A. Nollkaemper & E. De Wet (eds), *The Europeanisation of International Law* (The Hague: TMC Asser Press, 2008) 39–54.

unique but tells us nothing about what legal consequences flow from this. The idea is that the EU is so different from other forms of political and legal organization that it does not fit existing categories in international or constitutional law.[15] For most international lawyers, however, the idea that the EU belongs in its own legal category is either inaccurate[16] or unhelpful.[17] Schütze is highly critical of the sui generis 'theory' because it is conceptually useless – it cannot be used to analyse or measure the Union and its evolution.[18] The label is entirely negative.[19]

Yet international lawyers rightly question both the 'new legal order' and sui generis descriptions. Such conceptions imply that the EU is not only a highly distinctive legal order but also an *exceptional* one. Being unique can imply the need for special treatment. This has given rise to the discussion of European exceptionalism, a term that has been given multiple meanings in the literature.[20] European exceptionalism often implies the EU justifying certain legal exceptions for itself, both in its own case law and in its legal relationship with third states.[21] One consequence of this is that other states and organizations 'have to arrange themselves with particularities of the special status of the EU'.[22] International lawyers may be sceptical of the new legal order and sui generis narratives because the creation of a distinct legal order might have a negative effect on the universal application of international law. International law is often presented as a universal system applicable to all

[15] De Baere describes the EU as a sui generis legal concept, and that 'cannot be fitted easily within either constitutional or international law . . . ' G. De Baere, *Constitutional Principles of EU External Relations* (Oxford: Oxford University Press, 2008) 1.

[16] R. Schütze, *European Constitutional Law* (Cambridge: Cambridge University Press, 2012) 67: '[T]he *sui generis* "theory" is historically unfounded. All previously existing Unions of States lay between international and national law'.

[17] 'European lawyers are given to saying that the European Union is *sui generis* – which is true but not helpful'. E. Denza, *The Intergovernmental Pillars of the European Union* (Oxford: Oxford University Press, 2002) 1. P. Hay, *Federalism and Supranational Organizations: Patterns for New Legal Structures* (Illinois University Press, 1966) 44. Arguing that the notion of sui generis 'not only fails to analyze but in fact asserts that no analysis is possible or worthwhile'.

[18] Schütze (n16) 67.

[19] '[T]here exists only a consensus about what Community law does not represent (constitutional or international law). However, this conclusion offers no explanation about the nature of Community law. In particular, it does not provide answers to fundamental questions . . . ' Barents (n13) 45–46.

[20] G. Nolte & H. Aust, 'European Exceptionalism?' (2013) 2 *Global Constitutionalism* 407, 416; G. de Búrca, 'The Road Not Taken: The European Union as a Global Human Rights Actor' (2011) 105 *American Journal of International Law* 649, 690.

[21] Nolte & Aust (n20) 416. M. Ličková, 'European Exceptionalism in International Law' (2008) 19 *European Journal of International Law* 485.

[22] Nolte & Aust (n20) 407.

international legal persons; international law is thus reluctant to view an entity of somehow 'escaping' that system.[23] The EU's claims of autonomy can feed into anxieties about the fragmentation of international law caused by 'the emergence of specialized and (relatively) autonomous rules or rule-complexes, legal institutions and spheres of legal practice'.[24]

Despite these criticisms, the EU law perspective presents a relatively coherent conception of the EU. It is a body founded on international law instruments, which over time transformed into something else and fits neither into the realms of international nor municipal law.[25] It accepts that rules of international law (for the most part) no longer apply in the internal sphere to regulate the relations between the EU Member States in areas where EU law applies. Yet this internal narrative loses relevance when applied to the external sphere.

1.3 EXTERNAL VIEWS: INTERNATIONAL LAW

Whereas the EU's internal narrative presents a rather coherent picture of the EU, international law does not have such a clear understanding of the EU. In these debates, there is some confusion between discussing the nature of the EU legal order and the nature of the EU as a legal entity in international law. The first question relates to the internal sphere and is focused on whether EU law remains a 'creature of international law'. The second question relates to the external sphere and concerns the EU's status as an autonomous legal person acting on the plane of international law. In its internal dimension, the EU is a constitutional legal order, one that regulates the rights and responsibilities of the EU Member States in their mutual relations. At the international level, when the EU interacts with other subjects of international law, it is often considered to be an international organization.[26] As will be

---

[23]   A. Orakhelashvili, 'The Idea of European International Law' (2006) 17 *European Journal of International Law* 315, 344: '[T]he fact that the EEC Treaty differs from ordinary international agreements is no warrant for presuming that the law it establishes is not part of, and governed by, international law'.

[24]   'Fragmentation of International Law: Difficulties arising from the Diversification and Expansion of International Law', Report of the Study Group of the International Law Commission finalized by Martti Koskenniemi, 13 April 2006, UN Doc. A/CN.4/L.682, 1–256 and 18 July 2006, UN Doc. A/CN.4/L.702, para. 8. See M. Koskenniemi & P. Leino, 'Fragmentation of International Law? Postmodern Anxieties' (2002) 15 *Leiden Journal of International Law* 533.

[25]   Weiler and Haltern point out that '[t]here is no doubt that the European legal order started its life as an international organisation in the traditional sense, even if it had some unique features from its inception'. Weiler & Haltern (n5) 419.

[26]   Gardiner captures the internal/external dichotomy in relation to the EU: 'In its internal aspect, that is viewing relations between the member states themselves, the Community is

further elaborated in the following chapters, the EU's practice at the international level is often shaped by its internal legal order and characteristics.

1.3.1 *Self-contained Regime*

The EU is sometimes referred to as a 'self-contained regime' in international law. This narrative accepts the autonomy of the EU, but unlike the new legal order narrative, it still accepts that the EU is very much a part of the wider international legal order. According to one definition, a system can be considered 'self-contained'

> if it comprises not only rules that regulate a particular field or factual relations laying down the rights and duties of the actors within the regime (primary rules), but also a set of rules that provide for means and mechanisms to enforce compliance, to settle disputes, to modify or amend the undertakings, and to react to breaches, with the intention to replace and through this to exclude the application of general international law, at least to a certain extent.[27]

A self-contained regime is a 'sub-system' of international law; it not only regulates a certain sphere of activity but also contains its own secondary rules, largely or completely replacing the application of general international law. Some possible examples of self-contained regimes include the legal system of the World Trade Organization, the regime of diplomatic law, and various systems in international human rights law. One of the characteristics of a self-contained regime is that since they possess a complete system of rights and remedies, there is no 'fallback' to general rules. This is based on the concept of *lex specialis* – states are free to establish a sub-system of legal rules that is more specialized and displaces the application of general rules. The International Law Commission's (ILC) study on *Fragmentation of International Law* recognized that a system may develop into a self-contained regime over time:

> The establishment of a special regime in the wider sense (S.S. Wimbledon, any interlinked sets of rules, both primary and secondary) would also normally take place by treaty or several treaties (e.g. the WTO 'covered treaties'). However, it may also occur that a set of treaty provisions develops over time, without conscious decision by states parties, perhaps through the activity of

---

an organism for collective exercise of sovereignty in matters over which competence is transferred to the Community by treaty. In its external aspect, the Community functions as an international organization, entering into treaties in matters within its competences'. R. Gardiner, *Treaty Interpretation*, 2nd edn (Oxford: Oxford University Press, 2015) 129.

[27] E. Klein, 'Self-contained Regime', Rüdiger Wolfrum (ed), *Max Planck Encyclopedia of Public International Law* (online edn). https://opil.ouplaw.com/home/EPIL.

an implementing organ, into a regime with its own rules of regime-administration, modification and termination.[28]

The ILC's study lists 'EU law' as a possible self-contained regime.[29] The EU has been described as 'the most convincing example of a self-contained regime',[30] and there are a number of strong arguments that the EU should be considered as such. The main reason is that Union law provides an exhaustive system to deal with breaches of the EU Treaties.[31] It is now clear that EU Member States may not resort to traditional inter-state countermeasures against other Member States for breaches of EU law, thus excluding a key aspect of public international law from the powers of the Member States.[32] From a public international law perspective, the concept that general international law does not apply within scope of the EU Treaties is a revolutionary development. As Weiler points out, this is one of the key features that sets the EU legal order from international law:

> The Community legal order . . . is a truly self-contained legal regime with no recourse to the mechanism of state responsibility, at least as traditionally understood, and therefore to reciprocity and countermeasures, even in the face of actual or potential failure. Without these features, so central to the classic international legal order, the Community truly becomes something new.[33]

While there appears to be no more room for interstate countermeasures in the EU legal order, Simma and Pulkowski argue that these could still exist in certain narrow 'emergency' situations. These are (1) the continuous violation of EU law by a Member State and (2) state-to-state reparation for breaches of

---

[28]   Fragmentation of International Law (n24) para. 157.

[29]   *Id.*, para. 129.

[30]   Klein (n27) 27; B. Simma & D. Pulkowski, 'Leges Speciales and Self-contained Regimes, Responsibility in the Context of the European Union Legal Order' in J. Crawford, A. Pellet & S. Olleson (eds), *The Law of International Responsibility* (Oxford: Oxford University Press, 2010) 152.

[31]   Kuijper argues that upon establishing the European legal order, '[a]mong the Member States ... general international law is no longer applicable within the scope of "the Treaties"'. P. J. Kuijper, '"It Shall Contribute to ... the Strict Observance and Development of International Law" The Role of the Court of Justice' in A. Rosas, E. Levits & Y. Bot (eds), *The Court of Justice and the Construction of Europe: Analyses and Perspectives on Sixty Years of Case-law* (The Hague: TMC Asser Press, 2013) 589, 594.

[32]   See e.g. Judgment in *Commission v. Luxembourg & Belgium*, Joined cases 90/63 and 91/63, EU:C:1964:80, 631 in which the Court found the principle of *exceptio non adimpleti contractus* (enforcement of an obligation may be withheld if the other party has itself has failed to perform the same or related obligation) could not be applied in the EU legal order.

[33]   Weiler (n11) 2422.

EU law.[34] Even in these hypothetical scenarios, resort to public international law would only take place because the EU system would have effectively failed. The argument is that Member States have only given up their rights to institute interstate countermeasures to the extent that the procedures under EU law remain effective. In these situations, there would be a 'fallback' to the general system of state responsibility. One could argue that since international law can continue to operate as such a 'fallback', this would imply that the EU is not a fully self-contained system.[35]

International law tends to treat claims of self-containment with caution. As Special Rapporteur Arangio-Ruiz points out, '[g]enerally, the specialists in Community law tended to consider that the system constituted a self-contained regime, whereas scholars of public international law showed a tendency to argue that the treaties establishing the Community did not really differ from other treaties … '.[36] Indeed, whenever states create an international organization, they decide to create new legal relationships between themselves and derogate (to a certain extent) from general international law.[37] A reason that the self-contained regime label may be resisted is that it contributes to the fragmentation of international law, caused by 'the emergence of specialized and (relatively) autonomous rules or rule-complexes, legal institutions and spheres of legal practice'.[38] The

---

[34]   B. Simma & D. Pulkowski, 'Of Planets and the Universe: Self-contained Regimes in International Law' (2006) 17 *European Journal of International Law* 483, 518.

[35]   See G. Conway, 'Breaches of EC Law and the International Responsibility of Member States' (2002) 13 *European Journal of International Law* 679, 695 concluding that '[d]espite the uniqueness and comprehensiveness of the system created by the European Communities, it remains the case that the term "self-contained regime", strictly understood, cannot be applied to it'. K. S. Ziegler, 'International Law and EU Law: Between Asymmetric Constitutionalism and Fragmentation' in A. Orakhelashvili (ed), *Research Handbook on the Theory and History of International Law* (Cheltenham: Edward Elgar, 2011) 268, 285. ' … in principle, secondary norms of international law (for example, of the law of treaties or state responsibility) remain available as a subsidiary fallback position, because the EU Treaties foresee no mechanism beyond the penalty payments in Art 260 TFEU (ex Art 228 EC), leaving scope, for example, for the suspension of the Treaty in regard to a Member State according to Art 60(2) lit. a) VCLT which is in material breach of an obligation. This implies that the EU is not a fully self-contained regime'.

[36]   Quoted in Simma & Pulkowski (n30) 148.

[37]   'It was possible for the parties to the original EC Treaty to establish a system under which rules of general international law (at least those of the character jus dispositivum) would not apply; in fact, the point of establishing a new legal regime by means of a treaty is to derogate from the general law, so it could be expected that rules of general international law could play no more than a limited role within that regime'. O. Elias, 'General International Law in the European Court of Justice: From Hypothesis to Reality' (2000) 31 *Netherlands Yearbook of International Law* 3, 5.

[38]   Fragmentation of International Law (n24) para. 8.

consensus seems to be that, while the EU is probably the closest thing to a 'self-contained regime', the application of public international law has not been completely excluded, and international law would apply in order to solve problems not addressed by the EU Treaties, or to fill gaps. This means that the EU ' ... is very close to a genuine self-contained regime, but even here the umbilical cord to general public international law has not yet been cut'.[39] Like the new legal order and sui generis narratives, the 'self-contained regime' category has little explanatory value when seeking to understand the EU's relationship with other legal entities. Presenting the Union as a self-contained or closed system of law only describes how principles of public international law should apply within the EU legal order.

1.3.2 *Regional Economic Integration Organization*

The EU is also conceived as a 'Regional Economic Integration Organization' (REIO) in some instances. Whereas the new legal order and self-contained regime models discussed earlier focus on the internal sphere, the REIO model tells us more about how the EU relates with other subjects of international law. This model accepts that the EU is a type of international organization, albeit one with particular unique characteristics. The model is reflected in a number of international treaties that allow EU participation. Few multilateral treaties to which the EU is a party specifically mention the EU.[40] Instead, they tend to allow for participation of 'regional economic integration organizations' (REIO), or alternatively (recognizing the EU's competence beyond economic matters) 'regional integration organizations' (RIO).[41] The REIO model has only been applied in the EU's external relations and is not often used to describe the EU as a political entity outside that context. It captures the idea that the EU started as an international organization[42] but has transformed over time into a special type of organization.

---

[39]   Klein (n27).

[40]   For example, the EU (formerly European Communities) was a founding member of the WTO (Agreement Establishing the World Trade Organization, signed on 15 April 1994, 1867 UNTS 154).

[41]   See the discussion of REIO clauses in Chapter 2 on the law of treaties.

[42]   Weiler and Haltern point out that '[t]here is no doubt that the European legal order started its life as an international organisation in the traditional sense, even if it had some unique features from its inception'. Weiler & Haltern (n5) 419.

1.3.3 *Classic International Organization*

The EU has also been understood as a classic intergovernmental organization. This view downplays the unique characteristics of the EU and the constitutional character of the EU Treaties. It may accept that the EU possesses certain unique features, but rejects the notion that it is a qualitatively different entity from other international organizations or groups of states. Viewing the EU as 'just another' international organization may be conceptually appealing to international lawyers who see the compartmentalization of international organizations into discrete categories as a threat to the universal application of international law. Orakhelashvili reminds us that, despite its unique qualities, the EU is still an international organization:

> It is true that there is a substantive difference between the European Union and other international organizations as the former possesses specific aims of European integration and extensive powers to bind Member States and their nationals to that end. However, there are no consistent criteria for constructing a workable juridical distinction between supranational organizations and international organizations, especially in relation to general international law. Being a supranational organization means also being an international organization.[43]

The classic IO model thus also dismisses arguments for EU exceptionalism. Since the EU is, according to this view, merely an international organization, there is little need to develop specialized rules. It tends to view the EU, not as a distinct legal entity with its own personality and powers, but as a group of like-minded states. The EU has been described as an 'association of states'.[44]

If the 'new legal order' model overstates the EU's unique nature and its autonomy, the 'classic IO' model downplays it. Discussing the EU as just another international organization is also an unhelpful conceptual tool. As will be elaborated upon in further chapters, international lawyers tend to analyse the EU from this starting point, but often run into difficulties due to the unique features of the EU. Many EU lawyers would reject the notion that the EU is an intergovernmental organization, in the same category as, say, the

---

[43] Orakhelashvili (n23) 343.

[44] M. Shaw, *International Law*, 8th edn (Cambridge: Cambridge University Press, 2017) 192 The European Union is an association, of twenty eight states'. The EU is presented alongside the Commonwealth of Nations and the Commonwealth of Independent States (CIS). Likewise Triggs discusses the EU alongside ASEAN, the Arctic Council and the CIS and states that the 'most well-recognised association of states is the European Union'. G. D. Triggs, *International Law: Contemporary Principles and Practices* (Chatswood:LexisNexis Butterworths, 2006) 175.

World Meteorological Organization. Yet it should be acknowledged that when the EU acts on the international plane and interacts with other legal subjects, it is often confronted with this view. For example, within the United Nations General Assembly, where the EU Member States are a minority, the EU has struggled to be accepted as a distinct legal actor.[45] In this context, the EU is not widely viewed as a special or unique entity, but as another international organization or even a political bloc.[46] The EU's self-perception, that of a unique type of supranational organization, is not universally accepted, not least in many of the multilateral bodies where the EU seeks to enhance its participation and visibility.

1.3.4 *Models of European Union*

In 1961 McMahon wrote that 'although the [European] Communities were brought into being in the form of an international treaty, one should not allow the circumstances of their birth to obscure their real nature … '.[47] The discussion earlier shows how there are a number of ways that the EU is understood in EU and international law scholarship, and the 'real nature' of the EU remains contested. Generally, the 'EU law' view emphasizes the unique nature of the EU legal order and its autonomy and presents the Union as a 'new legal order'. The international law view stems from a different foundational myth, that of the unity and universalism of international law.[48]

According to the international law view, the EU is not a qualitatively unique entity from the perspective of public international law; while it

---

[45]   See E. Brewer, 'The Participation of the European Union in the Work of the United Nations: Evolving to Reflect the New Realities of Regional Organizations' (2012) 41 *International Organizations Law Review* 181–225; G. De Baere & E. Paasivirta, 'Identity and Difference: The EU and the UN as Part of Each Other' in H. de Weale & J. Kuijpers (eds), *The European Union's Emerging International Identity: Views from the Global Arena* (Leiden: Martinus Nijhoff, 2013) 42; J. Wouters, J. Odermatt & T. Ramopoulos, 'The Status of the European Union at the United Nations General Assembly' in I. Govaere, E. Lannon, P. Van Elsuwege & S. Adam (eds), *The European Union in the World. Essays in Honour of Marc Maresceau* (Leiden: Martinus Nijhoff Publishers, 2014) 212–213.

[46]   United Nations, Press Release, 'General Assembly, in Recorded Vote, Adopts Resolution Granting European Union Right of Reply, Ability to Present Oral Amendments', 3 May 2011: 'The European Union would be able to present oral proposals and amendments, which, however, would be put to a vote only at the request of a Member State. The bloc would have the ability to exercise the right of reply, restricted to one intervention per item'.

[47]   J. F. McMahon, 'The Court of the European Communities: Judicial Interpretation and International Organisation' (1961) 37 *British Yearbook of International Law* 320, 329.

[48]   See the discussion in A. Bianchi, *International Law Theories: An Inquiry into Different Ways of Thinking* (Oxford: Oxford University Press, 2016) 240.

TABLE 1.1 *Models of the European Union in International Law*

	Internal sphere	External sphere
Unique legal entity; high degree of autonomy	1. **'New Legal Order'** • EU has developed into a 'new' type of legal/political entity of a constitutional nature	3. **'Regional Economic Integration Organization' (REIO)** • EU is a 'special type' of international organization • Specialized rules are required to take into account its nature and autonomy
Fits within existing categories; low degree of autonomy	2. **'Self-contained Regime'** • EU is a part of international legal order, but has developed specialised internal rules	4. **'Classic' International Organization** • EU is not qualitatively different from other international organizations • Existing rules can be applied to the EU

may display some unique features, these are viewed as a difference of degree, not of kind.[49] These models illustrate the ends of the spectrum, and in reality there are nuances between them. Yet these diverging views continue to pervade this debate.[50] The table here captures the different models.

The four models differ with respect to a number of assumptions about the EU and its relationship with international law. The first axis relates to the extent to which the EU is viewed as a 'unique' entity in international law. The 'new legal order' model and the 'REIO' model both assume there is

[49] '[t]he difference between the legal orders of EC law and public international law is one of degree rather than of principle,' 165. G. Betlem & A. Nollkaemper, 'Giving Effect to Public International Law and European Community Law before Domestic Courts: A Comparative Analysis of the Practice of Consistent Interpretation' (2003) 14 *European Journal of International Law* 569, 588. 'The argument is advanced that no other group of states has pooled sovereignty to the degree that EU member states have done. No other entity would have brought about such a distinct form of supranational governance which also acts along-side its member states on the international level. This would have particular consequences on the international level, for instance when other states have to arrange themselves with particularities of the special status of the EU'. Nolte & Aust (n20).

[50] 'Public international lawyers generally presume the application of public international law and the character of the EU as an international organisation (i.e. focusing on its formal sources), while EU lawyers tend to adopt the perspective of the EU as an autonomous legal order or even a self-contained regime, stressing its sui generis nature, allowing the substantive perspective to prevail in the evaluation'. Ziegler (n35) 270.

something special about the EU, that sets it apart from other legal entities. The 'self-contained regime' model and 'classic IO' model see the EU as something that fits within existing international law categories; they either deny that the EU is unique at all, or reject that any legal consequences should flow from its unique features. The second axis relates to the 'sphere' that is concerned, either the perspective of the internal legal order of the EU, or the perspective of the EU's place within the wider international legal order. The 'new legal order' and 'self-contained regime' models are mostly concerned with the relationship between the EU and its Member States and are less concerned about the EU's relationship with other entities. The 'REIO' and 'classic IO' model focus on the EU's relationship with the wider world of international law. It should be stressed that these four models are not mutually exclusive, nor do they fully capture the range of views that exist. The models are useful because they capture the different conceptual 'starting points' that lawyers take when addressing legal questions dealing with the EU's place in international law. Section 1.4 examines some of the reasons for these diverging views.

1.4 EXPLAINING DIVERGING VIEWS

A practical illustration of the diverging views can be seen by the academic response to the line of *Kadi* judgments from the CJEU.[51] In this famous line of case law, the CJEU held that it was capable of exercising judicial review regarding EU measures intended to implement UN sanctions. *Kadi* is a landmark judgment in setting out the EU's relationship with the wider international legal order. Not only did the judgment spark intense scholarly debates among EU law experts, it also brought about debate in the international law scholarship. The diverging reactions to the case are often shaped by the perspective of the author, which often depends on whether it is analysed from an EU law or international law angle.[52] To many international lawyers, it was not the outcome in *Kadi* that was problematic, but the rather blunt way in which the Court dealt with international law. While many praised the outcome of the judgment for its approach to fundamental rights, it also led to

---

[51] Judgment in *Kadi and Al Barakaat International Foundation v. Council and Commission*, Joined Cases C-402/05 P & C-415/05 P, EU:C:2008:461.

[52] An edited volume on the Kadi cases includes separate sections on the 'public international law perspective' and 'constitutional perspective'. M. Avbelj, F. Fontanelli & G. Marinico (eds), *Kadi on Trial: A Multifaceted Analysis of the Kadi Trial* (London: Routledge, 2014).

a great deal of negative responses, mostly from those looking at the legal dispute from an international law perspective.[53] The judgment, it was argued, downplays the important and special character of the UN system for peace and security, and overemphasizes the separateness of the EU from the wider legal order.[54] Given the complex and controversial issues that the case dealt with, it is understandable that this scholarship led to such differing views. Yet this divergence stems not only from disagreements about the interpretation of the UN Charter or the status of certain human rights norms; it stems from a more fundamental disagreement about the EU's very legal character and its relationship with international law.[55] There is nothing particularly novel in pointing out that a legal assessment depends on one's points of reference or foundational assumptions.[56] Yet the *Kadi* example demonstrates a much broader problem when discussing the EU's role in the international legal order: highly divergent views about the very nature of that legal subject. Ličková points to this larger problem of 'partial inquiries' when conducting research at the intersection of EU law and international law.[57]

1.4.1 *Academic Specialization and Professional Communities*

One reason for the emergence of the different perspectives is academic and professional specialization, whereby communities identified as EU law or international law scholars have failed to engage with one another. This does

---

[53] G. de Búrca, 'The European Court of Justice and the International Legal Order after Kadi' (2010) 51 *Harvard International Law Journal* 1. See P. Margulies, 'Aftermath of an Unwise Decision: The UN Terrorist Sanctions Regime after Kadi II' (2014) 6 *Amsterdam Law Forum* 51–63, arguing that the Court failed in Kadi II to display the appropriate level of deference to Sanctions Committee decisions.

[54] A. Aust, *Handbook of International Law*, 2nd edn (Cambridge: Cambridge University Press, 2010) 198.

[55] P. J. Cardwell, D. French & N. D. White, 'Kadi: The Interplay between EU and International Law' (2009) 58 *International and Comparative Law Quarterly* 229–240. ' . . . the reason that the Kadi judgment should not be characterised as radical is because it reflects the long-standing view of the Court that the EU legal system is an autonomous legal framework independent of, and not reliant upon, public international law'.

[56] Cardwell et al (*id*) point out how *Kadi* 'highlights a growing sense of divergence in opinion between EU and public international lawyers, especially in terms of our respective normative "points of reference" – in the case of EU lawyers, the EU treaties, in the case of international lawyers, the UN Charter'. See C. Tomuschat, 'The *Kadi* Case: What Relationship is there between the Universal Legal Order under the Auspices of the United Nations and the EU Legal Order?' (2009) 28 *Yearbook of European Law* 654, 655.

[57] Ličková (n21) 463, 465. 'Only a tiny number of scholarly writings have examined the issue from both European and international sides. Rather, these two aspects have been dealt with separately. Such partial inquiries are useful, but they remain incomplete because both legal orders intervene and interplay when normative conflicts between them appear'.

not mean, however, that international lawyers have ignored the EU or that EU law specialists do not pay much attention to international law. Rather, the identification with a particular discipline tends to shape the conceptual starting points for these debates.[58] To those practicing and teaching EU law, the EU is not conceived as a specialized branch of international law, but as a separate discipline. Some other specialized legal disciplines, such as international human rights law, WTO law, or international environmental law, are still viewed as a sub-field of public international law. This is usually not the case with EU law. Academic disciplines are also associated with a broader project. Many scholars focusing on EU law, for example, are interested in and supportive of the broader European project. An 'EU lawyer' tends to accept some basic tenets and beliefs about what the EU is, and is part of an academic culture that applies and reasserts those principles.[59] This is not to say that EU law scholarship is uncritical of the EU institutions or the CJEU. Yet the conceptual starting point of the EU as a 'new legal order' is widely accepted in EU law scholarship.

A similar phenomenon takes place in international law scholarship. Of course, one should not lump together all international lawyers as having the same view. Yet just as EU lawyers have an attachment to the European project, much of international law scholarship is similarly connected to supporting and upholding an international legal system, or the 'project' of international law. International law as a legal discipline has long confronted questions regarding its existence and legitimacy. This has now given way to new questions of how to ensure that the legal order would not be pulled apart by competing and overlapping regimes of international law.[60] The increase in the number of international organizations, multilateral conventions, bilateral investment treaties, as well as the growth of international courts and tribunals

---

[58]   See Simma & Pulkowski (n30) 148, discussing how '[o]ften, a scholar's approach seems to depend on whether her intellectual home is the sphere of public international law or that of a specialized subsystem'.

[59]   On the 'managerial approach' to international law, see M. Koskenniemi, 'Constitutionalism, Managerialism and the Ethos of Legal Education' (2007) 1 *European Journal of Legal Studies* 1. ' What is significant about projects such as trade, human rights, or indeed "Europe", is precisely the set of values or purposes that we link with them. To be doing "trade law" or "human rights law", or "environmental law" or "European law" – as the representatives of those projects repeatedly tell us – is not just to operate some technical rules but to participate in a culture, to share preferences and inclinations shared with colleagues and institutions who identify themselves with that "box."'

[60]   Fragmentation of International Law (n24); G. Abi-Saab, 'Fragmentation or Unification: Some Concluding Remarks' (1999) 31 *New York University Journal of International Law and Politics* 919; M. Craven, 'Unity, Diversity and the Fragmentation of International Law' (2003) 3 *Finnish Yearbook of International Law* 14.

led to new concerns that the coherence and unity of the international legal order would be destabilized.[61] The community of international lawyers therefore has a similar interest in conceiving international law as a system and to be cautious of claims – like those made those by EU lawyers – that some entities have evolved and escaped that system. The divergences between EU law and international law scholarship is therefore not only spurred by different academic disciplines, but also by the interests of these disciplines in defending and promoting their underlying project.

Another possible reason may also be that the scholarship is embedded within a professional discipline. EU judges and officials tend to orient themselves towards the EU law perspective, but so does the academic community engaged in EU law scholarship. There is a tendency, then, to identify as an 'EU lawyer' or an 'international lawyer' (or even 'trade lawyer', or 'investment lawyer'), not only because they are academic specializations, but also because they are connected with a field within the legal profession or project. When legal questions surrounding the clash between EU law and international law arise, does one first turn to the EU Treaties or to the UN Charter? The answer to this question may depend on the professional discipline with which the scholar identifies.[62]

1.4.2 State-centrism

Another reason that international law has difficulty conceptualizing the EU is that international law remains a state-centric discipline. Although there has been a great debate about the role of non-state actors in international law, international law continues to view states as the principal unit of analysis. Corporations, armed rebel groups, NGOs and even international organizations are studied through the lens of the state; they are seen as exceptions to the rule that the international legal order remains one where states are the main drivers of law making. According to this traditional view, the EU is understood as a vehicle of its Member States, rather than an independent legal actor in its own right. International law's state-centrism prevents one from viewing how other legal subjects can also contribute to the development of international in addition to states. Schütze, for example, explains how international law is built

---

[61]   J. I. Charney, 'Is International Law Threatened by Multiple International Tribunals?' (1998) 271 *Recueil des Cours* 101, 347.

[62]   Fragmentation of International Law (n24) para. 483. 'This is the background to the concern about fragmentation of international law: the rise of specialized rules and rule-systems that have no clear relationship to each other. Answers to legal questions become dependent on whom you ask, what rule-system is your focus on'.

on the idea of the sovereign state, which prevents the discipline from fully understanding 'compound subjects' such as the EU.[63] This is symptomatic of a broader challenge of public international: understanding the role of legal entities that do not fit neatly into legal categories, such as state or international organization. The way international law deals with the EU therefore sheds some light on how non-State entities are conceived of in international law.

1.4.3 *Interests and Values*

The 'diverging views' cannot be explained only by academic specialization and the state-centric nature of international law. The four models discussed earlier are also reflective of deeper political tensions. They show how the acceptance of the EU in the international legal order is shaped by power relations. For instance, when the EU is accepted as a unique 'REIO' in international settings, it is usually because the EU has been able to successfully push for that model in international negotiations. In instances where the EU is viewed as a classic international organization, it is often because the EU is in a multilateral setting where it has less diplomatic influence to persuade other states.

The diverging approaches are not only symptomatic of professional and academic communities, but also the attachment to certain values in that community. Kennedy discusses international lawyers as a 'a group of people pursuing projects in a common professional language' and that in that project, international lawyers 'tend to think that international law is a good thing, and there should be more of it ... '.[64] The idea that international law is a 'good thing' should be challenged. In many instances, the EU legal order and EU law are put forward as normatively superior. In addition to contributing to the strict observance and the development of international law, the EU in its relations with the wider world should contributes to 'peace, security, the sustainable development of the Earth, solidarity and mutual respect among peoples, free and fair trade, eradication of poverty and the protection of human rights, in particular the rights of the child ... '.[65] This points to another

---

[63] 'Classic international law is built on the idea of the sovereign state. This State-centered structure of international creates normative difficulties for non-State actors. The European Union is a union of States, and as such still encounters normative hurdles when acting on the international scene. These normative hurdles have become fewer, but there remains situations in which the Union cannot externally act due to the partial blindness of international law towards compound subjects'. Schütze (n16) 217.

[64] D. Kennedy, 'One, Two, Three, Many Legal Orders: Legal Pluralism and the Cosmopolitan Dream' in P. Korkman & V. Mäkinenin (eds), *Universalism in International Law and Political Philosophy* (Helsinki: Helsinki Collegium for Advanced Studies, 2008) 257.

[65] Article 3(5) Treaty on European Union.

ambiguity about the EU and its place in the world. Is it an IO set up primarily for the benefit of its Member States and citizens, or can it also be regarded as an organization that is truly working for the 'greater good'? The EU was awarded a Nobel Peace Prize for having 'for over six decades contributed to the advancement of peace and reconciliation, democracy and human rights in Europe'.[66] The EU is often discussed in terms of being a 'normative power'.[67] Klabbers argues that 'the idea that the EU is an international organization created for the common good must be discarded: the common good the EU stands for is, by and large, the common good of itself and its 27 member states'.[68] While the EU is primarily a self-interested actor, the way in which it defines and pursues those interests does involve the pursuit of certain values. This tension also helps explains the EU's place in the international legal order.

Many of the legal conflicts between EU law and international law are, at a more basic level, conflicts over values. The classic example of collision between the EU and international legal orders, the *Kadi* saga, was more than a legal conflict over competing norms. Behind the legal conflict is a clash of values: between respect for individual human rights on the one hand and the respect for the UNSC system of international peace and security on the other. Many of the legal disagreements or clashes discussed in the next chapters reveal similar tensions about which legal order is 'normatively' superior. To those associated with the EU law view and the European project, EU law is put forward as more democratic and better able to protect fundamental rights and values. To those associated with the international law project, international law is viewed as the superior legal order, and can be used to challenge the validity of certain EU acts that allegedly violate international law. In fields where 'clashes' have emerged, such as in the fields of individual sanctions, data protection, animal welfare, climate change and investment arbitration, there are underlying questions about which legal order is best equipped to govern these topics. In some instances, the EU seeks to work with states and multilateral institutions to address these issues. However, in recent years the EU has sought to adopt its own approach in some areas, and has adopted more unilateral measures.[69]

---

[66] Statement of the Norwegian Nobel Committee, 'The Nobel Peace Prize for 2012', 12 October 2012, www.nobelprize.org/nobel_prizes/peace/laureates/2012/press.html.

[67] I. Manners, 'Normative Power Europe: A Contradiction in Terms?' (2002) *Journal of Common Market Studies* 235.

[68] J. Klabbers, *The European Union in International Law* (Paris: Pedone, 2012) 91.

[69] On EU unilateralism see J. Odermatt, 'Convergence through EU Unilateralism' in E. Fahey (ed), *Framing Convergence with the Global Legal Order: The EU and the World Hart* (Oxford: Hart, 2020) 49–63.

1.5 OVERCOMING DIVERGENT VIEWS

The models discussed earlier show different, often competing, conceptions of the EU. How can these divergent views be overcome?

1.5.1 *Multiple Nature of the EU*

One approach has been to accept the multiplicity and diversity of the international legal system, and to accept that the EU may exist in multiple states, depending on the forum and type of legal interaction involved. Rather than finding one model that applies to each set of circumstances, this approach requires one to examine the nature of the legal dispute and the forum in which it takes place. Under this relativistic approach, the EU's legal position depends on the perspective and the standpoint of the observer.[70] This was the approach adopted by the arbitral tribunal in *Electrabel SA v. The Republic of Hungary*.[71] The tribunal noted the 'multiple nature' of EU law, stating that 'EU law is a sui generis legal order, presenting different facets depending on the perspective from where it is analysed. It can be analysed from the perspectives of the international community, individual member states and EU institutions'.[72] It argues that 'many scholars' accept that 'EU law is international law because it is rooted in international treaties.'[73] The tribunal's reasoning demonstrates this relativistic approach: the nature of the EU and EU law depends on the legal site in question: national courts of EU Member States, the courts of non-EU states, the CJEU, international courts and tribunals or other legal forums.

This view attempts to capture the 'dual nature' of the EU. In *Kadi*, Advocate General Maduro sought to capture this duality when he described the EU legal order using the term 'municipal legal order of trans-national dimensions'.[74] Crawford and Koskenniemi also seek to capture the 'dual

---

[70] L. Kirchmair, 'The "Janus Face" of the Court of Justice of the European Union: A Theoretical Appraisal of the EU Legal Order's Relationship with International and Member State Law' (2012) 4 *Goettingen Journal of International Law* 677, 679. 'Depending on its perspective – and not on a different standpoint of the observer – the ECJ applies a monistic doctrine relating to its Member States and a dualistic doctrine relating to international law, two completely diverging doctrines'.

[71] *Electrabel SA v. The Republic of Hungary* (ICSID Case No. ARB/07/19) Decision on Jurisdiction, Applicable Law and Liability (2012) 4.117.

[72] *Id.*, 4.117.

[73] *Id.*, 4.120 and fn 7.

[74] Opinion of the Advocate General Maduro, *P Yassin Abdullah Kadi v. Council of the European Union and Commission of the European Communities*, Case C-402/05, EU:C:2008:11, para. 21.

nature' of the EU legal order as one that is both international and domestic in nature.[75] This captures the idea that the EU legal order has international law origins and dimensions, but possesses municipal law, even constitutional characteristics. This also recognizes that the EU legal order has both an internal and external dimension. Which model we apply in a given case will depend on which dimension is being discussed. Gardiner captures this internal/external dichotomy in relation to the EU:

> In its internal aspect, that is viewing relations between the member states themselves, the Community is an organism for collective exercise of sovereignty in matters over which competence is transferred to the Community by treaty. In its external aspect, the Community functions as an international organization, entering into treaties in matters within its competences.[76]

In its *internal dimension*, the EU can be thought of as a constitutional legal order, one that regulates the rights and responsibilities of the EU Member States in their mutual relations. From this perspective, it makes sense to treat the EU as a new legal order or self-contained regime. In these instances, the CJEU would be justified in treating the EU through the constitutionalist lens and to stress EU autonomy, since it is dealing only with the internal level. At the *external level*, however, a different set of assumptions apply. When the EU acts on the international scene, when it mediates with other subjects of international law (which are not bound by EU law) and enters into commitments on the plane of international law, it acts at the external level. Here, the EU is not in a position to assert the new legal order narrative, and must abide by rules of public international law along with other IOs. This internal/external divide allows the EU and the CJEU to continue to apply the 'new legal order' narrative and assert the EU's autonomy vis-à-vis the international legal order since in these instances internal constitutional law issues arise.[77] At the same time, when the EU acts on the international plane, the EU would be

---

[75]   J. Crawford & M. Koskenniemi, 'Introduction' in J. Crawford & M. Koskenniemi (eds), *The Cambridge Companion to International Law* (Cambridge: Cambridge University Press, 2012) 12.

[76]   Gardiner (n26) 129.

[77]   Elias (n37) 6: 'The distinction to be drawn, then, is between the role of public international law as a source of law governing legal relations within the Community on the one hand, and legal relations between the Community and third states on the other. In the latter context, general international law can be expected to have more relevance, given that such third parties are not bound by the EC Treaty, so that the relations between such third parties would be regulated primarily by international law'.

viewed more along the lines of a traditional IO. This internal/external divide may be conceptually appealing, but as the following chapters show, it is difficult to apply in practice. First, it is not always easy to divide the internal/external dimension of EU action. Second, the relativistic view tends to undermine legal certainty, since the legal status of the EU will often depend on the viewpoint of the observer. A litigant seeking to bring the EU or a Member State before an international dispute settlement body, for example, wants to know what the applicable rules will be; a discussion of the 'multiple nature' of EU law may not be helpful.

The legal view of the EU thus becomes dependent on these shifting power relations. The EU's legal status will depend on political, rather than objective legal conditions. International law can provide rules that are applicable equally to all subjects irrespective of power.[78] The relativistic approach means that the nature of the EU depends less on objective criteria, and more on how far the EU could push and persuade in treaty negotiations or within international organizations.

Pluralist visions accept that there may be multiple systems working at the global level, and tend to reject notions of unity and universality of public international law.[79] The idea of multiple sub-systems and regimes exercising autonomy, including the European Union, is not necessarily viewed as a problem, and accepts multiple overlapping orders, without hierarchy or a 'centre'. International Relations scholars seem to have less problem with the multiple nature of the EU, and can study it as a type of international organization, proto-state or federation. International law seems to have more difficulty with accepting multiple conceptions of the EU, as the labels given to the polity have legal consequences. As discussed in the following chapters, whether the EU is viewed as an international organization, a municipal legal order or something else, will often determine the legal framework that applies to that entity.

---

[78] C. Eckes & R. A. Wessel, 'The European Union from an International Perspective: Sovereignty, Statehood, and Special Treatment' in T. Tridimas & R. Schütze (eds), *The Oxford Principles of European Union Law – Volume 1: The European Union Legal Order* (Oxford: Oxford University Press, 2015) 74–102. 'International law, however, only works when it is applied across the board for certain categories of international actors. Its rationale is to offer clarity and set the conditions for a smooth cooperation between different subjects'.

[79] See, e.g., G. Shaffer, 'International Law and Global Public Goods in a Legal Pluralist World' (2012) 23 *European Journal of International Law* 669; M. Delmas-Marty, *Ordering Pluralism: A Conceptual Framework for Understanding the Transnational Legal World* (Oxford: Hart, 2009).

1.5.2 *Integrating the EU into the International Legal Order*

The constitutionalist vision, on the other hand, tends to view 'autonomous' regimes as a form of institutional fragmentation.[80] The EU may contribute to such fragmentation. A constitutionalist approach tends to find ways for the EU to 'fit' within this broader framework of international law. According to this approach, international law is undergoing a process of constitutionalization, one that mirrors a process that took place within the EU itself. It seeks to bring greater coherence to the disorder brought about by multiple overlapping legal regimes. The EU cannot 'escape' the international legal order; the task is to find ways to integrate sub-systems and resolve normative conflicts between legal orders. This has included discussions of various conflict management techniques, such as system integration, treaty interpretation (*lex posterior* and *lex specialis*) or normative hierarchy.[81] Much of the focus in this debate has been on the role of international and regional courts, including the CJEU. Yet the CJEU has not shown much interest in the unity of international law, and is more focused on preserving the autonomy of the EU legal order.[82]

Much of this debate has focused on the issue of conflict between legal orders. There is a tendency to focus on courts, and the 'clashes' that occur, especially in high-profile judgments. Much of the discussion, then, has been on finding techniques to be used by courts to promote integration or avoid conflicts. The present research seeks to go beyond an analysis of legal clashes and conflicts. Nor is the research intended to present ways of resolving normative conflict or to establish a formula for integrating the EU and public international law. The following chapters demonstrate how these various visions of the EU legal order play out in different international legal forums and legal debates. It is through these processes that the EU has had a role of influencing and developing international law.

---

[80] M. Prost, *The Concept of Unity in Public International Law* (Oxford: Hart, 2012); E. de Wet, 'The International Constitutional Order' (2006) 55 *International and Comparative Law Quarterly* 51, 59; E. de Wet, 'The Emergence of International and Regional Value Systems as a Manifestation of the Emerging Constitutional Order' (2006) 19 *Leiden Journal of International Law* 614; A. Peters & G. Ulfstein, *The Constitutionalization of International Law* (Oxford: Oxford University Press, 2009).

[81] A. Peters, 'The Refinement of International Law: From Fragmentation to Regime Interaction and Politicization' (2017) 15 *International Journal of Constitutional Law* 671.

[82] See J. Odermatt, 'The International Court of Justice and the Court of Justice of the European Union: Between Fragmentation and Universality of International Law' in A. Skordas (ed), *Research Handbook on the International Court of Justice* (Cheltenham: Edward Elgar, forthcoming, 2021).

1.6 CONCLUSION

This chapter has explained how EU law and international law scholarship have different views of the EU's place within the international legal order. These different conceptions have different assumptions and starting points. The EU law view starts from the understanding that the EU is an autonomous, municipal legal order; the EU's relationship with the international legal order is governed primarily by EU law. The international law view takes the starting point that the EU is a part of the international legal order, and whose special features can be taken into account in certain situations; the EU's relationship with the international legal order is governed by public international law. The following chapters will explore how these views of the EU in academic scholarship play out in different forums.

2

Customary International Law

2.1 INTRODUCTION

How can the European Union contribute to the development and identification of customary international law? Alongside treaties, customary international law is a key source of international obligations;[1] it has been described as 'the main mode of international regulation'.[2] Yet in comparison with the EU's treaty practice, the EU's contribution to the development and confirmation of customary international law has been the subject of less debate. There has been discussion about how customary international law applies in the EU legal order.[3] The EU Court of Justice has held that 'when [the EU] adopts an act, it is bound to observe international law in its entirety,

---

[1] Article 38(1)(b) Statute of the International Court of Justice sets out that the Court shall apply *inter alia* 'international custom, as evidence of a general practice accepted as law'.

[2] M. Hakimi, 'Making Sense of Customary International Law' (2020) 118 *Michigan Law Review* 1487, 1488.

[3] See, e.g., J. Wouters & D. van Eeckhoutte, 'Enforcement of Customary International Law through European Community Law' in J. M. Prinssen & A. Schrauwen (eds), *Direct Effect: Rethinking a Classic of EC Legal Doctrine* (Groningen: Europa Law Publishing, 2002) 223–225. P.-J. Kuijper, 'Customary International Law, Decisions of International Organisations and Other Techniques for Ensuring Respect for International Legal Rules in European Community Law' in J. Wouters, A. Nollkaemper & E. de Wet (eds), *The Europeanisation of International Law: The Status of International Law in the EU and Its Member States* (The Hague: TMC Asser Press, 2008) 183–234; C. Timmermans, 'The EU and Public International Law' (1999) 4 *European Foreign Affairs Review* 181; P.-J. Kuijper, 'From Dyestuffs to Kosovo Wine: From Avoidance to Acceptance by the Community Courts of Customary International Law as Limit to Community Action' in I. F. Dekker & H. H. G. Post (eds), *On the Foundations and Sources of International Law: Essays in Memory of Herman Meijers* (The Hague: TMC Asser Press, 2003) 151–171; A. Gianelli, 'Customary International Law in the European Union' in E. Cannizzaro, P. Palchetti & R. A. Wessel (eds), *International Law as Law of the European Union* (Leiden: Martinus Nijhoff, 2012).

including customary international law'.[4] The CJEU has applied principles of customary international law in fields such as the law of treaties;[5] international responsibility;[6] the law of the sea;[7] and privileges and immunities.[8] This debate has mainly focused on the conditions under which customary international law can be applied in the EU legal order, and whether it can be used to challenge the validity of EU acts.

This chapter focuses on a different question. To what extent can the EU also *contribute* to the development and identification of customary international law? If the EU is bound by rules of customary international law in its own right, does this mean that the EU also has the capacity to contribute, through its own practice and *opinio juris*, to the development of these rules? If so, does the EU contribute as a legal subject in its own right, or as a vehicle for the collective practice of the EU Member States? And to which kinds of rules of customary international law can EU practice contribute?

The chapter examines these issues in light of the International Law Commission's *Draft Conclusions on Identification of Customary International Law* (2018) ('Draft Conclusions'). The Draft Conclusions recognize that international organizations are capable of contributing to the formation of customary international law, albeit in a somewhat limited fashion compared to states. The first section discusses some of the conceptual issues faced during the ILC's study. It argues that the EU is capable of contributing to the formation of customary law, not only as a collective expression of the EU Member States, but also as an international actor in its own right. For example, EU practice can contribute to the development of specialized rules that apply in the relationship between states and international organizations, especially supranational bodies such as the EU.

The second part examines some examples of how the EU has contributed to the formation and identification of customary international law. Examples of EU practice have mostly related to the EU's diplomatic practice as an

---

[4] Judgment in *Air Transport Association of America and Others* v. *Secretary of State for Energy and Climate Change*, C-366/10, EU:C:2011:864, para. 101.

[5] See Judgment in *Brita* v. *Hauptzollamt Hamburg Hafen*, C-386/08, EU:C:2010:91, paras. 40–45.

[6] Judgment in *Walz* v. *Clickair SA*, C-63/09, EU:C:2010:251, para. 27.

[7] S. Boelaert-Suominen, 'The European Community, the European Court of Justice and the Law of the Sea' (2008) 23 *The International Journal of Marine and Coastal Law* 643–713.

[8] Judgment in *Hungary* v. *Slovakia*, C-364/10, EU:C:2012:630, para. 46: '[O]n the basis of customary rules of general international law … the Head of State enjoys a particular status in international relations which entails, inter alia, privileges and immunities'.

instigator of certain norms.[9] The ILC has also examined EU practice in relation to issues such as international responsibility and the law of treaties. This chapter also focuses on the role of supranational courts and whether the CJEU may also play a role in the development and identification of customary international law. The chapter lays the foundations for the discussion in later chapters on the EU's contribution in other areas of international law.

2.2 INTERNATIONAL ORGANIZATIONS AND THE FORMATION AND EVIDENCE OF CUSTOMARY INTERNATIONAL LAW[10]

In 2012, the International Law Commission (ILC) included the topic 'Formation and evidence of customary international law' in its programme of work. In 2013, this was changed to 'Identification of customary international law'. It appointed Sir Michael Wood, former Legal Adviser to the United Kingdom's Foreign and Commonwealth Office, to be the Special Rapporteur for the topic. The Special Rapporteur produced five reports, and in 2018 the ILC adopted its *Draft Conclusions on Identification of Customary International Law (Draft Conclusions)* with commentary.[11] The ILC's project and the Draft Conclusions aimed to set out an approach to the identification of customary international law, in particular to give guidance on identifying the two elements of customary international law: 'a general practice' and 'acceptance as law' (*opinio juris*).

During the study, the Special Rapporteur was faced with a number of conceptual questions related to customary international law. Many of these related to the role of international organizations in the identification of customary international law. Customary international law is usually associated with the practice of state actors; one thinks of customary law as including *state* practice, and the acceptance as law by *states*. The ILC Draft Conclusions and Commentary acknowledge that international organizations, including the European Union, can contribute to the formation of customary international law. Importantly, they accept that international organizations can

---

9 See F. Hoffmeister, 'The Contribution of EU Practice under International Law' in M. Cremona (ed), *Developments in EU External Relations Law* (Oxford: Oxford University Press, 2008) 37–127.

10 This section is based on J. Odermatt, 'The Development of Customary International Law by International Organizations' (2017) 66 *International Comparative Law Quarterly* 491.

11 International Law Commission, Draft conclusions on identification of customary international law, with commentaries, (2018) A/73/10, chapter V, para. 66 ('ILC Draft Conclusions'). For the ILC's output, see International Law Commission, 'Analytical Guide to the Work of the International Law Commission – Identification of customary international law', https://legal.un.org/ilc/guide/1_13.shtml.

contribute to practice and *opinio juris* 'as such', that is, as autonomous actors in international law, not only as the vehicles for their Member States. Whereas states remain the primary drivers of customary rules, the Draft Conclusions state that international organizations may contribute to practice 'in certain cases'.[12]

2.2.1 *ILC Methodology and International Organizations*

After having dealt with fundamental issues of public international law such as the law of treaties and international responsibility, the issue of how customary international law is formed and identified remained one of the key outstanding issues yet to be tackled by the ILC. The ILC's work on customary international law did not break new ground or seek to develop the law. Tasked with the codification and progressive development of international law, the ILC saw its role as one of giving 'practical guidance' in the identification of customary international law and its content. The ILC Draft Conclusions confirm the commonly accepted elements of identification of customary international law, such as the 'two-element' approach. Yet the lasting impact of the work may lie more with the way the ILC addressed, mainly at the latter stages of the study, a number of sub-issues, including the relevance of the practice of international organizations (IOs). The Special Rapporteur acknowledged from the outset that the practice of IOs could play a role in the identification and formation of customary international law, but it was not until the later stages that the precise role of IOs was addressed in more detail. The ILC's attention to IOs in this regard should be welcomed. Yet the ILC study still left a number of important questions unaddressed. This can be linked to the inconsistent way in which the ILC has dealt with international organizations (including the EU) in its work.

The ILC accepts that the practice of IOs can be relevant, yet its work remains somewhat state-centric, and thus finds it difficult to conceive of IOs *as such* contributing to the development of international custom. This represents an underlying tension in international law, between the view of IOs as independent actors, capable of contributing to its formation and development in an autonomous fashion, and the view of IOs representing little more than the collective will of their constituent members. While the Special Rapporteur acknowledges the possibility of the EU's practice contributing to the formation of customary international law, the work gives little detail on the type of organization practice that might be relevant, or the type of

---

[12]   ILC Draft Conclusion 4(2) (n11) 'In certain cases, the practice of international organizations also contributes to the formation, or expression, of rules of customary international law'.

rules to which this practice may contribute. Moreover, while the ILC study focuses on instances where a rule is 'accepted as law' (*opinio juris*), the question of how IOs may contribute to this aspect is less explored. The forms of evidence of that may be used to determine 'acceptance as law' mostly relate to the practice of states, such as official statements by governments, diplomatic correspondence and the jurisprudence of national courts.

The ILC's approach to the issue of customary international law suffers from a broader issue within the ILC, that is, an inconsistent approach to IOs. The ILC's state-centric approach is not surprising, since it is states that nominate and elect individual members of the ILC, and it is overwhelmingly the practice of states that contributes to the formation of custom. This does not mean that the ILC has ignored IOs in its work. The issue is more a methodological one, particularly the way in which IO practice is viewed and analysed. In the project on customary international law, IO practice was viewed as primarily representing the collective will of states. According to this view, states remain the driving force in international law making, and the capacity of IOs to contribute to the development of international law is reduced to their role in expressing the will of states.

This state-centric approach is also reflected in the ILC's work in other fields. Other ILC projects have similarly called upon it to examine the role of IOs, although few have focused on IOs specifically. The ILC tends to approach questions related to IOs in two main ways. The first model is to bifurcate its work, addressing separately the issues that arise in relation to states and those that arise in the context of IOs. This was the approach taken, for instance, with regard to the law of treaties, which resulted in two similar but separate codification conventions. This approach was applied with respect to the law of international responsibility, which resulted in a set of draft articles applicable to states, and another that applies to IOs and states within IOs. According to this approach, the rules applicable to states are fleshed out first, and these are later used as a basis for determining rules applicable to IOs, taking into account the relevant differences between the two. Such an approach allows the ILC to develop the law relating to IOs through analogy.[13] The second approach has been to deal with states and IOs together. For example, the ILC's Guide to Reservations to Treaties confirms that both states and IOs have the capacity to make reservation to treaties.[14]

[13] See F.-L. Bordin, *The Analogy between States and International Organizations* (Cambridge: Cambridge University Press, 2018).

[14] Article 1.1, ILC, Guide to Practice on Reservations to Treaties, adopted by the International Law Commission at its sixty-third session, in 2011, and submitted to the General Assembly as a part of the Commission's report covering the work of that session, UN Doc A/66/10, para. 75.

For the purposes of these guidelines, the ILC decided to treat IOs and states together.[15]

With regard to the ILC's work on customary international law, however, this methodological question was never addressed head on. While the Draft Conclusions and the Commentary refer to IOs, such references are not consistent throughout – a criticism that was acknowledged in the Fourth Report.[16] The ILC's work on customary international law thus suffers from this broader indeterminacy about the role of IOs in international law. The ILC's state-centric approach was also evident in the study: 'States remain the primary subjects of international law and, [. . .] it is primarily their practice that contributes to the formation, and expression, of rules of customary international law'.[17] Nonetheless, it is increasingly acknowledged that IO may also play an important role as law-makers, and the practice of IOs may be relevant in identifying customary international law. For instance, 'organization practice' may contribute to the development of customary international law in a number of ways.[18] The Special Rapporteur confirmed in his Fourth Report that '[i]n certain cases, the practice of international organizations also contributes to the expression, or creation, of rules of customary international law'.[19]

There should be nothing particularly controversial about the notion that IOs, alongside states, can contribute to the development of customary international law. Yet the examples given are usually instances where an IO, such as the EU, acts like a state. There is less discussion of how IOs might contribute in their own right, *as international organizations*.[20] If one shifts the focus away from the inter-state plane to the relationship between states and IOs, or between IOs, one can see more clearly how the practice of IOs may

---

[15]   On assimilating IOs to states, see D. Verwey, *The European Community, the European Union and the International Law of Treaties* (The Hague: TMC Asser Press, 2004) 129.

[16]   ILC, Fourth Report on Identification of Customary International Law by Michael Wood, Special Rapporteur, International Law Commission Sixty-eighth session, Geneva (2 May–10 June and 4 July–12 August 2016), UN Doc A/CN.4/695 ('Fourth Report'), para. 19: 'It was also noted that at present the reference to international organizations is not entirely consistent throughout the draft conclusions as a whole, since in places the latter refer explicitly to State practice alone'.

[17]   ILC, Third Report on Identification of Customary International Law by Michael Wood, Special Rapporteur, International Law Commission Sixty-seventh session, Geneva (4 May–5 June and 6 July–7 August 2015), UN Doc A/CN.4/682 ('Third Report'), para. 76.

[18]   See J. Crawford, *Brownlie's Principles of Public International Law*, 8th edn (Oxford: Oxford University Press, 2013) 192.

[19]   Fourth Report (n16) para. 20.

[20]   See Bordin (n13) who argues that IOs can contribute to customary law 'not because international organizations are analogous to States, but rather because doing otherwise would exclude from the picture practice stemming from the collective action of States,' 123.

contribute to the development of customary international law. Nonetheless, there has been certain resistance to the idea that IOs may also contribute to the development of customary international law in their own right, both from academic commentators and from some states themselves.[21]

There are a number of reasons why the practice of IOs may be considered as having less weight in the development of customary international law. IOs vary in terms of goals, functions, membership and powers, and therefore 'in each case their practice must be appraised with caution'.[22] Moreover, in contrast with states, there is simply less practice by IOs upon which to base rules of customary international law. The question is not so much whether the practice of IOs may contribute to customary international law, but how IO practice should be conceived; the type of practice that should be taken into account; the kinds of rules to which IO practice might contribute; and who is bound by such rules.

Another difficulty faced by the ILC is how to deal with legal actors such as the EU, which claim to be 'unique' or have special features. This also represents a tension between competing goals in the ILC's work: the aim of codifying rules of a general nature, applicable to all legal actors, and the need to reflect sufficiently the diversity of IOs. The work of the ILC regarding IOs has been criticized, for example, for neglecting the specific characteristics of supranational organizations, in particular the EU and its legal order. This primary focus on states is also evident in other codification projects, most notably the ILC's Articles on Responsibility of International Organizations (ARIO).[23] It was argued in this regard that the ILC largely ignored the wide-scale treaty practice of the EU and generally failed to consider the implications that such practice could imply for customary law.[24] The Draft Articles were thus criticized, among other things, for failing to take due account of 'unique' organizations such as the EU and its international practice.[25]

---

[21] See S. D. Murphy, 'The Identification of Customary International Law and Other Topics: The Sixty-Seventh Session of the International Law Commission' (2015) GW Law School Public Law and Legal Theory Paper No. 2015–2038, 9–11.

[22] Fourth Report (n16) para. 20.

[23] Draft Articles on the Responsibility of International Organizations with Commentaries, in Report of the International Law Commission, 63rd Session (26 April–3 June, 4 July–12 August 2011), UN Doc. A/66/10, at 52; GAOR, 66th Session, Supp. No. 10 (2011) ('ARIO').

[24] See E. Paasivirta & P.-J. Kuijper, 'Does One Size Fit All? The European Community and the Responsibility of International Organizations' (2005) 36 *Netherlands Yearbook of International Law* 169, 211–212.

[25] See Comments of the European Commission, Comments and Observations Received from International Organizations, 14 February 2011, UN Doc. A.CN.4/637, 8: 'for now the European Union remains unconvinced that the draft articles and the commentaries thereto adequately reflect the diversity of international organizations'.

Another issue faced by the ILC when dealing with IOs is the very definition of 'international organization'. The Special Rapporteur noted early on that it would be useful to define the term 'international organization' for the purposes of the Draft Conclusions.[26] The ILC has sought to define this term, for the purposes of its work, on a number of occasions. For instance, in ARIO 'international organization' is defined as:

> an organization established by a treaty or other instrument governed by international law and possessing its own international legal personality. International organizations may include as members, in addition to states, other entities.[27]

This definition was devised for the specific context of international responsibility, and was not intended to be a general definition. For the purposes of the customary international law study, the Special Rapporteur favoured a more general definition. The ILC adopted a definition that has been used in some codification conventions, such as the *Vienna Convention on the Law of Treaties between States and International Organizations or between International Organizations*[28] which set out simply that the term 'international organization' means an 'intergovernmental organization'. This definition was eventually included in the Commentary, rather than in the Draft Conclusions.[29]

By choosing to use this broad definition, the Special Rapporteur rejected the idea of creating separate categories of IOs.[30] This approach was initially considered, but ultimately rejected, by Special Rapporteur Gaja during the development of the ARIO. Rather than develop rules to apply to different categories of IOs, the ILC favoured a more all-encompassing definition, one that could apply to a broad range of IOs.[31] The EU was of the view, however, that such a broad definition would be inadequate, and argued consistently that

---

[26] ILC, Second Report on Identification of Customary International Law by Michael Wood, Special Rapporteur, International Law Commission, Sixty-sixth session, Geneva (5 May–6 June and 7 July–8 August 2014), UN Doc A/CN.4/672 ('Second Report'), para. 18.

[27] Article 2(a), ARIO (n23).

[28] Article 2, para. 1 (a)(i), Vienna Convention on the Law of Treaties between States and International Organizations or between International Organizations (21 March 1986) 25 ILM 543 (1986), not yet in force ('VCLT-IO').

[29] Third Report (n17) fn 159: 'The Special Rapporteur does not at present consider it necessary to include a definition in the draft conclusions, provided that an explanation is given in the commentary. This is a matter which the Drafting Committee may wish to consider further'.

[30] On the challenges of creating sub-categories of legal subjects such as 'regional integration organizations', see Bordin (n13) 116.

[31] See ILC, Report of the International Law Commission on the work of its fifty-fourth session (29 April–7 June and 22 July–16 August 2002), Official Records of the General Assembly, Fifty-fourth session, Supplement No. 10, UN Doc A/57/10, para. 470.

the draft articles should be more nuanced, taking into account the diversity of IOs. In the context of customary international law, the EU also expressed the view that a general definition of 'international organization' would be inadequate.

> ... the European Union considers that relying only on the formal notion of international organisation would not be helpful, but it is rather necessary to take a closer look at the organisations – or categories of organisations – concerned.[32]

Special Rapporteur Wood similarly did not seek to define different categories of IOs for the work on customary international law. While the EU is often considered to be 'a rather special international organization'[33] in the academic literature, the ILC has mostly rejected the idea of categorizing IOs for these purposes.[34] Rather, the approach has been to discuss the diversity of IOs, and the legal significance of this, in the Commentaries. One can understand the rationale for this. The ILC usually works on discrete legal issues, and thus it is not the place to explore some of the more underlying questions facing international law. To summarize, the ILC's work analyses IOs and states separately, but prefers to treat all IOs as belonging to a single legal category, irrespective of the diversity of IOs.

2.2.2 *Relevance of 'Organization Practice'*

The language of the Draft Conclusions and the Commentary continually refers to states. Although there are some references to IOs, it reveals that such practice is only relevant '[i]n certain cases'.[35] In the Commentary to the Draft Conclusions, the Special Rapporteur elaborates on what some of these 'certain cases' are. The Special Rapporteur points to some limits regarding how 'organization practice' should be dealt with. First, the practice of states within an organization should not be equated with that of the organization itself. It is important, therefore, to distinguish 'State practice' and 'organization practice'

---

[32] Statement on Behalf of the European Union and its Member States by Lucio Gussetti, Director, European Commission Legal Service at the General Assembly Sixth Committee on Item 83, 'Identification of Customary International Law', United Nations, New York, 4 November 2015, para. 5.

[33] N. Blokker & R. A. Wessel, 'Introduction: First Views at the Articles on the Responsibility of International Organizations' (2012) 9 *International Organizations Law Review* 1, 5.

[34] See J. Wouters & J. Odermatt, 'Are All International Organizations Created Equal?' (2012) 9 *International Organizations Law Review* 7–14.

[35] Fourth Report (n16) para. 20.

as separate elements, although this is admittedly easier said than done.[36] The second limit concerns what kind of 'organization practice' is relevant. The Special Rapporteur emphasizes that only the external practice of the organization is relevant, that is, the practice involving the organization's relationships with third states and organizations. While internal practice may be relevant in developing the 'rules of the organization', it is not considered relevant when contributing to the development of rules of customary international law.[37]

2.2.2.1 States Acting through International Organizations

The Special Rapporteur identified three main ways by which IOs can contribute to the formation of custom. The first is when states act through IOs, such as when they participate in the work of the UN General Assembly. For example, State conduct 'in connection with resolutions adopted by an international organization'[38] is considered a form of relevant practice, and as evidence of *opinio juris*.[39] However, a resolution adopted by an IO 'cannot, of itself, create a rule of customary international law'.[40] In these cases, the IO is a forum in which states act, thus developing practice or expressing *opinio juris* via the institution's organs. In this method, IOs remain an institutional setting in which states act. The *Third Restatement of the Law, Foreign Relations Law of the United States*, for example, sets out that '[t]he practice of states that builds customary law takes many forms and includes what states do in or through international organizations'.[41] Whether such behaviour should be regarded as sufficient State practice depends on a number of factors, including how widely supported the resolution or declaration was, and whether it has been supported by subsequent practice. When the UNGA adopts or 'takes note' of the work of the ILC, for example, it may be more likely to be considered a reflection of customary international law.[42] UNGA

---

[36]   Third Report (n17) para. 71.
[37]   Third Report (n17) para. 72.
[38]   ILC Draft Conclusion 6(2) (n11).
[39]   ILC Draft Conclusion 10(2) (n11).
[40]   ILC Draft Conclusion 12(1) (n11).
[41]   American Law Institute, *Restatement of the Law, Third, the Foreign Relations Law of the United States* (Philadelphia:American Law Institute Publishers, 1987) Section102 (Sources of International Law) Reporters' Notes 2.
[42]   See F.-L. Bordin, 'Reflections of Customary International Law: The Authority of Codification Conventions and ILC Draft Articles in International Law' (2014) 63 *International Comparative Law Quarterly* 535–567 arguing that courts and tribunals have increasingly cited ILC codification conventions and draft articles as reflections of customary international law.

resolutions may express *opinio juris*, but this is a reflection of the views of individual members of the UNGA, and not the institution as a separate actor in international law.

Draft Conclusion 12 relates to the 'Resolutions of international organizations and intergovernmental conferences' and sets out that a resolution of an IO cannot itself create a rule of customary international law. Rather, such a resolution may only 'provide evidence for establishing the existence and content of a rule of customary international law, or contribute to its development'.[43] This first method is the most common way in which IOs contribute to the development of customary international law. Yet scholars have cautioned against too easily equating organization practice with State practice, since State practice through an organization may be 'distorted'.[44]

2.2.2.2 International Organizations as 'Catalysts' of State Practice

The second method is when the acts of an IO serve to 'catalyse' State practice.[45] The examples given of this method include instances where IOs develop draft texts on which states provide their responses. This debate, spurred by the activity of IOs, can then lead to the development of customary international law. Another example is when IOs call upon states to act in a certain way, such as adopting certain national laws, which in turn can contribute to relevant practice. This form of contribution is closely linked with the first method described earlier. It accepts that, in addition to looking at the output of IOs such as declarations and resolutions, it is also important to examine closely the practice of states that led to their adoption.

The EU has been active in international legal forums where rules of international law are discussed, including the UN Sixth Committee and the International Law Commission.[46] The process by which the EU coordinates its positions on issues of public international law, such as discussion in the Council Working Group on Public International law (COJUR), has also helped to catalyse the expression of international law issues. Importantly, the

---

[43] ILC Draft Conclusion 12, point 2 (n11).

[44] J. Wouters & P. De Man, 'International Organizations as Law-Makers' in J. Klabbers & A. Wallendahl (eds), *Research Handbook on International Organizations Law: Between Functionalism and Constitutionalism* (Cheltenham: Edward Elgar, 2011). See Third Report (n17) fn 169 and the academic literature cited.

[45] Third Report (n17) para. 75.

[46] See J. Wouters & M. Hermez, 'The EU's Contribution to "the Strict Observance and the Development of International Law" at the UNGA Sixth Committee' in S. Blavoukos & D. Bourantonis (eds), *The EU in UN Politics: Actors, Processes and Performances* (London: Palgrave Macmillan, 2017) 190–224.

EU positions are not simply a reflection of the common views of the EU Member States, but also reflect the 'EU position' on certain issues, especially where they relate to the EU's practice in fields such as expulsion of aliens or the provisional application of treaties. In these circumstances, it may be difficult to ascertain whether such expressions represent the EU's contribution as such, or a collective expression of the views of the EU Member States. Much of the existing literature that deals with the EU's contribution to customary international law has focused on the EU as a 'catalyst'. Vanhamme provides examples of how the EU has been an 'instigator' in the development of customary international law in the fields of democracy and good governance, sustainable development and the precautionary principle.[47] However, even though it represents the position of 27 Member States, the EU's voice and influence within these bodies may be somewhat diluted compared to the positions made by states.

2.2.2.3 Contribution of International Organizations 'As Such'

The third method identified is when an IO contributes to practice and *opinio juris* 'as such', that is, as an independent and autonomous actor. The Special Rapporteur mentioned that the 'most clear-cut'[48] example of an IO whose practice can contribute to the formation of custom is the European Union. In these situations, the IO is more than a catalyst of State practice or forum for the expression of states' views; it is the organization's own practice which is of relevance. According to the Commentaries, this can only be the case where the subject matter of the rules falls within the mandate of the organization.[49] IO practice can thus contribute to the formation of customary law only 'where member states have transferred exclusive competences to the international organization'.[50] The Commentaries give some examples of types of practice that could contribute in such a fashion: 'the practice of international organizations when concluding treaties, serving as treaty depositaries, in deploying military forces (for example, for peacekeeping), in administering territories, or in taking positions on the scope of the privileges and immunities of the organization and its officials … '.[51] This position reflects the fact that IOs, possessing international legal personality, are capable of incurring rights and

---

[47]　J. Vanhamme, 'Formation and Enforcement of Customary International Law: The European Union's Contribution' (2008) 29 *Netherlands Yearbook of International Law* 127.

[48]　Third Report (n17) para. 77.

[49]　Commentary to ILC Draft Conclusion 4 (n11) 131.

[50]　Commentary to ILC Draft Conclusion 4 (n11) 131.

[51]　Commentary to ILC Draft Conclusion 4 (n11) 131.

responsibilities on the plane of international law.[52] As independent legal actors in their own right, they can thus contribute 'as such' to the formation of certain customary rules. The Special Rapporteur supports the concept that IOs can also contribute to the development of customary law in their own capacity. While the Report provides numerous references from academic literature to support this argument,[53] it does not refer to judicial practice that confirms this.[54]

The EU has functionally replaced its Member States in many fields of international relations, and the Special Rapporteur concludes that in these fields, 'such practice may be equated with the practice of States'.[55] If such practice were not equated with that of states, the Special Rapporteur reasons, not only would the organization's practice not be taken into account, but 'Member States would themselves be deprived of or reduced in their ability to contribute to State practice'.[56] The EU also considers that this conclusion 'makes practical and legal sense'.[57] In fields of EU exclusive competence, for example, EU Member States may be legally prevented from taking a separate position in international legal forums, especially when the Union has adopted a position on a certain subject.[58] The EU Member States should not be deprived of the opportunity to contribute to the development of customary international law because it was an IO, and not a State, acting at the international level.

The Commentaries suggest, however, that some caution should be exercised when considering organization practice. They emphasize that '[i]nternational organizations are not States',[59] and that it is 'primarily the practice of States that is to be looked to' when determining the existence of rules of customary international law. Moreover, they state that 'caution is

---

[52] Interpretation of the Agreement of 25 March 1951 between the WHO and Egypt, (Advisory Opinion) (1980) ICJ Rep 73, 89–90. 'International organizations are subjects of international law and, as such, are bound by any obligations incumbent upon them under general rules of international law . . . '

[53] Third Report (n17) fn 179.

[54] Murphy (n21) 7.

[55] Third Report (n17) para. 77.

[56] Third Report (n17) para. 77.

[57] Statement on Behalf of the European Union (n32) para. 5.

[58] J. Larik & A.-D. Casteleiro, 'The Duty to Remain Silent: Limitless Loyalty in EU External Relations' (2011) 36 *European Law Review* 524–541, 540: 'the duty of sincere cooperation in external relations manifests itself indeed rather often as a duty for the Member States to keep silent, unless told to speak by the EU institutions'. See M. Cremona, 'Defending the Community Interest: The Duties of Cooperation and Compliance' in M. Cremona & B. de Witte (eds), *EU Foreign Relations Law: Constitutional Fundamentals* (Oxford: Hart, 2008) 125–169.

[59] Commentary to ILC Draft Conclusions 4 (n11) 131.

required' when assessing the weight to be given to the practice of IOs, stressing that IOs vary greatly in terms of powers, membership and functions. The Draft Conclusions therefore recognize the possibility of IO practice contributing to the formation of customary rules, but then appear to suggest that such practice would arise in a very narrow set of circumstances, and that the weight of such practice is limited.

While areas of EU exclusive competences may be most visible, one need not limit this form of contribution to fields of exclusive competence. The EU contributes to the formation of custom in these fields due to its independent existence in the international legal order, and as such, it may contribute to the development of custom in other fields in which it has competence. It is not so much the fact that the EU has replaced the EU Member States with respect to certain policies, but that the EU exercises a certain independent will and function on the international plane. The issue of competence remains relevant, however, since the EU can only contribute to customary international law to the extent to which this lawmaking function has been transferred to the EU level. The ILC tends to restrict its analysis to the issue of the transfer of competences. It does not fully explore the circumstances under which the EU might be considered as acting as an organization 'as such'. EU action is most likely to be considered as 'organization practice' (in its own right) in the scenarios discussed subsequently, such as where the Union exercises its capacity to enter into international agreements in its own right, and through the jurisprudence of the CJEU.

The Draft Conclusions and Commentary accept that IOs may contribute 'as such' only in cases where they exercise powers that are analogous to that of a State, such as concluding treaties or deploying military forces. However, it overlooks the ways that IO practice may contribute *as international organizations*. Take, for instance, practice that leads to the formation of rules that apply between states and international organizations. Such practice is based in part upon the activities of both states and international organizations interacting. The 1986 *Vienna Convention on the Law of Treaties between States and International Organizations or between International Organizations* ('VCLT-IO')[60] to a large extent represents customary international law that is based on the practice of states *and* IOs. The VCLT-IO states that were the convention does not govern a certain issue; customary international law will continue to apply.[61] This implies that customary rules can be found by reference to the

---

[60] Fourth Report (n16) para. 20.
[61] Preamble, VCLT-IO (n28) states that 'rules of customary international law will continue to govern questions not regulated by the provisions of the present Convention'.

practice and *opinio juris* of states and IOs. When an IO concludes a treaty with a State, for example, the organization's practice might be taken into account when identifying rules applicable between those subjects.

It should be noted that this third category of contribution is far less common than the other two, and remains disputed. There are few examples of states conferring such extensive powers to an organization. As Murphy points out '[s]uch an example may well be valid, though the European Union is a rather unique international organization (often described more as a "supra-national" organization), and thus may not be exemplary of international organizations generally'.[62] Nonetheless, the practice of an IO acting in the field of competence conferred to it is rightly included in the Commentary. In areas such as the law of the sea and international fisheries or in WTO law, where the EU exercises significant competences conferred by its Member States, the Union could potentially contribute to the development of customary international law.[63]

When the EU contributes to customary international law in this way, it does so as a separate legal actor in international law. This practice should not be equated with State practice, as the Special Rapporteur suggests, since to do so would deny the separate and distinct legal personality of the Union. It has been pointed out that '[t]o depict [EU acts] as State practice would deny one of the main features of the [EU], i.e., its autonomous functioning on the basis of the legislative, executive and judicial powers delegated to it by the Member States'.[64] The EU is considered at the international level to be a legally distinct entity, separate from the Member States, and may contribute to the formation of customary international law as such.

It is now accepted that IOs play an important role in the development of international law alongside states.[65] In its recent work, the ILC has continued to face complex questions regarding the way principles of public international law apply to international organizations, especially those exercising autonomous powers, such as the EU. In doing so, the ILC has maintained a clear dichotomy between states and international organizations. Its work on the law

---

[62] Murphy (n21) 8.

[63] See, e.g., E. Paasivirta, 'Four Contributions of the European Union to the Law of the Sea' in J. Czuczai & F. Naert (eds), *The EU as a Global Actor – Bridging Legal Theory and Practice at the Turn of the 21st Century. Liber Amicorum in Honour of Ricardo Gosalbo Bono* (Leiden: Brill Nijhoff, 2016) 241–265.

[64] Vanhamme (n47) 131.

[65] As Brölmann points out, '[o]rganisations are involved in almost all fields of human cooperation, where they present themselves not only as institutional fora for states, but also as independent international actors'. C. Brölmann, *The Institutional Veil in Public International Law: International Organisations and the Law of Treaties* (Oxford: Hart, 2007) 1.

of treaties, and its more recent work on international responsibility, for example, is premised on this distinction. One particular criticism is that 'such projects [VCLT-IO and ARIO] suggest an approach by the Commission previously that separates rules relating to states from rules relating to international organizations, not a mixing of the two into a single system'.[66] One may question whether it is appropriate to continue with this sharp distinction when examining the issue of sources of international law.

2.3 THE EU'S CONTRIBUTION TO THE FORMATION AND IDENTIFICATION OF CUSTOMARY INTERNATIONAL LAW

How do principles developed primarily to apply to states, such as the rules of international responsibility, the law of treaties, jurisdiction, nationality and so on, apply to a regional integration organization such as the EU? The answer to these questions can be found largely by looking at international practice which involves the EU acting on the international plane. This not only includes the practice of the EU, but also of the EU Member States and the reaction by non-EU states. Over time, this international practice helps to develop rules of customary international law pertaining to how entities such as the EU fit within the wider international legal order. For example, the EU could be considered as contributing to customary international law through its treaty practice, which is discussed in more detail in Chapter 3. Similarly, the activity of the EU and the Member States in the context of international organizations (Chapter 4) and international dispute settlement bodies (Chapter 5) may also be relevant. EU practice has been discussed in the context of identifying rules of responsibility in the context of international organizations (Chapter 6).Section 2.2.1 will briefly discuss whether the courts of the EU could also be relevant in the identification of customary international law.

2.3.1 *Judicial Practice*

Alongside the EU's practice on the plane of international law, the EU may also contribute to customary international law through the Court of Justice of the EU (CJEU). In a statement at the UN General Assembly's Sixth Committee, the EU Delegation observed that 'it is far from exceptional or rare for the EU judiciary to deal with public international law issues'.[67] As the EU becomes

---

[66] Murphy (n21) 9.
[67] Statement on Behalf of the European Union (n32) para. 8.

more active in a broad range of fields, this can also give rise to a range of issues faced by the CJEU related to public international law, such as fields of state responsibility, diplomatic and consular law, the law of the sea, territory and jurisdiction, and nationality and citizenship. Can such practice also contribute to the formation of customary international law? The ILC's Draft Conclusions recognize the role of courts in the identification of customary international law. Yet their role largely depends on whether the court is a national or an international/regional court.

National courts, as organs of the State, are capable of contributing to the 'general practice' element. State practice in this context refers to the conduct of the State, including its 'executive, legislative, judicial or other functions' and forms of practice including 'decisions of national courts'.[68] The Commentary sets out that the term 'national courts' can include courts 'with an international element operating within one or more domestic legal systems, such as courts or tribunals with mixed national and international composition'.[69] This recognizes that states are the main drivers of the formation of customary international law, and that national courts are an act of the State to be considered when examining State practice.

Decisions of national courts can also be evidence that a particular rule of customary international law is 'accepted as law' (*opinio juris*). The examples of such evidence in the Commentary mostly refer to the acts of the executive and legislative branches, including official documents and publications, diplomatic correspondence and national legislation. While there is no hierarchy of forms of evidence, the Commentary appears to diminish the potential role of national courts in *opinio juris*: '[d]ecisions of national courts may also contain such statements when pronouncing upon questions of international law'.[70] This reflects the fact that, in many cases, it is the official acts of executive organs that establishes whether a particular rule is accepted as law. Nonetheless, there are certain areas where the practice of national courts has also been influential, such as in the field of sovereign immunity.

Decisions of national courts are also a subsidiary means for the determination of customary international law where they relate to the 'existence and content' of those rules.[71] It should be emphasized that 'subsidiary' does not mean 'unimportant'. It just means that these court decisions do not directly

---

[68] ILC Draft Conclusion 6 (n11).
[69] Commentary to ILC Draft Conclusion 6 (n11) 134, fn 705. This would apply to so-called hybrid courts that have an international composition but operate in one or more national systems.
[70] Commentary to ILC Draft Conclusion 10 (n11) 140.
[71] ILC Draft Conclusion 13(2) (n11).

contribute to the formation of customary international law.[72] Article 38 (1) (d) of the ICJ Statute also considers jurisprudence of international courts as a subsidiary means, but this likewise does not mean that ICJ jurisprudence is not highly influential in the development of the law. A national court thus plays a dual role; it may contribute directly as a form of State practice and as evidence of *opinio juris*, and may also be a subsidiary means of determining the existence and content of customary international law.

The impact of international courts is more limited. According to the Draft Conclusions, such international judicial practice is considered a subsidiary means for determining the rules.[73] The Commentary gives some examples of what is meant by an 'international court'. In addition to the ICJ and Permanent Court of International Justice (PCIJ) the Commentary also refers to 'specialist and regional courts, such as the International Tribunal for the Law of the Sea, the International Criminal Court and other international criminal tribunals, regional human rights courts and the World Trade Organization Dispute Settlement Body'.[74] Although the CJEU is not mentioned, it would fall within the category of a regional court for these purposes. The Commentary notes, furthermore, that the distinction between national and international courts is not always 'clear-cut'.[75]

Where does the CJEU fit? On the one hand, the CJEU could fall within the category of an international court. It is a court of an international organization established by international treaties, and its role is to 'ensure that in the interpretation and application of the Treaties the law is observed'.[76] On the other hand, the CJEU is not usually considered as an ordinary international court, in the same way that the European Union is not considered an ordinary international organization. The very reasons that the Union is considered to be a 'sui generis' organization, such as the fact that Union law is integrated into the law of the EU Member States, could be used to argue that the CJEU is very much a 'sui generis' court, one that sits between that of a national and an international court. This is supported by the role of the CJEU, whose function resembles that of a national court. While it does deal with issues of public international law occasionally, its primary role is to interpret and apply the EU Treaties, and in that role resembles that of a national constitutional court.

[72] Commentary to ILC Draft Conclusion 13 (n11).
[73] '[d]ecisions of international courts and tribunals, in particular of the International Court of Justice, concerning the existence and content of rules of customary international law are a subsidiary means for the determination of such rules'. ILC Draft Conclusion 13(1) (n11).
[74] Commentary to ILC Draft Conclusion 13 (n11) 150.
[75] Commentary to ILC Draft Conclusion 13 (n11) 150.
[76] Article 19, Treaty on European Union (TEU).

The focus, however, should not be on the character or the CJEU, but rather on the role it plays in a given case. This means that the CJEU may be considered an international court in certain instances, and analogous to a national court in others.

First, the CJEU may reflect State practice and *opinio juris* of the EU Member States. For example, where the CJEU opines on the position of EU Member States on a particular issue of customary international law, that legal opinion could be considered as evidence of *opinio juris* in the same way as a national court could reflect a states' expression of *opinio juris*. This follows the same rationale for allowing IOs to contribute to state practice and *opinio juris*: in certain cases, especially where the Union exercises exclusive competences, it is the CJEU, rather than the courts of the EU Member States, that will decide on legal issues associated with customary international law. Judgments of the CJEU would then contribute to State practice and expression of *opinio juris* in the same way as a national court. In such cases, the CJEU would be expressing this on behalf of some or all of the EU Member States, and thus the weight given to such practice should reflect the fact that it is formed by a number of states.

Second, the CJEU may also contribute to the formation of customary rules that apply in the relations between states and IOs. This would be the case, for instance, when rules are being developed about how regional integration organizations, such as the Union, participate in international law. As discussed earlier, rules may have to be adapted to take into account the unique nature of the EU. Take, for instance, the development of rules relating to international responsibility. When examining the rules that apply to the responsibility of IOs (and states acting within those organizations), the ILC examined the practice of the EU, including the case-law of the CJEU. The ILC Commentaries to the Draft Articles refer to *Costa v. ENEL*, in the discussion on whether 'rules of the organization' are to be considered 'international obligations'.[77] They refer to the concept of 'damage', citing *Walz*.[78] The issue of mixed agreements is discussed with reference to the *Parliament v. Council*.[79] The commentary on lawful countermeasures discusses the judgment in *Commission v. Luxembourg*, where the CJEU found

---

[77] ARIO (n23) Commentary to Article 10, p. 63: 'Another view, which finds support in practice, is that international organizations that have achieved a high degree of integration are a special case'.

[78] ARIO (n23) Commentary to Article 10, p. 77. In *Walz* the CJEU referred to these draft articles on State responsibility as indicative of customary international law. Judgment in *Walz v. Clickair SA*, C-63/09, EU:C:2010:251, para. 27.

[79] ARIO (n23) Commentary to Article 48, p. 89.

that the EU Member States could no longer resort to inter-state counter-measures to enforce obligations under the EU Treaties.[80] In these cases, the CJEU jurisprudence contributes to the development of EU law, but may also contribute 'as such' to the formation of rules of customary international law relating to IOs.

Consider the case of *Wightman*,[81] which dealt with the question of whether the United Kingdom could unilaterally revoke its intention to withdrawal from the European Union. In deciding this case, the CJEU first and foremost applied EU law. Yet it may contribute indirectly to the law of international organizations and the law of treaties. The CJEU decided the case mostly with reference to the EU Treaties themselves, without resorting to the application of the VCLT. The CJEU notes that its conclusion – that a Member State's notification of intention to withdrawal does not inevitably lead to the withdrawal of that State – 'is corroborated by the provisions of the Vienna Convention on the Law of Treaties, which was taken into account in the preparatory work for the Treaty establishing a Constitution for Europe'.[82] Such practice may simultaneously develop EU law as well as add to the scarce international practice on State withdrawal from an IO. Of course, the specific case of Article 50 TEU and the nature of EU law would have to be taken into account when examining the significance of such practice, but this does not exclude the fact that it may be relevant in the formation of customary international law.

Third, the CJEU may interpret and apply customary international law while acting in the capacity of an 'international court'. In such cases, the CJEU is not reflecting the position of EU Member States, or contributing to rules that apply to international organizations, but is identifying and applying rules of customary international law in a way that is analogous to that of the ICJ or another international court. For instance, the CJEU has interpreted and applied provisions of the VCLT that it considers to be a reflection of customary international law. In these cases, the CJEU jurisprudence should be viewed as a subsidiary means for the determination of rules of customary international law. This reflects the fact that, like domestic courts that apply and interpret customary international law, the CJEU deals with customary international law within a very specific legal context. In these cases, it is primarily focused on resolving a dispute that arose in the context of EU law, and will often apply international law as means of applying EU law. Moreover,

---

[80] ARIO (n23) Commentary to Article 52, p. 94.
[81] Judgment in *Wightman*, Case C-621/18, 10 December 2018, EU:C:2018:999.
[82] *Id.*, para. 70.

judges of the EU Court of Justice are not necessarily competent to deal with issues of public international law. They are chosen from those who 'possess the qualifications required for appointment to the highest judicial offices in their respective countries or who are jurisconsults of recognised competence'.[83] The Panel that is responsible for assessing whether candidates meet the criteria established under the EU Treaties will assess whether a candidate has adequate basic knowledge of EU law, but it does not assess whether he or she has experience or knowledge in international law.[84] The lack of expertise on issues of public international law within the CJEU would also diminish the weight of its contribution. The Commentary reflects this:

> National courts operate within a particular legal system, which may incorporate international law only in a particular way and to a limited extent. Their decisions may reflect a particular national perspective. Unlike most international courts, national courts may sometimes lack international law expertise and may have reached their decisions without the benefit of hearing argument advanced by states.[85]

Similarly, while the CJEU may identify and apply rules of customary international law, this should be understood in the context of the CJEU's role. This does not mean that the CJEU's jurisprudence should be disregarded, but it does affect the weight that should be given to it. The Commentary to Conclusion 13 on the decisions of courts and tribunals discusses how the value of decisions will vary greatly, depending on the 'quality of the reasoning (including primarily the extent to which it results from a thorough examination of evidence of an alleged general practice accepted as law)'.[86]

2.3.1.1 Identification of Customary International Law

There are a number of cases where the CJEU has been called upon to identify and apply rules and principles of customary international law. The CJEU rarely explicitly applies the two-element test to identify customary international law, preferring to refer to sources such as the work of the International Law Commission, the UN General Assembly and judgments and opinions of the

---

[83] Article 235, TEU.
[84] See Fifth Activity Report of the panel provided for by Article 255 of the Treaty on the Functioning of the European Union, 18 February 2018. See J.-M. Sauvé, 'Selecting the European Union's Judges: The Practice of the Article 255 Panel' in M. Bobek (ed), *Selecting Europe's Judges: A Critical Review of the Appointment Procedures to the European Courts* (Oxford: Oxford University Press, 2015) 78–85.
[85] Commentary to ILC Draft Conclusion 13 (n11) para. 7.
[86] Commentary to ILC Draft Conclusion 13 (n11) 149.

International Court of Justice. This is not surprising. Examining the customary international law-identification methods used by domestic courts, Ryngaert and Hora Siccama found that 'rarely does a domestic court thoroughly examine relevant state practice and *opinio juris* at length'.[87] A similar review of CJEU cases reveals that the CJEU also prefers a short-cut route to the identification of customary international law. The CJEU will first see whether a particular rule appears in any written sources, such as a codification treaty, UNGA resolution or the ARIO. In other instances, the CJEU will accept the customary law status of a rule if none of the parties dispute that, or if it has been accepted by the EU institutions and intervening Member States. The ICJ is also an important source in the CJEU's reasoning.[88] In particular, the opinions of the Advocates General often reveal a high level of engagement with these international law sources.

A full examination of the CJEU's methodology when identifying customary international law is beyond the scope of this book. The cases reveal an approach which tends to prefer references to written legal sources, such as codification conventions, or references to the ICJ/PCIJ confirming the customary law status of a particular rule. In this regard, the CJEU's approach mirrors that of many domestic courts, which do not engage in an in-depth analysis of State practice and *opinio juris*. Even the ICJ does not always engage in the 'two-step' process of identification of customary international law. Tomka notes that 'in practice, the [ICJ] has never found it necessary to undertake such an inquiry for every rule claimed to be customary in a particular case and instead has made use of the best and most expedient evidence available to determine whether a customary rule of this sort exists ...'.[89] Moreover, whereas the CJEU has been confident and active in identifying general principles of EU law, it has not showed the same approach when identifying customary international law.[90]

As discussed earlier, the value and legal weight to be given to the decisions of courts and tribunals depend in part on the quality of the reasoning, and the

---

[87]   C. M. Ryngaert & D. Hora Siccama, 'Ascertaining Customary International Law: An Inquiry into the Methods Used by Domestic Courts' (2018) 65(1) *Netherlands International Law Review* 1, 5.

[88]   R. Higgins, 'The ICJ, the ECJ, and the Integrity of International Law' (2003) 52(1) *International Comparative Law Quarterly* 1, 10: 'the International Court of Justice's findings as a useful short-route to identifying what customary international law on a given topic may be'.

[89]   P. Tomka, 'Custom and the International Court of Justice' (2013) 12 *The Law and Practice of International Courts and Tribunals* 195, 197.

[90]   Higgins (n88) 9. Higgins argues that the CJEU's approach to customary international law appears to be 'in marked contrast to the confidence shown as to its capabilities in international law shown by the Court in other cases'.

extent to which the court carries out an examination of the two elements. The capacity of the CJEU to contribute in this way is diminished by the lack of consistent engagement with these two-elements. This does not mean that the CJEU cannot contribute to the identification of customary international law. As explained earlier, the potential contribution may arise through the application of international law to the context of a supranational organization.

2.3.2 *Regional Custom*

Can EU practice also contribute to the development of regional custom?[91] Draft Conclusion 16 refers to 'Particular customary international law' and recognizes that in certain cases, a rule of customary international law may apply to a limited number of states, such as a regional customary rule.[92] In order to ascertain whether such regional customary rules exist, it is necessary to apply the two-element test to determine whether those particular rules are accepted by the general practice and *opinio juris* of those particular states.[93] The ICJ has recognized in principle the concept of regional custom.[94] The Conclusions and Commentary refer to 'particular customary international law', rather than regional customary international law, recognizing that, while such custom usually has a geographical element, this is not required.

The question also arises whether the CJEU jurisprudence would contribute to the formation of 'regional custom' in Europe. Alongside the European Court of Human Rights, the CJEU has produced a rich jurisprudence on human rights in Europe. While these rights are established in treaty law, specifically the *European Convention for the Protection of Human Rights and Fundamental Freedoms* and the *Charter of Fundamental Rights of the*

---

[91] S. Besson, 'General Principles and Customary Law in the EU Legal Order' in S. Vogenauer & S. Weatherill (eds), *General Principles of Law European and Comparative Perspectives* (Oxford: Hart, 2017) 128: 'Contrary to what is the case in domestic and international law, customary law has been largely neglected in the EU legal order . . . '

[92] ILC Draft Conclusion 16(1) (n11): 'A rule of particular customary international law, whether regional, local or other, is a rule of customary international law that applies only among a limited number of States'.

[93] ILC Draft Conclusion 16(1) (n11): 'To determine the existence and content of a rule of particular customary international law, it is necessary to ascertain whether there is a general practice among the States concerned that is accepted by them as law (*opinio juris*) among themselves'.

[94] See, e.g., *Military and Paramilitary Activities in and against Nicaragua*, 105, para. 199. 'the Court finds that in customary international law, whether of a general kind or that particular to the inter-American legal system, there is no rule permitting the exercise of collective self-defence in the absence of a request by the State which regards itself as the victim of an armed attack . . . '

European Union, the EU Treaties also recognize that fundamental rights stemming from the constitutional traditions of the EU Member States 'constitute general principles of the Union's law'.[95] The term 'general principles' here may appear to be analogous to 'general principles of law' found in the Article 38 of the ICJ Statute. 'General principles' in the ICJ Statute have been used mostly to close the gap of *non liquet*, and have mostly been used in the fields of 'procedure, evidence and the machinery of the judicial process'.[96] They include principles of equity, good faith and proportionality. In the context of EU law, general principles also include substantive rights. In *Kadi*, the CJEU recognized that the right to property is a general principle of Union law,[97] and that the imposition of the restrictive measures (sanctions) was an unjustified restriction on Mr Kadi's right to property.[98] It has been argued that the right to property binds states in Europe under regional customary law, supported by both state practice and *opinio juris*.[99]

Besson discusses the idea of 'EU customary law', defined as 'as a normative practice, ie (i) a general, coherent and regular practice (ii) regarded as law and hence as legally binding'.[100] Besson notes that the method by which the CJEU identifies general principles resembles the way in which domestic and international courts establish whether state practice constitutes customary international law.[101] Such EU customary law may develop through the practice of the EU Member States and the institutions; it can also develop 'bottom up' from the constitutional traditions of the Member States: 'EU fundamental rights could actually be approached as customary in source'.[102] EU customary law has relatively little relevance in practice. One reason for this is the progressive codification of practice over time.[103] In its judicial reasoning, the CJEU has shown a preference for examining and applying legal texts, primarily the EU Treaties and legislation, over the practice of the Member States or institutions.

---

[95] Article 6(3), TEU: 'Fundamental rights, as guaranteed by the European Convention for the Protection of Human Rights and Fundamental Freedoms and as they result from the constitutional traditions common to the Member States, shall constitute general principles of the Union's law'.

[96] M. Shaw, *International Law*, 8th edn (Cambridge: Cambridge University Press, 2017).

[97] Judgment in *Kadi and Al Barakaat International Foundation v. Council and Commission*, Joined Cases C-402/05 P & C-415/05 P, EU:C:2008:461, para. 355.

[98] *Id.*, para. 370.

[99] See L. Mardikian, 'The Right to Property as Regional Custom in Europe' (2018) 9(1) *Transnational Legal Theory* 56–84.

[100] Besson (n91) 115.

[101] Besson (n91) 125.

[102] Besson (n91) 126.

[103] Besson (n91) 121.

2.4 CONCLUSION

Rules of customary international law can be developed, not only by states, but also through the *interaction* between states and international organizations or between international organizations. Some of the fields where such inter-action can develop custom include the law of treaties, international responsi-bility of IOs and the law of succession between international organizations.[104] The practice of developing such rules will include, in addition to states and their national courts, international organizations and their courts. In such instances, the court of an international organization should be considered as having the same capacity to influence customary international law – in identifying practice and *opinio juris* – as that of a national court. This would mean that when international organizations and states interact, such as when they conclude treaties, the courts of both parties have an equal capacity to contribute to custom related to that practice. This means that in certain circumstances, the CJEU's judicial practice can contribute in the same way as a 'national court'.

While it has been accepted generally that international organizations, including the Union, may contribute to the development of customary inter-national law, there has been less debate about the types of rules to which they may contribute, and the types of practice that may be relevant. Much of the focus has been on instances where the EU practice reflects the common position of the EU Member States, or where EU practice has been a catalysis towards the development of custom. Konstadinides concludes that 'although the EU's practice alone has not generated by itself any new custom yet [. . .] it has reinforced and consolidated some otherwise emerging international cus-tomary rules'.[105]

Yet there is a form of IO practice that is often overlooked, that is, the practice of organizations as such. Compared with the others, this form of contribution may be considered relatively marginal. There is now a wealth of practice emanating from the EU: treaties to which the EU is a party, and the practice connected to those treaties; statements made on behalf of the EU in international forums; EU practice within international dispute settlement

---

[104] T. Treves, 'Customary International Law' in Rüdiger Wolfrum (ed), *Max Planck Encyclopedia of Public International Law* (online edn), http://opil.ouplaw.com/home/EPI L, para. 51.

[105] T. Konstadinides, 'The Meso Level: Means of Interaction between EU and International Law Customary International Law as a Source of EU Law: A Two-Way Fertilization Route?' (2016) 35 *Yearbook of European Law* 513, 530.

bodies; the actions of the EU legislative organs; and the jurisprudence of the CJEU, can all be considered relevant forms of practice. Such practice may be highly relevant when examining the development of rules that apply to international organizations (or supranational organizations) and in the relationship between the EU and third states and organizations.

3

The Law of Treaties

3.1 INTRODUCTION

There has been discussion in recent years about 'the end of treaties' and how international cooperation is now often achieved through methods other than the formal treaty-making process.[1] Over the past decade, states have sought to deal with global challenges ranging from financial stability to climate change and nuclear non-proliferation, not through binding international instruments, but through non-binding commitments, diplomacy and unilateral domestic measures. This has brought into doubt the continued relevance of treaties, which can be viewed as rigid and slow moving compared with other forms of international co-operation.

Yet treaties still play a large role in diplomatic life, and remain very much the cornerstone of modern international law.[2] For the EU, treaties are a key method by which it acts on the international scene. Although the EU is able to take autonomous measures, and is developing its own diplomatic representation, the main method by which the EU has acted internationally is through the negotiation and conclusion of international agreements. International treaties remain a central part of the EU's foreign policy. Much of the EU's foreign policy towards its Eastern and Southern neighbours is pursued through the negotiation of agreements with those states. The 2014 unrest in Ukraine, for example, was sparked in part by the refusal of Ukraine's President Viktor Yanukovych to sign an Association Agreement with the European

---

[1] J. P. Rubin, 'Farewell to the Age of the Treaty', *The New York Times*, 21 November 2010. See the discussion on this issue at American Journal of International Law, AJIL Unbound, The End of Treaties? An Online Agora, www.asil.org/blogs/end-treaties-online-agora.

[2] O. Dörr & K. Schmalenbach (eds), *Vienna Convention on the Law of Treaties: A Commentary* (Heidelberg: Springer, 2012) v. '[t]he law of treaties forms the backbone of the international legal order'.

Union.[3] The negotiation and conclusion of trade agreements have been subject to intense political scrutiny.

Major international issues where the EU seeks to play an important role, including trade and development, maritime issues, aviation, the protection of the environment, human rights, global economic governance and investment are all governed, in large part, by treaty regimes. The EU is a party to a long and ever-expanding list of multilateral and bilateral treaties. According to the EU's Treaties Office Database, the EU is party to some 982 bilateral treaties and 289 multilateral treaties.[4] The range of fields in which the EU has entered into treaties is also expanding. Once focused mainly on issues such as trade, the EU is now an active treaty partner in fields such as international security, human rights, health and environmental protection. In 2010, the EU became a party to the UN Convention on the Rights of Persons with Disabilities (CRPD),[5] the first time the EU has joined an international treaty focused solely on human rights protection.[6] The EU is still in the long and difficult process of becoming the first non-state party to the European Convention on Human Rights and Fundamental Freedoms.[7] The European Union's relationship with the former Member State, the United Kingdom, is managed through a Withdrawal Agreement and Trade and Cooperation Agreement negotiated between the EU and UK.

This expanding treaty practice brings new challenges for the EU, its Member States, and its international partners. It has spawned a growing literature in EU external relations law,[8] much of which focuses on the internal institutional issues faced by the EU. This includes discussion of complex constitutional issues such as competences, the duty of loyalty and sincere

---

[3]   The Association Agreement and Deep and Comprehensive Free Trade Area (DCFTA) will replace the current Partnership and Cooperation Agreement Ukraine that was signed with the EU in 1998.

[4]   See European Union, Treaties Office Database, http://ec.europa.eu/world/agreements/default .home.do. This includes an inventory of all agreements to which the European Union (EU), the European Community (EC), the European Economic Community (EEC), or the European Atomic Energy Community (EURATOM) is a party.

[5]   Council Decision 2010/48/EC of 26 November 2009 concerning the conclusion, by the European Community, of the United Nations Convention on the Rights of Persons with Disabilities [2010] OJ L23/35.

[6]   European Commission, 'EU ratifies UN Convention on disability rights', Press Release, 5 January 2011, http://europa.eu/rapid/press-release_IP-11-4_en.htm.

[7]   J.-P. Jacqué, 'The Accession of the European Union to the European Convention on Human Rights and Fundamental Freedoms' (2011) 48 *Common Market Law Review* 1019.

[8]   See G. De Baere, *Constitutional Principles of EU External Relations* (Oxford: Oxford University Press, 2008); P. Eeckhout, *EU External Relations Law* (Oxford: Oxford University Press, 2011).

cooperation in external affairs, and issues regarding the EU's external representation in international negotiations and international organizations.
This chapter examines the international law issues that arise from the EU's
expanding and developing treaty practice. Rather than focusing on internal
constitutional questions that arise from the EU becoming party to international agreements, it focuses on questions that arise under international
law. To what extent do the EU's internal legal issues become externalized
through the conclusion of agreements by the EU and its Member States? In
what ways has the EU contributed to the development of international law
through its treaty practice?

The law of treaties remains a fundamental issue in public international law.
It has dominated much of the work of the International Law Commission
(ILC), whose work has resulted in the 1969 Vienna Convention on the Law
of Treaties (VCLT)[9]; the 1986 Vienna Convention on the Law of Treaties
between states and International Organizations or between International
Organizations (VCLT-IO)[10]; and the 1978 Vienna Convention on
Succession of states in respect of Treaties.[11] In December 2013, the UN
General Assembly took note[12] of the ILC's Guide to Practice on
Reservations to Treaties (2011).[13] In 2018, it adopted Draft Conclusions on
Subsequent Agreements and Subsequent Practice in Relation to the
Interpretation of Treaties,[14] and its Guide on the Provisional Application of
Treaties.[15] The EU has also sought to contribute to the ILC's work on these
and other topics, by making observations or comments.[16]

While the law of treaties remains an important topic for international law,
there has been relatively little attention paid to how legal entities other than

---

[9]   Vienna Convention on the Law of Treaties (23 May 1969) 1155 UNTS 331, entered into force
      27 January 1980 ('VCLT').
[10] Vienna Convention on the Law of Treaties between States and International Organizations or
      between International Organizations (21 March 1986) 25 ILM 543 (1986), not yet in force
      ('VCLT-IO').
[11] Vienna Convention on Succession of States in Respect of Treaties (23 August 1978) 1946
      UNTS 3, entered into force 6 November 1996.
[12] UNGA Res. 68/111 (16 December 2013).
[13] International Law Commission, Guide to Practice on Reservations to Treaties, adopted by the
      International Law Commission at its sixty-third session (2011).
[14] International Law Commission, Draft conclusions on subsequent agreements and subsequent
      practice in relation to the interpretation of treaties, A/73/10, chapter IV (2018).
[15] International Law Commission, Guide on the Provisional Application of Treaties, A/73/10
      (2018).
[16] On this practice, see J. Wouters & M. Hermez, 'The EU's Contribution to "the Strict
      Observance and the Development of International Law" at the UNGA Sixth Committee' in
      S. Blavoukos & D. Bourantonis (eds), *The EU in UN Politics: Actors, Processes and
      Performances* (London: Palgrave Macmillan, 2017) 147–163.

states participate in treaties. The law of treaties has developed upon the assumption that the state is the usual treaty party. Other entities, such as international organizations, are recognized as being capable of entering into international agreements, but they do so in a way that differs substantially from that of states. As Reuter points out, international organizations 'radically differ from states, for they never possess a full and unqualified capacity to be parties to any kind of treaty'.[17] The law of treaties is premised on an important distinction. States possess full competence to enter into binding agreements on a range of issues, whereas international organizations exercise only limited powers, and may only enter into agreements in a limited capacity, such as headquarters agreements. However, the agreements to which the EU is a party fall more in the first category, that is, its commitments are much more 'state-like' in nature. This practice calls into question the logic of the dichotomy between states and international organizations.

How should the law of treaties deal with international organizations such as the EU entering into 'state-like' agreements? In *Modern Treaty Law and Practice*, Aust puts it bluntly: 'Anything to do with the European Union (and its predecessors) is complex'.[18] Klabbers also notes that '[t]he treaty practice of the EU is a highly fascinating, if somewhat under-explored, area of international and European law'.[19] As the EU enters into agreements in new fields, such as human rights and investment, these issues are becoming ever more complex and challenging. This chapter explores the main issues that arise from this expanding treaty practice, and how international law has dealt with these unique legal issues. Building on the discussion in Chapter 2, it examines how the EU's treaty practice may also contribute to the development of international law.

The chapter deals with treaties to which the EU is a party, both alongside the EU Member States ('mixed agreements') or without ('EU-only agreements'), or where issues of EU law are relevant to the treaties concluded by the EU Member States. It does not deal with the question of how the law of treaties may apply to the EU's founding instruments, since in these cases EU constitutional law applies internally, and international law plays a limited role. Article 5 1969 VCLT states that the Convention applies to the constituent

---

[17]   P. Reuter, *Introduction to the Law of Treaties*, 2nd edn (London: Kegan Paul International, 1995) 76.
[18]   A. Aust, *Modern Treaty Law and Practice*, 3rd edn (Cambridge: Cambridge University Press, 2013) 359.
[19]   J. Klabbers, *Treaty Conflict and the European Union* (Cambridge: Cambridge University Press, 2009) 59.

treaties of international organizations.[20] Yet Article 5 VCLT is a reservation clause, and for the most part the EU has developed its own internal law about how the EU Treaties are to be applied and interpreted. The rules relating to the interpretation and application of treaties to which the EU is a party are governed by international law.

The chapter first discusses what laws govern treaties to which the EU is a party. It discusses some of the features of the EU and its legal order. Section 3.1.1 turns to the phenomenon of 'EU-specific' clauses. These are clauses that are included in agreements with the EU or the EU Member States that are supposedly required to take into account the unique nature of the EU and its legal order. It discusses to what extent these clauses are indeed justified, and whether other methods could be employed to take into account the special nature of the EU. The third part then examines a number of international law issues that arise from the EU's treaty practice. It examines classic public international law concepts, such as territory and jurisdiction, consent to be bound, and discusses how they are applied in relation to the EU. In many cases, these legal concepts can be applied to the EU without modification. However, there are occasions when they have to be modified or adapted in order to be applied to the EU as a treaty party. The chapter ends with a discussion about whether the law of treaties is adequately equipped to deal with composite legal entities such as the EU. It argues that the law of treaties is flexible enough to take into account entities that do not fit into the neat legal categories of state and international organization.

3.1.1 *Which Rules Apply to Treaties to Which the EU is a Party?*

At the international level, treaties to which the EU is a party are governed by international law, not EU law.[21] Although the EU may be considered a 'new legal order', it cannot apply its legal order outside of that legal sphere. This is because EU law is *res inter alios acta* and is not opposable to non-EU states that enter into agreements with the EU. They cannot be bound by EU law, to which they have not given their explicit consent. What law governs treaties to which the EU is a party?

---

[20] Article 5, VCLT (n9): 'The present Convention applies to any treaty which is the constituent instrument of an international organization and to any treaty adopted within an international organization without prejudice to any relevant rules of the organization'.

[21] International agreements entered into by the EU become part of the EU legal order upon their entry into force. EU law also governs the effects of such agreements within the EU legal order.

Two main instruments have sought to codify the international law of treaties. The 1969 VCLT is designed to apply to states,[22] whereas a separate treaty, the 1986 VCLT-IO[23] applies to international organizations and states in their relations with international organizations. The two treaties closely resemble each other in many respects. The development of two separate legal regimes underscores the dichotomy that pervades international treaty law, between states and international organizations. The applicable law, either the provisions of the VCLT or the VCLT-IO, largely depends on the legal characterization of the party to the treaty. One might presume then, that since the EU is not a state but an international organization, the VCLT-IO would be the applicable law. However, there are several reasons why the VCLT-IO is not necessarily appropriate to the agreements of the Union, and the VCLT rules would be more appropriate.

First, the Court of Justice of the European Union (CJEU) has generally applied the provisions of the 1969 VCLT when interpreting agreements to which the EU is a party. The Court justifies this on the basis that its provisions represent customary international law.[24] In *Brita*, the Court explained why it applies the rules in the 1969 VCLT, to the extent that they represent customary international law, regarding agreements of the EU:

> Under Article 1 thereof, the Vienna Convention applies to treaties between states. However, under Article 3(b) of the Vienna Convention, the fact that the Vienna Convention does not apply to international agreements concluded between states and other subjects of international law is not to affect the application to them of any of the rules set forth in that convention to which they would be subject under international law independently of the convention.[25]

The VCLT, according to its own terms, only applies regarding agreements between states. Article 3(b) VCLT, to which the Court refers, was included so that 'no legal conclusions whatsoever can be drawn from the Convention's pragmatic step to focus on written interstate treaties'.[26] It sought to ensure that rules of customary international law would still apply to agreements between states and other subjects of international law. There are a number of subjects of international law that possess agreement-making capacity, including bodies

[22] Article 1, VCLT (n9): 'The present Convention applies to treaties between States'.
[23] VCLT-IO (n10).
[24] See Judgment in *Racke* v. *Hauptzollamt Mainz*, C-162/96, EU:C:1998:293.
[25] Judgment in *Brita* v. *Hauptzollamt Hamburg Hafen*, C-386/08, EU:C:2010:91, para. 40.
[26] K. Schmalenbach, 'Article 3 – International agreements not within the scope of the present Convention' in Dörr & Schmalenbach (n2) 50.

as diverse as units of federal states, dependent territories, the Holy See, the International Committee of the Red Cross (ICRC), International Non-governmental Organizations, liberation or opposition movements and indigenous peoples. There is currently no treaty that covers agreements made between states and these bodies, and so customary international law applies. There is, however, a treaty applicable to IOs. By referring to Article 3(b) VCLT, the Court does not fully answer the question of why the VCLT is applicable, and not the VCLT-IO. The Court explained that 'the rules laid down in the Vienna Convention apply to an agreement concluded between a state and an international organization ... in so far as these rules are an expression of customary international law ... '[27] without elaborating why the VCLT-IO provisions are not more appropriate. It appears from the practice of the Court and EU institutions that the VCLT is now considered to represent the applicable law.

Second, the EU is not a party to the 1986 VCLT-IO. The EU was sceptical about the VCLT-IO when it was drafted, and has not to become a party to the Convention. Moreover, the VCLT-IO has not yet entered into force, and it is unlikely that it will gain the necessary 35 ratifications needed. The provisions of the VCLT-IO may still be applied in the meantime, but only to the extent that they are considered to represent customary international law. Third, although the VCLT-IO is designed to apply to international organizations, one can argue that the EU does not fall within the category of international organizations to which the VCLT-IO was designed to apply. As discussed earlier, EU treaty practice differs from that of 'traditional' international organizations such as the UN; its treaty practice resembles that of a state. Under these agreements, the EU is expected to fulfil certain obligations within its jurisdiction and may incur international responsibility in cases where the EU breaches these obligations. This contrasts with the treaty practice of other international organizations, which is confined mostly to the realm of head-quarters agreements, or agreements on cooperation and exchange of information. For these reasons, one may consider the VCLT, insofar as it represents customary international law, as the applicable law regulating treaties to which the EU is a party.

This confusion may also relate to the 'state-centric' approach of the ILC discussed in Chapter 2, and the lack of attention paid to the characteristics of supranational organizations such as the EU.[28] In the case of the law of treaties,

---

[27] *Brita* (n25) paras 40–41.
[28] J. M. Cores Martin, 'European Exceptionalism in International Law? The European Union and the System of International Responsibility' in M. Ragazzi (ed), *The Responsibility of International Organizations: Essays in Memory of Sir Ian Brownlie* (Leiden: Brill Publishing, 2013) 192: 'from a historical point of view, it is not unprecedented that the characteristics of

the ILC first dealt with the law relating to states, before moving to international organizations. Rather than develop specific rules applicable to supranational organizations like the EU, the VCLT-IO applies to the wide variety of IOs that exist.

3.2 TREATY-MAKING AND THE EU LEGAL ORDER

International law does not generally pay much heed to the internal legal orders of its subjects. It is for those subjects of international law to determine how they will meet their international obligations. Yet when the EU enters into international agreements, the internal EU legal order is often highly relevant. When states enter into international agreements, it is uncommon for there to be specific clauses that take into account the state's internal law. It is a principle of international law that a state cannot invoke its internal law to circumvent an international obligation.[29] When analysing the EU's treaty practice, however, one must bear in mind the internal legal issues that are involved when the EU enters into international agreements. The EU often has to negotiate the inclusion of specialized rules to take into account certain features of EU law. This section briefly examines the EU's internal lawmaking powers, and how these issues may be externalized when the EU enters into international agreements.

3.2.1 *The Evolution of the EU's Treaty Practice*

It is now well accepted that IOs have the capacity to enter into binding legal obligations, primarily through entering into treaties.[30] From early on in the life of the European Community, it was accepted that there was a need to enter into agreements with third states and organizations. The treaty-making powers of the Union are explicitly included in the EU Treaties,[31] and these

---

supranational organizations have been neglected from the Commission's work, which was also the case of the project that resulted in the adoption of the 1986 Vienna Convention on the Law of Treaties between States and International Organizations and between International Organizations'.

[29] Article 26, VCLT (n9): 'A party may not invoke the provisions of its internal law as justification for its failure to perform a treaty'.

[30] Reparation for Injuries Suffered in the Service of the United Nations (Advisory Opinion) [1949] ICJ Rep 174.

[31] Article 216(1), TFEU: 'The Union may conclude an agreement with one or more third countries or international organisations where the Treaties so provide or where the conclusion of an agreement is necessary in order to achieve, within the framework of the Union's policies,

agreements are binding upon the EU and the Member States.[32] Just like domestic legal orders, the EU has developed internal legal rules regarding the exercise of treaty-making powers. These touch upon the issues such as legal basis, institutional balance and respect for autonomy of the EU legal order. Unlike a state, however, the EU or its treaty partner will request these issues to be addressed in the agreement.

One factor that influences the EU's treaty practice is the difference between bilateral and multilateral treaties. Even when the EU concludes an agreement alongside its Member States ('mixed agreement'), the agreement is considered bilateral if it is structured so as the EU and the Member States are parties to the treaty on the one part, and a third state (or group of states) are parties on the other.[33] It is in the field of bilateral agreements where the EU developed much of its early treaty practice, and where the EU has generally been able to exert more influence internationally. The EU has also taken part in numerous multilateral conventions. At first, these were mostly in the field of trade and fisheries, but have more recently extended to a much wider range of issues. The EU's treaty practice is heavily influenced by this contrast between multilateral and bilateral treaties.[34] The extent to which the EU is capable of negotiating 'EU-specific' clauses is determined in large part by whether the treaty is a multilateral or bilateral agreement. Another factor is whether it is a 'European' international agreement (e.g. under the auspices of the Council of Europe or other European organization) or one with a wider participation (e.g. under the auspices of the United Nations).

A second factor is that the EU's treaty making is subject to almost constant change. As the EU's internal machinery regarding its treaty-making powers has

---

one of the objectives referred to in the Treaties, or is provided for in a legally binding Union act or is likely to affect common rules or alter their scope'.

[32] Article 216(2), TFEU: 'Agreements concluded by the Union are binding upon the institutions of the Union and on its Member States'.

[33] 'When a treaty is structured in a bilateral way such as this, the rights and obligations are owed to one another on each side, rather than mutual obligations among all parties'. K. Schmalenbach, 'Article 2 – Use of terms' in Dörr & Schmalenbach (n2) 31. See the Cotonou Partnership Agreement between the Members of the African, Caribbean and Pacific Group of States, of the One Part, and the European Community and its Member States, on the Other Part [2000] OJ L 317, 3.

[34] D. Verwey, *The European Community, the European Union and the International Law of Treaties* (The Hague: TMC Asser Press, 2004) 193. 'bilateral practice is in sharp contrast to the multilateral setting. What usually happens, and this should be deplored, is that the position of the Community in a multilateral setting is usually a disadvantageous one. Its position is defined in relation to that of its Member States and not as an independent entity endowed with competences separate from the Member States'.

evolved over the decades, so too has the type of agreement to which the EU has become a party. As the competence of the EU has expanded with successive EU Treaty changes, the Union has become capable of entering into agreements in a wider range of fields. The (then) Community began by concluding bilateral agreements largely regulating trade liberalization, including partnership agreements and a number of commodity agreements. The EU's treaty practice expanded rapidly when it concluded agreements in the field of CFSP. It is no longer confined to the economic arena, and now concludes agreements in the field of energy, development, human rights, security and the environment.[35]

Not only has the subject matter widened, but the type of treaty to which the EU enters has also evolved. The EU takes part in treaties with a general law-making character, such as the UN Convention on the Law of the Sea (UNCLOS), which codified much of international law of the sea. This evolution in the type of agreements has also had an effect on the EU's treaty practice. Agreements with law-making objectives are more likely to lay down general rules that may overlap with the EU's own internal law, increasing the likelihood that EU law will conflict with the EU's own legislative efforts. Many of the recent challenges to the legality of EU measures, for example, have been based on alleged violations of international agreements of a general law-making character. The EU differs from other IOs in this regard since it is the only IO that enters into such law-making agreements, which are typically confined to states.[36] The participation of the EU in these types of treaties presents new challenges for international law. The EU and its partners have developed a number of tools to address the challenges that arise from the EU's participation in multilateral agreements of a law-making character.

Reuter distinguishes between 'ordinary international organizations' and 'international organizations exercising State functions'.[37] The EU is the only international organization that truly falls within the latter category. While the EU's treaty practice differs substantially from other IOs, it also differs from states. The issue of competences looms large over the EU's treaty practice, and

---

[35] As Mendez notes, '[t]oday few parts of the world remain unconnected to the EU by some form of bilateral or regional trade-related agreement'. M. Mendez, *The Legal Effects of EU Agreements: Maximalist Treaty Enforcement and Judicial Avoidance Techniques* (Oxford: Oxford University Press, 2013) xvii.

[36] K. Schmalenbach, 'Article 6 – Capacity of States to conclude treaties' in Dörr & Schmalenbach (n2) 112. 'For several reasons, international organizations are rarely parties to multinational law-making treaties. An increasing number of multilateral treaties, eg in the field of environmental protection, are open to the participation of "regional economic integration organizations", but so far only the European Union has acceded on such a basis'.

[37] Reuter (n17) 114.

this has led to the EU concluding many agreements as 'mixed' ones, even in cases where it may not have been legally required. Constitutional issues, especially regarding the autonomy of the EU legal order, also cast a shadow over the treaty practice of the EU. The EU's treaty-making practice is also subject to constant change, through changes in the EU Treaties and judgments of the CJEU.

3.3 EU-SPECIFIC CLAUSES

The EU is not a normal treaty partner. It can be treated neither as a state for the purposes of international treaty law, nor as an ordinary international organization. When negotiating international agreements, the EU will often seek to include certain clauses that would take into account the specific nature of the EU legal order. The EU's treaty partners may also seek certain clauses in these agreements, for instance, to reassure them that the EU or the Member States can be held responsible in the event of the non-fulfilment of treaty obligations. Each treaty is different, and clauses must be adapted to the aims and purposes of that treaty. Over time, the use of these clauses has developed a certain pattern of EU treaty practice. The EU has developed techniques that allow it to take part in treaties, to avoid conflicts between international law and treaty law, and to safeguard the EU's *acquis*.

These 'EU-specific' clauses are now included in many bilateral and multilateral treaties to which the EU (and its Member States) is a party. These include relatively uncontroversial clauses, such as the 'regional economic integration organization' (REIO) clause, as well as more controversial ones, such as the 'disconnection clause'. International law proves to be adaptable and flexible when it comes to accepting international organizations such as the EU as a treaty partner. More often than not, the obstacles the EU encounters are more political than legal. In certain situations, the EU's treaty partners may be reluctant to allow special treatment to the EU and its Member States. The EU faces a challenge, therefore, not only of finding a legally acceptable solution in any given case, but also one that will be accepted by other parties to the agreement. The extent to which the EU is permitted 'special treatment' may often be explained more by the EU's negotiating power than by legal considerations.

3.3.1 *EU Participation Clause*

Treaty making is a power that has traditionally been exercised by states. Although other legal entities are capable of entering into international agreements, this is usually seen as a deviation from what is viewed as a practice that is primarily exercised by sovereign entities. This is demonstrated by the fact that when the EU becomes a party to a multilateral convention, a specific clause often has to be included to allow for EU participation.

The first method is for the treaty to refer to the Union specifically. This is the case, for instance, in the WTO Agreement, where the EU is included as a founding member of the organization.[38] Conventions concluded through the Council of Europe often refer to the EU specifically as a party.[39] The European Convention on Human Rights was amended to allow participation by the EU by including a specific clause stating that '[t]he European Union may accede to this Convention'.[40] In other multilateral settings, however, the EU's treaty partners are reluctant to include language that mentions the EU specifically.

The more common option is for the instrument to include a 'Regional Economic Integration Organization' (REIO) or 'Regional Integration Organization' (RIO) clause. While there is no legal difference between a 'REIO' and a 'RIO' clause, the elimination of the term 'economic' illustrates how the EU has transformed in to more than an IO involved in economic matters.[41] Some treaties, such as UNCLOS are open to signature by 'international organizations'.[42] These clauses allow accession by organizations, including the EU, if they meet certain criteria. While these criteria differ

---

[38]   Article XI, Agreement establishing the World Trade Organization, signed on 15 April 1994, 1867 UNTS 154.
The WTO Agreement open not only to states but also 'separate customs territory possessing full autonomy in the conduct of its external commercial relations' (Article XII).

[39]   Article 12(3), Convention on the Elaboration of a European Pharmacopoeia (No 50, Council of Europe) simply states that '[t]he European Economic Community may accede to the present Convention'. The Council of Europe Convention on Preventing and Combating Violence against Women (2011) Article 75(1), Council of Europe Convention on Preventing and Combating Violence against Women and Domestic Violence (2011) also specifically refers to the EU: 'This Convention shall be open for signature by the member States of the Council of Europe, the non-member States which have participated in its elaboration and the European Union'.

[40]   See Article 17(2), European Convention on Human Rights Convention for the Protection of Human Rights and Fundamental Freedoms ('ECHR'), entered into force 3 September 1953, 213 UNTS 222 (amended by Protocol No. 14 to the Convention). In the case of the EU's accession to the ECHR, it was decided that there should be a specific clause mentioning the EU, rather than 'regional organizations' generally.

[41]   Convention on the Rights of Persons with Disabilities ('CRPD'), New York, 13 December 2006, entry into force 28 May 2008, UNTS 2514, 3.

[42]   Article 305(f), United Nations Convention on the Law of the Sea ('UNCLOS'), signed at Montego Bay, 10 December 1982, entry into force 16 November 1994, UNTS 1833, 3: 'This Convention shall be open for signature by international organizations, in accordance with Annex IX'.

from treaty to treaty, they usually require the organization to have transferred competences under the relevant treaty to that regional organization.[43] A typical example of such a RIO clause is found in the CRPD: "'Regional integration organization" shall mean an organization constituted by sovereign states of a given region, to which its member states have transferred competence in respect of matters governed by this Convention'.[44] According to this clause, a regional organization must satisfy two criteria. It must be composed of sovereign states and those states must have transferred some, but not necessarily all, competences to that organization with respect to issues covered by the convention.

Some treaties set the threshold a little higher. For instance, the Agreement on the International Dolphin Conservation Programme (AIDCP) requires that the REIO have 'authority to make decisions binding on its member states in respect of those matters'[45] covered by the agreement. The Convention Concerning International Carriage by Rail (COTIF) allows participation by REIOs 'which have competence to adopt their own legislation binding on their Member States'.[46] REIO/ RIO clauses may stipulate further conditions. For instance, the United Nations Convention against Corruption requires that at least one member of the regional organization is also a party to the convention.[47] The Convention for the strengthening of the Inter-American Tropical Tuna Commission stipulates that:

> [N]o member State of such [regional economic integration organizations] may sign this Convention unless it represents a territory which lies outside the territorial scope of the treaty establishing the organization and provided that such member State's participation be limited to representing only the interests of that territory.[48]

---

[43] Annex IX, Article 1, UNCLOS (n42).

[44] Article 44, CRPD (n41).

[45] Article I.5, Agreement on the International Dolphin Conservation Programme (AIDCP), ILM 37, 1246 (1998).

[46] Article 38, Convention Concerning International Carriage by Rail ('COTIF') of 9 May 1980, as amended by the Vilnius Protocol of 3 June 1999.

[47] Article 67(2), United Nations Convention against Corruption, signed at New York, 31 October 2003, entry into force 14 December 2004, UNTS 2349, 41: 'This Convention shall also be open for signature by regional economic integration organizations provided that at least one member State of such organisation has signed this Convention in accordance with paragraph 1 of this Article'.

[48] Article XXVII, Convention for the Strengthening of the Inter-American Tropical Tuna Commission established by the 1949 Convention between the United States of America and the Republic of Costa Rica ('Antigua Convention').

The International Convention for the Conservation of Atlantic Tunas (ICCAT Convention) sets out that when a REIO becomes a contracting party, 'the member states of that organization and those that adhere to it in the future shall cease to be parties to the Convention . . . '.[49]

While REIO/RIO clauses allow for the possibility of membership by other international organizations, the EU is practically the only organization that makes use of them. The abstract language of the REIO/RIO clause avoids the treaty referring to the EU specifically. It also allows for the possibility of other regional organizations to join in the future, if and when they meet the criteria set out in the relevant treaty. That the EU is the only organization that makes use of these clauses is understandable, since they are usually drawn up with the specific intention of including the EU/EC. However, the use of REIO/RIO clauses raises the interesting question of whether they could allow other international organizations to become a party in the future. To what extent would an organization wishing to join have to resemble the EU? The organization would have to display a certain degree of supranational decision-making. This would likely exclude many regional organizations in their current form, such as the African Union or ASEAN, which despite being active on the global stage do not exercise the same level of supranational decision-making as the EU. Yet there is a certain reluctance on the part of states to see a more formalized role for other regional organizations. The REIO/RIO clause thus allows regional organizations to participate in a multilateral treaty, but in reality confines this mostly to the EU.

Other regional organizations have also entered into treaties,[50] and some may seek to participate in other multilateral conventions in the same way as the EU. The debate about the conditions under which other regional bodies can participate in an international organization was illustrated during negotiations on a draft UN General Assembly Resolution to allow the EU to participate as an 'enhanced observer' in that body. An initial draft of the Resolution tabled by the EU set out some conditions under which other regional bodies could be granted similar status in the General Assembly in the future:

> when an organization for regional integration develops common external policies and establishes permanent structures for their conduct and

---

[49] Article XIV(6), Protocol to the Final Act of the Conference of Plenipotentiaries of the States Parties to the International Convention for the Conservation of Atlantic Tunas.

[50] On ASEAN treaty practice, see M. Cremona, D. Kleimann, J. Larik, R. Lee & P. Vennesson (eds), *ASEAN's External Agreements: Law, Practice and the Quest for Collective Action* (Cambridge: Cambridge University Press, 2015).

representation, the General Assembly may benefit from the effective participation in its deliberations of that organization's external representatives
speaking on behalf of the organization and its member States, without
prejudice to the ability of each organization to define the modalities of its
external repetition.

This would have required the regional organization to (1) have developed
external policies and to (2) have permanent structures for its representation.
The Resolution that was eventually adopted looks much different:

> following a request on behalf of a regional organization that has observer
> status in the General Assembly and whose member States have agreed
> arrangements that allow that organization's representatives to speak on behalf
> of the organization and its member States, the Assembly may adopt modal-
> ities for the participation of that regional organization's representatives, such
> as those set out in the annex to the present resolution.

According to the eventual language adopted, the regional organization seeking enhanced observer status only needs to allow the organization's representatives to speak on its behalf. This is much less restrictive, and would
potentially allow a greater number of regional bodies granted observer status.
While this debate did not concern participation in a multilateral treaty,[51] it
does reflect the types of issues that would be raised if regional bodies other
than the EU were to seek to join multilateral treaties. The interpretative
statement by Caribbean Community (CARICOM) upon the adoption of
the UN Resolution demonstrates how contentious this issue can be: '[t]he
conferral of identical rights [to those given to the EU] is not dependent on
a duplication of the European Union's modalities of integration, nor is it
premised on the achievement of any perceived "level" of integration'.[52] Other
regional organizations may argue that they need not emulate the European
model of integration in order to participate. In practice, however, the participation of organizations like ASEAN or the AU in multilateral treaties will
depend more on the political will of other contracting parties than on such
legal constraints.

---

[51] The UN General Assembly is based on an international treaty, the UN Charter, to which only
states may join. This instance involved the EU's participation in a body established by
a multilateral treaty.
[52] Annex to the Letter Dated 9 May 2011 from the Permanent Representative of the Bahamas to
the United Nations addressed to the Secretary-General Interpretive declaration by the
Bahamas on behalf of CARICOM, 3 May 2011, in connection with General Assembly
resolution 65/276, entitled 'Participation of the European Union in the work of the United
Nations', para. (b).

Allowing a RIO/REIO to participate in a multilateral convention is relatively straightforward, at least from a legal point of view. More complicated questions arise regarding the participation of that RIO/REIO in the convention, especially when it is premised on 'state-centric' language. For instance, even where the EU is a party to a convention, it will often continue to refer to 'State Parties'. In this case, the agreement will often include a separate clause that specifies that 'state party' also includes regional integration organizations. For example, Article 44(2) of the UN CRPD states that 'References to State Parties in the present Convention shall apply to such organizations [RIOs] within the limits of their competence'.[53] This language shows that the participation by an international organization is still somewhat anomalous. More neutral language, such as 'contracting parties' could be used instead.

The issue of 'state centric' language posed a problem regarding the EU's accession to the ECHR. The ECHR was designed with the assumption that human rights would be guaranteed by the contracting state, and therefore the treaty employs a great deal of 'state-centric' language. The draft Accession Agreement, designed to allow the EU to accede to the ECHR, set out that the terms 'State', 'State Party', 'States' or 'States Parties' in certain parts of the Convention and Protocols are to be understood as referring also to the European Union.[54] While this will be a practical solution in most situations, there may be instances where state-centric terminology cannot be applied easily to the context of a regional organization. Terms used in human rights treaties such as 'domestic law', 'administration of the state', 'jurisdiction', 'territory', 'territorial integrity', 'national security' or 'life of the nation' would have to be adapted and interpreted within the context of the EU. This is not an issue that applies only in the field of human rights. For instance, the term 'flag state' has been adapted to apply to the context of a regional organization.[55]

From an international law perspective, it makes no difference whether the EU is specifically mentioned in a treaty, or whether it joins as an 'international organization' or 'regional integration organization'. The fact that the EU's

---

[53] CRPD (n41).
[54] Article 1, para. 5. Fifth Negotiation Meeting between the CDDH ad hoc Negotiation Group and the European Commission on the Accession of the European Union to the European Convention on Human Rights, 'Final report to the CDDH', 47+1(2013)008rev2, Strasbourg, 10 June 2013, Appendix I 'Draft revised agreement on the accession of the European Union to the Convention for the Protection of Human Rights and Fundamental Freedoms' ('EU-ECHR Accession Agreement').
[55] Article 1(4), Antigua Convention (n48): '"Flag State" means, unless otherwise indicated: (a) a State whose vessels are entitled to fly its flag, or (b) a regional economic integration organization in which vessels are entitled to fly the flag of a Member State of that regional economic integration organization'.

treaty partners have preferred the latter in multilateral conventions points to two things. First, with the exception of the field of trade or European conventions, third states are reluctant to mention the EU specifically. Second, as argued in Chapter 1, it shows that the EU's treaty partners do not really consider the EU as a sui generis body, but as a species of international organization.

3.3.2 *Declaration of Competence Clause*

EU participation clauses allow the EU to become a party to a treaty, but they do not give any guidance about how the EU will participate in the treaty regime. Nor do they resolve questions regarding who will be responsible, either the EU or the Member States or both, in cases of a breach of the obligations under the agreement. This issue is made even more complicated due to the nature of competences in EU law and the practice of concluding 'mixed agreements'. It is for this reason that treaties to which the EU is a party will often require the EU to make a declaration at the time of signature, ratification, acceptance, approval or accession, setting out the extent to which the EU or the Member States have competence with respect to the matters governed by the treaty. The Constitution of the Food and Agriculture Organization, for example, sets out that:

> Each regional economic integration organization applying for membership in the Organization shall, at the time of such application, submit a declaration of competence specifying the matters in respect of which competence has been transferred to it by its Member States.[56]

By requiring the EU to submit a declaration of competences, an internal EU law issue (the balance of competences) becomes externalized, and relevant to the EU' treaty partners.[57] The main rationale for a declaration of competence clause is twofold: to assure the EU's treaty partners that the treaty obligations will be complied with and to inform them who will be responsible for implementing those obligations. The declaration of competence may be important for determining responsibility in cases of breach of the agreement, however it will not always be determinative. Other than assisting in determining responsibility at the international level, the declaration may also be used to determine who will speak or exercise the right to vote in the context of an

---

[56] Article II(5), Constitution of the Food and Agricultural Organization (with Annexes) (adopted 16 October 1945, entered into force 16 October 1945), 145 BSP 910.

[57] A. Delgado Casteleiro, 'EU Declarations of Competence to Multilateral Agreements: A Useful Reference Base?' (2012) 17 *European Foreign Affairs Review* 491, 492.

international organization or treaty body. The extent to which these declarations should have internal relevance for the purposes of EU law is another point of contention.[58]

Declarations of Competence differ depending on the type of agreement, but they follow a similar structure. Below is the declaration made under Article 24(3) of the Kyoto Protocol[59]:

> The European Community declares that, in accordance with the Treaty establishing the European Community, and in particular Article 175(1) thereof, it is competent to enter into international agreements, and to implement the obligations resulting therefrom, which contribute to the pursuit of the following objectives:
>
> - preserving, protecting and improving the quality of the environment;
> - protecting human health;
> - prudent and rational utilisation of natural resources;
> - –promoting measures at international level to deal with regional or worldwide environmental problems.
>
> The European Community declares that its quantified emission reduction commitment under the Protocol will be fulfilled through action by the Community and its member states within the respective competence of each and that it has already adopted legal instruments, binding on its member states, covering matters governed by the Protocol.
>
> The European Community will on a regular basis provide information on relevant Community legal instruments within the framework of the supplementary information incorporated in its national communication submitted under Article 12 of the Convention for the purpose of demonstrating compliance with its commitments under the Protocol in accordance with Article 7(2) thereof and the guidelines thereunder.

First, declarations will often begin with a general statement stating the EU has competence in the field covered by the international agreement. The declaration will also include language that stresses the dynamic nature of EU law regarding competences. For example, the declaration made regarding the UN

---

[58] For a discussion of the relevance of declarations of competence for EU law, see Delgado Casteleiro (n57) 496–505.

[59] Article 24(3), Kyoto Protocol to the United Nations Framework Convention on Climate Change ('Kyoto Protocol'), signed at Kyoto, 11 December 1997, entry into force 16 February 2005, UNTS 2303, 162: '[i]n their instruments of ratification, acceptance, approval or accession, regional economic integration organizations shall declare the extent of their competence with respect to the matters governed by this Protocol. These organizations shall also inform the Depositary, who shall in turn inform the Parties, of any substantial modification in the extent of their competence'.

CRPD states that 'The scope and the exercise of Community competence are by their nature, subject to continuous development [...]'.[60] The declaration may also seek to demonstrate the extent to which the EU has exercised competence in the field covered by the agreement, for example, by providing a list of relevant EU legislation.

Due to this dynamic nature of EU law on competences, declarations of competence quickly become out of date. Not long after the declaration is made, EU legislation to which it refers is often replaced or updated. The balance of competences may have shifted, through EU practice, the interpretation by CJEU, or through a change in the EU Treaties. It is for this reason that declaration of competences clauses usually require the EU to keep them up-to-date, and to inform the treaty partners of changes. UNCLOS, for example, requires that '[t]he international organization and its Member States which are States Parties shall promptly notify the depositary of this Convention of any changes to the distribution of competence, including new transfers of competence'.[61] Since declarations of competence are meant to be informative for third parties, the rationale for updating them over time is clear.

Despite this obligation on the part of the EU to communicate updates regarding the distribution of competences, this is rarely done in practice. The only example of the EU updating its declaration of competences was with regard to its FAO membership.[62] The EU joined that organization in 1994 and did not update its Declaration until more than twenty years later. One of the main reasons for this is that declarations of competence are notoriously difficult for the EU to produce. The allocation of competence is rarely a clear-cut issue; it is not only a complex legal issue under EU law but also a delicate political topic. EU Member States are reluctant to 'codify' the balance of competences in a legal document, fearing that it could be used to expand further EU competences at the expense of the Member States. Despite these practical difficulties, however, the EU remains under an international law obligation to update declarations of competence.

---

[60] Declaration Concerning the Competence of the European Community with Regard to Matters Governed by the United Nations Convention on the Rights of Persons with Disabilities under Disabilities (Declaration made pursuant to Article 44(1) of the Convention).

[61] Article 5(4), Annex IX, UNCLOS (n42).

[62] Draft Declaration of competences by the European Union in respect of matters covered by the Constitution of the Food and Agriculture Organization of the United Nations (FAO), in Communication from the Commission to the Council, The role of the European Union in the FAO after the Treaty of Lisbon: Updated Declaration of Competences and new arrangements between the Council and the Commission for the exercise of membership rights of the EU and its Member States, COM(2013) 333 fin, annex 2, 13.

The issue of declarations of competence becoming out-of-date points to a more general problem. While they are designed to inform third parties about the nature of EU competences, in reality they do little to clarify this issue. They are often laconic statements setting out the extent of EU law in a certain field at a given moment in time, stressing that EU law is dynamic and subject to change. An official of a non-EU state who is not trained in EU law could not be expected to determine, based on a declaration of competences, who has responsibility in a given field. Declarations of competences were initially designed for this very purpose, to inform third parties about the nature of competences. They do not fulfil this intended purpose. Olson argues that declarations of competence are not practically useful for the EU's treaty partners, pointing out that '[d]eclarations rarely, if ever, include something which would be far more informative: an article-by-article [...] analysis informing treaty partners clearly and in detail which entity will be exercising which rights and performing which obligations'[63] Such an article-by-article listing, however, would probably not be helpful to third states either, since it can only ever be a snapshot of the legal situation at the time that the agreement was concluded. This means that EU declarations of competence will be couched in terms that are in reality too vague to be of any use to third states.[64] As Talmon notes, declarations of competences 'are often formulated in such general and nebulous terms that it may be difficult for the other treaty parties to determine whether a certain obligation is incumbent upon the organization or upon its member states'.[65] Hoffmeister defends the drafting of declarations in this way: 'First, it illustrates that the identification of EU competences in a given field is not a question of mathematics or a pre-defined

---

[63]   P. M. Olson, 'Mixity from the Outside: The Perspective of a Treaty Partner' in C. Hillion & P. Koutrakos (eds), *Mixed Agreements Revisited: The EU and its Member States in the World* (Oxford: Hart, 2010) 331, 345.

[64]   M. Klamert, *The Principle of Loyalty in EU Law* (Oxford: Oxford University Press, 2014) 196. '[...] declarations of competence tend to be very terse, and if they consist of a list of legislative acts relevant for demarcating the scope of Union competence (qua ERTA), the list in most cases is "illustrative" (a euphemism for non-exhaustive) and often rather short'.

[65]   S. Talmon, 'Responsibility of International Organizations: Does the European Community Require Special Treatment?' in M. Ragazzi (ed), *International Responsibility Today: Essays in Memory of Oscar Schachter* (Leiden: Brill Publishing, 2005) 419. Talmon gives the example of the Declaration made by the EC pursuant to Article 35(3) of the WHO Framework Convention on Tobacco Control. In relation to environmental agreements, Nollkaemper points out that 'the EU has submitted a declaration of competence that seeks to make clear externally how competences are divided internally more often than not such declaration do not provide clarity to third parties'. A. Nollkaemper, 'Joint Responsibility between the EU and Member States for Non-Performance of Obligations under Multilateral Environmental Agreements' in E. Morgera (ed), *The External Environmental Policy of the European Union* (Cambridge: Cambridge University Press, 2012) 304, 321.

catalogue of competences in the Treaty, but a matter for case-by-case analysis. Secondly, it underlines the fact that Union competence in the field covered by the Convention is not status but may evolve over time'.[66] If declarations must be worded so vaguely that they cannot provide third states with any useful information about competences, then what is the point of such clauses?

From the EU perspective, the requirement to submit and update declarations of competence is an unnecessary burden. Given the number of treaties to which the EU and the Member States are parties, the requirement to constantly inform third parties about the nature of EU competences can impede the EU's ability to function effectively on the international stage.[67] Verwey argues that declaration of competences and the need to update them, also 'denies the Community its position as a subject of international law alongside states and entitled to exercise the full range of its competences at international level'.[68] Other subjects of international law, such as federal states, are not required to inform treaty partners about who is responsible for fulfilling obligations under a treaty. The difference regarding the EU, however, is that both the EU and its Member States are international legal subjects, and are both responsible for the fulfilment of the obligations under the treaty. The aim of declarations of competence could be fulfilled using other less onerous legal techniques.

Despite the problems associated with declaration of competence clauses, they nevertheless remain a part of the EU's treaty practice. They seek to fulfil a basic demand of the EU's treaty partners: to know whether international obligations will be implemented, and by whom. In many cases it may be questioned whether declarations of competence are actually necessary. In some contexts, such as the WTO, where the EU enjoys exclusive competence under the CCP no declaration of competence clause has ever existed. In other fields, such as environmental governance or human rights protection, where competences are often shared between the EU and Member States, a declaration of competence will have little practical utility.[69]

---

[66] F. Hoffmeister, 'Curse or Blessing? Mixed Agreements in Recent Practice' in C. Hillion & P. Koutrakos (eds), *Mixed Agreements Revisited: The EU and its Member States in the World* (Oxford: Hart, 2010).

[67] 'The requirement of constant statements of competences seems to form an obstacle to an efficient functioning of the EU in the FAO'. K. E. Jørgensen & R. A. Wessel, 'The Position of the European Union in (Other) International Organizations: Confronting Legal and Political Approaches' in P. Koutrakos (ed), *European Foreign Policy Legal and Political Perspectives* (Cheltenham: Edward Elgar, 2011) 271.

[68] Verwey (n34) 194.

[69] Delgado Casteleiro (n57) 500.

One option would be for the EU and its Member States to take them more seriously, and ensure that they are updated to adequately reflect the status of EU law and practice. The problem with this, as discussed earlier, is that these declarations can be very difficult to draft, and almost impossible to update. Once drafted, the EU seems to be reluctant to re-open this issue. Another option would be to find ways to encourage or compel the EU to update declarations of competence. This could be achieved by including a clause providing that where the EU and the Member States fail to clarify the division of competences, they will be subject to joint and several liability. For example, UNCLOS allows third states to request the EU to clarify who has responsibility on a specific matter. The EU is encouraged to fulfil this request since failure to do so will result in joint and several liability.[70]

A better option would be to do away with these declarations. Kuijper and Paasivirta argue that declarations of competence are no longer strictly necessary in EU law after Lisbon.[71] They argue that the declaration has two main functions: to express that the EU can conclude the agreement with the Member States and to provide guidance on responsibility in the result of breach. The first objective, they argue, can be met by demonstrating that the EU has significant competence in the field covered by the agreement, which can be done without a formal treaty clause. As for the second objective, this can be better met by using a clause, such as that in UNCLOS, which obliges the EU to clarify the division of responsibility at the request of a treaty partner.[72] This is an alternative to the more time-consuming process of drawing up, and then revising and updating, a declaration of competence.

An alternative to the declaration of competence can be seen in the Accession Agreement regarding the EU's accession to the ECHR. Unlike other international agreements that apply to a specific field or policy area, the ECHR enshrines human rights across these areas. It would be impossible to draw up an accurate declaration of competence for a treaty such as the ECHR, which seeks to protect human rights across all areas of government

---

[70] Annex IX, Article 6, UNCLOS (n42). '[f]ailure to provide this information within a reasonable time or the provision of contradictory information shall result in joint and several liability'.

[71] P.-J. Kuijper & E. Paasivirta, 'EU International Responsibility and its Attribution: From the Inside Looking Out' in M. Evans & P. Koutrakos (eds), *The International Responsibility of the European Union: European and International Perspectives* (Oxford: Hart, 2013) 35, 70.

[72] E.g. Article 5(5), Annex IX, UNCLOS (n42): 'Any State Party may request an international organization and its member States which are States Parties to provide information as to which, as between the organization and its member States, has competence in respect of any specific question which has arisen. The organization and the member States concerned shall provide this information within a reasonable time. The international organization and the member States may also, on their own initiative, provide this information'.

action. Rather than attempting to delineate the apportionment of responsibility of the EU and the Member States *ex ante*, such as through a declaration of competence, the Accession Agreement leaves the issue to the EU and the Member States to determine. While this may be an alternative to the declaration of competence, it would need to ensure that no international body other than the CJEU would be capable of ruling on the division of competences, otherwise this would violate the autonomy of the EU legal order (Section 5.2.2).

3.3.2.1 Declarations of Competence under International Law

How should declarations be understood from the viewpoint of international law? Although declarations of competence are a unique phenomenon under international law, the 1969 VCLT can take into account their use. Article 31(2) VCLT states that for the purposes of interpretation, a treaty comprises of the text itself, its annexes and preamble, as well as 'any instrument which was made by one or more parties in connection with the conclusion of the treaty and accepted by the other parties as an instrument related to the treaty'. Since the declaration of competence was made in accordance with the provisions of the treaty, it is more than a unilateral declaration made by the EU. Third parties also give their consent to be bound by the declaration. The declaration has more than an informative role, but can also be given legal effect on the international law plane.

For example, Article 4(2), Annex IX, UNCLOS sets out that 'an international organization shall be a Party to this Convention to the extent that it has competence *in accordance with the declarations*, communications of information or notifications'.[73] Here the declaration of competence has more than informative value; it sets out that the EU's declaration will be taken into consideration when determining the extent of the EU's obligations under the agreement. It is the EU's declarations that are determinative in this regard, not the internal law of the EU, which is subject to change and interpretation.[74] As Talmon argues, '[...] it is not the division of competence as laid down in the rules of the organization that is decisive but the division of competence *as declared to the other parties to the treaty*'.[75] The declaration of competence is a method by which the EU and the Member States limit their consent to be bound by the agreement, that is, to the extent to which they possess

---

[73] Emphasis added.
[74] Talmon (n65) 418.
[75] Talmon (n65) 418.

competence on a field covered by the agreement.[76] This would be critical in cases where there is a mismatch between the EU's declaration of competences on the one hand, and the reality of the EU's internal law on the other.

Declarations of competence aim to provide clarity to third states, yet they do not achieve this aim. They unnecessarily complicate the EU's external powers by elevating a purely internal issue, the balance of competences, to the international level. Although non-EU states have an interest in knowing that the international commitments will be complied with, the declaration of competence is an overly burdensome method to achieve this.

3.3.3 *Disconnection Clause*

When the EU Member States enter into a treaty, it raises the question of how the treaty is to be applied in the relations between the EU Member States themselves. There is a possibility that EU Member States may enter into international obligations that conflict with their obligations under EU law, thereby undermining the effectiveness of the latter. One of the methods by which the EU Member States have sought to prevent this form of treaty conflict is by negotiating the inclusion of 'disconnection clauses' in treaties to which the EU Member States are party. These clauses provide that EU Member States will continue to apply EU law between themselves, rather than the provisions of the agreement. The disconnection clause is designed to ensure that EU *acquis* would not be prejudiced by an international treaty touching upon issues concerning EU law. It has been described as the 'first, oldest and most well-known technique for safeguarding the *acquis*'.[77] An early example of such a clause can be found in the Article 27 of the Joint Council of Europe/OECD Convention on Mutual Administrative Assistance in Tax Matters:

> Notwithstanding the rules of the present Convention, those Parties which are members of the European Economic Community shall apply in their mutual relations the common rules in force in that Community.[78]

Similarly, the Council of Europe Convention on Laundering, Search, Seizure and Confiscation of the Proceeds from Crime and on the Financing of Terrorism sets out that:

---

[76] Talmon (n65) 417.

[77] J. Klabbers, 'Safeguarding the Organizational *Acquis*: The EU's External Practice' (2007) 4 *International Organizations Law Review* 57, 70.

[78] Joint Council of Europe/OECD Convention on Mutual Administrative Assistance in Tax Matters, CETS No. 127, entry into force 1 April 1994.

Parties which are members of the European Union shall, in their mutual relations, apply Community and European Union rules in so far as there are Community or European Union rules governing the particular subject concerned and applicable to the specific case, without prejudice to the object and purpose of the present Convention and without prejudice to its full application with other Parties.[79]

These clauses are most often found in treaties that have been developed under the auspices of the Council of Europe, but are also found in other treaties.[80]

In the COTIF Accession Agreement[81] the EU sets out some of the reasons why a disconnection clause is necessary for the EU and its Member States. Its preamble states 'a disconnection clause is necessary for those parts of the Convention which fall within the competence of the Union, in order to indicate that Member States of the Union cannot invoke and apply the rights and obligations deriving from the Convention directly among themselves'.[82] The EU has elsewhere clarified the reasons for the inclusion of these clauses:

> The European Community/European Union and its Member States reaffirm that their objective in requesting the inclusion of a 'disconnection clause' is to take account of the institutional structure of the Union when acceding to international conventions, in particular in case of transfer of sovereign powers from the Member States to the Community.[83]

Disconnection clauses differ from similar conflict clauses such as 'without prejudice' or 'non-affect' clauses that are well known in international law. This is because, unlike those clauses, disconnection clauses operate automatically and do not require any conflict to arise.[84]

---

[79] Article 52(4), Council of Europe Convention on Laundering, Search, Seizure and Confiscation of the Proceeds from Crime and on the Financing of Terrorism, CETS No.198, entry into force 1 May 2008.

[80] For example, Article 3 of the COTIF (n46) sets out that: 'The obligations resulting from § 1 for the Member States [international cooperation], which are at the same time Members of the European Communities or States parties to the European Economic Area Agreement, shall not prevail over their obligations as members of the European Communities or States parties to the European Economic Area Agreement'.

[81] Agreement between the European Union and the Intergovernmental Organisation for International Carriage by Rail on the Accession of the European Union to the Convention concerning International Carriage by Rail (COTIF) of 9 May 1980, as amended by the Vilnius Protocol of 3 June 1999.

[82] COTIF Accession Agreement, preamble, 7th recital (n81)

[83] See Explanatory Report of the Council of Europe Convention on the Prevention of Terrorism, CETS no. 196, para. 272.

[84] M. Cremona, 'Who Can Make Treaties? The European Union' in D. B. Hollis (ed), *The Oxford Guide to Treaties* (Oxford: Oxford University Press, 2012) 109. Arguing that disconnection clauses

The disconnection clause applies only in the relations between the EU Member States in their mutual relations, and does not apply to the relationship between EU Member States and third parties. In this way, the disconnection clause allows the simultaneous application of two separate legal regimes. It is for this reason that they have been criticized, especially since their inclusion in treaties may contribute to the fragmentation of international law. The use of disconnection clauses can lead to different treatment afforded to different treaty parties, and therefore may undermine the effectiveness of the treaty regime. Ličková argues that disconnection clauses 'seem to challenge, if not contradict, the well-established principle of relative effect of treaties by making intra-EU rules internationally opposable to third states'.[85]

The disconnection clause was one of the 'special clauses' discussed by the International Law Commission in its 2006 Report on the Fragmentation of International Law.[86] The Report states, 'the effect of the proliferation of such clauses to the coherence of the original treaty has seemed problematic'.[87] The ILC Study pointed to two main issues. First, they are only applicable to one class of treaty participant, that is EU Member States, and are therefore not open to all treaty parties. The second issue is that EU law is subject to change, and therefore may lead to uncertainty about the precise application of the clause. When agreeing to a disconnection clause, third states do not know how EU law may evolve in the future. As the ILC Study points out, however, these clauses have been accepted by non-EU parties, and their inclusion in treaties has become relatively common. However, it points out that these parties may not be fully aware of the potential impact that the disconnection clause may have, particularly as within the EU 'rules can develop rapidly and are subject to changing interpretation or that they can include technically complex wordings'.[88] It is for this reason that the ILC notes that, '[f]rom the perspective

---

'operate automatically and are peremptory: they do not merely allow the Member States to apply EU law instead of the Convention's rules, but require them to do so'.

[85] M. Ličková, 'European Exceptionalism in International Law' (2008) 19 *European Journal of International Law* 463, 485.

[86] 'Fragmentation of International Law: Difficulties arising from the Diversification and Expansion of International Law', Report of the Study Group of the International Law Commission finalized by Martti Koskenniemi, 13 April 2006, UN Doc. A/CN.4/L.682, 1–256 and 18 July 2006, UN Doc. A/CN.4/L.702, 1–25.

[87] *Id.*, para. 291.

[88] Council of Europe, Committee of Legal Advisers on Public International Law (CAHDI), 'Report on the consequences of the so-called "disconnection clause" in international law in general and for Council of Europe conventions, containing such a clause, in particular', 10 December 2008, para. 27.

of other treaty parties, the use of disconnection clause might create double standards, be politically incorrect or just confusing'.[89]

The Council of Europe's Committee of Legal Advisers on Public International Law (CAHDI) was requested to examine the legal issues concerning the use of disconnection clauses. It noted

> [C]riticism has also been generated by fears that indiscriminate and frequent use of such clauses may inadvertently lead to the erosion of the object and purpose of important standard-setting treaties, or inspire similar practices with regard to the relations inter se between states engaged in integration processes in other regions.[90]

Another criticism of the disconnection clause is that under a multilateral agreement, it is difficult to legally separate the obligations between different members. As Ličková argues, 'Some multilateral treaties regulate subjects such as the prevention of arms sales or illegal drug trafficking, and their efficiency clearly depends on the co-operation of all parties involved. Any fragmentation of the established regime may thus threaten the success of this objective'.[91] Even if EU rules are more developed or more stringent than those of the underlying convention, the fact that different sets of rules apply to different treaty partners may affect the coherence of that multilateral system. A multilateral treaty is more than just a web of multiple bilateral treaties; it creates a system of co-operation among treaty parties.[92]

Although the use of disconnection clauses has been criticized, there is no question about whether they are in conformity with international law. Disconnection clauses are part of the international agreement, to which non-EU states have given their consent, and are thus willing to accept the effect of the disconnection clause on the treaty regime. The ILC did discuss whether the disconnection clause was 'illegal' under international law.[93] Yet the continued use and acceptance of disconnection clauses by the EU's treaty partners suggests that they are legal by virtue of state consent and the fact that they are not prohibited by any other rule. The law of treaties allows for

---

[89] Fragmentation of International Law (n86) para. 294.
[90] CAHDI (n88) para. 9.
[91] Ličková (n85) 486.
[92] Ličková (n85) 486, arguing that 'one can ask whether it will always be easy to draw a clear line between "legal relations between EU Member States *inter se*", on the one hand, and their relations towards third states, on the other'.
[93] Certain members of the ILC were of the opinion that 'such clauses might be illegal inasmuch as they were contradictory to the fundamental principles of treaty law' Report of the International Law Commission, Fifty-seventh session (2 May–3 June and 11 July–5 August 2005), UN Doc A/60/10, para. 464.

provisions that permit states to apply the treaty amongst themselves in a certain way. In this way, disconnection clauses are not that different from *inter se* agreements, where treaty parties are permitted to modify a treaty regarding their mutual relations. While the ILC Study treats the disconnection clause in the family of conflict clauses,[94] they are better viewed as a form of *inter se* agreement under Article 41 VCLT.[95]

In many cases disconnection clauses will not be problematic since EU law will require a higher or more stringent standard than that required under an international treaty. But what if EU law were to include provisions that were substantially different from those of the treaty, to the extent that they were to defeat the object and purpose of the underlying treaty? Article 41(1) of the VCLT on *inter se* agreements sets out that '[t]wo or more of the parties to a multilateral treaty may conclude an agreement to modify the treaty as between themselves alone'. However, Article 41 sets out that such an arrangement is only valid if it (1) 'does not affect the enjoyment by the other parties of their rights under the treaty or the performance of their obligations' and (2) 'does not relate to a provision, derogation from which is incompatible with the effective execution of the object and purpose of the treaty as a whole'. Any *inter se* modification must respect the object and purpose of the treaty. Indeed, some disconnection clauses specifically state that they are 'without prejudice to the object and purpose of the present Convention'. It is difficult to envisage, however, how EU law could develop in a way that undermines the object and purpose of the agreement in such a way that it would call into question the validity of the disconnection clause.

The disconnection clause is another example of an EU-specific clause, designed to take into account the particular nature of the EU legal order. The use of the clause may be justified to safeguard the EU *acquis* and principles of EU law. In the instance where the clause was first employed – in the OECD Tax Convention – the disconnection clause avoids the possibility of the Member States applying the Convention in their mutual relations, which could have jeopardized EU law principles such as the free movement of capital. However, such clauses may become problematic if they were to be

---

94 '[Disconnection clauses] are thus best analyzed as conflict clauses added to treaties with the view to regulating potential conflicts between Community law and the treaty'. 'Fragmentation of International Law' (n86) para. 292.

95 M. Fitzmaurice & P. Merkouris, 'Uniformity versus Specialisation (1): The Quest for a Uniform Law of Inter-State Treaties' in C. J. Tams, A. Tzanakopoulos & A. Zimmermann (eds), *Research Handbook on the Law of Treaties* (Cheltenham: Edward Elgar, 2014) 341–374. Fitzmaurice and Merkouris pose the question: 'how is this different than the *inter se* agreements provided for in Article 41 of the VCLT?'

used in a widespread manner by a multitude of other international organizations. While the clause seeks to protect the coherence of EU law, it may also undermine the coherence of the multilateral system that the international agreement seeks to establish. The EU Member States could employ less radical methods to achieve the same aim. For example it has used 'without prejudice' and 'non-affection' clauses, which provide that other treaties may apply as long as they offer more favourable treatment or protection.[96] In cases where a disconnection clause is not established, the EU Member States may still make a declaration to that effect.[97] The EU Member States may do this in situations where other treaty parties may not accept a disconnection clause to be added to the text of a treaty.

Even if the disconnection clause is legally justified, it still constitutes a form of special treatment afforded to the EU and its Member States that is not afforded to other treaty parties. It is not uncommon for a treaty to set out that parties may apply more extensive rules than those in the treaty. What makes the disconnection clause different is that it allows this for only one category of treaty partner. Furthermore, it complicates issues for non-EU states, who will not necessarily know the intricacies of EU law or follow the development of EU law after the international agreement enters into force. From the perspective of non-EU states, disconnection clauses 'leave EU's treaty partners in an even greater state of uncertainty'.[98] The disconnection clause is one of several legal techniques that the EU Member States could employ to safeguard the EU *acquis*. It is a rather radical type of clause since it gives automatic precedence to EU law, described as the 'most blatant form of this "reverse primacy"'[99] in EU treaty practice. While the EU could employ other less invasive methods to ensure the *acquis* is safeguarded by international agreements, it insists that such a clause is necessary to ensure that EU law is not undermined by international legal developments. It therefore constitutes another type of 'special treatment' for the EU Member States, based on internal legal considerations.

---

[96] See M. Cremona, 'Disconnection Clauses in EU Law and Practice' in C. Hillion & P. Koutrakos (eds), *Mixed Agreements Revisited: The EU and its Member States in the World* (Oxford: Hart, 2010) 164.

[97] Klabbers (n77) 57, 77: 'A more traditional way of safeguarding the position of Community law is to make reservations or, as the case may be, declarations, to be attached to an agreement with third parties'.

[98] Olson (n63) 337.

[99] B. de Witte, 'International Law as a Tool for the European Union' (2009) 5 *European Constitutional Law Review* 265, 282.

3.3.4 *Relationship to Other Treaties*

Treaties are often part of a wider network of interlinking agreements. Since the EU has only a limited capacity to enter into international agreements it may be only capable of joining a limited set of agreements that are part of that wider network. It is not uncommon for a treaty to refer to the provisions of another treaty setting out its relationship with other agreements. The best known of these is Article 103 of the UN Charter, which sets out its relationship to other international agreements. Other examples include Article 311 of the United Nations Conventions on the Law of the Sea[100] and Article 16 of the Energy Charter Treaty, which deal with the treaty's relationship with prior and subsequent agreements.

In most cases, these clauses will not pose any particular legal issues for the EU. However, it may cause problems when the EU is only capable of entering one treaty that is part of a wider framework. This is the case, for instance, with agreements concluded under the auspices of the Council of Europe. The EU is capable of acceding to the European Convention on Human Rights, but it is not capable of joining two agreements that are closely linked with that Convention. The European Agreement relating to Persons Participating in Proceedings of the European Court of Human Rights (ETS No. 161) is a separate international agreement that requires Parties to ensure that persons participating in proceedings instituted under the ECHR enjoy immunity from legal process in respect of their acts before the Strasbourg Court.[101] Similarly, the Sixth Protocol to the General Agreement on Privileges and Immunities of the Council of Europe (ETS No. 162) relates to privileges and immunities granted to the judges of the European Court of Human Rights (ECtHR). The EU cannot accede to these conventions since they are only open to Member States of the Council of Europe. To resolve this issue, Article 9 of the EU's Draft Accession Agreement stated that the EU will, within the limits of its competence, 'respect the provisions of' the relevant articles of these treaties.[102] It also states that the Contracting Parties 'shall treat the European Union as if it were a Contracting Party to that Agreement or Protocol'. Under this scenario, the EU would not have become a party to the agreements under international law, but would have declared to abide by their provisions. In

---

[100]   Article 311, UNCLOS (n42).
[101]   European Agreement Relating to Persons Participating in Proceedings of the European Court of Human Rights, CETS No. 161, entry into force 1 January 1999.
[102]   Article 9, EU-ECHR Accession Agreement (n54).

this way, the EU could thus be seen as having unilaterally assumed the obligations under international law.[103]

3.3.5 *Territorial Application*

Article 29 VCLT sets out that 'Unless a different intention appears from the treaty or is otherwise established, a treaty is binding upon each party in respect of its entire territory'.[104] How should the state-centric concept of territory be applied to the context of the EU? This is a complex issue since the EU falls somewhere between a state, which possesses territory by definition, and an ordinary international organization, which does not. International agreements to which the EU is a party employ the terminology of territory, yet the application of this notion of territory must be applied differently in cases where the EU is a party.[105]

There is a presumption that the application of a treaty applies to the entire territory of a state. However, as Reuter points out, '[s]uch a presumption cannot extend to international organizations since they do not have a "territory"'.[106] While the term 'EU territory' is sometimes used, the EU does not, strictly speaking, have its own 'territory'. Rather, Article 52 TEU sets out that the EU Treaties shall apply to the EU Member States. Article 355 TFEU defines in more detail the specific territorial scope of the EU Treaties. Since the EU does not have its own territory, many international agreements to which the EU is a party set out the agreement's territorial application.[107] A typical example of such a clause sets out that:

> This Agreement shall apply, on the one hand, to the territories in which the Treaty on European Union is applied and under the conditions laid down in that Treaty, and, on the other hand, to the territory of the Republic of Korea.[108]

---

[103] See North Sea Continental Shelf (*Federal Republic of Germany* v. *Denmark and Federal Republic of Germany* v. *Netherlands*) (Merits) [1969] ICJ Rep 4, para. 27.

[104] Article 29, VCLT-IO (n10) uses similar language, but refers to 'a treaty between one or more States and one or more international organizations'.

[105] Verwey (n34) 135. '[I]t must be borne in mind that the concept of territory when applied to the Community is not the same as when applied to states. But the state-like character of the Community gives the concept a meaning that is different from that of a typical international organization'.

[106] Reuter (n17) 99.

[107] 'Because the Community is neither a state nor a traditional international organisation, the use of provisions defining the territorial application of agreements to which it is a party, therefore, becomes very meaningful'. Verwey (n34) 198.

[108] Article 52, Framework Agreement between the European Union and its Member States, of the one part, and the Republic of Korea, of the other part, signed on 10 May 2010 in Brussels.

The agreement does not apply to 'EU territory' but to the *territories in which EU law is applied*, as defined in the TEU. This links the territorial application of the agreement to EU law regarding the territorial application of the EU Treaties. Agreements generally do not refer to 'EU territory' or use other state-centric language. Article 1(10) of the Energy Charter Treaty uses the term 'area'.[109]

Since the application of the agreement is linked to the application of the EU Treaties, there is a potential for the territorial application of the agreement to be modified significantly, especially when states join or leave the EU. At the time of concluding an agreement with the EU, it is difficult to foresee where the agreement may potentially apply in the future. For states, territory is more or less fixed. Change in the territorial application tends to take place through monumental shifts, such as dissolution (Yugoslavia), secession of one part of the state (South Sudan) or the merger of two states (re-unification of Germany). Whereas for states the change in territory is relatively rare, for the EU, territorial application undergoes almost constant change. This has mostly taken place through enlargement, but also when the United Kingdom left the EU.

3.3.5.1 Accession of a New Member State

The territory to which the EU Treaties applies expands with the accession of every new EU Member State. When a new Member State joins the EU, unless stated otherwise, agreements to which the EU is a party will apply to the territory of that new Member State. In this case, the Commission will notify treaty partners that there has been a change to the territorial application of the agreement. The EU often does this unilaterally, without the consent of the other treaty partners. In the case of mixed agreements, the EU and the Member States will often conclude a separate protocol to an agreement that takes into account the accession of the new Member States. For example, the EC-Russian Federation Partnership and Cooperation Agreement[110] sets out in Article 10 that the agreement applies to Russia and the territories on which the European Treaties apply. With the accession of new EU Member States in

---

[109]   Article 45, Energy Charter Treaty, 2080 UNTS 95, entry into force 16 April 1998. 'to a Regional Economic Integration Organization which is a Contracting Party, area means the areas of the Member States of such Organization, under the provisions contained in the agreement establishing that Organization'.

[110]   Agreement on Partnership and Cooperation Establishing a Partnership between the European Communities and their Member States, of one part, and the Russian Federation, of the other part, OJ L 327, 28 November 1997, 3.

2004 and 2007, the EU and its Member States concluded protocols specifically including the new Member States as parties to the agreement.[111]

3.3.5.2 Change in Status of Territory

The territory on which EU law applies will also change when there is a change in the legal status of a part of the territory of an EU Member State, such as one of the Member States' overseas territories or other territories covered by special arrangements.[112] Denmark, France, the Netherlands, Spain and Portugal have overseas territories, which are subject to specific conditions under EU law.[113] Through a change in the status of one of these territories, the territory on which the Treaties apply, and thus the territorial application of EU agreements, may expand or contract. According to Article 355(6) TFEU, the Council may adopt a decision amending the status of certain overseas countries and territories, upon an initiative of the Member State involved, and after consultation of the Commission. On 1 January 2014, Mayotte became an 'outermost region' of the EU within the meaning of Article 349 TFEU.[114] Upon the entry into force of the Council Decision, EU law began to apply to the territory (subject to certain transitional arrangements). Treaties to which the EU is a party also are applicable in respect of that territory.

One prominent example of a change in status is the 'withdrawal' of Greenland from the EU. Since Greenland was not an EU member in its own right, it could not technically withdraw from the Union. Rather, Denmark sought to modify the territorial application of substantial parts of the Treaties to exclude Greenland. Special arrangements, such as those regarding fisheries and trade rights, were developed, and the other EU Member States and institutions were consulted at each stage.

---

[111] See Protocol to the Partnership and Cooperation Agreement establishing a partnership between the European Communities and their Member States, of the one part, and the Russian Federation, of the other part, to take account of the accession of the Czech Republic, the Republic of Estonia, the Republic of Cyprus, the Republic of Latvia, the Republic of Lithuania, the Republic of Hungary, the Republic of Malta, the Republic of Poland, the Republic of Slovenia, and the Slovak Republic to the European Union, [2006] OJ L 185/17.

[112] These include Article 355(5)(a) (Faroe Islands); Article 355(5)(c) TFEU (Channel Islands and the Isle of Man), Article 355(5)(b) TFEU (UK Sovereign Base Areas of Akrotiri and Dhekelia).

[113] For a discussion of how Union law principles apply to overseas territories, see D. Kochenov (ed), *EU Law of the Overseas: Outermost Regions, Associated Overseas Countries and Territories, Territories Sui Generis* (Alphen aan den Rijn: Kluwer Law International, 2011).

[114] European Council Decision of 11 July 2012 amending the status of Mayotte with regard to the European Union, [2012] OJ L 204/131. See Commission Opinion on outermost status: www.parlament.gv.at/PAKT/EU/XXIV/EU/08/45/EU_84522/imfname_10032623.pdf .

Another example of a change in status is the re-unification of Germany in 1990. One question in this regard was whether the reunification of Germany would entail the automatic entry of the former GDR into the European Community. According to one view, reunification was merely a change in the territory of a Member State, and therefore a change in the territorial application of the Treaties. According to another view, reunification in essence created a new state, and therefore it would need to apply for admission.[115] Since the EU Treaties gave little guidance on this issue, resort had to be made to principles of international law.[116] A related question was the extent to which previous international agreements entered into by the EC and by the Federal Republic of Germany were applicable to the territory of the former GDR.

Similar questions would arise if a part of an EU Member State were to secede and form a new state. In the lead up to the 2014 Scottish independence referendum, there was discussion about whether an independent Scotland would have to apply to become a new EU Member State. Crawford and Boyle argued that the EU Treaties would no longer apply with respect to an independent Scotland, viewing the issue as one of change of territorial scope of the EU Treaties.[117] A related question was whether agreements entered into by the EU would apply in respect of an independent Scotland. This is a different scenario from the withdrawal of an EU Member State. If Scotland had voted to leave the UK, it would have effectively withdrawn from the EU without using the procedure in Article 50 TEU. Unlike the UK, Scotland would not have been in a position to negotiate a withdrawal agreement, unless the UK authorized Scotland to do so under internal constitutional arrangements. There are other independence movements in Europe, such as Catalonia in Spain or Flanders in Belgium. The EU Treaties would cease to apply to these new states, who would be required to apply for admission as new EU Member States.

---

[115] J.-P. Jacqué, 'German Unification and the European Community' (1991) 2 *European Journal of International Law* 1.

[116] Jacqué (n115) 5: 'Community law gives no obvious answer to the question whether the operation can only be accomplished by amending the Treaty. Falling a specific solution, it is appropriate to refer to international law'.

[117] J. Crawford & A. Boyle, 'Opinion: Referendum on the Independence of Scotland – International Law Aspects', 11 February 2013, para. 160: 'it is open for the UK to change the territorial scope of the treaties unilaterally by granting Scotland independence. The [EU] treaties would continue to apply to the reduced territory of the [remainder of the UK] but would, on their face, cease to apply to an independent Scotland unless amended'.

3.3.5.3 Withdrawal of a Member State

On 31 January 2020, the United Kingdom became the first EU Member State to leave the European Union. Upon the UK's withdrawal, the UK's relationship with the EU was governed by the EU-UK Withdrawal Agreement, which established an implementation period during which EU law continued to apply in respect of the UK. The Brexit process uncovered a wide range of legal questions for the EU, UK and third states, many of which are at the cusp of EU and public international law. This section will not examine these issues in detail, and have been discussed extensively in legal literature.[118] One of these legal questions related to the fate of international agreements concluded by the EU and whether they would continue to apply in respect of the UK after withdrawal. Most commentators agreed that EU-only agreements would no longer apply in respect of the UK, since the UK is not a party to these agreements. Some had argued, however, that the UK could continue to be bound by certain EU-only agreements by way of succession. According to this argument, EU-only agreements were concluded on behalf of the EU Member States, and that these legal obligations would flow back to the leaving Member State upon withdrawal. Bartels made this argument in relation to the WTO's 2014 Government Procurement Agreement, a plurilateral agreement to which the EU is a party, but the UK is not.[119] The argument is partly based on the practice of the dissolution of unions and federations, and that customary international law on the succession of states to treaties can be applied to the context of a supranational organization. The automatic succession argument denies the separate legal personality of the EU in international law, and the fact that EU-only agreements are concluded by the EU in its own right, not on behalf of its Member States.[120] There are also practical problems, especially as many EU-only agreements are structured bilaterally, and it would be difficult to disentangle the obligations of a leaving Member State from those of the EU.

---

[118] See K. Bradley, 'On the Cusp: Brexit and Public International Law' in I. Govare & S. Garben (eds), *The Interface between EU and International Law: Contemporary Reflections* (Oxford: Hart, 2019); J. Larik, 'Brexit, The EU-UK Withdrawal Agreement, and Global Treaty (Re-) Negotiations' (2020) 114 *American Journal of International Law* 443; J. Odermatt, 'Brexit and International law: Disentangling Legal Orders' (2017) 31 *Emory International Law Review* 1052; R. A. Wessel, 'Consequences of Brexit for International Agreements concluded by the EU and its Member States' (2018) 55 *Common Market Law Review* 101; P. Koutrakos, 'Negotiating International Trade Treaties after Brexit' (2016) 41 *European Law Review* 475.

[119] L. Bartels, 'The UK's Status in the WTO after Brexit' in R. Schütze & S. Tierney (eds), *The United Kingdom and the Federal Idea* (Oxford: Hart, 2018).

[120] A. Łazowski & R. A. Wessel, 'The External Dimension of Withdrawal from the European Union' (2017) 227–250 *Revue des Affaires européennes*.

In the case of mixed agreements, the UK would continue to be bound by such an agreement under international law, in certain circumstances. This is also the position of the UK government.[121] For multilateral agreements, such as the WTO agreement, the UK would continue to be bound as long as it is a party in its own right. More complications arose in relation to bilateral mixed agreements, which are structured in a way so that EU Member States and the EU are parties together on the same side of the agreement. The Cotonou Agreement, which involves the EU and the Member States as well as seventy-nine countries from Africa, the Caribbean and the Pacific, is structured as a bilateral treaty.[122] One strategy would have been to examine these agreements and understand how the 'parties' are defined in each agreement. In some cases, an agreement will apply to the EU and its Member States as a single party.[123] In such cases, the EU and the Member States are acting *jointly*, and the UK would not continue to be bound upon its withdrawal from the Union.[124] The strategy adopted by the UK has been to 'rollover' bilateral EU agreements, rather than seek the continued application of EU bilateral agreements. In these cases, the UK enters into a separate agreement with a third state, but the agreement largely replicates the existing EU agreement, with relevant changes. The benefit of this approach is that by concluding a new agreement, the UK has the explicit consent of the third state. In some cases, the third state will not wish to rollover the existing EU agreement, but to negotiate a new agreement.

3.3.5.4 Defining Territorial Application

Although the international law of treaties presumes that treaties apply with respect to the entire territory of its parties, those parties may choose to define the agreement's territorial application.[125] EU agreements often include

---

[121]　S. Fella, 'UK replacement of the EU's external agreements after Brexit', House of Commons Library, Number 8370, 19 September 2019.

[122]　See Cotonou Partnership Agreement between the Members of the African, Caribbean and Pacific Group of States, of the one part, and the European Community and its Member States, of the other part, 23 June 2000, 2000 OJ L 317, 3.

[123]　*See, e.g.*, Trade Agreement between the European Union and its Member States, of the one part, and Colombia and Peru, of the other part, 26 June 2012, 2006 OJ L 354, 3.

[124]　This was also reflected in the European Council Guidelines. See European Council (Article 50) guidelines following the United Kingdom's notification under Article 50 TEU, EUCO XT 20004/17, 29 April 2017, para. 13. 'The United Kingdom will no longer be covered by agreements concluded by the Union or by Member States acting on its behalf or by both acting jointly'.

[125]　Article 29, VCLT-IO (n10) 'Unless a different intention appears from the treaty or is otherwise established, a treaty between one or more States and one or more international organizations is binding upon each State party in respect of its entire territory'.

specific 'territorial application clauses' to clarify issues arising from EU law. For a number of reasons, the EU may seek to limit the territorial application of an agreement to a certain part of the EU territory.[126] For example, agreements may stipulate that they only apply with respect to the 'European territory' of the EU Member States, thereby excluding its application to overseas territories.[127] The EU may also limit the application of an agreement regarding a particular Member State or Member States. In agreements relating to the Area of Freedom, Security and Justice (AFSJ) special provisions exist regarding Ireland or Denmark due to their opt-outs in this field. For example, EU readmission agreements include a provision stating that the agreement 'shall not apply to the territory of the Kingdom of Denmark'.[128] Readmission agreements often contain a special clause inviting Denmark to conclude a bilateral agreement mirroring the one concluded by the EU.[129]

There are certain circumstances where a treaty may apply to the *jurisdiction* of the contracting parties, as is the case with several human rights treaties. For example, Article 1 ECHR sets out that '[t]he High Contracting Parties shall secure to everyone within their jurisdiction the rights and freedoms defined in Section I of this Convention'. The concept of jurisdiction is broader in scope than that of territory. The 'extra-territorial' application of human rights treaties and other international instruments has been the focus of academic attention in recent years.[130] The territorial application of the ECHR will be an important legal issue once the EU accedes to the human right treaty. The EU-ECHR Accession Agreement sought to deal with this issue – it set out that the term 'jurisdiction' will be understood 'as referring to persons within the territories of

---

[126] See Verwey (n34) 135.
[127] Article 5 of the Agreement between the European Community and Antigua and Barbuda on the short-stay visa waiver, L/169, 30/06/2009, 10, provides that: 'As regards the French Republic, the provisions of this Agreement shall apply only to the European territory of the French Republic, 2. As regards the Kingdom of the Netherlands, the provisions of this Agreement shall apply only to the European territory of the Kingdom of the Netherlands'.
[128] See, e.g., Article 21, Agreement between the European Community and Bosnia and Herzegovina on the readmission of persons residing without authorisation [2007] OJ L334/66.
[129] See C. Matera, 'Much Ado about Opt-Outs? The Impact of Variable Geometry in the AFSJ as a Global Security Actor' in S. Blockmans (ed), *Differentiated Integration in the EU: From the Inside Looking Out* (Brussels: Centre for European Policy Studies, 2014) 87.
[130] See M. Milanović, *Extraterritorial Application of Human Rights Treaties: Law, Principles, and Policy* (Oxford: Oxford University Press, 2011); S. Ghandhi, 'Al-Skeini and the Extra-territorial Application of the European Convention on Human Rights' in A. Burrows, D. Johnston & R. Zimmermann (eds), *Judge and Jurist: Essays in Memory of Lord Rodger of Earlsferry* (Oxford: Oxford University Press, 2013) 575–590; M. den Heijer & R. Lawson, 'Extraterritorial Human Rights and the Concept of "Jurisdiction"' in M. Langford (ed), *Global Justice, State Duties: The Extraterritorial Scope of Economic, Social and Cultural Rights in International Law* (Cambridge: Cambridge University Press, 2013) 153–191.

the member states of the European Union to which the TEU and the TFEU apply'.[131]

One can envisage that after accession the ECtHR will be faced with complex legal questions regarding how concepts of jurisdiction and territory may apply to the EU. This may arise, for instance, when the EU is involved in CSDP missions. Under Article 41(2) TEU, the Union 'may use [civilian and military assets] on missions outside the Union for peace-keeping, conflict prevention and strengthening international security . . . '.[132] The Explanatory Report on the Accession Agreement states that Article 1 of the Agreement 'applies to acts, measures or omissions in whichever context they occur, including with regard to matters relating to the EU common foreign and security policy'.[133] Jacqué argues that 'it is possible that substantive action committed by the Union's missions might constitute a breach of the Convention'.[134]

The EU's 'territory' is not fixed, and is not entirely defined by the EU.[135] Rather, the territorial scope of EU law, and thereby the territorial application of agreements to which the EU is a party, can change in a number of ways. Under EU law, the EU Treaties apply to the territory of the Member State, which is defined by the constitutional order of that state.[136] Moreover, the Union is made up of different levels of integration, meaning that the application of an agreement to which the EU is a party may not always apply to the entire Union legal space. This 'flexibility in space'[137] sets the EU apart from states as subjects of international law that have much more fixed and defined territory. This is another example of an internal EU law issue – the scope of EU law – being externalized through the EU's treaty practice. It often means that the scope of an international agreement will depend on questions of EU law. Unlike some other EU-specific clauses, however, EU territorial application clauses have not given rise to significant complications for third states.

---

[131]   Article 1, para. 6, EU-ECHR Accession Agreement (n54).
[132]   Article 41(2), TEU.
[133]   EU-ECHR Accession Agreement (n54) 'Explanatory Report', para. 23.
[134]   Jacqué (n17) 995, 1006.
[135]   J. Ziller, 'The European Union and the Territorial Scope of European Territories' (2007) 38 *Victoria University Wellington Law Review* 51, 52. As Ziller points out, 'in the case of the EU, the definition of the "territory" is not in the hands of the Union itself'.
[136]   Judgment in Case C-148/77 *Hansen v. Hauptzolamt Flensburg*, EU:C:1978:73, point 10.
[137]   J. Ziller, 'Flexibility in Geographical Scope of EU Law: Diversity and Differentiation in the Application of Substantive Law on Member States' Territories' in G. de Búrca & J. Scott (eds), *Constitutional Change in the EU – From Uniformity to Flexibility?* (Oxford: Hart, 2000) 114.

3.4 LAW OF TREATIES APPLIED TO EU TREATY PRACTICE

The previous section examined how the EU, the Member States and their treaty partners seek to resolve issues arising from international law and EU law through EU-specific clauses. This section examines a related issue, how principles of the law of treaties are applied in the context of the EU's treaty practice. In most cases these principles, enshrined in the VCLT and VCLT-IO, can be applied in a rather straightforward manner to the EU context with no need for adaptation. However, there may be situations where these rules may be modified to take into account the special nature of the EU legal order and the EU's specific treaty-making practice.

3.4.1 *Conclusion of Agreements by the Union*

Article 218 TFEU sets out a procedure by which the EU concludes agreements between it and third countries or international organizations.[138] This section goes through the stages by which the EU concludes these agreements, discussing international law issues that arise at each stage.

3.4.1.1 Negotiation

The first formal step is for the Council to authorize the opening of negotiations, and to adopt 'negotiating directives' addressed to the party or parties undertaking the negotiations.[139] In most cases, this will be the European Commission, who will have first made a recommendation to the Council for the opening of negotiations.[140] Where the envisaged agreement relates solely or predominantly to CFSP, the High Representative of the Union for Foreign Affairs and Security Policy may make such a recommendation to the Council.[141] The European Parliament is to be fully informed of the process

---

[138] Article 218, TFEU: 'Without prejudice to the specific provisions laid down in Article 207, agreements between the Union and third countries or international organisations shall be negotiated and concluded in accordance with the following procedure'.

[139] Article 218(2), TFEU: 'The Council shall authorise the opening of negotiations, adopt negotiating directives, authorise the signing of agreements and conclude them'.

[140] Article 207(3), TFEU ' ... The Commission shall make recommendations to the Council, which shall authorise it to open the necessary negotiations. The Council and the Commission shall be responsible for ensuring that the agreements negotiated are compatible with internal Union policies and rules'.

[141] Article 218(3), TFEU: 'The Commission, or the High Representative of the Union for Foreign Affairs and Security Policy where the agreement envisaged relates exclusively or principally to the common foreign and security policy, shall submit recommendations to the Council, which shall adopt a decision authorising the opening of negotiations and, depending on the

from this step on.[142] The Council will nominate an EU negotiator or negotiation team and issue a set of negotiating directives. It may also establish a committee to ensure that the negotiations take place within the framework set out by the Council. The external representation of the Union, and the procedures surrounding the negotiation of agreements, is a complex issue in EU external relations law. At the negotiation stage, these legal issues remain predominantly internal legal issues for the EU, rather than those touching upon international law.[143] This does not mean, however, that international law issues are not considered at this stage. The Commission may mention issues of public international law in its recommendation. Its recommendation to open negotiations on a Global Pact for the Environment mentions that '[t]he aim of EU participation in the negotiations is to maximise the international instrument's alignment with relevant EU and other international law' to justify its choice of legal basis.[144]

The topic of representation during the negotiation phase is governed by public international law. For the purpose of providing legal certainty and stability, it is important to ensure that negotiators actually possess the legal power to represent the legal person (a state, a group of states or an international organization) on whose behalf they are negotiating. It relates to the questions of who is capable of representing the sovereign internationally. Article 7 VCLT deals with the question of who is capable of representing a *state* in treaty making: when they produce appropriate full powers, or where from practice or from circumstances it was the intention of the parties concerned to consider that person as representing the state for such purposes.[145] For states, the Heads of State, Heads of Government and Ministers for Foreign Affairs do not need to present full powers, as they are considered to be representatives of their state. There is no corresponding provision for ex officio full powers by the delegates of international organizations, however. This reflects the fact that,

---

subject of the agreement envisaged, nominating the Union negotiator or the head of the Union's negotiating team'.

[142] Article 218(10), TFEU.

[143] Verwey (n34) 103. 'International treaty law governs neither the negotiating process nor the negotiating powers of international law'.

[144] Recommendation for a Council Decision authorizing the opening of negotiations on a Global Pact for the Environment, COM (2018) 138 final.

[145] Article 7(1), VCLT (n9): 'person is considered as representing a State for the purpose of adopting or authenticating the text of a treaty or for the purpose of expressing the consent of the State to be bound by a treaty if: (a) he produces appropriate full powers; or (b) it appears from the practice of the States concerned or from other circumstances that their intention was to consider that person as representing the State for such purposes and to dispense with full powers'.

for international organizations, there are no similar positions where the office holder is considered to represent the organization in international affairs. It remains at the discretion of the state to determine who is capable of exercising full powers in treaty-making procedures. The VCLT-IO, on the other hand, simply sets out that '[t]he capacity of an international organization to conclude treaties is governed by the rules of that organization'.[146] This is defined in the EU Treaties and case law. Art 7 VCLT-IO deals with the question of who is deemed to represent an IO for the purposes of authenticating the text of a treaty or expressing the IO's consent to be bound. A person is considered to represent an IO if that person has appropriate 'full powers' or if it appears from the circumstances that the parties intended to consider that person as representing the IO, in accordance with the rules of the organization.[147] The VCLT-IO defines 'full powers':

> a document emanating from the competent authority of a State or from the competent organ of an international organization designating a person or persons to represent the State or the organization for negotiating, adopting or authenticating the text of a treaty, for expressing the consent of the State or of the organization to be bound by a treaty, or for accomplishing any other act with respect to a treaty.[148]

For international organizations, full powers are generally issued by the secretariat of the organization, such as the UN Secretary General in the case of the United Nations.[149] There is no consistent practice of international organizations in this regard. In the context of the EU, it is a well-established practice that the European Commission has powers to represent the EU internationally. In the case of negotiations of mixed agreements, however, the exact limits of the powers of the EU and the Member States may not always be clear to third parties. In such cases, the Member States should be viewed as having delegated their powers of negotiation to the Commission/High Representative, within the defined boundaries of the EU Treaties. Over time, this contributes to practice whereby the representatives of an IO are considered capable of not only representing that organization, but also the members of that organization.

---

[146] Article 6, VCLT-IO (n10).

[147] 'A person is considered as representing an international organization for the purpose of adopting or authenticating the text of a treaty, or expressing the consent of that organization to be bound by a treaty, if: (a) that person produces appropriate full powers; or (b) it appears from the circumstances that it was the intention of the States and international organizations concerned to consider that person as representing the organization for such purposes, in accordance with the rules of the organization, without having to produce full powers'.

[148] Article 2(c), VCLT-IO (n10).

[149] F. Hoffmeister, 'Article 7 – Full powers' in Dörr & Schmalenbach (n2) 123.

While this is recognized under the EU's internal rules, such practice has also been recognized and accepted by non-EU states.

3.4.1.2 Signature

Once an agreement has been negotiated, the EU must then give its consent to be bound by that agreement. The first step involves the text of the agreement being submitted to the Council. At this point, if it approves the text of the agreement, the Council with authorize the signing of the agreement. This procedure is covered by Article 218(5) TFEU.[150] At this point, signature of the agreement does not have legal effect unless the agreement itself explicitly provides as such, or the agreement is to be applied provisionally (Section 3.4.1.5). In most cases signature indicates that the parties agree to the text and indicate they will submit the agreement for approval according to their own constitutional arrangements.[151] Under international law, the text of the agreement is generally established as authentic and definitive at the point of signature.[152] Moreover, from the point of signature, the EU has an obligation under international law not to act so as to defeat the object and purpose of the treaty before its entry into force.[153]

Third states may want to be assured that the party that has signed the agreement is actually capable of representing the Union. Before the entry into force of the Lisbon Treaty, the Treaties gave no guidance on who was capable of signing an agreement on behalf of the Union/Community.[154] Under the TFEU, while the Council is responsible for taking 'a decision authorising the signing of the agreement'[155] it does not specify which party is actually responsible for signature at the conclusion of negotiations. It has been argued that the Council therefore has wide discretion as to designating the party responsible for signature. However, the post-Lisbon Treaties are clear that the external representation of the Union in the negotiation of

---

[150] 'The Council, on a proposal by the negotiator, shall adopt a decision authorising the signing of the agreement and, if necessary, its provisional application before entry into force'.

[151] Eeckhout (n8): 'The prevailing practice as regards significant treaties or agreements is that through their signature, the representatives of the contracting parties agree to submit the agreement for domestic approval'.

[152] See Article 10, VCLT (n9).

[153] Article 18, VCLT (n9) (Obligation Not to Defeat the Object and Purpose of a Treaty Prior to Its Entry into Force). See also Judgment in *Opel Austria* v. *Council*, T-115/94, EU:T:1997:3, paras 90–94.

[154] M. Gatti & P. Manzini, 'External Representation of the European Union in the Conclusion of International Agreements' (2012) 49 *Common Market Law Review* 1724.

[155] Article 218(5), TFEU.

international agreements is to be undertaken by the Commission or the High Representative (in the fields of non-CFSP and CFSP respectively). Consequently, it has been argued that no other entity should do so.[156] In the post-Lisbon period the Member State holding the rotating Presidency has still been involved in signing agreements. One question post-Lisbon is whether the Presidency is representing the EU or only the Member States in a mixed agreement. While this may be an issue for the EU in terms of presenting itself as a unified body to the world, this has no international law significance – the EU may designate a party to have full powers to sign the instrument.

3.4.1.3 Consent to Be Bound

Article 11(2) VCLT-IO states how an international organization may express its consent to be bound by an international instrument:

> The consent of an international organization to be bound by a treaty may be expressed by signature, exchange of instruments constituting a treaty, act of formal confirmation, acceptance, approval or accession, or by any other means if so agreed.

This article reproduces the means of expressing consent under Article 11 VCLT,[157] except that the term 'ratification' used in the VCLT is replaced with 'act of formal confirmation' with regard to IOs. It allows consent to be expressed by 'any other means if so agreed'. In this way, the VCLT-IO provides international organizations with the same degree of flexibility as states. There are numerous ways in which an international legal person can express its consent to be bound under international law.[158] It has been noted that 'approval', rather than ratification, is the common method by which international organizations give their consent to be bound by an international instrument.[159] The terminology often used is that the EU 'concludes' an agreement. Whereas the VCLT/VCLT-IO uses the term 'conclusion' to

---

[156] Gatti & Manzini (n154) 1726. 'No other entity, and in particular the rotating Presidency, should play any role in this area'.

[157] Draft Articles on the Law of Treaties between States and International Organizations or between International Organizations, with Commentaries (1982), Commentary to Article 11, 29.

[158] 'International treaty law is silent on the manner in which an international organisation and its members are to express their consent to be bound in the event that they act together as a contracting party'. Verwey (n134) 168.

[159] F. Hoffmeister, 'Article 14. Consent to be bound by a treaty expressed by ratification' in Dörr & Schmalenbach (n2) 189.

refer to the entire treaty-making process[160] the term 'conclusion' in the EU context refers to a procedure by which the EU expresses its consent to be bound. This resembles ratification in domestic jurisdictions.[161]

When the EU expresses its consent to be bound, it generally does so through a Council Decision in which it states that the convention 'is hereby approved on behalf of the Union'. The Council Decision will also include in its preamble the legal basis for the agreement (which it is obliged to do under EU law) and the procedural history of the agreement. The Decision may also include instructions regarding the notification of other parties to the agreement.[162] It may also specify who is to represent the Union in dispute resolution procedures or organs established by the agreement. This process takes place according to Article 218(6) TFEU. For most types of agreements, formal consent of the European Parliament is also required.[163]

3.4.1.4 Entry into Force

Article 24 VCLT-IO states that:

> A treaty enters into force in such manner and upon such date as it may provide or as the negotiating States and negotiating organizations or, as the case may be, the negotiating organizations may agree.

This mirrors Article 24 VCLT. Agreements to which the EU is a party will often include clauses setting out in detail when the agreement will enter into force. Where no specific clause exists, the treaty will enter into force when the negotiating parties have expressed their consent to be bound by the agreement.[164] Treaties entered into by the Union then become binding

---

[160]   See VCLT (n9), Section 1 'Conclusion of Treaties'.
[161]   See Gatti & Manzini (n154).
[162]   For example, in Council Decision of 14 April 2014 on the conclusion on behalf of the European Union of the Political Dialogue and Cooperation Agreement between the European Community and its Member States, of the one part, and the Republics of Costa Rica, El Salvador, Guatemala, Honduras, Nicaragua and Panama, of the other part, as regards Article 49(3) thereof (2014/210/EU), the President of the Council is instructed to give the notifications provided for in Article 54 of the Agreement, behalf of the EU.
[163]   Article 218(6)(a) TFEU sets out the types of agreements that require approval of the European Parliament. These are (i) association agreements, (ii) agreement on Union accession to the European Convention for the Protection of Human Rights and Fundamental Freedoms; (iii) agreements establishing a specific institutional framework by organising cooperation procedures; (iv) agreements with important budgetary implications for the Union; (v) agreements covering fields to which either the ordinary legislative procedure applies, or the special legislative procedure where consent by the European Parliament is required'.
[164]   Article 24(2), VCLT (n9).

upon the Union and the Member States[165] from the moment it enters into force.[166]

3.4.1.5 Provisional Application

This two-stage procedure can lead to the situation whereby there is a significant delay between the moment of signing the agreement on behalf of the EU and the decision of the Council to conclude the agreement. In the case of multilateral treaties that do not enter into force until a certain number of states have ratified the agreement, there can be a long period between the moment of signing and the moment when it enters into force. In the case of mixed agreements, the process can also be delayed when the approval of all EU Member States is required.[167] The Council may decide in certain cases to declare provisional application of the agreement in accordance with Article 25 VCLT.[168] Article 218(5) TFEU allows the Council to authorize the provisional application of an agreement prior to its entry into force.[169] For example, Article 45 of the Energy Charter Treaty sets out that each signatory will apply the treaty provisionally pending its entry into force.[170]

For mixed agreements, the requirement to include the ratification procedures of the EU Member States may result in a delay of several years. In his *Marrakesh Opinion*, Advocate General Wahl mentioned that one of the

---

[165]   Article 216(2), TFEU: 'Agreements concluded by the Union are binding upon the institutions of the Union and on its Member States'.

[166]   Judgment in *R. & V. Haegeman v. Belgian State*, C-181/73, EU:C:1974:41, para. 5: 'The provisions of the agreement, from the coming into force thereof, form an integral part of Community Law'. See Judgment in *Anklagemindigheden v. Poulsen and Diva Navigation*, C-286/90, EU:C:1992:453, paras 9–10.

[167]   F. Hoffmeister, 'Article 14. Consent to be bound by a treaty expressed by ratification', in Dörr & Schmalenbach (n2) 193: 'Mixed agreements between the European Union and its Member States, on the one hand, and a third State, on the other, nowadays need 29 instruments of ratification, acceptance or approval (27 from the Member States, one from the Union, one from the third State) before they enter into force. This process takes on average 3–4 years'. See L. Bartels, 'Withdrawing Provisional Application of Treaties: Has the EU Made a Mistake?' (2012) 1 *Cambridge Journal of International and Comparative Law* 112–118.

[168]   Article 25(1), VCLT (n9): 'A treaty or a part of a treaty is applied provisionally pending its entry into force if: (a) the treaty itself so provides; or (b) the negotiating States have in some other manner so agreed'.

[169]   See, e.g., Council Decision 2010/397/EU of 3 June 2010 on the signing, on behalf of the European Union, and on provisional application of the Fisheries Partnership Agreement between the European Union and Solomon Islands, OJ L 190, 22 July 2010, 1–2.

[170]   Article 45, Energy Charter Treaty (n109). 'Each signatory agrees to apply this Treaty provisionally pending its entry into force for such signatory in accordance with Article 44, to the extent that such provisional application is not inconsistent with its constitution, laws or regulations'.

reasons for choosing not to conclude an agreement (in the field of shared or parallel competences) as mixed would be 'because of the urgency of the situation and the time required for the 28 ratification procedures at national level, seriously risk compromising the objective pursued, or cause the Union to breach the principle *pacta sunt servanda*'.[171] The urgency of the situation may be a political reason to conclude the agreement as an EU-only agreement; however, the long delay in ratification by the Member States is not a 'breach' of the principle of *pacta sunt servanda* for the Union. The EU and its Member States are distinct legal subjects, including for the purposes of ratification. Cremona also questions the propriety of the practice of 'indefinite extension' of mixed agreements (via provisional application), especially in cases where there is little hope of the Member States ratifying the agreement.[172] A practice of the EU/MS may cause problems in practical terms, but this does not necessarily mean that it has violated international law.

Provisional application allows the terms of a treaty to be applied before the treaty has officially entered into force. In the case of mixed agreements, it allows the EU to apply the parts of the agreement applicable to it to be applied, while those related to the EU Member States are not. This can also clearly give rise to complex questions under EU and international law. Third states will seek to understand which parts of the convention apply to the Union and subject to provisional application. The practice of provisional application of parts of an agreement, especially when it takes place for an extended period, exposes third states to an unnecessary level of legal uncertainty and complexity.

Article 25 VCLT allows a treaty, or part of a treaty, to be applied provisionally where (a) the treaty itself allows for provisional application, or (b) where the negotiating parties to the treaty have otherwise agreed. The VCLT does not set out strict rules about how treaties may be applied provisionally, as it gives room for the parties to agree to this in the treaty itself. Many agreements entered into by the Union thus include provisional application clauses, using language such as '[t]his Agreement shall be provisionally applied from the date of signature' or otherwise setting out a date from which the agreement will be applied provisionally. Some provisional application clauses contain much more detailed procedural steps. The Comprehensive Economic and Trade

---

[171]   Opinion of A. G. Wahl, *Marrakesh Treaty*, EU:C:2016:657, para. 121.
[172]   M. Cremona, 'Distinguished Essay: A Quiet Revolution – The Changing Nature of the EU's Common Commercial Policy' (2017) 8 *European Yearbook of International Economic Law* 32: 'difficulties may be encountered in ratifying an agreement which has been signed and is being provisionally applied, raising questions as to the propriety of an indefinite extension of provisional application'.

Agreement (CETA) between the EU and the Member States and Canada, for example, sets out details about the notification and termination of the agreement's provisions.[173] In some cases, the provisional application may apply to only one part of a treaty, rather than the entire instrument.[174]

In a mixed agreement, the Union may be authorized to decide which parts of the agreement to apply provisionally. For example, the Cooperation Agreement on Partnership and Development between the European Union and its Member States and Afghanistan sets out that 'the Union and Afghanistan agree to provisionally apply this Agreement in part, *as specified by the Union*, as set out in paragraph 3 of this Article, and in accordance with their respective internal procedures and legislation as applicable'.[175] Here it is the Union, one side of the agreement, that can decide which parts of the agreement are to be applied provisionally. In the Council Decision on the signing of that agreement, the EU sets out further that 'the following parts of the Agreement shall be applied provisionally . . . but only to the extent that they cover matters falling within the Union's competence . . . '[176]

While the VCLT gives flexibility and scope to the parties, the practice in relation to the EU has given rise to legal questions. The rules on provisional application, moreover, have gained more attention in recent years. In 2011, the ILC decided to include the topic of "Provisional application of treaties" in its long-term programme of work.[177] The EU welcomed the fact that the study included both the practice of states and international organizations, pointing out that 'the European Union is an actor who is actively contributing to

[173] See Article 30.7 of the Comprehensive Economic and Trade Agreement (CETA) between Canada, of the one part, and the European Union and its Member States, of the other part, OJ [2017] L 11/23.

[174] For example, see Article 22 of the Agreement between the European Union and the Swiss Confederation on the linking of their greenhouse gas emissions trading systems (OJ [2017] L 322/3), which provides that '[b]efore the entry into force of this Agreement, Articles 11 to 13 shall be applied on a provisional basis as from the date of signature of this Agreement'.

[175] See Article 59 of the Cooperation Agreement on Partnership and Development between the European Union and its Member States, of the one part, and the Islamic Republic of Afghanistan, of the other part, OJ [2017] L 67/3 (emphasis added).

[176] Council Decision 2017/434 on the signing, on behalf of the Union, and provisional application of the Cooperation Agreement on Partnership and Development between the European Union and its Member States, of the one part, and the Islamic Republic of Afghanistan, of the other part, OJ [2017] L 67/1.

[177] In 2012, the International Law Commission decided to include the topic 'Provisional application of treaties' in its programme of work, on the basis of the recommendation of the Working Group on the long-term programme of work. See UNGA Res. 67/92 (2013) Report of the International Law Commission on the work of its sixty-third and sixty-fourth sessions.

shaping the practice in the field of provisional application of treaties'.[178] The Union and its Member States provided the ILC with substantial examples of its practice of provisional application of treaties with regard to mixed agreements. As with the law of treaties, one of the questions was the relevance of internal law of states and international organizations. In its *Guide to Provisional Application of Treaties*[179] Draft Guideline 12 sets out that the guidelines are without prejudice to the right of 'a State or an international organization to agree in the treaty itself or otherwise to the provisional application of the treaty or a part of the treaty with limitations deriving from the internal law of the state or from the rules of the organization'.[180] This is reflected in Union practice, such as the decision on the signing and provisional application of the cooperation agreement with Afghanistan, referred to earlier. The parts that are to be provisionally applied with respect to the Union are based on Union competence.[181] The Union provided examples of agreements that state that provisional application is 'without prejudice' to the parties' constitutional requirements.[182]

The Memorandum by the Secretariat on Provisional application of treaties, which reviews state practice in respect of bilateral and multilateral treaties deposited or registered with the Secretary General in the last twenty years that provide for provisional application, gives only brief mention to the practice of 'mixed agreements'. It is interesting to note that the Memorandum does not use the distinction between bilateral and multilateral mixed agreements that is used in much of the literature. 'While mixed agreements are typically registered as bilateral treaties, they require the ratification, approval or acceptance of the European Union and each of its member states. Accordingly, mixed agreements share certain structural characteristics with bilateral and multilateral treaties, particularly those multilateral treaties with limited

---

[178] Statement on behalf of the European Union by Lucio Gussetti, Director, European Commission, Legal Service, at the 73rd Session of the United Nations General Assembly Sixth Committee on Item 82: Report of the International Law Commission on the work of its seventieth session: Provisional application of treaties, http://eueuropaeeas.fpfis.slb.ec.europa .eu:8084/delegations/un-new-york/54130/eu-statement-%E2% 80%93-united-nations-6th-committee-provisional-application-treatiesen.

[179] International Law Commission, Provisional application of treaties Texts and titles of the draft guidelines adopted by the Drafting Committee on first reading, UN Doc. A/CN.4/L.910.

[180] *Id.*, Draft guideline 12.

[181] See Council Decision 2017/434.

[182] See Article 19(4) of the Agreement between the European Union and the Kingdom of Norway on supplementary rules in relation to the instrument for financial support for external borders and visa, as part of the Internal Security Fund for the period 2014 to 2020 (OJ [2017] L 75/3) which provides: 'Except for Article 5, the Parties shall apply this Agreement provisionally as from the day following that of its signature, without prejudice to constitutional requirements'.

membership'.[183] While bilateral mixed agreements could technically be described as 'multilateral', as they are composed of more than two states, they remain bilateral in nature because they are structured between two sides of the agreement.

When the EU applies an agreement provisionally, it does so with the understanding that eventually, the EU Member States will also ratify and be bound by that agreement. What are the legal implications of an EU Member State, or Member States, indicating that they will not, or cannot, ratify the agreement? There has been discussion whether the refusal or failure of a Member State to ratify the agreement would mean the Union would be legally required to discontinue provisional application. From the perspective of international law, the fact that a Member State refuses to ratify a mixed agreement would not require the EU to stop provisional application. This is because the agreement is applied provisionally only with respect to the parts of the agreement pertaining to EU competences. The decision to end provisional application would require a decision of the EU itself, via a Council decision notifying the other treaty partners. The analysis may be different, however, in cases where it is rendered impossible – for instance under the law of an EU Member State, to ratify the agreement.[184] This question is not just a theoretical one. For instance, following the referendum in the Netherlands on the EU Association Agreement with Ukraine, questions arose regarding the non-ratification of mixed agreements due to a constitutional 'impossibility'.[185] Suse and Wouters argue in this regard that 'the question whether the EU is under a legal obligation to discontinue the provisional application of an agreement once it has become clear that a Member State has permanently and definitively failed to ratify a mixed agreement remains open'.[186] As argued earlier, there do not appear to be legal reasons based in international law, that the EU should discontinue provisional application in such circumstances, especially given that the EU and the Member States are distinct parties in these instances. Moreover, it is difficult to identify when a Member State has 'permanently and definitively' failed to ratify a mixed agreement. The

---

[183]   International Law Commission, Provisional application of treaties – Memorandum by the Secretariat, UN Doc. A/CN.4/707, para. 5.
[184]   See A. Suse & J. Wouters, 'Exploring the Boundaries of Provisional Application: The EU's Mixed Trade and Investment Agreements' (2019) 53 *Journal of World Trade* 3, 411 arguing that 'from an international law perspective, a Member State's notification of its intention not to ratify the agreement cannot preclude the EU from provisionally applying the agreement'.
[185]   See G. van der Loo & R. A. Wessel, 'The Non-Ratification of Mixed Agreements: Legal Consequences and Solutions' (2017) 54 *Common Market Law Review* 742–743.
[186]   Suse & Wouters (n184).

problem is less a legal one for the Union, and more a practical and political one, since non-ratification of mixed agreements and long delay have negative consequences for the EU's treaty partners. Such practice exposes the EU's treaty partners to the complexities of EU competence questions in a way that negatively impacts those parties.

3.4.1.6 Effect of Ratification

The ratification of an international agreement has effects both for the party ratifying the treaty as well as for the overall treaty regime. Ratification is especially important in cases where a treaty will only come into force when a certain number of parties have ratified the treaty. Should the act of accession by a regional organization like the EU count towards the total number of ratifications? This issue is dealt with differently in different treaties. Some do not count the EU's ratification towards the number needed for entry into force. For example, the United Nations Convention to Combat Desertification in Countries Experiencing Serious Drought and/or Desertification, Particularly in Africa enters into force upon the fiftieth ratification, but an instrument deposited by a regional organization does not count towards this.[187] Other conventions do not include such a clause, leaving the issue ambiguous. For example, it may use the term 'parties' or 'entities', in which case ratification by the EU should count towards the Convention's entry into force. Practice in this field is varied. In certain cases, the EU is viewed as a separate and distinct treaty party, in which case its accession counts as any other party. However, in situations where the EU is viewed as a sum of its Member States, rather than a distinct legal person, EU ratification does not count towards the convention's entry into force.[188]

3.4.2 *Reservations*

Article 2(1)(d) of the VCLT-IO defines a treaty reservation as:

> a unilateral statement, however phrased or named, made by a State or by an international organization when signing, ratifying, formally confirming, accepting, approving or acceding to a treaty, whereby it purports to exclude

---

[187]   Article 36(3) of the Convention sets out that 'any instrument deposited by a regional economic integration organization shall not be counted as additional to those deposited by States members of the organization'.

[188]   Verwey (n34) 177–178.

or to modify the legal effect of certain provisions of the treaty in their application to that State or to that organization.[189]

The International Law Commission's Guide to Reservations to Treaties confirms that both states and international organizations have the capacity to enter into reservations to treaties.[190] While the ILC generally prefers separate rules for states and international organizations, it decided to treat international organizations and states together for the purposes of these guidelines.[191] The EU is capable of making reservations, just as a state can, as long as they are in conformity with international law and the agreement itself. In practice, however, this is actually quite rare, and nearly all practice of international organization making reservations refers to the European Union.[192] One of the reasons for this is that many of the multilateral treaties where reservations are of importance are not open to international organizations.[193] The exception to this is the EU, which has become a party to a number of multilateral conventions (Section 3.3.1). As the EU enters into more multilateral conventions of a law-making character, the issue of reservations by the EU will likely emerge in the future. The EU may also make a reservation at the time of concluding the agreement according to Article 218 TFEU. It may not do so in cases where the treaty itself expressly prohibits this or if the reservation defeats the object and purpose of the treaty.[194] The EU made a reservation when becoming a party to the UN CRPD relating to the right of EU Member States to exclude non-discrimination on the grounds of disability with respect to employment in the armed forces.[195] This is a rare

---

[189] The VCLT (n9) uses the same definition in Article 2(1) but does not use the term 'international organization'.

[190] Article 1.1, International Law Commission, Guide to Practice on Reservations to Treaties, adopted by the International Law Commission at its sixty-third session, in 2011, and submitted to the General Assembly as a part of the Commission's report covering the work of that session (A/66/10, para. 75). '"Reservation" means a unilateral statement, however phrased or named, made by a State or an international organization when signing, ratifying, formally confirming, accepting, approving or acceding to a treaty ... '

[191] 'Although the International Law Commission had some reservations on equating the rules applicable to international organizations to those applicable to states, it was decided in the end to assimilate international organizations to states'. Verwey (n34) 129.

[192] '[P]ractice shows that international organizations rarely make use of reservations. In fact, these rules primarily concern the treaty practice of the European Community'. Verwey (n34) 129.

[193] See P. Reuter, 'Fourth Report on the Question of Treaties Concluded between States and International Organizations, or between Two or More International Organizations' (1975/11) *Yearbook of the International Law Commission* 25–46, 36–38.

[194] Article 19, VCLT (n9) and VCLT-IO (n10).

[195] Council Decision of 26 November 2009 concerning the conclusion, by the European Community, of the United Nations Convention on the Rights of Persons with Disabilities,

example of an EU reservation to a universal multilateral treaty. Most practice of EU reservations takes place within the context of 'European' treaties, such as those under the auspices of the Council of Europe.

The possibility of EU reservations also arose during negotiations on the EU's accession to the ECHR. Article 57 ECHR allows contracting states to make a reservation in respect to a particular provision of the convention at the time of signature or ratification.[196] Should the EU also be capable of making reservations to the ECHR and its protocols? Since the EU should join the ECHR on the same footing as other contracting states, it was decided that the EU would have this right.[197] It is not clear, however, whether the EU intends to make any reservations, or to which articles any reservation might relate. EU Member States had discussed the possibility of excluding certain aspects of the ECtHR's jurisdiction by way of reservation,[198] for instance, by shielding the EU from cases in the field of CFSP or touching upon EU primary law.[199] It is doubtful, however, whether such a reservation would be legally permitted given that reservations of a general character are not permitted under Article 57 ECHR. If the EU does make a reservation, it must be in conformity with general international law and the rules established under the ECHR system.[200]

OJ L23, 27 January 2010, 35. Annex III, Reservation by the European Community to Article 27(1) of the UN Convention of the Rights of Persons with Disabilities: 'The European Community states that pursuant to Community law (notably Council Directive 2000/78/EC of 27 November 2000 establishing a general framework for equal treatment in employment and occupation), the Member States may, if appropriate, enter their own reservations to Article 27(1) of the Disabilities Convention to the extent that Article 3(4) of the said Council Directive provides them with the right to exclude non-discrimination on the grounds of disability with respect to employment in the armed forces from the scope of the Directive. Therefore, the Community states that it concludes the Convention without prejudice to the above right, conferred on its Member States by virtue of Community law'.

[196]   Article 57, ECHR (n40): 'Any State may, when signing this Convention or when depositing its instrument of ratification, make a reservation in respect of any particular provision of the Convention'.

[197]   Article 2(2), EU-ECHR Accession Agreement (n54). The following provision would have been added to Article 57(1), ECHR: 'The European Union may, when acceding to this Convention, make a reservation in respect of any particular provision of the Convention to the extent that any law of the European Union then in force is not in conformity with the provision'.

[198]   Council of the European Union, 'Accession of the European Union to the European Convention for the protection of Human Rights and Fundamental Freedoms (ECHR): State of Play' 16385/11, Brussels, 8 November 2011.

[199]   See P. Gragl, 'A Giant Leap European Human Rights? The Final Agreement on The European Union's Accession to the European Convention on Human Rights' (2014) 51 *Common Market Law Review* 13, 47.

[200]   See *Belilos* v. *Switzerland*, Admissibility, merits and just satisfaction, App. No 10328/83, Case No 20/1986/118/167, A/132, [1988] ECHR 4, (1988) 10 EHRR 466, IHRL 76 (ECHR 1988), 29 April 1988.

The issue of reservations to treaties is made more complicated in the case of mixed agreements.[201] Is a declaration of competence (Section 3.3.2) made by the EU specifying that the convention only applies to the EU in regard to areas in which it is competent to be regarded as a 'reservation' from the viewpoint of international law? Since their aim is to 'exclude the legal effect of certain provisions with regard to the Community or the member states'[202] it could be argued that they are reservations 'expressly authorized by a treaty'. According to the VCLT-IO, these reservations do not require any subsequent acceptance by contracting states or organizations.[203] However, it is still arguable that a third state or organization could object to a declaration of competence submitted by the EU, for example, if certain obligations under the treaty were not covered by either the EU or the Member States.[204] As discussed in Section 3.3.2 on Declarations of Competence, these statements cannot be viewed as normal reservations, since they are specifically required by the agreement.

The aims of some other 'EU-specific' clauses discussed earlier can also be achieved through a unilateral declaration made by the EU at the time of conclusion. The aim of a disconnection clause or the territorial application clause, for instance, can be achieved by way of reservation made at the time of conclusion of the agreement.[205]

3.4.3 *Prior Treaties of EU Member States*

In some instances, the EU Member States appear to have conflicting legal obligations, since they are bound by an international agreement and obligations under Union law. Article 351 TFEU sets out a method to resolve this form of treaty conflict. The first paragraph states that:

> The rights and obligations arising from agreements concluded before 1 January 1958 or, for acceding States, before the date of their accession, between one or more Member States on the one hand, and one or more third countries on the other, shall not be affected by the provisions of the Treaties.

International agreements entered into by the Member States (or more accurately, the rights and obligations arising under them) before they joined the

---

[201] Verwey (n34) 185.
[202] See S. Spiliopoulou Åkermark, 'Reservation Issues in the Mixed Agreements of the European Community' (2002) 10 *Finnish Yearbook of International Law* 359.
[203] Article 20(1), VCLT-IO (n10).
[204] Spiliopoulou Åkermark (n202) 360.
[205] Klabbers (n77) 77.

Union will continue to apply. This provision confirms the *pacta sunt servanda* principle and preserves the existing obligations of the EU Member States before they became members of the EU, clarifying that those existing obligations are not displaced merely through EU membership. The wide-sweeping nature of the first paragraph is nuanced by the second paragraph. It stipulates that, where inconsistencies exist, Member States 'shall take all appropriate steps to eliminate the incompatibilities established'.

This provision seeks to strike a balance between two principles: the respect for prior agreements of the Member States and the need to ensure that these agreements do not undermine the integrity of EU law. The CJEU has interpreted the Member States' obligation to avoid incompatibilities in a somewhat expansive fashion, finding incompatibilities to exist even where they remain hypothetical.[206] Klabbers argues that the CJEU

> has been less than generous in applying the rule: while ostensibly safeguarding anterior member state agreements, the clause has always been more about achieving a balance between the protection of those earlier treaties and the protection of the autonomy of the EC's legal order – and that is a charitable reading.[207]

While Article 351 may seem 'friendly' towards international law at first glance, it has been used much more as a tool to safeguard the autonomy of the EU legal order than to protect the prior commitments of the EU Member States.[208] Article 351 TFEU may appear to find a balance between respect for pre-existing Member States' international obligations and the goal of preserving the integrity of EU law. The CJEU's recent case law suggests an emphasis on the latter goal, and in cases where applicants have sought to rely on Article 351 TFEU to limit Union acts, these arguments were given short shrift.[209]

---

[206] See Judgment in *Commission v. Austria*, C-205/06, EU:C:2009:118; Judgment in *Commission v. Sweden*, C-249/06, EU:C:2009:119; Judgment in *Commission v. Finland*, C-118/07, EU:C:2009:715. See N. Lavranos, 'Protecting European Law from International Law' (2010) 15 *European Foreign Affairs Review* 265.

[207] J. Klabbers, 'Beyond the Vienna Convention: Conflicting Treaty Provision' in E. Cannizzaro (ed), *The Law of Treaties beyond the Geneva Convention* (Oxford: Oxford University Press, 2011) 203.

[208] J. Klabbers, *The European Union in International Law* (Paris: Pedone, 2012) 64. Klabbers argues that Article 351 TEU is not as friendly towards international law as it first seems: 'The construction is reminiscent of a federal structure, not of that of an international organization based on conferred powers'.

[209] See Judgment in *Kadi and Al Barakaat International Foundation v. Council and Commission*, Joined Cases C-402/05 P & C-415/05 P, EU:C:2008:461, para. 304: 'Article 307 EC [now Art 351 TFEU] may in no circumstances permit any challenge to the principles that

There are numerous avenues that can be taken under international law in the event of conflict with EU law. The Member States could, for instance, suspend, renegotiate or denounce agreements with third states in the event of conflict with EU law.[210] The Court has found, however, that these processes would take too long. The Court's interpretation of Art 351 TFEU is an example of how a conflict clause that was seemingly designed to protect the prior commitments of the EU Member States has been applied in a way that limits their continued international role.

Article 351 TFEU applies as a conflict clause within the EU legal order. But does this clause also apply to disputes outside that legal order? This question arose in relation to bilateral investment treaties (BITs) that were concluded by states before becoming EU Member States. What should be the fate of these agreements after a state joins the EU? These BITs were not expressly terminated by the parties. The European Commission has made the argument before a number of investment tribunals, that this situation is covered by the law of treaties, namely Article 30 VCLT (Application of successive treaties relating to the same subject-matter)[211] and Article 59 VCLT (Termination or suspension of the operation of a treaty implied by conclusion of a later treaty).[212] These provisions enshrine the *lex posterior* rule, whereby a later treaty may supersede an incompatible provision on the same subject matter.

In *Eastern Sugar*,[213] the Czech Republic argued that since it had become an EU Member State, the 1991 Czechoslovakia/Netherlands BIT was no longer applicable beyond 1 May 2004.[214] The Czech Republic argued that the BIT had been terminated in accordance with Article 59 VCLT, since a later treaty

---

form part of the very foundations of the Community legal order'. Judgment in *Bogiatzi*, C-301/08, EU:C:2009:649, paras 17–19: 'it is equally settled case-law that the provisions of an agreement concluded prior to the entry into force of the Treaty cannot be relied on in intra-Community relations'.

[210] B. Van Vooren & R. A. Wessel, *EU External Relations Law: Text, Cases and Materials* (Cambridge: Cambridge University Press, 2014) 70.

[211] Article 30(3), VCLT (n9): 'When all the parties to the earlier treaty are parties also to the later treaty but the earlier treaty is not terminated or suspended in operation under article 59, the earlier treaty applies only to the extent that its provisions are compatible with those of the later treaty'.

[212] Article 58(1), VCLT (n9): 'A treaty shall be considered as terminated if all the parties to it conclude a later treaty relating to the same subject matter and (a) it appears from the later treaty or is otherwise established that the parties intended that the matter should be governed by that treaty'.

[213] *Eastern Sugar BV v. Czech Republic*, 27 March 2007, SCC Case 088/2004, Partial Award. *Rupert Joseph Binder v. Czech Republic*, 6 June 2007, Award on Jurisdiction.

[214] *Id.* para. 97.

on the same subject matter had been concluded which was incompatible with the BIT. The Czech Republic's argument was not that the BIT was expressly terminated; rather, it was implicitly superseded by the *acquis communautaire* upon that country's accession to the EU, an argument the tribunal perceived as 'novel'.[215] The tribunal rejected this argument. Although both EU law and the BIT deal with intra-EU cross-border investment, they did not 'not cover the same precise subject-matter'.[216] The tribunal found that Article 42 VCLT[217] relating to the termination of agreements applied, and that the BIT could only be terminated in accordance with that provision.

A similar argument that a BIT had been terminated in accordance with Article 59 VCLT was rejected in *Eureko BV* v. *The Slovak Republic*.[218] Here, the tribunal found that Article 59 VCLT is subject to the provisions of Article 65 VCLT ('Procedure to be followed with respect to invalidity, termination, withdrawal from or suspension of the operation of a treaty'). The tribunal found that 'it is therefore clear from the text of the VCLT that the invalidity or termination of a treaty must be invoked, according to the Article 65 procedure'.[219] The tribunal found that there had been no notification of termination of the BIT for the purposes of Article 65 VCLT. While both EU Member States had clearly intended that EU law would apply between them, there was 'no evidence of any intention that the provisions of EU law should result in the termination of the entire BIT'.[220] Article 59 VCLT deals with the termination or suspension of an *entire treaty*. This is a drastic step and can have serious consequences. It is understandable, then, that there is a high threshold for finding a treaty to be terminated by the conclusion of a treaty on the same subject matter. As the tribunal found, there was no clear indication that the BIT would be terminated by any legal documents produced by the parties, such as the Association Agreement, the Accession Treaty or the Lisbon Treaty.

The EU law issues arising in investment arbitration are discussed in more detail in Section 5.3.3. The application of the law of treaties in these cases shows how the European Commission's arguments, often based on the supremacy and primacy of EU law, are not often accepted by these

---

[215] *Id.* para. 155.

[216] *Id.* para. 160.

[217] Article 42(2), VCLT (n9): 'The termination of a treaty, its denunciation or the withdrawal of a party, may take place only as a result of the application of the provisions of the treaty or of the present Convention. The same rule applies to suspension of the operation of a treaty'.

[218] *Eureko BV* v. *The Slovak Republic*, Award on Jurisdiction, Arbitrability and Suspension, 26 October 2010, para. 233.

[219] *Id.* para. 234.

[220] *Id.* para. 244.

tribunals.[221] These cases illustrate the complex interaction between EU law and the law of treaties. The CJEU and the European Commission are more likely to support the invalidity of prior agreements, based on the supremacy of EU law and concerns over the autonomy of the EU legal order. International tribunals seem less likely to be persuaded by such arguments and have found that such treaties can continue to have legal effect.

3.4.4 *Validity of Treaties*

Treaty conflict deals with the question of which law will have effect when two valid treaties provisions apply. The question is not about validity, but primacy. There may be situations, however, where the provisions of an international agreement are challenged due to a legal deficiency. The issue of the validity of treaties is dealt with in the 1969 VCLT.[222] By providing an exhaustive list of grounds for invalidity, the VCLT intends to ensure stability in treaty relations and reinforce the principle of *pacta sunt servanda*. It also deals with the consequences of a treaty being found to be invalid. A treaty is presumed to be valid[223] unless one of these grounds set out by the VCLT applies: consent expressed in violation of a provision of internal law;[224] specific restrictions on the authority to express the consent;[225] error;[226] fraud;[227] corruption;[228] coercion;[229] threat or use of force;[230] and conflict with *jus cogens* norms.[231] How are these rules applied when the EU is a party to the agreement in question?

---

[221] See European Commission Observations (7 July 2010) quoted in *Eureko BV* (n218) para. 180.

[222] Article 42, VCLT (n9): '1. The validity of a treaty or of the consent of a State to be bound by a treaty may be impeached only through the application of the present Convention. 2. The termination of a treaty, its denunciation or the withdrawal of a party, may take place only as a result of the application of the provisions of the treaty or of the present Convention. The same rule applies to suspension of the operation of a treaty'.

[223] 'The Commission accordingly considered it desirable, as a safeguard for the stability of treaties, to underline in a general provision … that the validity and the continuance in force of a treaty is the normal state of things … ' International Law Commission, Draft Articles on the Law of Treaties with commentaries, *Yearbook of the International Law Commission*, vol. II (1966), Commentary to Art 39, 236, para. 1.

[224] Article 46, VCLT (n9).

[225] Article 47, VCLT (n9).

[226] Article 48, VCLT (n9).

[227] Article 49, VCLT (n9).

[228] Article 50, VCLT (n9).

[229] Article 51, VCLT (n9).

[230] Article 52, VCLT (n9).

[231] Article 53, VCLT (n9).

The first category is where a representative of a state or IO did not have the legal capacity to express its consent to be bound, either because it violated domestic law, or because it exceeded its authority. International relations require a certain degree of certainty in treaty-making, and it would be problematic if states and other legal bodies were able to claim that a treaty was invalid because it violated the internal law of that state. Article 46(2) VCLT-IO sets out that:

> An international organization may not invoke the fact that its consent to be bound by a treaty has been expressed in violation of the rules of the organization regarding competence to conclude treaties as invalidating its consent unless that violation was manifest and concerned a rule of fundamental importance.[232]

This mirrors Article 46 VCLT relating to 'Provisions of internal law regarding competence to conclude treaties', which has been interpreted restrictively in practice. Both the VCLT and VCLT-IO require that the internal law of a state/rules of an organization can only be invoked under very limited circumstances, that is, where there has been a manifest violation of these internal rules. VCLT-IO defines a manifest violation:

> A violation is manifest if it would be objectively evident to any State or any international organization conducting itself in the matter in accordance with the normal practice of States and, where appropriate, of international organizations and in good faith[233]

One can envisage a situation whereby a representative of the EU expresses its consent to be bound by an international legal instrument where it has no legal authority to do so under the EU Treaties. Similarly, a Member State could enter into an agreement in violation of EU law. Due to the complex nature of EU law, however, it would be very unlikely that such a breach of internal EU rules could be described as 'manifest'.[234] It is difficult for non-members to keep themselves up-to-date with the relevant provisions of the EU Treaties, the evolving case law and relevant practice of the EU institutions and Member States.[235]

---

[232]   Article 46(2), VCLT-IO (n10).
[233]   Article 46(3), VCLT-IO (n10).
[234]   Aust (n18) 274.
[235]   T. Rensmann, 'Article 46 – Provisions of internal law regarding competence to conclude treaties' in Dörr & Schmalenbach (n2) 801. 'For non-members, the rules of an international organization are, in principle, not more easily ascertainable than the internal law of a State. Just as States or international organizations do not have a general legal obligation to keep themselves informed of legal developments in other States, they also cannot be expected to

There would be very few situations where such a breach of internal EU law is manifestly evident. Examples of EU law include the lack of competence by an EU institution, the incorrect legal basis for the conclusion of an agreement, or the adoption of the agreement according to the incorrect procedure. However, such violations of EU internal law would not be enough to affect the validity of the agreement under international law unless they were manifestly evident.[236] If an EU Member State were to conclude an agreement in a field that was clearly in the exclusive competence of the EU, such as trade, this might be an objectively evident violation of EU law that would render the treaty invalid.

In *France* v. *Commission*, the CJEU found that an agreement concluded by the European Commission with the US was in violation of EU law, but this finding did not affect the validity of the agreement under international law.[237] Since EU law is not opposable to third states and organizations, a legal deficiency under EU law cannot affect the EU's continued legal obligations under the treaty. Again, particular problems are posed in this regard by the practice of mixed agreements by the EU and the Member States.[238]

The EU Member States may not invoke their membership of the EU to evade their international responsibilities. Article 46(1) VCLT deals with the 'internal law' of competences of states to conclude treaties. It provides that:

> A State may not invoke the fact that its consent to be bound by a treaty has been expressed in violation of a provision of its internal law regarding competence to conclude treaties as invalidating its consent unless that violation was manifest and concerned a rule of its internal law of fundamental importance.

have familiarized themselves with the constituent instrument, secondary law or relevant practice of an international organization to which they do not belong'.

[236] P.-J. Kuijper, 'The Court and the Tribunal of the EC and the Vienna Convention on the Law of Treaties 1969' (1998) 25 *Legal Issues of European Integration* 1, 12: '[i]n such cases the lack of competence of the Community institution in question, either because of its inherent incompetence (Commission) or because of the selection of an incorrect legal basis and thereby of an incorrect procedure (Council), cannot stand in the way of the honouring of the obligations contracted under the international agreement in question, unless the violation of internal law regarding competence to conclude treaties was manifest, i.e. objectively evident to anyone conducting itself in the matter in accordance with normal practice and in good faith'.

[237] Judgment in *France* v. *Commission*, C-327/91, EU:C:1994:305, para. 25.

[238] T. Rensmann, 'Article 46. Provisions of internal law regarding competence to conclude treaties' in Dörr & Schmalenbach (n2) 802.

'Internal law' here not only concerns a state's constitutional law. It may also include limitations imposed by membership in an international organization, such as the European Union.[239]

3.4.5 *Termination and Suspension*

Closely related to the issue of validity is the issue of termination and suspension of treaties. Whereas treaties have only rarely been found to be invalid, the issue of termination and suspension of treaties has more practical relevance in modern treaty practice. The validity of a treaty relates mostly to whether there were legal deficiencies in the treaty-making process. Termination and suspension, on the other hand, relate to the cessation of rights and obligations from a certain period. In some cases treaties will set out rules regarding their suspension and termination, or establish that they are to remain in force for a specified period. In the absence of such provisions, international law applies, as codified in the VCLT.[240]

3.4.5.1 Suspension of Treaties

Article 218(9) TFEU covers the situation whereby the EU may suspend an international agreement:

> The Council, on a proposal from the Commission or the High Representative of the Union for Foreign Affairs and Security Policy, shall adopt a decision suspending application of an agreement and establishing the positions to be adopted on the Union's behalf in a body set up by an agreement, when that body is called upon to adopt acts having legal effects, with the exception of acts supplementing or amending the institutional framework of the agreement.

One example of the EU unilaterally denouncing a treaty was after the outbreak of the war in Yugoslavia.[241] At that time, there was no specific Treaty provision regulating suspension of a treaty by the EU.[242] A more recent

---

[239] *Id.*, 788.

[240] Verwey (n34) 11.

[241] Council Regulation (EEC) No 3300/91 of 11 November 1991 suspending the trade concessions provided for by the Cooperation Agreement between the European Economic Community and the Socialist Federal Republic of Yugoslavia, OJ 1991 L 315, 1. See *Racke* (n24) para. 52. See Verwey (n34) 148–149.

[242] Eeckhout (n8) 209: 'After having fared somewhat badly with the suspension of a co-operation agreement with Yugoslavia at the time of the war in and between the various Republics of the former Yugoslavia, because the agreement did not contain a suspension clause, the institutions developed the practice of including suspension provisions in agreements with third countries'.

example of the EU suspending a treaty was when the Council applied Article 218(9) TFEU to partially suspend application of the Cooperation Agreement with the Syrian Arab Republic[243] in response to the outbreak of hostilities in that country.

According to Article 60 VCLT, an agreement may be terminated or suspended in whole or in part where there has been a 'material breach' of the agreement.[244] Some agreements concluded by the EU, such as cooperation agreements, include an 'essential clause' that deal with respect for human rights, democracy and the constitutional state.[245] The violation of this clause may result in a 'material breach' of the agreement.

3.4.5.2 Termination of Treaties

The EU Treaties do not provide a specific procedure for the termination of agreements to which the EU is a party. In the absence of specific guidelines, which procedure should apply to the termination and withdrawal? For example, for agreements that require consent of the European Parliament, does the Parliament also need to provide its consent? Kuijper et al. argue that, in the absence of specific rules in the EU Treaties, one can also rely on the principles common in the EU Member States, the practice of the EU institutions and the principle of institutional balance.[246] There is, however, no common approach to this issue within the law of the EU Member States. Some require parliamentary approval of termination whereas others allow denunciation by executive prerogative.[247]

---

[243] Council Decision (2011/523/EU) of 2 September 2011 partially suspending the application of the Cooperation Agreement between the European Economic Community and the Syrian Arab Republic, OJ L 228 (2011), 19 and Council Decision 2012/123/CFSP of 27 February 2012 amending Decision 2011/523/EU partially suspending the application of the Cooperation Agreement between the European Economic Community and the Syrian Arab Republic, OJ L/54 (2012), 18.

[244] See *Legal Consequences for States of the Continued Presence of South Africa in Namibia (South West Africa) notwithstanding Security Council Resolution 276 (1970)* (Advisory Opinion) [1971] ICJ Rep 16, para. 96.

[245] See Article 9, Partnership Agreement between the Members of the African, Caribbean and Pacific Group of States of the one Part, and the European Community and its Member States, of the other Part (signed 23 June 2000, entered into force 1 April 2003) [2000] OJ L317/3 ('Cotonou Convention').

[246] P.-J. Kuijper, J. Wouters, F. Hoffmeister, G. De Baere & T. Ramopoulos, *The Law of EU External Relations: Cases, Materials and Commentary on the EU as an International Legal Actor* (Oxford: Oxford University Press, 2013) 93. 'recourse can be had to constitutional principles common to the Member States, EU practice, and the general institutional balance established by the Treaty in external relations'.

[247] *Id.*, 93–95.

One approach would be for the termination of an agreement to mirror the practice of concluding an agreement (*actus contrarius* theory).[248] This would mean, for example, that if the European Parliament were required to give its consent to the conclusion of an agreement, its consent would also be required in the case of termination. Application of the *actus contrarius* theory may lead to problems when there is a need to act quickly. Kuijper et al. argue against such a mechanical application of the *actus contrarius* theory to the EU level, favouring a process that seeks to respect the institutional balance in EU external relations, 'taking due account of the specific content of the agreement and the circumstances surrounding its termination'.[249] EU practice tends to show that the Parliament's involvement in the termination of treaties depends largely on the policy field in question. Termination of a treaty is often a highly political act, one that is tied to foreign policy decisions. In this sense, one might argue that the Parliament need not be involved in the decision to terminate an agreement. Such an argument is not convincing. Just as the conclusion of an international agreement gives rise to important legal consequences for the EU and its Member States, so does its termination. There is no reason why this process should not involve the same EU bodies that were involved in deciding upon its conclusion.

3.4.6 *Succession of Treaties*

Succession of states is an important issue in international treaty law, and is one on which the EU and the Member States has contributed to 'state practice'.[250] Succession in international treaty law mostly concerns succession of international obligations by *states*. The ILC Draft Articles sets out that 'Succession of States' means the replacement of one state by another in the responsibility for the international relations of territory'.[251] Yet international law gives little guidance on the topic of succession of obligations regarding international organizations.

---

[248] Eeckhout (n8) suggests 'one would expect the same procedure to apply as that governing the conclusion of the agreement', 209.

[249] Kuijper et al. (n246) 97.

[250] P.-J. Kuijper, 'The Community and State Succession in Respect of Treaties' in D. Curtin & T. Heukels (eds), *Institutional Dynamics of European Integration: Essays in Honour of H. G. Schermers* (Dordrecht: Nijhoff, 1994) 640.

[251] Article 2(1)(b), International Law Commission, Draft Articles on Succession of States in respect of Treaties (1974). Text adopted by the International Law Commission at its twenty-sixth session, in 1974, and submitted to the General Assembly, *Yearbook of the International Law Commission* (1974) vol. II, Part One.

3.4.6.1 Succession by International Organizations

The rules relating to the succession of states cannot be automatically applied to other legal persons, such as international organizations. The ILC's 1974 Draft articles on Succession of states in respect of Treaties (1974) make it clear that the articles 'apply to the effects of a succession of states in respect of treaties between states'[252] and as such are not intended to apply to succession involving other subjects of international law, such as international organizations.[253] Regarding the issue of succession by *international organizations*, the ILC chose not to include it as a subject in its long-term programme since 'the scope for codification and progressive development of the law with regard to this matter would appear to be limited'.[254] Not only is there little practice upon which to base a project of codification, the topic is mired in conceptual difficulties and disagreements on a number or topics.

International law accepts that one international organization may 'succeed' another. In *Namibia*, the ICJ found that the United Nations was the legal 'successor' of the League of Nations.[255] In other contexts, the WTO succeeded the GATT, and the OECD is the successor of the Organization for European Economic Cooperation (OEEC).[256] Succession of states and succession of international organizations are entirely different concepts. The former applies to changes in territorial sovereignty, and seeks to avoid the situation whereby the creation of a new legal entity leads to a legal vacuum. Succession by international organization, on the other hand, is more concerned with ensuring legal continuity and stability. Given these important differences, rules developed in relation to state succession are not necessarily appropriate to the situation of international organizations.

Unlike a state, which possesses 'the totality of international rights and duties recognized by international law', the rights and duties of an international organization 'must depend upon its purposes and functions as specified or

[252] Article 1, Draft Articles on Succession of States (n251).
[253] Draft Articles on Succession of States (n251), Commentary to Article 1: 'the present articles have not been drafted so as to apply to the effects of a succession of States in respect of treaties to which other subjects of international law, and in particular international organizations, are parties'.
[254] International Law Commission, 'Review of the Commission's Long-Term Programme of Work' (1971) 2 *Yearbook of the International Law Commission* Part II, 79–80.
[255] Legal Consequences for States of the Continued Presence of South Africa in Namibia (South West Africa) Notwithstanding Security Council Resolution 276 (1970) (Advisory Opinion) [1971] ICJ Rep 16, 49.
[256] The OEEC was replaced by the Organization for Economic Co-operation and Development (OECD) in 1961.

implied in its constituent documents and developed in practice'.[257] This has consequences for succession. In the context of an international organization, succession can only take place in relation to the functions that had been transferred to it by its members: 'instead of territory there is a function, and instead of a sovereignty, a competence'.[258] Another issue that complicates the succession of international organizations is the fact that international organizations are bound to their membership; succession can only take place with the consent of the states that have brought the organization to life.

3.4.6.2 Succession of one Organization to Another

The European Union has undergone several treaty changes, which have transformed its legal identity, and has contributed to international law and practice in the field of succession of IOs. In 2002, the European Coal and Steel Community (ECSC) was dissolved after fifty years, in accordance with its treaty,[259] and its functions were taken over by the European Community. The Council decided that 'the EC shall succeed to the rights and obligations flowing from the international agreements concluded by the ECSC with third countries'.[260] It instructed the Commission to 'undertake all necessary technical amendments in order to make the agreements compatible with EC rules' including negotiating amendments to those agreements.

Perhaps one of the most important changes from the perspective of international law came about through the Lisbon Treaty. Two separate legal bodies, the European Community and the European Union were both subsumed into one formal organization, the European Union. Article 1 of the TEU provides that '[...] The Union shall replace and succeed the European Community'. From a public international law perspective, it is more accurate to say that the EU and European Community merged into a single international legal person. Myers sets out five main types of succession of international organizations: replacement, absorption, merger, separation and

---

257 Reparation for Injuries Suffered in the Service of the United Nations (Advisory Opinion) [1949] ICJ Rep 174, 180.
258 A. G. Mochi-Onory, 'The Nature of Succession between International Organizations: Functions and Treaties' (1968) 21 *Revue hellénique de droit International* 37.
259 Article 97, Treaty establishing the European Coal and Steel Community (Paris, 18 April 1951) entered into force on 23 July 1952 and expired on 23 July 2002: 'The present Treaty is concluded for a period of fifty years from the date of its entry into force'.
260 Council Decision 2002/596/EC of 19 July 2002 on the consequences of the expiry of the Treaty establishing the European Coal and Steel Community (ECSC) on the international agreements concluded by the ECSC of 19 July 2002, OJ EU L 194/36.

transfer of specific functions.[261] The change that took place under the Lisbon Treaty can probably be best described as a 'merger' under this conceptualization since it involved two existing organizations coming together under a single legal personality, rather than one organization replacing or absorbing the tasks of another. Merger takes place where the new organization combines the functions from each of the predecessor organizations. Myer defines merger as a situation where 'the organizations being combined have different functions and capacities but operate in fields that are closely related'.[262]

The succession of one international organization to another is mainly an issue for the members of the organization. Members of both the former organization and the new one must give their consent to the transfer. In the EU context, this is done through the normal process in line with other Treaty reforms, whereby a reform treaty is agreed upon and ratified by the EU Member States. These changes under the various treaties have mostly had internal consequences for the EU Member States, but have not really posed issues for the EU's treaty partners. Third states have generally accepted the transfer of personality. Yet the EU will inform third states and organizations of the legal change that took place. For example, on 9 February 2010, the Council of the European Union deposited with ICAO a *note verbale* stating that, upon the entry into force of the Lisbon Treaty, the EU had succeeded the European Community. It states 'As a consequence, as from 1 December 2009, the European Union has replaced and succeeded the European Community ... and has exercised all rights and assumed all obligations of the European Community whilst continuing to exercise existing rights and assume obligations of the European Union'. Similar notes have been deposited in the context of other treaty bodies and organizations where the European Community was a party.[263]

---

[261] P. Myers, *Succession between International Organizations* (London: Kegan Paul International, 1993).

[262] *Id.*, 28.

[263] For example, the European Union made the following Declaration of Succession in relation to Convention on Choice of Court Agreements (29 January 2010): ' ... as from 1 December 2009, the European Union has replaced and succeeded the European Community (Article 1, third paragraph, of the Treaty on European Union as it results from the amendments introduced by the Treaty of Lisbon) and has exercised all rights and assumed all obligations of the European Community whilst continuing to exercise existing rights and assume obligations of the European Union. The General Secretariat of the Council of the European Union, therefore has the honour to notify the Permanent Representation of the Netherlands to the European Union that, as from 1 December 2009, the European Community has been replaced and succeeded by the European Union in respect of all Conventions/Agreements for which the Ministry of Foreign Affairs of the Kingdom of the Netherlands is the depositary and to which the European Community, replaced from 1 December 2009 by the European Union, is a contracting party'.

These communications are intended to announce the EU's change in personality, rather than to request the consent of third parties. To date no treaty partner has refused to recognize such a change, since it is more of an internal formality for the EU and its Member State than a fundamental change in the nature of the treaty partner. Would the situation be different, however, were the EU to undergo a more fundamental treaty change, one that would alter the nature of the legal entity that is party to the agreement? In such circumstances it could be argued that the other treaty parties would need to give their consent in order for the EU to continue as a party to the agreement. One argument would be that a fundamental change in the nature of the EU would be tantamount to a modification to the treaty, governed by Arts 39 and 40 VCLT. In this case, the successor organization would require the consent of treaty partners to remain bound by the treaty. In reality, however, the EU's treaty partners have accepted the EU's internal constitutional changes and revisions, since they do not fundamentally affect its ability to fulfil its functions and obligations under a treaty.

The EU has also been a successor international organization to the Western European Union (WEU). The WEU decided that it would transfer its capabilities and functions to the EU. This would fall into Myer's categories as a transfer of specific functions,[264] described as a situation 'when organizations which have the same or similar member-ships and overlapping functions and capacities decide that only one of the institutions should continue to perform certain functions'.[265] This is designed to avoid the duplication of tasks that occurs when two inter-national organizations work in a similar field with similar membership. Since the WEU has also ceased to exist, this could also be viewed as a form of succession.

Practice in the EU context shows that, unlike state succession, the succession of international organizations is usually a relatively smooth affair, giving rise to few legal complications under international law. Unlike state succession, which takes place during a momentous shift in the life of a state, often during war or state upheaval, succession of organizations takes place through the consent of parties involved, and can be managed by the parties. Moreover, the EU's treaty partners have accepted the changes in the EU Treaties and the various changes in its international legal personality.

---

[264] Myers (n261) 34.
[265] Myers (n261) 34.

3.4.6.3 Succession of an Organization to the Member States

A more complicated question arises when the succession is not from one organization to another, but from an organization to its *constituent members*. The CJEU has recognized the concept of 'functional succession', whereby the EU may become a 'successor' to the Member States' legal obligations under a treaty in certain circumstances.[266] An interesting question is whether legal obligations could go in the other direction? The issue was addressed in Section 3.3.5.3 in relation to the 'succession' of the obligations from the EU to the UK upon its withdrawal from the EU. Can a Member State continue to be bound by obligations entered into by the EU, once that state is no longer an EU Member State? What if the EU were to be dissolved?

International law on the succession of treaties gives no clear guidance. The *Vienna Convention on Succession of States in Respect of Treaties*, for example, applies only 'to the effects of a succession of states in respect of treaties between states'[267] and these rules cannot be applied by analogy to a state leaving an international organization. The question arises whether examples such as unions of states and federations can be used by analogy to the context of the EU. In his report on succession in respect of treaties, Sir Humphrey Waldock cautioned against treating economic organizations as unions of states.[268] For the purposes of succession, it was argued the EEC was to be dealt with as an intergovernmental organization. Here again, the legal analysis depends largely on what kind of entity one conceives the EU to be. Viewed as a union of states or federation, succession may make sense, but when viewed as an intergovernmental organization, these rules cannot be so easily applied to the withdrawal of an EU Member State. Autonomic succession arguably has the benefit of allowing greater continuity in treaty relations. However, it may not always be possible to continue to apply certain agreements with respect to a non-EU member, and as argued earlier, such theory tends to deny the separate legal personality of the Union, distinct from its Member States.

---

[266] See Judgment in *International Fruit Company and Others v. Produktschap voor Groenten en Fruit*, Joined Cases 21 to 25/72, EU:C:1972:115; R. Schütze, '"The Succession Doctrine" and the European Union' in A. Hull, C. Barnard, M. Dougan & E. Spaventa (eds), *A Constitutional Order of States? Essays in EU Law in Honour of Alan Dashwood* (Oxford: Hart, 2011) 462–467.

[267] Article 1, Vienna Convention on Succession of States in Respect of Treaties, 23 August 1978, 1946 UNTS 3 (entered into force 6 November 1996).

[268] Sir Humphrey Waldock, Special Rapporteur, *Fifth Report on Succession in Respect of Treaties*, [1972] 2 Y. B. Int'l L. Comm'n 18, UN Doc. A/CN.4/SER.A/1972/Add.1. 'there are some hybrid unions which may appear to have some analogy with a union of States but which do not, in the opinion of the Special Rapporteur, form part of the present topic . . . One such hybrid is EEC [European Economic Community]'.

Similar questions arise regarding the dissolution of the European Union. Unlike a Member State withdrawing from the Union, the EU Treaties provide no legal mechanism for the EU to be dissolved or disbanded. Among the countless legal complications that would arise from such an event, one would be the continuing legal obligations of the (former) European Union. This question is especially problematic in regard to 'EU only' agreements, which are binding upon the Member State only by virtue of Union law. Would the treaty law on succession of states apply to this scenario? Reuter discusses the complex question of what happens to treaties entered into by an international organization upon dissolution of the organization:

> It could perhaps be assumed in the case of a 'mixed treaty' that the member States which are parties to such a treaty 'succeed' to the organization when it ceases to exist or is altered so as no longer to be in a position to perform the treaty; but there is no general rule to the effect that member States 'inherit' the treaties of the international organization once it has ceased to exist.[269]

Indeed, international law has little to say on this matter, in part due to the lack of practice. According to one view, upon dissolution of the EU, the former EU Member States would no longer be bound by international commitments entered into by the EU. This is because the EU is a separate and distinct legal entity under international law.[270] Wessel for instance argues that '[a]utomatic succession to existing agreements by the (then former) EU Member States is not obvious because of their distinct legal personalities and the consequences of the new situation need to be discussed with third parties'.[271] It is true that the EU is a separate and distinct legal entity, but does this really mean that the Member States would no longer be encumbered by the obligations of the former EU? When entering into an international agreement, the EU is exercising powers that have been transferred to it by Member States. One could make the argument, as outlined earlier, that the EU had entered into the agreement on behalf of the Member States, and that they remain bound by the international obligations of the treaty (if not the treaty itself) upon the EU's dissolution. Schermers and Blokker argue that '[i]t would not be acceptable to declare that all such Community trade agreements would terminate if ever the EC were dissolved. The rules for state succession are much more appropriate

[269] Reuter (n17) 121.
[270] R. A. Wessel, 'Dissolution and Succession: The Transmigration of the Soul of International Organizations' in J. Klabbers & A. Wallendahl (eds), *Research Handbook on the Law of International Organizations* (Cheltenham: Edward Elgar, 2011) 354.
[271] *Id.*, 354.

and, accordingly, should be applied'.[272] In such a situation it is likely that the EU and Member States would negotiate appropriate arrangements to deal with the EU's external agreements. Failing this, international treaty law gives little useful guidance.

3.4.7 *Additional Protocols and Other Instruments*

When entering into a treaty, the EU may also decide whether to enter into additional protocols and other instruments related to that agreement. For example, along with the European Convention on Human Rights, the jurisdiction of the Strasbourg Court extends to the interpretation and application of the additional protocols.[273] When acceding to the ECHR, the EU must decide whether it will also accede to these protocols, and if so, which ones. The EU Member States' commitments under the Convention differ due to the fact that their accession to these various protocols is inconsistent. The approach followed in the original Accession Agreement was that the EU would accede to the First Protocol to the Convention as well as Protocol No. 6.[274] This is because these are the only protocols to which all EU Member States are party. Article 59(2) ECHR would be amended to allow the EU to accede to the other additional protocols in the future.[275] As protocols are separate legal instruments under international law, the EU's accession to the further protocols would require a similar process to that of accession to the ECHR, including a separate accession agreement.[276]

Although the EU decided only to accede to Protocols 1 and 6, this raises the question whether the EU would be legally permitted also to accede to other protocols. Under EU law, international agreements entered into by the Union are binding, not only on the EU institutions, but also on the EU Member States.[277] It could be argued that if the EU were to accede to protocols to which only some EU Member States had joined, then these Member States would be bound by international agreements to which they had not given their explicit

---

[272] H. G. Schermers & N. M. Blokker, *International Institutional Law*, 4th edn (Leiden: Martinus Nijhoff, 2003) 1057.

[273] Article 32(1), ECHR (n40): 'The jurisdiction of the Court shall extend to all matters concerning the interpretation and application of the Convention and the Protocols thereto which are referred to it as provided in Articles 33, 34, 46 and 47'.

[274] Article 1(1), EU-ECHR Accession Agreement (n54).

[275] Article 1(2), EU-ECHR Accession Agreement (n54).

[276] EU-ECHR Accession Agreement (n54) 'Explanatory Report', para. 16: 'Subsequent accession by the EU to other Protocols would require the deposit of separate accession instruments'.

[277] Article 216(2), TFEU: 'Agreements concluded by the Union are binding upon the institutions of the Union and on its Member States'.

consent. While this is an acceptable position, it goes against the understanding of the EU as a separate and distinct legal order. The EU's accession to the additional protocols need not be conditioned by whether all the Member States have acceded to them. There is no legal impediment to the EU acceding to protocols to which only some EU Member States have ratified, as long as these protocols apply only with respect to EU law.

Another option would have been for the EU to accede to the protocols that covered rights that were already protected via the EU Charter of Fundamental Rights. These rights are already binding upon the EU Member States by virtue of EU law, and therefore would not have posed a problem of extending obligations to the EU Member States. Alternatively, the EU could accede to additional Protocols, making clear at the time of accession that these only apply to fields of Union competences and Union law. However, the idea of acceding to any Protocols other than only those which all Member States had ratified was strongly opposed by the Member States.[278] This means that even upon the EU's accession, there will still be legal gaps in human rights protection. There will be instances where a right enshrined in one of the protocols is binding upon an EU Member State that has ratified the protocol, but is not binding upon the Union.

3.5 CONCLUSION

The EU has entered into international agreements from its earliest days, and a well-developed treaty practice has now emerged. The international law of treaties is premised on a dichotomy between states and international organizations, as shown by the two separate conventions that seek to regulate the law of treaties. Since the EU is neither a state nor a traditional international organization, one might assume that the EU's treaty practice poses particular challenges to the law of treaties, or that new rules might need to be developed to take into account such practice. Some argue that neither the VCLT nor the VCLT-IO is appropriate to take into account the unique nature of the EU. Verwey concludes that 'neither the Vienna Conventions on the international law of treaties nor customary international law, are equipped to fully take into account the unique nature of the European Community'.[279] Verwey, for instance, argues in favour of a revision of these instruments to

---

[278]   X. Groussot, T. Lock & L. Pech, 'EU Accession to the European Convention on Human Rights: A Legal Assessment of the Draft Accession Agreement of 14th October 2011' (2011) 218 *European Issues* 3, 4.

[279]   Verwey (n34) 206.

allow for participation by the EU on the international level in its own right.[280]

Yet this chapter has shown that, rather than pose obstacles, the law of treaties is flexible enough to accommodate the EU's treaty practice.[281] Over time, such practice can also contribute to the development of customary international law (Chapter 2). Many of these obstacles have been addressed through innovative solutions within the international agreements themselves. This chapter has discussed the different types of 'EU-specific' clauses that find their way into such agreements. Some of these are demanded by the EU, for instance, clauses to protect the integrity and autonomy of the EU legal order, whereas others are requested by the EU's treaty partners, in order to identify which party will be responsible for the implementation of obligations under the agreement. The use and acceptance of such clauses over time may also contribute to the development of customary international law.

While the CJEU is of the opinion that the VCLT applies to the interpretation of EU agreements (to the extent it represents customary international law), there are occasions where the VCLT-IO rules are more appropriate to the EU's treaty practice. This is especially the case regarding procedural issues relating to the process by which the EU negotiates and gives its consent to be bound by an agreement. Yet there are fields where international treaty law gives little guidance, and the EU has developed its own practice. The issue of succession is an example of such a field where international law gives no clear answers, and the practice of the EU will further contribute to the development of international law. Similarly, the unique ways in which the EU approaches treaty conflict, which prioritizes the integrity of EU law, further develops the law of treaties in this area. The Vienna Conventions are not straightjackets that limit the flexibility of the EU and its Member States when entering into agreements; rather EU practice shows the use of pragmatic solutions.

Innovative clauses such as the disconnection clause, or the use of mixed agreements, are examples of this flexibility. While the disconnection clause has been criticized for undermining the coherence of international law, it has been accepted by the EU's treaty partners. The EU will continue to face challenges regarding how it navigates international treaty law. It continues to join multilateral treaties of a lawmaking character (such as the CRPD), those

---

[280] Verwey (n34) 206, arguing that challenges facing the Union 'will require changes in the rules that will allow the Community to act as a full member of the international community in its own right'.

[281] Klabbers (n208) 38. Klabbers concludes, that since the EU is bound by the customary rules of the law of treaties, 'the plan sometimes launched in the literature to adapt the law of treaties to the peculiar characteristics of the EU is not all that persuasive'.

that involve external legal review (such as the European Convention on Human Rights or treaties including investor-state dispute settlement) and where it replaces the former competence of the Member States. This may require further practice of 'EU-specific' clauses or other innovative arrangements. The EU should be careful not to stretch these too far. States may not be willing to accept 'EU-specific' clauses in these agreements, however, leading the EU to find new ways to abide by Union law and protect its internal *acquis*. The EU's treaty-making practice will continue, and in doing so will further develop international legal practice on how composite legal entities behave on the international plane. As the EU has acknowledged, '[b]ecause of the regularity with which it is admitted to participate in multilateral treaties the European Union has shaped treaty law and practice in a significant manner'.[282]

There is now a wealth of practice in connection with EU agreements. In many respects, the EU is able to exist as a 'normal' treaty partner alongside states. Legal questions mostly arise in relation to the practice of the EU and its Member States both being parties to an agreement. This practice is likely to continue, both for (internal) legal and political reasons. Rather than view such practice as an aberration in international law, EU treaty practice can also be conceived as developing customary law in relation to composite legal entities and 'joint parties' to international agreements.[283]

---

[282]   Statement on behalf of the European Union by Lucio Gussetti, Director, Principal Legal Adviser, European Commission, at the UN General Assembly 6th Committee (Legal) 66th Session: Report of the International Law Commission on the work of its sixty-third session on Responsibility of International Organizations, 24 October 2011, New York.

[283]   This argument has been developed further in relation to mixed agreements; see J. Odermatt, 'Facultative Mixity in the International Legal Order – Tolerating European Exceptionalism?' in M. Chamon & I. Govaere (eds), *EU External Relations Post-Lisbon: The Law and Practice of Facultative Mixity* (Leiden: Brill Nijhoff, 2020) 291–316; See S. Schäfer and J. Odermatt, 'Nomen est Omen? The Relevance of 'EU Party' in International Law', in N. Levrat, Y. Kaspiarovich, C. Kaddous, and R.A. Wessel (eds.), *The EU and Its Member States' Joint Participation in International Agreements* (forthcoming 2022, Oxford: Hart Publishing).

4

International Organizations

4.1 INTRODUCTION

The EU's participation in international agreements has been the main method by which it acts on the international law plane. Yet the EU is also a participant in a growing number of international organizations (IOs) and international forums.[1] Early in the life of the EU, it became evident that it was not enough that it participate in treaty making, but also engage with, and even participate in IOs. This chapter focuses on the legal issues that arise from the EU's participation in IOs and other international forums. Many of these challenges are identical to those discussed in Chapter 3 regarding treaties. Legal issues regarding the nature of competences and the issue of 'mixity' also arise in the context of IOs. This is because when the EU joins an IO, it almost always does so by becoming party to a multilateral treaty. Yet there are a number of unique challenges that arise in the context of joining and participating in IOs. These challenges arise from both the lack of guidance regarding the EU's engagement with IOs in the EU Treaties, as well as the external political and legal environment the EU faces when it seeks to join or participate in IOs. While many of these are legal issues that challenge the state-centric nature of international law, the main problems arise from an international environment that remains unreceptive to the EU's presence in IOs, as well as recalcitrance from some EU Member States. The difficulties the EU faces when joining and participating in IOs does not stem from international law, but from political pushback.

---

[1] For work on the EU in particular organizations, see R. A. Wessel & J. Odermatt (eds), *Research Handbook on the European Union and International Organizations* (Cheltenham: Edward Elgar, 2019); C. Kaddous (ed), *The European Union in International Organisations and Global Governance: Recent Developments* (Oxford: Hart, 2015); K.-E. Jørgensen & Katie Laatikainen (eds), *Routledge Handbook on the European Union and International Institutions: Performance, Policy, Power* (London:Routledge, 2013).

In order to examine the EU's relationship with IOs, it is useful to discuss briefly what is meant by 'international organization'. An international organization is generally described in international law as a body established by a treaty, which has states among its members. One commonly used definition regards international organizations as 'forms of co-operation (i) founded on an international agreement; (ii) having at least one organ with a will of its own; and (iii) established under international law'.[2] This legal definition places importance on the separate legal personality of the organization. For the purposes of this chapter, a broader notion of international organization is used. This is because a focus on only intergovernmental organizations with legal personality would leave out a much larger array of bodies that, although not IOs from the perspective of international law, develop norms that have an effect on the EU legal order. In this sense, international organizations include more than just the intergovernmental bodies such as the United Nations, the World Trade Organization or the International Monetary Fund (IMF), but also include a vast array of international bodies whose output has an effect on the EU. In the field of international economic law, for example, the landscape includes less formal bodies such as the Group of 20 (G20),[3] the Financial Stability Board (FSB), the Basel Committee on Banking Supervision (BCBS) or the International Organization of Securities Commissions (IOSCO).[4] Even if these organizations do not qualify as international organizations under international legal definitions, they are bodies that continue to have influence on the development of EU law, and the types of bodies where the EU seeks to exert greater influence. In order to fully understand the EU's participation at the international level, therefore, it is important to not only look at the traditional intergovernmental organizations, but to also take into account the range of

---

[2] H. G. Schermers & N. M. Blokker, *International Institutional Law: Unity within Diversity*, 5th edn (Leiden: Martinus Nijhoff, 2011) 37.

[3] See F. Amtenbrink & R. Repasi, 'G7, G20 and Global Summits: Shortcomings and Solutions in Informal International Governance' in R. A. Wessel & J. Odermatt (eds), *Research Handbook on the European Union and International Organizations* (Cheltenham: Edward Elgar, 2019) 388–359; J. Wouters, S. Van Kerckhoven & J. Odermatt, 'The EU at the G20 and the G20's Impact on the EU' in B. Van Vooren, S. Blockmans & J. Wouters (eds), *The EU's Role in Global Governance: The Legal Dimension* (Oxford: Oxford University Press, 2012) 259–271.

[4] See S. Donnelly, 'Financial Stability Board (FSB), Bank for International Settlements (BIS) and Financial Market Regulation Bodies: ECB and Commission Participation Alongside the Member States' in R. A. Wessel & J. Odermatt (eds), *Research Handbook on the European Union and International Organizations* (Cheltenham: Edward Elgar, 2019) 360–385; J. Wouters & J. Odermatt, 'International Banking Standards, Private Law and the European Union' in M. Cremona & H. Micklitz (eds), *The External Dimension of European Private Law* (Oxford: Oxford University Press, 2015) 171–199.

normative activity in other forums, including treaty bodies, committees, standard-setting bodies, advisory bodies, etc.[5]

4.1.1 *Why Join International Organizations?*

Why should the EU become a member of, or participate in, international organizations? It is now undeniable that IOs now play an important role in global governance and world politics. If the EU seeks to promote its interests and values on the international scene, one of the most effective ways it can do this is through engagement with IOs. As High Representative Ashton noted in her December 2012 communication to the Commission, often 'the ability of the EU to promote and defend its values and its interests is impaired by its limited status in organisations and fora where important decisions are taken'.[6] Closer co-ordination with IOs, and EU representation within these bodies, is a key method by which the EU can pursue its interests on the international plane.

One reason for EU participation in IOs is the fact that the EU and its Member States are increasingly influenced by the normative activity of international organizations and bodies. The decisions, rules, best-practices and guidelines that are developed within these bodies often find their way into legislation at the EU or Member State level, or are referred to in case law. Since the 2008/2009 financial crisis, much of the international response has taken place in international forums including the G20, Financial Stability Board and other informal bodies. EU representation at these bodies allows the Union to assert its position and shape the development of rules that are likely to have an effect in the EU legal order. The CJEU has recognized that even 'recommendations' that are adopted in an organization to which the EU is not a party are 'taken into consideration for the purposes of drawing up rules of EU law'[7] and therefore 'are capable of decisively influencing the content of the legislation adopted by the EU legislature'.[8] By becoming a member of these bodies in its own right, therefore, the EU is

---

[5] J. Wouters & J. Odermatt, 'Norms Emanating from International Bodies and Their Role in the Legal Order of the European Union' in R. A. Wessel & S. Blockmans (eds), *Between Autonomy and Dependence: The EU Legal Order under the Influence of International Organisations* (The Hague: T. M. C. Asser Press/Springer Verlag, 2013) 47.

[6] Communication to the Commission from the President in Agreement with Vice-President Ashton, Strategy for the progressive improvement of the EU status in international organizations and other fora in line with the objectives of the Treaty of Lisbon (C(2012) 9420 final) ('Barroso-Ashton Strategy') 1.

[7] Judgment in *Germany v. Council* ('OIV case'), C-399/12, EU:C:2014:2258, para. 62.

[8] *Id.*, para. 63.

capable of influencing the development of these norms that may find their way into EU law and policy.

The other reason for the EU to join IOs in its own right is similar to the case for joining international agreements, that is, the EU's competence in the field dealt with by the IO. Many IOs deal with issues where the EU has considerable or exclusive competences, including trade or maritime resources. Moreover, where the EU exercises considerable competences in a certain field, but is not bound by the international agreement in that field (but the Member States are), this can give rise to legal complications. The EU Member States will be bound by the obligations under agreement or under the IO, but the EU will be the body that is capable of implementing those obligations. Full EU membership in that body helps remove this discrepancy. The legal complications that arose in some high-profile cases, such as *Air Transport Association*,[9] or *Intertanko*,[10] stem in part from gaps created by the EU's non-membership in IOs where it exercises considerable competence. For instance, in *Air Transport Association*, the EU's non-membership of ICAO, a UN specialized agency, meant that the EU was not formally bound by a significant body of international law regulating air transport. Removing these gaps would be another reason for the EU to join bodies active in other fields where the EU exercise competences, such as the International Maritime Organization (IMO) (Section 4.5.2) or the International Civil Aviation Organization (ICAO).

EU membership also means that the EU is not entirely dependent on its Member States to assert its position at the international level. It is a well-established goal of the EU to assert itself as an international actor in its own right, and since Lisbon has strengthened the institutional actors that are designed to represent the EU internationally. The creation of the positions of High Representative for Foreign Affairs and Security Policy and the European Council President as well as the establishment of the European External Action Service, were designed to improve the EU's presence at the international level. It makes sense, then, that the EU would wish to put these mechanisms to work in international organizations, where the EU is able to increase its visibility and improve its effectiveness. However, since 2009 the EU has not been highly successful at upgrading its status or improving its visibility in IOs. Even relatively small changes such as gaining an EU name plate, or having statements made in the name of the EU, were initially met

---

[9] Judgment in *Air Transport Association of America and Others v. Secretary of State for Energy and Climate Change*, C-366/10, EU:C:2011:864.
[10] Judgment in *Intertanko and Others*, C-308/06, EU:C:2008:312.

with resistance. Moreover, even where the EU succeeds at gaining member-ship, observer status or other forms of involvement, this does not always translate into greater EU influence within those bodies, and in some cases can even hinder effective EU action.

4.1.2 *Existing Studies on the EU in International Organizations*

The EU's presence within international organizations has received attention in academic literature from both legal and political science scholars. Much of the work on the EU in international organizations is within the International Relations and European Studies disciplines.[11] These studies are concerned with understanding inter alia what kind of influence the EU is able to exert within international organizations. It examines issues such as the effectiveness of the EU within international forums, and asks how the EU can become a more coherent actor at the international level. Much of this work is therefore problem-driven; it seeks to understand how the EU can play a more effective role in particular organizations or with respect to certain policies. These studies seek to understand how the EU can achieve 'effective multilateralism', or act as a 'normative power'. It often relies upon case studies of the EU's presence at a certain organization or set of bodies in order to measure EU influence. These studies often do not distinguish between the two ways in which the 'EU' acts in an IO: (1) as the EU Member States behaving in a concerted manner or (2) as a separate legal actor participating in its own right.[12] This chapter focuses mainly on the latter role. This chapter is not concerned so much with the effectiveness of the EU's action in these bodies, but on the legal issues that arise when it seeks to participate in IOs.

Much of the legal scholarship examining the EU and international organ-izations is primarily concerned with issues that arise within the EU legal order: the EU's representation in international bodies; the legal effects of decisions of IOs within the EU legal order; or legal issues regarding the

[11] See e.g. K. V. Laatikainen & K. E. Smith (eds), *The European Union at the United Nations: Intersecting Multilateralisms* (Basingstoke: Palgrave, 2006); S. Blavoukos & D. Bourantonis (eds), *The EU Presence in International Organizations* (London: Routledge, 2010); R. Kissack (ed), *Pursuing Effective Multilateralism: The European Union, International Organizations and the Politics of Decision Making* (Basingstoke: Palgrave Macmillan, 2010); K. E. Jørgensen (ed), *The European Union and International Organizations* (London: Routledge, 2009).

[12] T. Gehring, S. Oberthür & M. Mühleck, 'European Union Actorness in International Institutions: Why the EU is Recognized as an Actor in Some International Institutions, but Not in Others' (2013) 51 *Journal of Common Market Studies* 849.

competence to join an IO.[13] Most of these issues are addressed in the field of EU external relations law. These studies seek to understand the internal issues that arise from the EU's activity in IOs, and focus on issues such as the extent to which EU participation in international organizations affects the 'autonomy' of the EU.[14]

The EU's participation in IOs has received less attention from international lawyers. This may be surprising, since it is one of the very few examples of an IO becoming a full member of another IO, and challenges the assumption that IOs consist exclusively of states. The EU is by no means the only IO that has joined or participated in another organization or body. But like with international agreements, the *type* of IOs that the EU has joined and participates in is different. Moreover, the role of the EU in these organizations, such as the World Trade Organization, is often comparable to that of a state. Like its participation in international treaties, the EU's presence within these bodies also poses a number of challenges to international law.

Section 4.2 turns to the internal elements regarding the EU's relationship with international organizations. As with international agreements, the way in which the EU joins and takes part in international organizations is conditioned upon the EU Treaties and the case law. Although there are numerous references to IOs and multilateralism in the Treaties, they give little guidance on important questions regarding how the EU is to engage with these bodies. Section 4.3 then turns to the challenges facing the EU in participating in international organizations. While many of these are legal obstacles, they often stem from political opposition to the EU joining or taking part in IOs. Section 4.4 then looks at the different legal issues that arise from the EU's participation in IOs. While many of these issues are similar to those regarding the EU and the law of treaties (mixity, EU-specific clauses) there are also a number of issues that are unique to IOs. Section 4.5 then turns to how the EU seeks to upgrade its status at IOs. Given the obstacles discussed in the previous sections, it looks at some of the strategies the EU may develop in order to achieve its goal of having more visibility and influence in IOs. The topic is one where legal issues are closely intertwined with political ones, both of which the EU must address if it is to effectively engage with IOs.

---

[13] F. Hoffmeister, 'Outsider or frontrunner? Recent Developments under International and European law on the Status of the European Union in International Organizations and Treaty Bodies' (2007) 44 *Common Market Law Review* 41, 67.

[14] R. A. Wessel & S. Blockmans (eds), *Between Autonomy and Dependence: The EU Legal Order under the Influence of International Organisations* (The Hague: TMC Asser Press, 2013); N. Tsagourias, 'Conceptualizing the Autonomy of the European Union' in R. Collins & N. D. White (eds), *International Organizations and the Idea of Autonomy* (London: Routledge, 2011) 339.

4.2 INTERNATIONAL ORGANIZATIONS AND EU LAW

The EU's ability to join and participate in international organizations is conditioned upon the EU Treaties and EU law. Indeed, the Lisbon Treaty sought to equip the EU to play a greater role on the international plane, including closer cooperation with international organizations. How do the EU Treaties and EU law regulate the Union's participation in IOs?

4.2.1 *International Organizations in the EU Treaties*

The starting point for discussing the EU's relationship with international organizations is the EU Treaties themselves. First, the EU Treaties demonstrate the EU's commitment to multilateralism and the importance of international organizations in global governance. Article 21(2) TEU sets out that the Union 'shall seek to develop relations and build partnerships with [. . .] international, regional or global organisations' and to 'promote multilateral solutions to common problems, in particular in the framework of the United Nations'.[15] One of the objectives of the EU's external action is to 'promote an international system based on stronger multilateral cooperation and good global governance'.[16] As the EU itself is a form of multilateral cooperation, it has an interest in building 'a stronger international society, well-functioning international institutions and a rule-based international order'.[17] This not only involves participating in this multilateral system but also playing a leading role in shaping and developing it:

> At a global level, Europe must lead a renewal of the multilateral order. The UN stands at the apex of the international system. Everything the EU has done in the field of security has been linked to UN objectives. We have a unique moment to renew multilateralism, working with the United States and with our partners around the world.[18]

It is clear from the Treaties that the EU is generally committed to participating in, and shaping international organizations. Beyond this general commitment to international organizations, however, the EU Treaties provide little guidance on the EU's legal relationship with (other) international organizations.

[15] Article 21(1) TEU para. 2.
[16] Article 21(2)(h) TEU.
[17] European Council, European Security Strategy: A Secure Europe in a Better World, 12 December 2003.
[18] Council of the European Union, Report on the Implementation of the European Security Strategy: Providing Security in a Changing World, S407/08, 11 December 2008, 2.

Second, there are numerous specific references to international organizations in the EU Treaties. The Treaties set out a number of issue areas where the Union and Member States are to foster cooperation with third countries and international organizations.[19] Much of this cooperation is with the Council of Europe, an organization where many issues overlap with EU competences. In the field of development cooperation, the EU and the Member States are to cooperate with third countries and international organizations[20] and to consult on their aid programmes 'including in international organisations and during international conferences'.[21] The Union is to maintain 'appropriate forms of cooperation' with certain international organizations, especially the UN, Council of Europe, the Organization for Security and Co-operation in Europe (OSCE) and the Organisation for Economic Co-operation and Development (OECD).[22]

It is clear from the EU Treaties that the UN is of key importance to the Union.[23] Article 3(5) TEU mentions 'respect for the principles of the United Nations Charter' as one of the principles guiding its relations with the world. Article 21(1) TEU sets out that the EU's action on the international scene will be guided by inter alia 'respect for the principles of the United Nations Charter'. The UN and UN bodies are referred to throughout the Treaties, including an obligation to comply with commitments and take into account objectives approved in the UN context.[24] These references are mostly concerned with *cooperation* with the UN and respect for the Charter's *principles*. They give little guidance on the EU's participation within the UN and UN system, or the legal relationship between EU law and decisions of UN bodies, such as the resolutions of the UN Security Council.

---

[19] The EU and the Member States are to facilitate cooperation with international organizations in the fields of education and sport (Article 164(3) TFEU); vocational training (Article 166(3) TFEU); culture (Article 167(3) TFEU); public health (Article 168(3) TFEU); research and technological development (Article 180(b) TFEU); the environment (Article 190(4) TFEU); economic, financial and technical cooperation measures (Article 212(1) TFEU); humanitarian aid (Article 214(7) TFEU).

[20] Article 211 TFEU.

[21] Article 210(1) TFEU.

[22] Article 220(1) TFEU.

[23] Other than Article 21(1) TEU, the UN/UN Charter is referred to in 14 other instances: Article 3(5), Article 21(2)(c), Article 34(2), Article 42(1) and (7) TEU, 7th recital of the preamble of the TFEU, Article 208(2), Article 214(7), Article 220(1) TFEU, 3th and 8th recital preamble, as well as Article 1(b) Protocol No. 10 on permanent structured cooperation, 3rd paragraph Declaration No. 13 concerning CFSP, Declaration No 14. concerning CFSP.

[24] Article 208(2) TFEU: 'The Union and the Member States shall comply with the commitments and take account of the objectives they have approved in the context of the United Nations and other competent international organisations'.

4.2.1.1 Power to Join IOs

Despite the numerous references to international organizations in the EU Treaties, there is no *express* power for the EU to join international organizations. It is now accepted that the power to conclude international agreements includes the ability to join an international organization or treaty body. This legal right to join IOs is based on the implied power of the EU.[25] Based on the doctrine developed in *ERTA*, the EU has the capacity to join IOs based on the external dimension of its internal competence, now confirmed in Article 216(1) TFEU. This provision empowers the Union to conclude agreements with 'one or more third countries or *international organisations*'.

There are no provisions in the EU Treaties that regulate how the Union should go about joining international organizations. The process can be dealt with for the most part by the existing provisions relating to the conclusion of international agreements, namely the procedural steps set out in Article 218 TFEU. Legal issues regarding competences, legal basis, mixity and the role of the different EU institutions, all of which are relevant to the concluding of agreements are therefore also present in relation to the joining of international organizations.[26] However, this only covers the EU participating in formal organizations that are based on an international treaty and does not cover EU involvement in a multitude of bodies that are not based on a formal instrument. Although this has not prevented the EU from joining informal bodies such as the G20 and Financial Stability Board, it does mean that this process is not regulated by the EU Treaties.

At the time of the creation of the EEC, the idea that the Community would join another international organization was not really envisaged.[27] Although the participation in IOs is now accepted part of the EU's international action, there has never been a specific Treaty clause governing the EU's participation in IOs.

[25] *Opinion 1/76*, EU:C:1977:63, para. 5: 'The Community is therefore not only entitled to enter into contractual relations with a third country ... but also has the power, while observing the provisions of the Treaty, to cooperate with that country in setting up an appropriate organism such as the public international institution which it is proposed to establish ... The Community may also ... cooperate with a third country for the purpose of giving the organs of such an institution appropriate powers of decision and for the purpose of defining, in a manner appropriate to the objectives pursued, the nature, elaboration, implementation and effects of the provisions to be adopted within such a framework'.

[26] See P. Eeckhout, *EU External Relations Law* (Oxford: Oxford University Press, 2011) 222–223.

[27] J. Sack, 'The European Community's Membership of International Organizations' (1995) 32 *Common Market Law Review* 1227, 1228.

4.2.1.2 Representation

The EU Treaties also regulate to some extent how the EU and the Member States are to be represented in international organizations. For example, in the field of CFSP, the EU High Representative for Foreign Affairs 'shall express the Union's position in international organisations and at international conferences'.[28] Article 221 TFEU is the legal basis for Union delegations, which are to represent the Union in third countries, as well as various international organizations and multilateral forums.[29] Union Delegations are to work in close cooperation and are to share information with the diplomatic services of the Member States to ensure that decisions defining Union positions and actions are complied with and implemented.[30] Currently, the EU is represented abroad by 141 Delegations and Offices around the world, nine of which are to multilateral organizations.[31]

Member States are obliged to coordinate their action in international organizations and uphold the Union position.[32] This includes upholding EU positions 'in international organisations and at international conferences where not all the Member States participate'.[33] There are also specific obligations regarding the EU Member States who are members of the UN Security Council,[34] who must keep the High Representative and other Member States informed of developments, and to invite the High Representative to present the Union position where there is a defined Union position on a subject on the agenda. For example, on 28 May 2020, High Representative Josep Borrell addressed the UN Security Council on the topic of preservation of international peace and security at the invitation of Estonia, which held the rotating presidency of the Security Council.

The CJEU also continues to develop jurisprudence relating to representation in international organizations. These cases examine issues such as the

---

[28] Article 27(2) TEU.

[29] Article 221(1) TFEU.

[30] Article 35 TEU and Art 5., Council Decision 2010/427/EU of 26 July 2010 establishing the organization and functioning of the EEAS, OJ L 201, 3 August 2010, 30–40 ('EEAS Decision').

[31] See a list of Union delegations to multilateral organizations at: European External Action Service, 'EU in the World', https://eeas.europa.eu/headquarters/headquarters-homepage/are a/geo_en.

[32] Article 34(1) TEU.

[33] Article 34 TEU.

[34] Article 34(2) TEU: 'Member States which are also members of the United Nations Security Council will concert and keep the other Member States and the High Representative fully informed. Member States which are members of the Security Council will [...] defend the positions and the interests of the Union, without prejudice to their responsibilities under the provisions of the United Nations Charter'.

extent of the duty of sincere cooperation on the part of the Member States and the interpretation of articles in the Treaties concerning the EU and international organizations. Despite the Treaties giving guidance on the issues of representation, there remain legal disputes about who is capable of representing the Union in these bodies, especially regarding the continued role of the EU Member States. Although the Lisbon Treaty sought to address some of these questions, the post-Lisbon era has seen these legal disputes continue, and for some new ones to emerge. Again, these issues can be traced back to issues over competences and the desire of EU Member States to retain their positions and visibility in international affairs.

4.2.2 *Issues Not in the EU Treaties*

While the Treaties show a commitment to multilateralism and cooperation, the EU Treaties do not give any further guidance regarding which organizations the EU should join or strengthen its relationships. There are some references to the UN system and some other specific organizations. Article 6(2) TEU stipulates EU accession to the European Convention on Human Rights. Article 189(3) TFEU obliges the Union to 'establish any appropriate relations with the European Space Agency', but this leaves open all options regarding the precise nature of this relationship.[35] These provisions do not guide the EU when deciding where to invest time and energy in joining or upgrading its status in international organizations. The EU is simply not able to join every organization where it has an international interest or where it exercises competences. This has meant that the EU has had to become more strategic in deciding which organizations to join or pursue closer relations.[36]

Another issue that is not addressed in the EU Treaties is the legal effect of decisions of international organization in the EU legal order. The EU Treaties set out that international agreements concluded by the EU are binding on the EU and the Member States, and there is well-developed jurisprudence on the conditions under which international treaties are given effect in the EU legal order. There is less guidance, however, on what effect should be given to the normative output of international organizations and institutions, which is very rarely in the form of a formal binding instrument. Rather, international organizations and other bodies produce an array of decisions that have been

---

[35] J. Wouters, 'Space in the Treaty of Lisbon' (2009) *Yearbook on Space Policy*, European Space Policy Institute (ESPI), Vienna, 116–124.

[36] See J. Wouters, A. Chané, J. Odermatt & T. Ramopoulos, 'Improving the EU's Status in the UN and the UN System: An Objective without a Strategy?' in C. Kaddous (ed), *The European Union in International Organisations and Global Governance* (Oxford: Hart, 2015) 45–74.

described as soft law or informal law making. International law is beginning to recognize the importance of these regulatory processes, yet it is still not clear what effect they should have within the EU legal order.

The Lisbon Treaty sought to provide the EU with better tools to join and be represented in international organizations. In the years following Lisbon, complex questions about the EU's presence in IOs are still being elaborated upon by the Court, and there remain disagreements within the EU about representation in IOs. This may be linked partially with the fact that the EU's involvement in IOs is not sufficiently dealt with in the Treaties themselves.

It is not evident that the EU's uncertain relationship with IOs would be rectified by a Treaty amendment or the inclusion of a specific chapter on IOs. Eeckhout has argued, for instance '[t]here is an obvious case for basic legal texts on how to conduct co-operation in the framework of international organizations'.[37] The multiple references to international organizations and multilateralism in the EU Treaties has done little to answer some of the more thorny legal questions. Moreover, as the case law on Article 218 TFEU relating to the conclusion of international agreements demonstrates, including more provisions in the EU Treaties does not solve these internal legal questions, and in reality create ground for new 'battles' to take place over the interpretation and application of these provisions. Providing more guidance on joining and participating in IOs is likely to give rise to further disagreement and even litigation.

4.3 CHALLENGES FACING THE EU IN INTERNATIONAL ORGANIZATIONS

Whereas the EU has a long history of becoming a party to bilateral and multilateral treaties, it faces a number of unique obstacles when seeking to join international forums. These obstacles stem from legal and political issues within the EU, as well as from the external environment. Many of the challenges are found in the structure of international law itself and the nature of international organizations. This book examines how the EU confronts the 'state-centric' structure of international law. It is in international organizations where this state-centrism remains highly pervasive. There is a strong reluctance to allow participation by entities that are not sovereign states. This is not a challenge faced only by the EU. Other regional organizations, non-state actors, non-recognized states and entities short of statehood, NGOs and civil society groups, have also sought to gain greater representation within international organizations with varying levels of success.

---

[37]   Eeckhout (n26) 255.

Representation at international organizations, especially those within the United Nations system, is closely linked with state sovereignty and the sovereign equality of states. In older organizations, especially those part of the UN system, the Union has faced significant challenges in gaining representation. Although this problem is less pronounced in newer and informal organizations, EU participation is still viewed as an anomaly in IOs.

As with joining international agreements, problems stem from the *type* of international organization that the EU is and the form of participation it seeks. It is not uncommon for an international organization to attend the meetings of another international organization as an observer. In these cases, the observer organization may provide input and comments, but does not seek to function like a state member. When the EU takes part in international organizations, it often does not seek observer status in order to play this informative or consultative role; it seeks to take part in a way that bears greater resemblance to a Member State of the organization. This will include, for instance, the right to speak behind an EU nameplate or to exercise the right to vote. Its involvement in the IO will often be motivated by the fact that the EU exercises competence in the field covered by the organization and seeks to influence developments in the body. It is this 'state-like' involvement that often causes friction.

One must also bear in mind the fact that European states are already viewed as being overrepresented in the international legal order. One can understand the reluctance of non-EU states to allow what is perceived to be even more European representation, in addition to the existing European members. As Lowe points out,

> The European Community is a party to many international agreements and often attends conferences alongside member States, causing concern that the European States are over-represented – a view based largely upon the misconception that the interests of the Commission, which represents the Community, and the Member States are necessarily the same.[38]

Although in some instances the Union position and that of the EU Member States will not be identical, in many cases EU representation will lead to the EU in effect being given greater representation. This may have the consequence of urging other regional groups to pursue their own path towards regional representation. Bodies such as the Caribbean Community (CARICOM) and the African Union (AU) have indicated they would also push for representation by their groups. There is a difference, however, between the EU and these other regional bodies. The EU is a more integrated

---

[38]   V. Lowe, *International Law* (Oxford: Oxford University Press, 2007) 230.

organization; it possesses international legal personality and exercises competences linked to a number of international organizations. EU representation is necessitated, not only by the interest of EU Member States in concerted representation, but also by the fact that it is the EU that often has legislative capacity in the fields covered by the international organization and has developed its own modalities of representation. This is a rather legalistic argument, however. It is unlikely to be accepted by those who see EU representation as little more than an attempt to entrench European influence, and as a threat to the state-centric system of IOs.

The EU therefore faces a steep political hurdle when seeking to join or upgrade its status in international organizations. It should be pointed out that this reluctance is not spread evenly across all fields and the degree to which the EU has been accepted as an international actor in its own right differs from organization to organization. The World Trade Organization, for instance, stands out as a body where the EU has been accepted as an international actor in its own right, although frictions still exist. In the United Nations and the UN system, where the EU seeks to have closer relations and greater influence, the EU has encountered much more resistance.

The obstacles preventing the EU from joining international organizations are not entirely political, however. In many cases, the EU will seek to join an existing international organization which only allows states as members. This is the case with many of the bodies that are part of the UN system. EU membership in these bodies requires a specific amendment to the constituent treaty of the organization to allow participation by the EU or by a 'regional economic integration organization' (Section 3.3.1).

Allowing for participation by the EU or a regional organization in the constituent treaty of an IO is a relatively straightforward (legal) task. It requires the constituent treaty to be amended to include an REIO clause, or to state the EU may become a member. The more complex questions arise, however, regarding the modalities of the EU's participation in the legal order of that organization. The organization will have developed its own rules and practices over time, based on the assumption that its membership comprises states. Membership by the Union, especially when it is in addition to the EU Member States, creates a set of issues for the organization. These include voting, the calculation of financial contributions, the exercise of speaking rights, the ability to put forward candidates for positions and the EU's role in dispute resolution mechanisms. Section 4.4 examines how international organizations and the EU have sought to solve these issues. International law can find solutions to EU involvement in IOs, but this requires certain modifications to allow EU participation. Whereas we find numerous EU-specific clauses in international agreements (Section 3.3), there is far less political will to find similar legal concessions to the EU in the field of international organizations.

4.4 THE EU'S PARTICIPATION IN INTERNATIONAL ORGANIZATIONS AND INSTITUTIONS

4.4.1 *Membership*

The first issue pertains to the conditions for membership. The EU enjoys a variety of different statuses in international organizations. Full membership remains very much the exception, with the EU enjoying various levels of representation short of full membership status. The EU's status in a given organization depends on a number of factors, the first of which is competence. The EU is more likely to pursue membership in an organization where it has substantial or exclusive competence. For instance, the EU's full membership of the World Trade Organization corresponds with its exclusive competence in the field of common commercial policy.[39] The same is the case with the status of the Union in many fisheries management organizations.[40] Yet the EU is not a full member of all organizations where it exercises exclusive competence. Moreover, the EU's significant competences and law-making activity in fields such as air and maritime transport have not led to membership in important organizations such as the IMO or ICAO where EU membership should be pursued.

The second issue is the external environment faced by the EU, that is, the legal and political situation in the organization where EU seeks participation. The EU has had success, for instance, in cooperating with other 'European' (or Western-dominated) organizations, such as the Council of Europe or OECD. In these situations, the EU is in a much stronger negotiating position. Here the EU is negotiating with other European states, many of which will be members of the Union, or more willing to accept the EU's international role. In organizations with a broader or near universal membership, such as those within the UN system, the EU has been less successful,

---

[39] Article 3(1)(e) TFEU.
[40] See P. Heckler, 'Regional Fisheries Management Organisations: Defining the EU and Member State Roles' in R. A. Wessel & J. Odermatt (eds), *Research Handbook on the European Union and International Organizations* (Cheltenham: Edward Elgar, 2019) 429–445. See J. Wouters, S. de Jong, A. Marx & P. De Man, *Study for the Assessment of the EU's Role in International Maritime Organisations*, Research Report for the European Commission, Directorate General for Fisheries and Maritime Affairs (2009).

and states that are less responsive to the EU position can play a spoiler role. The presence of EU Member States in an organization does not necessarily improve the EU's chance of membership, however. A notable example is the Arctic Council, where the presence of EU Member States (as full members and observers) has not helped the EU to pursue formal representation. In organizations where the Member States have their own political and strategic interests, EU Member States may be more reluctant to see the EU participate in its own right.

4.4.1.1 Full Membership

Despite the obstacles mentioned earlier, the EU has managed to gain full membership in a number of organizations. In addition to being a founding member of the WTO,[41] the EU has also become a member of the Hague Conference on Private International Law[42] and is a founding member of the European Bank for Reconstruction and Development (EBRD).[43] The EU's full membership of the European Organisation for the Safety of Air Navigation (EUROCONTROL) is still pending.[44] In 2007, the Council of the World Customs Organization (WCO) accepted the EU's request to become a member, but accession will only take place when the organization's 172 members ratify an amendment allowing economic and customs unions to join. The EU currently enjoys status 'akin to WCO membership'.[45] The EU is a full member of quite a number of regional fisheries management organizations (RFMOs).[46] The EU is generally a member of these bodies without the presence of the EU Member States, except in certain instances where France

---

[41]   Agreement Establishing the World Trade Organization (WTO Agreement), signed on 15 April 1994, 1867 UNTS 154.

[42]   Council Decision of 5 October 2006 on the accession of the Community to the Hague Conference on Private International Law, 2006/719/EC, OJ L 297, 26 October 2006, 1–14.

[43]   Article 3, Agreement Establishing the European Bank for Reconstruction and Development: 'Membership in the Bank shall be open: (i) to (1) European countries and (2) non-European countries which are members of the International Monetary Fund; and (ii) to the European Economic Community and the European Investment Bank'.

[44]   Protocol on the accession of the European Community to the EUROCONTROL International Convention relating to Cooperation for the Safety of Air Navigation of 13 December 1960, as variously amended and as consolidated by the Protocol of 27 June 1997 (not yet in force).

[45]   A list of World Customs Organization Members is available at: www.wcoomd.org/en/about-us /wco-members/membership.aspx. See T. Yamaoka, 'The De Facto Accession of the European Communities to the World Customs Organizations: Process and Significance' (2013) 8(4) *Global Trade and Customs Journal* 92.

[46]   See Heckler (n40).

or Denmark are members, due to their overseas territories. This also coincides with the exclusive competence of the Union in the field.

The EU is a member of the Food and Agriculture Organization (FAO)[47] and Codex Alimentarius Commission.[48] Membership in these bodies also coincides with competence, agriculture being one of the core competences of the EU since its earliest days, where the Treaty tasked the EEC with the creation of a common agricultural policy.[49] Although the EU has achieved the status of a 'Member Organization'[50] at the FAO, its effective representation continues to face challenges. The EU does not enjoy the same rights as other members. It may not hold office in the Conference, the Council and their subsidiary bodies,[51] it has no voting rights for elective places[52] or budget matters,[53] and no participation rights in the restricted committees[54] and the bodies dealing with the internal working of the conference.[55] Full membership can mean that actual participation rights remain restricted.

In addition to being a member of international organizations, the EU is also a full party to a number of 'treaty regimes'. In these instances, the EU is a party to a convention and takes part in its meetings of its parties, but a formal IO has not been established. This is the case, for instance, with a number of environmental agreements, including the UN Framework Convention on Climate Change. The EU is a party to multilateral treaties such as the UN Convention Rights of Persons with Disabilities and the UN Convention against Corruption, where it takes part in the conference of parties. Many of the similar obstacles facing EU representation in IOs also occur when the EU takes part in treaty regimes.

4.4.1.2 Observer Status

In most cases where the EU seeks to institutionalize its involvement with an international organization, it has sought a status short of full membership, such

---

[47] Constitution of the Food and Agriculture Organization (with Annexes) (adopted 16 October 1945, entered into force 16 October 1945). Council Decision of 25 November 1991; OJ C of 16 December 1991, 238.

[48] Codex Alimentarius Commission, established by WHO and FAO.

[49] Article 3(d) 38–47 EEC Treaty.

[50] Article II(3) FAO Constitution (n47).

[51] Article II(9) FAO Constitution (n47); Rules XLIII(3), XLIV FAO General Rules.

[52] Rule XLV(2) FAO General Rules.

[53] Article XVIII(6) FAO Constitution (n47).

[54] Programme Committee, Finance Committee, Committee on Constitutional and Legal Matters, Article II(9) FAO Constitution, Rule XLVI, FAO General Rules.

[55] See Credentials Committee, General Committee, Rule XLIII(2), FAO General Rules.

as observer status. There are different levels of observer status, depending on the actual rights enjoyed. The EU may seek 'enhanced observer' or 'full participant' status that comes close to full membership. This should come as no surprise given the fact that the basic instruments of most IOs provide for membership only by states, and the amendment of these instruments is often an onerous procedure. This is the case, for instance, with the United Nations, where EU membership would require an amendment to Article 4(1) of the UN Charter. Rather, the EU has gained observer status in many of these bodies, allowing the EU to act as far as possible as a member of the organization, but without full membership rights, such as voting. This compromise allows the EU to act within an IO that only allows states to become members without having to officially amend the founding instrument of the organization. Rather, it may involve an amendment to the rules of procedure of the organ involved.

Being an 'observer' does not always imply that the EU plays a passive role. Indeed, the role of 'observer' has changed significantly over time, especially due to the role of the EU, which in practice can be better described as 'full participant' in a number of bodies.[56] The actual rights enjoyed by the EU will depend largely on the attitude of third states that are full members of the organization.[57] This attitude towards the EU, and the willingness to let it participate as an observer, may change over time. Fearful that they play too large a role in the IO, members may seek to define and limit the participation rights of non-members. For instance, the EU has enjoyed enhanced observer status at the OECD,[58] where its participation 'comes quite close to full membership',[59] yet in 2004 the OECD updated its policy on participation by non-members.[60] On a separate occasion, after gaining 'enhanced observer'

---

[56]   Hoffmeister (n13) 54.

[57]   S. Gstöhl, '"Patchwork Power" Europe: The EU's Representation in International Institutions' (2009) 14 *European Foreign Affairs Review* 385, 401.

[58]   Convention on the Organisation of Economic Co-operation and Development (Convention on the OECD), 14 December 1960, 88 UNTS 180, Supplementary Protocol No. 1: 'The Commissions of the European Economic Community and of the European Atomic Energy Community as well as the High Authority of the European Coal and Steel Community shall take part in the work of that Organisation'. See M. Emerson, R. Balfour, T. Corthaut, J. Wouters, P. M. Kaczyński & R. Renard, *Upgrading the EU's Role as a Global Actor: Institutions, Law and the Restructuring of European Diplomacy*, Centre for European Policy Studies (Brussels: CEPS, 2011) 96–97, https://www.ceps.eu/ceps-publications/upgrading-the-eus-role-as-global-actor-institutions-law-and-the-restructuring-of-european-diplomacy/

[59]   See R. A. Wessel, 'The Legal Framework for the Participation of the European Union in International Institutions' (2011) 33 *European Integration* 621, 628.

[60]   Organisation for Economic Co-operation and Development Council (OECD) (2004) 'Resolution of the Council Concerning the Participation of Non-Members in the Work of Subsidiary Bodies of the Organisation', adopted by the Council at its 1091st Session on 8 July 2004, C(2004)132/FINAL.

status at the UN General Assembly (UNGA), the EU still had to push to have this status accepted in practice by UN Members (Section 4.5.1.1). While enhanced observer status provides a useful formal legal avenue for EU participation where membership is not legally or politically possible, it often still requires a sustained effort from the EU to safeguard its position in the IO. Observer status may allow the EU to participate in the work of an IO and to present itself as an international actor, but it will be legally prevented from exercising some of the more important functions. This means that the EU must still rely on the EU Member States, acting as agents of the EU, to vote and pursue EU positions.

4.4.1.3 Status Less Than Observer

The last category is where the EU is not a member and enjoys no official observer or similar status in the organization. In some situations, this is not a problem for the Union, since the EU has little or no interest in the operation of the organization. In cases where the EU does have an interest in the workings of the IO, the EU must rely upon its Member States to pursue its interests. In these cases, internal EU law has developed to ensure that the Member States pursue the Union interest. A notable example of such a body is the UN Security Council, where the EU has no official representation, but has a strong interest in developments, particularly regarding the EU's Common Foreign and Security Policy. As discussed earlier, the EU Treaties set out certain obligations on the part of Member States in the UNSC. Rule 39 of the UNSC's Provisional Rules of Procedure provides that it may invite 'members of the Secretariat or other persons, whom it considers competent for the purpose, to supply it with information or to give other assistance in examining matters within its competence'.[61] The EU representative issues statements on a regular basis at the UNSC in its public sessions.

In a similar vein, the EU has to rely on its Member States to represent it in a number of international financial institutions and conferences. Especially since the financial crisis, the work of the IMF has been particularly important to the Union. Pursuant to Article 138(1) TFEU the Council 'shall adopt a decision establishing common positions on matters of particular interest for economic and monetary union within the competent international financial institutions and conferences'.[62] Article 138(2) TFEU seeks a unified

---

[61] Provisional Rules of Procedure of the United Nations Security Council, UN Doc S/96/Rev.7.

[62] On the EU at the IMF, see J. Wouters, S. Van Kerckhoven & T. Ramopoulos, 'The EU and the Euro Area in International Economic Governance: The Case of the IMF' in F. Amtenbrink & D. Kochenov (eds), *The European Union's Shaping of the International Legal Order* (Cambridge: Cambridge University Press, 2013) 306–327.

representation of the euro area in IFIs. Despite the clear legal framework, internal political considerations and legal constraints imposed by the founding instruments of some IFIs has led to inaction by the EU institutions and the euro area Member States.

4.4.1.4 Parallel Membership

Most international agreements entered into by the EU are 'mixed agreements' where the EU is present alongside all or some EU Member States. The same is true for most IOs where the EU is present, the EU being a member alongside all or some of the Member States, rather than replacing them. Many of legal problems of 'mixity' that arise in the context of international agreements are therefore also present in the case of IOs. Unique issues arise in IOs, especially regarding issues of representation and voting.

The EU and its Member States often face internal problems originating from their parallel membership in an IO. An example of such a case is at the FAO, where the EU and the Member States have had parallel membership for more than two decades. This situation is governed by internal arrangements[63] developed at the EU level that deal with internal coordination for the preparation and exercise of membership rights, including voting and speaking rights. These arrangements have been the subject of litigation before the CJEU.[64] Similar arrangements exist for the participation of the EU and its Member States in the Codex Alimentarius Commission.[65] The experience at the FAO demonstrates the complexities of parallel membership. The Commission, for example, does not consider the experience from these arrangements in FAO to have been successful: 'their application has constantly led to time-consuming discussions on the division of competences. This has not left sufficient time for the relevant Council preparatory bodies to elaborate on the substance of the positions to be taken in view of FAO meetings'.[66] Since the EU acceded to the

---

[63] Council (1991) Council Document 10478/91, 18 December 1991, revised by Council Document 9050/92, 7 October 1992, and Council Document 8460/95, 26 June 1995.

[64] Judgment in *Commission* v. *Council*, C-25/94, EU:C:1996:114.

[65] Council, 'Arrangement between the Council and the Commission regarding preparation for Codex Alimentarius', Annex III to Council Decision 2003/822/EC of 17 November 2003 on the accession of the European Community to the Codex Alimentarius Commission [2003] OJ L 309/14.

[66] European Commission, 'Communication from the Commission to the Council, The role of the European Union in the Food and Agriculture Organisation (FAO) after the Treaty of Lisbon: Updated Declaration of Competences and new arrangements between the Council and the Commission for the exercise of membership rights of the EU and its Member States', Brussels, 29 May 2013, COM(2013) 333 final, 4

FAO alongside its Member States, speaking and voting rights have to be exercised on an alternative basis.[67]

In addition to internal arrangements, the issue of parallel membership is also governed at the international level. For example, in the FAO, the EU and the Member States are required to submit a declaration of competence[68] and to notify the Director-General of any subsequent changes.[69] The EU first submitted a declaration of competences in 1994.[70] It was only with the 2013 FAO Communication, that the Commission submitted an updated draft declaration to the Council, in order to bring it in line with the provisions of the Lisbon Treaty.[71] As discussed in Chapter 3, such declarations are notoriously difficult to update, mainly due to political sensitivities about the division of competences. For this reason, the Commission stresses that '[n]either the new Declaration of competences, nor the new arrangements affect in any way the division of competences between the EU and its Member States as provided for under the Treaties'.[72] The updated declaration attracted criticism from the side of EU Member States, since it does not include 'any recognition of the extent to which the EU has not exercised its competence under shared competence areas'.[73]

---

[67] Article II(8), (10) FAO Constitution (n47). On the exercise of voting rights see J. Heliskoski, 'Internal Struggle for International Presence: The Exercise of Voting Rights within the FAO' in A. Dashwood & C. Hillion (eds), *The General Law of EC External Relations* (London: Sweet & Maxwell, 2000) 79–99.

[68] Article II(5) FAO Constitution (n47) (Section 3.3.2).

[69] Article II(7) FAO Constitution (n47).

[70] Council Decision of 25 November 1991, Declaration of Competence by the European Union in respect of matters covered by the constitution of the Food and Agriculture Organization of the United Nations (Pursuant to the General Rules of the Organization) (O.J. 1991 C 238); updated by a letter sent on 4 October 1994 from the President of the Council to the Director-General of the FAO, cf. Communication from the Commission to the Council on the notification of a change in the distribution of competence between the EC and its Member States pursuant to Article II(7) of the FAO Constitution, SEC 94 (437) final. See F. Schild, 'The Influence of the Food and Agriculture Organization (FAO) on the EU Legal Order' in R. A. Wessel & S. Blockmans (eds), *Between Autonomy and Dependence: The EU Legal Order Under the Influence of International Organisations* (The Hague: TMC Asser Press, 2013) 226.

[71] Annex 1, 'Draft Declaration of competences by the European Union in respect of matters covered by the Constitution of the Food and Agriculture Organisation of the United Nations (FAO)', Communication from the Commission to the Council, The role of the European Union in the Food and Agriculture Organisation (FAO) after the Treaty of Lisbon: Updated Declaration of Competences and new arrangements between the Council and the Commission for the exercise of membership rights of the EU and its Member States, COM (2013) 333 final.

[72] FAO Communication (n71).

[73] United Kingdom, Department for International Development, Explanatory Memorandum on COM (2013) 333 final, Doc. No. 10368-13, 27 June 2013, para. 3.

The FAO Constitution also sets out how the EU or its Member States are to indicate before each meeting the division of competences for each agenda item and to declare which entity shall vote.[74] This is a significant additional burden to the functioning of the EU in the FAO. The Commission states that it considered 'the systematic submission of such an information note [to be] not required for meetings or specific agenda points thereof where either a vote is not envisaged or the division of competence between the EU and its Member States results directly from the present declaration of competence'.[75] Such as view was criticized by Member States, including the UK.[76] The FAO rules explicitly require an indication of competence 'before any meeting of the Organization'.[77] Although the new declaration of competences seeks to clarify the situation, it remains too vague to give useful guidance to third states on who has competence on a specific agenda item.

Parallel membership has been rather more successful in the WTO. The EU was already deeply engaged with the GATT, the predecessor to the WTO and the EU/Community presence in the organization has been accepted.[78] Second, the EU Member States are more willing to let the EU take the lead in nearly all aspects of the WTO's activity. Not only does the EU possess exclusive competence in the common commercial policy, it has built up experience and expertise in the field. This is in stark contrast to the situation at other organizations such as the FAO, where parallel membership has caused more difficulties. Even where the Union has obtained full membership status, its participation in the work of the organization is still conditioned by the extent to which the EU Member States are still involved in the IO. The example of the FAO shows that, despite EU full membership, its actual participation remains restricted.[79] This is not only due to the limitations stemming from the FAO Constitution and the General Rules of Procedure, but primarily results from EU internal procedures and quarrels.[80]

Rather than providing an exhaustive account of the EU's membership in IOs, this section points out how the EU's actual involvement in IOs is highly varied and dependent on a number of factors. Full membership remains the

---

74   Rule XLII(2) of the General Rules of the FAO.
75   FAO Communication (n71) annex 1.
76   United Kingdom, Explanatory Memorandum (n73) para. 4.
77   Rule XLII(2) of the General Rules of the FAO.
78   Judgment in *International Fruit Company and Others* v. *Produktschap voor Groenten en Fruit*, Joined Cases 21 to 25/72, EU:C:1972:115, paras 14–15. See K. Lenaerts & P. Van Nuffel, *European Union Law* (London: Sweet & Maxwell, 2011) 973–974.
79   I. Govaere, J. Capiau & A. Vermeersch, 'In-Between Seats: The Participation of the European Union in International Organisations' (2004) 9 *European Foreign Affairs Review* 155, 165.
80   See Eeckhout (n26) 229.

exception, and even in those cases, the actual strength of the EU's position varies. Moreover, formal status does not mean influence. In many cases it will be the strength of the EU position being put forward that is more decisive than the EU's position in the IO.[81] The idea that formal status and competence are necessarily linked should be questioned. The need for EU participation is not obvious to the EU's external partners, who may continue to view the EU as gaining an extra seat.

4.4.2 *Funding*

Most international organizations require funds in order to operate, and these funds are usually raised through the assessed contributions of their members. Assessed contributions are calculated differently from organization to organization. A question that arises from EU participation is whether, and in what way, the EU should also contribute to the funding of the IO. Since EU participation can lead to increased expenditures of the IO, the EU should in principle pay something towards these increased costs. Moreover, if the EU seeks to be treated on an equal footing with other members, then it too should shoulder the burden of funding the IO. On the other hand, the EU is often a member alongside its Member States. It would be unfair to ask those Member States to effectively pay twice, once as a member of the IO and again via the contributions of the EU. In addition to the direct funding of the organization, there is also the issue of financing particular programmes run by the organization within the framework of a particular treaty regime.

International organizations have developed a variety of techniques to contend with this situation. For example, in the WTO, contributions are based on each Member's share of international trade. It would arguably be unfair if the EU would make a contribution in addition to that of the individual Member States. The EU itself does not directly contribute to the WTO budget. In the FAO, where the EU is a full member, the EU does not contribute to the budget in the same manner as the members that are states.[82] Rather, Article XVIII, paragraph 6 states that '[a] Member Organization shall not be required to contribute to the budget as specified in paragraph 2 of this Article, but shall pay to the Organization a sum to be

---

[81] See G. De Baere & E. Paasivirta, 'Identity and Difference: The EU and the UN as Part of Each Other' in H. de Weale & J. Kuijpers (eds), *The European Union's Emerging International Identity: Views from the Global Arena* (Leiden: Martinus Nijhoff, 2013) 42.

[82] Article XVIII FAO Constitution (n47) para. 2 (Budget and Contributions).

determined by the Conference to cover administrative and other expenses arising out of its membership in the Organization'.[83] In 2011, this annual payment made to the FAO was €270,000.[84] A similar clause can be found in Article 9(2) of the Statute of the Hague Conference on Private International Law, which provides that the member organization shall not contribute to the budget but shall pay a sum to be determined by the Conference, 'to cover additional administrative expenses arising out of its membership'.[85] The EU does not make contributions to International Tribunal for the Law of the Sea (ITLOS), since the expenses of the Tribunal are borne by the States Parties.[86] When the EU or another non-state entity is a party to a case, the Tribunal will decide upon an amount for that party to pay in order to contribute towards the Tribunal's expenses.[87]

The ECHR Accession Agreement also dealt with the issue of funding. One of the complicated issues was that the EU would join the ECHR, but not become a party to the Council of Europe, the body that is responsible for funding the ECtHR. Under Article 50 ECHR, the expenditure of the ECHR is to be borne by the Council of Europe.[88] It was decided that the EU would provide an annual contribution to take into account the additional expenditures that would arise from its participation in the Convention, especially those related to the ECtHR.[89]

---

[83]   Article XVIII FAO Constitution (n47) para. 6.

[84]   See 'EU Financial Contribution to the Food and Agriculture Organization', http://eeas .europa.eu/delegations/rome/eu_united_nations/work_with_fao/ec_financial_contribution_ fao/index_en.htm.

[85]   Article 9(2), Hague Conference on Private International Law, 'Statute of the Hague Conference on Private International Law' (done 31 October 1951, entered into force 15 July 1955) 220 UNTS 121.

[86]   Article 19(1), Statute of the International Tribunal for the Law of the Sea (ITLOS Statute), Annex VI to the United Nations Convention on the Law of the Sea (concluded 10 December 1982, entered into force 16 November 1994) 1833 UNTS 561: 'The expenses of the Tribunal shall be borne by the States Parties and by the Authority on such terms and in such a manner as shall be decided at meetings of the States Parties'.

[87]   Article 19(2) ITLOS Statute (n86): 'When an entity other than a State Party or the Authority is a party to a case submitted to it, the Tribunal shall fix the amount which that party is to contribute towards the expenses of the Tribunal'.

[88]   Article 50, Convention for the Protection of Human Rights and Fundamental Freedoms (signed 4 November 1950, entered into force 3 September 1953) 213 UNTS 221.

[89]   Article 8, Council of Europe, Final Report to the CDDH, Appendix I, Draft revised agreement on the accession of the European Union to the Convention for the Protection of Human Rights and Fundamental Freedoms (2013) ('Draft ECHR Accession Agreement'). The EU shall 'pay an annual contribution dedicated to the expenditure related to the functioning of the Convention'. On the method of assessing contributions, see J. Odermatt, 'The EU's Accession to the European Convention on Human Rights: An International Law Perspective' (2014) 47(1) *New York University Journal of International Law & Politics* 59, 92–94.

A rather unique case is the European Bank for Reconstruction and Development (EBRD), its membership comprising 64 countries, as well as the European Union and the European Investment Bank (EIB).[90] The EU and EIB are both shareholders and are represented by an Executive Director, in addition to the EU Member States. This is an example of how the EU is able to gain representation in bodies that are relatively new (established in 1991) and are European in character. An explanatory note sets out the reasoning for EU/EIB involvement:

> Delegates agreed that both the European Economic Community and the European Investment Bank (EIB) should be members, given the importance accorded to their role by the European Community Heads of State or Government who had first endorsed the idea of the Bank. It was not intended that their membership would be a precedent for other organizations or Banks to become members of the Bank, or that their membership would be used as a precedent for them to become members of other organizations or other banks.[91]

This shows how EU membership, funding and membership on the Board of Directors is still viewed as an exceptional situation, justified by the unique nature of the EBRD, rather than a precedent for other similar bodies.

There is no common approach to the funding of IOs. The EU is generally willing to pay its share for the increased expenditures of an IO, but will not pay assessed contributions in the same manner as other members. In certain instances, this may mean that the EU is excluded from decision-making on budgetary affairs of the organization, such as at the FAO. Moreover, the European Union will often contribute to extra-budgetary resources of an organization, such as funding specific programmes and projects.

4.4.3 *Voting*

More contentious issues arise regarding the EU's participation in IOs where voting takes place. The right to vote is viewed as being linked with the sovereign equality of states. In the majority of international organizations where voting takes place, a one member, one vote rule applies, meaning that countries with a relatively small population or economic power have the same voting rights as the large and economically powerful states. An

---

[90] Article 3 (membership); Article 5 (subscription of shares); Article 26 (Board of Directors), Agreement Establishing the European Bank for Reconstruction and Development.
[91] Article 3, European Bank of Reconstruction and Development, Basic Documents of the EBRD (Explanatory Notes).

obvious exception to this rule is the United Nations Security Council and the veto rights of its five permanent members. The Bretton Woods institutions are other notable exceptions, the IMF and World Bank both using weighted voting based on a system of quotas, where voting power is intended to reflect a member's economic significance in the world economy. The EU is however not a member of these bodies.

In international organizations where voting takes place, the IO is faced with the issue of how to reconcile the fact that on the one hand, the EU is a separate legal entity that should prima facie have the right to vote, and the fact that the EU is constituted by other Member States who will retain their right to vote. The sovereign equality of states is taken seriously. Allowing an international organization such as the EU to exercise voting rights can be viewed as a threat to this system. Another concern is that the European states may be seen as unjustly gaining a vote. A third issue relates to the EU's internal legal order. Under EU law, EU Member States are under a duty of loyalty and are legally obliged to support EU positions. Bloc voting by the EU Member States might help the EU push forward its agenda, but can have a negative effect on the overall organization of the IO, by encouraging other regional groups to engage in bloc voting, making negotiation and compromise more difficult.

Most organizations seek to avoid the issue of 'double representation' through alternate voting. This means that when the EU Member States exercise their right to vote, the EU is precluded from doing so, and vice versa. The decision of who will exercise these voting rights, either the EU or as the EU Member States, is an internal question for the EU and the Member States, and will often be tied to the issue of competence. The FAO Constitution contains a typical example of an alternate voting clause:

> A Member Organization shall exercise membership rights on an alternative basis with its Member States that are Member Nations of the Organization in the areas of their respective competences and in accordance with rules set down by the Conference.[92]

Article 4(4) of Annex IX of the United Nations Convention on the Law of the Sea (UNCLOS) states that 'Participation of . . . an international organization shall in no case entail an increase of the representation to which its Member States which are States Parties would otherwise be entitled, including rights in decision-making'.[93] The Statute of the International Renewable Energy Agency (IRENA) states that, regarding a regional economic integration

---

[92]   Article II FAO Constitution (n47).
[93]   Article 4(4) of Annex IX, UNCLOS.

organization, '[t]he organisation and its Member States shall not be entitled to exercise rights, including voting rights, under the Statute concurrently'.[94] Article 9 of the WTO Agreement states that '[w]here the European Communities exercise their right to vote, they shall have a number of votes equal to the number of their Member States which are members of the WTO'.[95] This remains a more theoretical issue, since voting rarely occurs in the WTO, which generally acts through consensus.[96] All these instruments stress that the EU will in no way gain an extra vote through its membership and participation in the organization.

An interesting deviation from the alternate voting model is found in the draft agreement for EU accession to the European Convention on Human Rights.[97] One of the questions faced by the drafters was whether the EU should exercise the right to vote in the Committee of Ministers. One of the problems was that, in the field of human rights, it would be difficult to divide issues along the lines of competence, as is the case with most mixed agreements. It was decided that both the EU and the Member States would have a right to vote and could exercise their right to vote simultaneously in the Committee of Ministers. The Accession Agreement set out the topics on which the EU would be entitled to participate as a voting party, all of which related to the functioning of the European Court of Human Rights.[98]

Since the EU and the EU Member States could exercise voting rights concurrently, this raised concerns regarding potential 'bloc voting'. The EU and the Member States could potentially use their combined voting power to prevent decisions that would be unfavourable to the EU or its Member States. This would have been likely since Member States are under an obligation to act in a co-ordinated manner when expressing statements and voting within international forums.[99] While the precise nature of this obligation is still being developed in the case law of the CJEU, it is likely that the EU Member States

---

[94] Article XI, Statute of the International Renewable Energy Agency (IRENA) (2009).

[95] Article 9 WTO Agreement (n41).

[96] As Article IX(1) WTO Agreement (n41) sets out: 'Except as otherwise provided, where a decision cannot be arrived at by consensus, the matter at issue shall be decided by voting'.

[97] See Draft ECHR Accession Agreement (n89).

[98] These are Article 26(2) (to reduce, at the request of the plenary Court, the number of judges of the Chambers); Article 39(4) (the execution of the terms of a friendly settlement); Article 46(2) to (5) (execution of judgments); Article 47 (advisory opinions) and Article 54(1) (Powers of the Committee of Ministers).

[99] This stems from the principle of sincere cooperation' under Article 4(3) TEU. See G. De Baere, '"O, Where is Faith? O, Where is Loyalty?' Some Thoughts on the Duty of Loyal Co-operation and the Union's External Environmental Competences in the light of the PFOS Case' (2011) 36 *European Law Review* 405.

would have been under an obligation to coordinate their vote. This led to the concern that the combined votes of the EU Member States and the European Union could impede the effective functioning of the Committee of Ministers, especially in cases where it exercises supervision of judgments. The draft accession agreement introduced special voting rules regarding the situation where the Committee of Ministers exercises its supervisory function related to obligations upon the EU alone or upon the EU and one or more of its Member States jointly. A Draft Rule was to be added to the Rules of the Committee of Ministers for the supervision of the execution of judgments and of the terms of friendly settlements in cases to which the Union is a party. This rule effectively set out different voting requirements for certain decisions involving the EU. For instance, decisions by the Committee of Ministers under Rule 17 (Final Resolution) shall be adopted 'if a majority of four fifths of the representatives casting a vote and a majority of two thirds of the representatives entitled to sit on the Committee of Ministers are in favour'[100] rather than majority voting that is set out in Article 20.d of the Statute of the Council of Europe.[101] The accession agreement would have introduced a more complicated voting system, deviating from the established practice of alternate voting in most IOs. Some EU Member States, particularly France,[102] argued that these special voting rules might set a dangerous precedent for future situations where the EU seeks to take part in other international forums.[103]

4.4.4 *Candidates for Positions*

In addition to the right to vote, some international organizations' members also have the right to put forward candidates for certain positions. The EU is generally not given the right to put forward candidates in its own right, although candidates will come from EU Member States. The ITLOS Statute, for example, allows members to put forward candidates for election. The Tribunal is composed of twenty-one members, elected via secret ballot after having been nominated by a State Party.[104] The EU is therefore

---

[100]   Draft ECHR Accession Agreement (n89) Annex III.
[101]   Article 20(d) Statute of the Council of Europe: 'All other resolutions of the Committee ... require a two-thirds majority of the representatives casting a vote and of a majority of the representatives entitled to sit on the Committee'.
[102]   Council of the European Union, 'Accession of the European Union to the European Convention for the Protection of Human Rights and Fundamental Freedoms (ECHR): – State of Play' 16385/11, Brussels, 8 November 2011.
[103]   T. Lock, 'End of an Epic? The Draft Agreement on the EU's Accession to the ECHR' (2012) 31 *Yearbook of European Law* 162.
[104]   Article 2 ITLOS Statute (n86).

precluded from putting forward a candidate, and the Statute forbids two or more members of the Tribunal being nationals of the same state.[105] Similarly, in the WTO there are no members representing the EU taking part in the Dispute Settlement Body.[106] Article 8(1) of the Dispute Settlement Understanding simply provides that 'Panels shall be composed of well-qualified governmental and/or non-governmental individuals … '. The FAO Constitution states that '[a] Member Organization shall not be eligible for election or designation to any such body, nor shall it be eligible for election or designation to any body established jointly with other nations. A Member Organization shall not have the right to participate in bodies of restricted membership specified in the rules adopted by the Conference'.[107]

The first proposal for an 'EU judge' can be found in the draft ECHR Accession Agreement. Article 20 ECHR states that the number of Judges shall be equal to the number of contracting parties,[108] which implies that there should also be a judge with respect to the Union. It was decided that there should be a judge in respect of the EU, who would sit alongside the judges from the other Council of Europe Member States. Article 22 ECHR sets out that 'judges shall be elected by the Parliamentary Assembly with respect to each High Contracting Party'.[109] This means that there would be no need for a formal amendment to the Convention to allow a judge in respect of the EU. There was some discussion about whether the 'EU judge' should exercise the same rights and duties as the other judges, or whether special rules should apply in respect of this judge. For instance, the 'EU judge' might only take part in cases where the EU is a party to the proceedings, or where the case involves questions of EU law. This may have prevented the appearance of 'double representation' whereby the EU is represented via an EU Member State and an EU judge. Some argued that an 'EU judge' was necessary in order to allow EU representation and to ensure there is knowledge of EU law at the Court.[110] The problem with this argument, however, is that while that judge will be nominated by the EU, he or she would in no way 'represent' the EU in the ECHR system. Judges are to

---

[105] Article 3 ITLOS Statute (n86).
[106] See T. Cottier, 'Dispute Settlement in the World Trade Organization: Characteristics and Structural Implications for the European Union' (1998) 35 *Common Market Law Review* 325, 348.
[107] Article 2(9) FAO Constitution (n47).
[108] Article 20 ECHR.
[109] Article 22 ECHR.
[110] X. Groussot, T. Lock & L. Pech, 'EU Accession to the European Convention on Human Rights: A Legal Assessment of the Draft Accession Agreement of 14th October 2011' (2011) 218 *European Issues* 3.

be independent and sit in their personal, not national, capacity.[111] It is also clear from the Explanatory Report that the judge in respect of the EU will participate on an equal footing with the other judges.[112] The judge in respect of the EU would have been elected by the Parliamentary Assembly of the Council of Europe upon candidates being nominated by the European Parliament.

In UNGA Resolution 65/276, which gives greater the EU participation rights in the UN General Assembly, the right to put forward candidates was one of the rights explicitly excluded in respect of the EU.[113] Outside the ECHR accession context, the EU has not pushed for the right to put forward candidates.

4.5 UPGRADING THE EU'S ROLE IN INTERNATIONAL ORGANIZATIONS

One of the aims of the Lisbon Treaty was to strengthen the EU's ability to act as a unified actor on the world stage. There was an assumption that this would include greater visibility and participation within IOs and other bodies. Since Lisbon, the EU has been rather unsuccessful in seriously upgrading its status within IOs, outside the UNGA context. In 2012 European Commission President Barroso and Vice-President Ashton issued a 'Strategy for the progressive improvement of the EU status in international organisations and other fora in line with the objectives of the Treaty of Lisbon'.[114] As the title suggests, this Strategy set out some of the ways in which the Union could meet the Lisbon objectives of closer cooperation with, and greater representation at international organizations and bodies. This remains an 'objective without a strategy', and the aims of 'upgrading' legal status in IOs appear to have been replaced with greater engagement and cooperation with IOs. This can be explained partly by the external environment in which the EU finds itself, one where multilateralism is under strain and there is less willingness to allow the EU to have a formal status in IOs and multilateral forums. This does not mean, however, that the EU should no longer seek to join or upgrade its status in these institutions, but it does mean the EU must be more strategic when deciding on which bodies to focus its

---

[111] Article 21(2) ECHR: 'Judges shall sit on the Court in their individual capacity'.

[112] Draft ECHR Accession Agreement (n89) Appendix V (Explanatory Report) 77.

[113] UN General Assembly Resolution 65/276, Annex, para. 3: 'The representatives of the European Union shall not have the right to vote, to co-sponsor draft resolutions or decisions, or to put forward candidates'.

[114] Barroso-Ashton Strategy (n6).

diplomatic attention. The following sections discuss the issues related to upgrading EU status, with the examples of the EU's efforts to improve its representation in the UN General Assembly, and its relations with the International Maritime Organization.

4.5.1 *UN and UN System*

The UN and the UN system is an evident example of a body that could be targeted by the EU for greater representation rights. First, the UN tackles a number of issues that fall completely or predominantly within the competences of the Union. Many of the EU's key foreign policy goals require some kind of engagement with the UN and the UN system. These include issues such as climate change policy, eradication of global poverty, humanitarian assistance and security issues such non-proliferation. Thus, achieving an effective representation of the Union in the UN and the UN system is in the interest of the EU, and is a significant political priority. As discussed earlier, the EU Treaties also put great emphasis on the importance of the UN and the UN system for the EU. The EU already has gained observer status in many UN forums.[115] Across the wide range of UN bodies, the Union holds a variety of different legal statuses, ranging from no representation to full membership. The type of status depends not only on the competences of the EU but also on the institutional framework of the respective UN bodies, which is in turn based on political issues.

4.5.1.1 UN General Assembly

The UNGA was the main body in which the EU has upgraded its status since the Lisbon Treaty. It provides a good example of the pitfalls that occur when the EU seeks to upgrade its status in an IO.[116] The EU has had a long relationship with the UNGA, and was one of the first non-state actors to enjoy observer status at the UNGA. In 1974, the UNGA requested the UN Secretary-General 'to invite the European Economic Community to

---

[115]   Hoffmeister (n13) 41–68.
[116]   On the saga involving the EU's UNGA upgrade, see E. Brewer, 'The Participation of the European Union in the Work of the United Nations: Evolving to Reflect the New Realities of Regional Organizations' (2012) 9 *International Organizations Law Review* 181–225; J. Wouters, J. Odermatt & T. Ramopoulos, 'The Status of the European Union at the United Nations General Assembly' in I. Govaere, E. Lannon, P. Van Elsuwege & S. Adam (eds), *The European Union in the World. Essays in Honour of Marc Maresceau* (Leiden: Martinus Nijhoff Publishers, 2014) 212–213.

participate in the sessions and work of the General Assembly in the capacity of observer'.[117] Following the entry into force of the Lisbon Treaty, it was decided that the EU would seek 'enhanced observer status' at the UNGA, to align the EU's status with the Lisbon Treaty, and to provide greater visibility to the EU within the UNGA. Given the high visibility of the UNGA and the importance of the body in addressing global issues, the UNGA was seen as a good candidate for the EU to upgrade its status.[118] The UNGA is one of the primary organs of the UN, and an upgraded status within that body could have helped pave the way for further enhanced status both inside and outside the UN system.

The EU had been previously represented at the UNGA by the Member State holding the rotating Presidency. Upon the entry into force of the Lisbon Treaty, this was no longer seen as an adequate solution, especially since the EU had now put in place permanent positions for its representation in international forums, such as the President of the European Council. The EU's first diplomatic efforts suffered a serious setback in September 2010 when a first draft resolution was met with opposition by non-EU states and was not adopted.[119] It was only after increased outreach and substantive amendments that the UNGA adopted Resolution 65/276 granting the EU 'enhanced observer' status. If one compares the first resolution tabled by the Union, and the resolution that was finally adopted, it can be seen that the participation rights the EU actually achieved were substantially lower than those that had first been proposed. Of course, it is only natural in international negotiations that concessions are made and changes adopted. But it also highlights the problems the EU faces when seeking to upgrade its status in IOs. Securing an upgraded status in international organizations is neither simple nor automatic process, but one that requires a serious and sustained diplomatic effort.

The UNGA upgrade also highlights the fact that even once an enhanced status is achieved, the EU may still have to fight for its place at the table to make sure the upgrade is given full effect. The EU has still had to push to have this status accepted in practice by other UN members. Moreover, enhanced membership in one organ does not necessarily flow on to others. Since the UNGA upgrade, the EU has had little success in pushing for enhanced status

---

[117]   Status of the European Economic Community in the General Assembly, UN Doc. A/RES/3208, UNGA Res. 3208, 1974, Status of the European Economic Community in the General Assembly, 11 October 1974.
[118]   De Baere & Paasivirta (n81) 26.
[119]   See M. Emerson & J. Wouters, 'The EU's Diplomatic Debacle at the UN: What Else and What Next?', Commentary, Centre for European Policy Studies, 1 October 2010.

in other IOs or UN organs. Although UNGA Resolution 65/276 is touted as a diplomatic success, since 2011 there has been no comparable effort to replicate the EU's upgraded status in other international organizations or UN bodies. The Barroso-Ashton Strategy recommends continued efforts to ensure the full implementation of UNGA Resolution 65/276, as well as an evaluation of its possible extension to other UNGA subsidiary bodies. Until now, however, the Union has had less success in translating this to the work of other UN bodies.

The EU also faces obstacles from its own Member States when it seeks to upgrade its status in international arena. One significantly problematic issue has been the question in whose name statements are to be made at international forums. In particular, disagreement centred on the seemingly trivial issue of whether statements before the UN should be preceded by a short clause indicating if the statement was delivered 'on behalf of the EU', 'on behalf of the EU and its member states' or 'on behalf of the member states of the European Union'. In the second half of 2011, the United Kingdom blocked a number of EU statements in an attempt to safeguard its national competences in the field of shared competences.[120] This move was seen as having considerably hindered the EU's external action during this period.[121] The issue was resolved through the adoption of 'general arrangements' on EU statements in multilateral organizations by the Council on 24 October 2011.[122] These state that 'Member States agree on a case-by-case basis whether and how to coordinate and be represented externally'.[123] The Commission was critical of these arrangements[124] arguing that they risk creating confusion for third countries regarding the allocation of competences within the EU. This saga demonstrates again that the obstacles faced by the EU when taking part in IOs often stem from internal disagreements, rather than from the international legal order.

---

[120] T. Vogel, 'Split Emerges over Remit of the EU's Diplomatic Service', *European Voice*, 24 May 2011; J. Borger, 'EU Anger over British Stance on UN Statements', *The Guardian*, 20 October 2011; S. Barkowski & K. Wiatr, 'External Representation of the European Union and Shared Competences – an Unsolved Puzzle' (2012) 15 *Yearbook of Polish European Studies* 155.

[121] European External Action Service, Report by the High Representative to the European Parliament, the Council and the Commission, 22 December 2011, point 17.

[122] Council of the European Union, EU Statements in Multilateral Organizations – General Arrangements, Doc. No. 15901/11, 24 October 2011 ('General Arrangements').

[123] General Arrangements (n122).

[124] Statement by the Commission to be entered into the minutes of the Council session endorsing the General Arrangements, Council of the European Union, EU Statements in Multilateral Organizations – General Arrangements (n122).

4.5.1.2 International Maritime Organization

The IMO has been suggested as another IO where the EU may seek to become a member in the future.[125] The scope of the IMO Convention would fall under shared competences. The EU has now adopted a great deal of legislation that falls within the scope of the IMO activity, and IMO decisions have a bearing on the development of EU rules. The Union increasingly focuses on work of the organization, especially with regard to working on international environmental issues (particularly reduction in CO_2 emissions) and issues of ship safety. While the EU currently has an emissions trading system that covers other fields of transport, including airlines operating in EU Member States,[126] it has not yet implemented a system that regulates emissions from maritime transportation.[127] Despite the slow pace of discussions on maritime emissions within the IMO, the Union still views the IMO as the best international forum to regulate emissions from shipping, which currently constitute around 3 per cent of global greenhouse gas emissions. The EU also plays an active role in other areas relevant to the IMO, such as maritime pollution and maritime safety. Apart from EU legislation in these fields, in 2003 the European Maritime Safety Agency (EMSA) was established to provide specialized technical assistance. Lastly, the EU and the IMO are both becoming active in the field of maritime security and piracy,[128] a topic that is increasingly important to the Union from a security standpoint. Work undertaken by the IMO has led to amendments of the International Convention for the Safety of Life at Sea, 1974 (SOLAS Convention) and the International Ship and Port

---

[125] See C. Cinelli, 'Law of the Sea Framework: Is EU Engagement a Sine Qua Non for Influence?' in R. A. Wessel & J. Odermatt (eds), *Research Handbook on the European Union and International Organizations* (Cheltenham: Edward Elgar, 2019) 464.

[126] European Parliament and Council Directive 2008/101/EC of 19 November 2008 amending Directive 2003/87/EC so as to include aviation activities in the scheme for greenhouse gas emission allowance trading within the Community (OJ 2009, L8/3).

[127] Directive (EU) 2018/410 of the European Parliament and of the Council of 14 March 2018 amending Directive 2003/87/EC to enhance cost-effective emission reductions and low-carbon investments, and Decision (EU) 2015/1814 OJ L 76, preamble: 'The IMO has set up a process to adopt in 2018 an initial emission reduction strategy to reduce greenhouse gas emissions from international shipping. The adoption of an ambitious emission reduction objective as part of this initial strategy has become a matter of urgency and is important for ensuring that international shipping contributes its fair share to the efforts needed to achieve the objective of well below 2 °C agreed under the Paris Agreement'.

[128] See IMO, Piracy and Armed Robber against Ships, 'Guidance to shipowners and ship operators, shipmasters and crews on preventing and suppressing acts of piracy and armed robbery against ships', MSC.1/Circ.1334, 23 June 2009; European Commission, Recommendation of 11 March 2010 on measures for self-protection and the prevention of piracy and armed robbery against ships, 2010/159/EU.

Facility Security Code (ISPS Code). It is clear from this that the EU has significant legislation in the field of the IMO and an interest in the work of the IMO, and is thus an organization where enhanced status of the Union could be pursued.

The European Commission (not the Community or the Union) has been an observer at the IMO since 1974. Although the Commission recommended to the Council to pursue full membership of the then EC in both the IMO and the ICAO in 2002,[129] the Member States did not support this.[130] In the face of opposition from EU Member States that are IMO members, the Commission is now seeking instead to change the Commission's representation to that of the 'European Union' in accordance with the Lisbon Treaty. There are also significant external constraints that prevent the EU from becoming a full IMO member.[131] The IMO Convention is only open to states,[132] and EU membership would require the inclusion of an REIO clause. There is little incentive, however, to go through the process of treaty modification that would be necessary to amend the Convention, which would require the ratification of two-thirds of the IMO membership.[133] The Barroso-Ashton Strategy included the IMO as one of the organizations where the EU has a strategic and economic interest. Moreover, the IMO is viewed as one of the organizations for which an EU status upgrade appears realistic in the short or medium term. The Strategy points out, however, 'Member States fear that EU membership would erode their presence and rights in the IMO'.[134] Indeed, the Commission has proposed to the Council to negotiation EU membership in the IMO, but has not been successful,[135] and it may be more practicable to pursue first observer status for the time being.

---

[129] European Commission, Recommendation from the Commission to the Council in order to authorize the Commission to open and conduct negotiations with the International Civil Aviation Organization (ICAO) on the conditions and arrangements for accession by the European Community, SEC/2002/0381 final.

[130] De Baere argues that observed that 'external sovereignty seems to be regarded as rather more sacred than internal sovereignty: the Member States are quite happy to accept Community-imposed restrictions on their regulatory competences with regard to internal policy areas, while refusing to accept parallel restrictions for the external aspects of the same areas', G. De Baere, *Constitutional Principles of EU External Relations* (Oxford: Oxford University Press, 2008) 249–250.

[131] For further discussion on these constraints, see L. Nengye & F. Maes, 'Legal Constraints to the European Union's Accession to the International Maritime Organization' (2012) 43 *Journal of Maritime Law & Commerce* 279.

[132] Article 4, Convention on the Intergovernmental Maritime Consultative Organization (IMO Convention) (done 6 March 1948, entered into force 17 March 1958) 289 UNTS 3.

[133] Article 66 IMO Convention (n132).

[134] Barroso-Ashton Strategy (n6).

[135] Barroso-Ashton Strategy (n6).

There is a good legal case for full membership at the IMO. First, the EU's non-membership of the IMO has led to some legal difficulties within the EU legal order, some of which have given rise to litigation before the Court of Justice.[136] As discussed earlier, when the EU is not a formal member of an IO where significant Union competences are concerned, this can create a gap in legal obligations between the EU and its Member States. Given the considerable competences exercised by the EU in maritime issues, IMO membership would go a long way to filling this gap. Moreover the Union's membership in global regulatory bodies such as IMO is important for it to safeguard its own significant regulatory framework. However, the prospects for status upgrade look rather dim, as illustrated by the 2013 information note on the implementation of the Barroso-Ashton-Strategy, which states that 'little or no progress could be achieved due to a changed political context' and recommends that '[s]ervices will sustain their efforts in order to unlock the situation'.[137] The case of the IMO demonstrates some of the challenges that the EU faces when seeking to upgrade its status in IOs, especially where there is a clear legal and political rationale for its membership. A 2016 Communication on the EU and international ocean governance sets out the EU's aim 'to promote and build capacity for better ocean governance, conservation and restoration of biodiversity, and sustainable blue economies with its partners, including with international organisations'.[138] The emphasis here is on cooperation and coordination with IOs, rather than joining or upgrading the EU's status in them. Although the IMO was once viewed as an organization that the EU might join in the future, EU strategy puts more emphasis on partnerships and dialogue.

4.6 CONCLUSION

The EU's engagement with and participation in international organizations has given rise to questions under international law and the law of international

---

[136] Some key judgments relating to the IMO and its Conventions include Judgment in *Commission v. Greece*, C-45/07, EU:C:2009:81; Judgment in *Commune de Mesquer*, C-188/07, EU:C:2008:359; and Judgment in *Intertanko and Others*, C-308/06, EU:C:2008:312.

[137] Note to the College of Commissioners from President Barroso and Vice-President Ashton on the implementation of the 'Strategy for the progressive improvement of the EU status in international organisations and other fora in line with the objectives of the Treaty of Lisbon, C(2012) 9420 final', INFO(2013) 115, 3.

[138] Joint Communication of the Commission and the High Representative of the Union for Foreign Affairs and Security Policy, 'International Ocean Governance: An Agenda for the Future of Our Oceans' Join (2016) 49 final.

institutions.[139] This is sometimes presented as a clash between two types of legal orders, the EU's supranational legal order and the more state-centric system of international law in which traditional IOs operate.[140] Yet international institutions appear to allow a deal of flexibility with regard to the EU. When there is a clear rationale of Union participation, and where it is in the interests of the IO to include the EU, the organization's rules and practices can be adapted to include EU participation. The challenge for the Union has been to make a clear case for membership and participation, which is more an issue of diplomacy than of public international law. In cases where the EU has joined an IO, the issues regarding funding, voting and dispute settlement have been addressed through pragmatic solutions. Much of the existing literature on the EU and IOs has focused on the internal legal issues that arise for the Union and Member States, such as co-ordination, representation, competences and the legal effects of IO decisions within the EU legal order. At the international level, the participation of the EU in these bodies will continue to give rise to new rules and practices, thus indirectly shaping international rules.

The EU's recent engagement with international organizations has been affected by two related trends. The first has been the broader challenge faced by multilateral institutions. In this environment, the EU faces a difficult task to improve its status in IOs. The EU's ability to participate in an IO is determined less by issues such as EU competence, and more by whether third countries accept this role. The second trend has been a move towards governance in informal bodies that are not constituted as international organizations with legal personality. This includes global summits, such as the G7 and G20,[141] as well as less formal bodies such as the Financial Stability Board (FSB).[142] Amtenbrink and Repasi note that in informal bodies, 'the EU's status in informal international governance fora depends solely on whether the subjects discussed by these fora fall within the scope of [EU] competences'[143] and thus the EU's role may be more prominent in such informal bodies than in formal institutions. In contrast to the EU's participation in international agreements and within international institutions, the EU Treaties and EU law give far less guidance about how the EU institutions are to operate in informal bodies.

---

[139] Hoffmeister (n13) 67. Hoffmeister points out that '[a]gainst the backdrop of this mixed picture of factual developments, some interesting questions under international law came to the forefront'.

[140] J. Wouters & A. Chané, 'Brussels Meets Westphalia: The European Union and the United Nations' in P. Eeckhout & M. Lopez-Escudero (eds), *The European Union's External Action in Times of Crisis* (Oxford: Hart, 2015) 299–324.

[141] See Amtenbrink & Repasi (n3).

[142] Donnelly (n4).

[143] Amtenbrink & Repasi (n3) 341.

The opposition to the EU's presence in IOs is sometimes presented as either due to misunderstanding of the nature of the EU or a rather petty way to frustrate the EU's international ambitions. However, the opposition towards greater EU involvement in IOs can perhaps be better understood when one considers just how fundamental a change EU membership is for many IOs. Allowing EU membership changes the character of the IO from one where states dominate, to one where states exist beside other bodies. As discussed earlier, changes will often need to be made to accommodate the EU's presence, such as changing voting rules. This adds a layer of complexity to an organization, and can make negotiations and decision-making more complex. Third states will be more likely to accept the EU's presence when this adds something to the organization, rather than creating more complexities for its practice.[144]

Membership and participation in IOs is a way for states to maintain visibility and presence on the international stage. In some instances, the EU Member States have no problem with the European institutions being active in international forums, such as in less 'high profile' organizations, or where it is in their interests for the Union to speak with one voice. It is not only the external environment that poses a problem for the Union when seeking to upgrade its status in IOs but also the EU Member States themselves, who do not want to lose that international role. The parallel membership or participation by the EU and the Member States, will also continue to pose legal issues, both externally and internally.

---

[144]   It has been argued that 'EU participation will become attractive for third parties only if this actor can significantly contribute to the related co-operation project separately from its member states'. Gehring et al. (n12) 851.

5

International Dispute Settlement

5.1 INTRODUCTION

One of the significant changes in the landscape of international law in recent decades has been the increase in the number of international courts and other forms of international dispute settlement.[1] Not only has the number of such bodies increased, but their role and function has changed significantly, and include compulsory procedures and may allow a role for individuals (and other actors) in a realm once dominated by inter-state procedures. The European Union has contributed to this changing landscape. The Court of Justice of the European Union has been a model for other regional courts.[2] Yet the EU has also influenced the design and function of other dispute settlement bodies through its participation and interaction within those bodies. This chapter focuses on this form of influence.

The EU has pushed for the inclusion of dispute settlement chapters in its agreements, particularity in trade and investment, and has joined multilateral treaties that include dispute settlement mechanisms. Whereas the EU Treaties govern the process for negotiating and concluding agreements, they give less guidance on the way the EU and its Member States are to engage with international dispute settlement bodies. This has meant that the CJEU has played a quite active role in determining the modalities of the EU's engagement with dispute settlement bodies. A line of case law from the CJEU sets out conditions for the EU and Member States to join and participate in

---

[1] See K. J. Alter, *The New Terrain of International Law: Courts, Politics, Rights* (Princeton: Princeton University Press, 2014) Chapter 5; C. P. R. Romano, 'The Proliferation of International Judicial Bodies: The Pieces of the Puzzle' (1999) 31 *New York University Journal of International Law and Politics* 709.

[2] See K. J. Alter, 'The Global Spread of European Style International Courts' (2012) 35 *West European Politics* 135.

international dispute settlement bodies. The EU has shown a preference for resolving disputes through judicial means, which can help strengthen enforcement procedures in international law. The EU's participation in international dispute settlement has been described as an 'effective means for the EU to be an active player on the international scene in line with its own objectives, not only in terms of its role as rule-promoter but also as rule-complier and rule-enforcer'.[3] Yet this support is conditioned by the caveats that are required to preserve EU autonomy. These caveats can have far-reaching effects for the EU's treaty partners. In some cases, it will require an agreement to be amended to include certain safeguards to protect EU autonomy.

The practice of the EU and the Member States establishing international dispute settlement bodies, taking part in international dispute settlement, and the application of judgments and awards in the EU legal order, all give rise to issues under international and EU law. This chapter discusses various forms of judicial or quasi-judicial dispute settlement that exist at the international level and the participation of the EU and/or Member States. In some cases, the EU itself may join or establish a treaty that creates a dispute settlement body, and will participate more or less on an equal footing with states. In other instances, the EU itself will not be a party to an agreement establishing a dispute settlement body, but issues of EU law may still arise, for instance, when disputes involve EU Member States or where issues related to EU law arise. This chapter focuses on forms of dispute settlement where a tribunal or dispute settlement body is established by a treaty. In these cases, the court or tribunal is usually tasked with providing authoritative interpretations of the treaty and to resolving legal disputes arising between the parties. The chapter does not examine the role of the EU in the settlement of disputes more broadly, such as through diplomatic or other political procedures.[4]

Using this definition of international dispute settlement, the EU already has a quite well-developed system of dispute resolution: the CJEU. The CJEU can be considered a type of international court.[5] It is a supranational judicial

---

[3] C. Hillion & R. A. Wessel, 'The European Union and International Dispute Settlement: Principles and Conditions' in M. Cremona, A. Thies & R. A. Wessel (eds), *The European Union and International Dispute Settlement* (Oxford: Hart, 2017) 24.

[4] See F. Hoffmeister, 'The European Union and the Peaceful Settlement of International Disputes' (2012) 11(1) *Chinese Journal of International Law* 77. Hoffmeister argues that the EU has 'a quasi-constitutional mandate to strive for the peaceful settlement of international disputes in accordance with Article 33 of the UN Charter . . . '

[5] 'The Court of Justice of the European Union (CJEU) is certainly itself an international court but it is also in a real sense a "domestic" court for the EU's own legal order; in both roles it may find itself in competition with other international courts and tribunals' M. Cremona, A. Thies

institution established by the EU Treaties, tasked to provide authoritative interpretation and application of those instruments and secondary law. The CJEU is not an ordinary international court, however, and its methods of practice more closely resemble those of national court. Yet any discussion of the EU's role in international dispute settlement must involve the CJEU, since many of the legal issues in this chapter arise from the co-existence of the CJEU and 'other' international courts. This is especially the case where international dispute settlement bodies have the power to render judgments that are binding on the EU and the Member States, and can possibly jeopardize the autonomy of the EU legal order. The CJEU has held that the EU/MS may join or establish international agreements that include binding dispute settlement mechanisms, and that such agreements are in principle compatible with EU law.[6] However, the CJEU has also added a number of conditions that must be met to satisfy the requirement of respecting the EU's autonomy.[7] This chapter discusses how some of these internal issues are externalized when the EU/MS participate in international dispute settlement. In many cases, the EU law view has been more contested.

The EU has influenced international dispute settlement in two main ways. First, we find that the design of dispute settlement bodies has taken into account the requirements of EU autonomy. For instance, in *Opinion 1/17*, the CJEU found that the safeguards included in a trade agreement with Canada were sufficient to preserve EU autonomy.[8] Second, we see how arguments based on EU law have been presented before international dispute settlement bodies, often by EU Member States or the EU Commission. In recent cases, there appears to be a reluctance to accept such arguments based on the primacy of EU law.

& R. A. Wessel, 'Introduction' in M. Cremona, A. Thies & R. A. Wessel (eds), *The European Union and International Dispute Settlement* (Oxford: Hart, 2017) 1–4. But see A. Rosas, 'International Responsibility of the EU and the ECJ' in M. Evans & P. Koutrakos (eds), *The International Responsibility of the European Union* (Oxford: Hart, 2013) 159. See J. Allain, 'The European Court of Justice Is an International Court' (1999) 68 *Nordic Journal of International Law* 249.

6 *Opinion 1/17*, EU:C:2019:341, para.106. See *Opinion 1/91*, EU:C:1991:490: 'An international agreement providing for such a system of courts is in principle compatible with Community law'. para. 40.

7 See *Opinion 1/91* (EEA Agreement) EU:C:1991:490, para. 40: 'An international agreement providing for such a system of courts is in principle compatible with Community law. The Community's competence in the field of international relations and its capacity to conclude international agreements necessarily entails the power to submit to the decisions of a court which is created or designated by such an agreement as regards the interpretation and application of its provisions'.

8 *Opinion 1/17* (n6) discussed in section 2.3 on investment disputes (Section 5.3.3).

5.2 EU LAW RELATED TO INTERNATIONAL DISPUTE SETTLEMENT BODIES

International dispute settlement bodies differ substantially in terms of their institutional design and set-up. Some, such as the International Court of Justice, were active before the establishment of the EU, and do not address the role of supranational institutions. More recent dispute settlement bodies allow participation by the Union itself. At the time of the EU's creation, it was not envisaged that the EU would appear in its own right before such bodies. The EU Treaties therefore focus more on the role of the EU Member States and dispute settlement.

5.2.1 *Article 344 TFEU*

Article 344 TFEU sets out that only the CJEU may hear disputes relating to the interpretation and application of the EU Treaties:

> Member States undertake not to submit a dispute concerning the interpretation or application of the Treaties to any method of settlement other than those provided for therein.

This provision forbids EU Member States from utilizing dispute settlement mechanisms in instances where that body would interpret and apply the EU Treaties and Union law.[9] It thus preserves the CJEU's judicial monopoly over the interpretation of EU law. There is a clear rationale for this: if EU Member States were to submit disputes relating to EU law to other courts and tribunals, EU Member States may be bound by multiple, contradicting interpretations of EU law. Yet the effect of this provision depends on whether the CJEU interprets it in a narrow or expansive manner. Does this provision mean, for instance, that the Member States are prevented from bringing claims to an international tribunal on issues of EU law, or does it prevent the EU and the Member States from even taking part in cases where issues of EU law *might* be involved? Would Article 344 TFEU be violated if the dispute settlement body addresses EU law issues in a more incidental manner, such as when determining its jurisdiction or standing? What if a dispute settlement body is not called upon to interpret EU law as such, but provisions that closely resemble, or which seek to replicate, EU law? What should be understood as a 'method of settlement', especially when there is a vast array of dispute settlement

---

[9]   Judgment in *Commission v. Ireland*, C-459/03, EU:C:2006:345 ('MOX Plant').

mechanisms, both judicial and non-judicial, at the international level?[10] These questions are not clear from the text of Article 344 TFEU itself, and have been clarified through applications by the CJEU. The CJEU interprets this article in a more expansive manner.[11] For example, the Court has interpreted Article 344 TFEU to mean that the Union may not join a dispute settlement body where there is a *possibility* that a Member State might bring a dispute involving EU law. The case law shows how the CJEU interprets the provision as expressing a more general principle concerning the exclusive jurisdiction of the CJEU, and Article 344 TFEU as a means of preserving EU autonomy.

A number of these issues were addressed in the MOX *Plant* case.[12] The case arose from a dispute between the UK and Ireland regarding a nuclear facility situated on a site at Sellafield, UK, on the coast of the Irish Sea. Ireland instituted arbitral proceedings against the UK, pursuant to the dispute settlement provisions in UNCLOS.[13] The European Commission regarded Ireland's use of arbitral proceedings as a violation of EU law and brought infringement proceedings against Ireland for inter alia failing to fulfil its obligations under Article 292 TEC (now Article 344 TFEU). While the arbitral tribunal considered that it had prima facie jurisdiction, it noted that the dispute between Ireland and the UK before the CJEU would be binding under EU law, and might therefore lead to conflicting decisions. The Tribunal decided to suspend the proceedings.[14]

The Commission argued that the dispute between Ireland and the UK was essentially a dispute concerning the interpretation of EU law, and that the CJEU therefore had exclusive jurisdiction to hear the dispute. The CJEU found that Ireland, by submitting the dispute to the arbitral tribunal, had breached its obligation under Art 292 TEC. The judgment drew a certain amount of criticism, from academics in both EU law and

---

[10] See *European American Investment Bank AG (EURAM)* v. *Slovak Republic*, Award on Jurisdiction, 22 October 2012, para. 257: 'Concerning arbitration between one Member State and nationals of another Member State . . . it is the view of the Tribunal that it does not come under Article 292 of the EC Treaty (now Article 344 TFEU) and is therefore perfectly compatible with EU law'.

[11] M. Klamert, *The Principle of Loyalty in EU Law* (Oxford: Oxford University Press, 2014) 15. It has been argued that '[a]lthough Article 344 TFEU does not deal with the classic form of norm conflict, it is a conflict clause nonetheless'.

[12] *MOX Plant* (n9).

[13] Article 287, United Nations Convention on the Law of the Sea (UNCLOS) and Article 1, Annex VII, UNCLOS.

[14] See President's Statement of 13 June 2003, *Ireland* v. *United Kingdom* ('MOX Plant Case') w ww.pca-cpa.org/showpage.asp?pag_id=1148, para. 11.

international law.[15] Klabbers, for instance, argued that 'the Court's attitude is worrisome: it does aspire to build a fence around EU law, thus running the risk of placing the EU outside international law'.[16] Prost argued that the judgment 'artificially "Communitarises" whole portions of the law of the sea and asserts, in absolute terms, the autonomy and superiority of the Community system over the universal regime of the UN'.[17] It has been put forward as an example of the CJEU acting as a 'selfish court'[18] safeguarding its own role at the expense of other judicial bodies in the international legal order. Much of the criticism stemmed from the fact that the Court examined the issues solely through the lens of EU law, without acknowledging that the wider dispute concerned issues of international law and dispute settlement.[19] The judgment is also important in that the Court invoked the principle of autonomy in order to determine the relationship between EU law and the international legal order more generally. It held that an international agreement could not 'affect the allocation of responsibilities defined in the Treaties and, consequently, the autonomy of the Community legal system'.[20] Autonomy is not used here just to preserve the role of the Court, but as a way to protect the allocation of responsibilities in the EU legal order.

The CJEU went a step further in *Opinion 2/13*, finding that the very possibility of Member States bringing inter-state disputes before the European Court of Human Rights (ECHR) would violate EU autonomy. Article 33 of the ECHR allows Contracting Parties to bring inter-state disputes regarding alleged breaches of the Convention. The CJEU found that the 'very existence of such a possibility' of the EU or Member States utilizing Article 33

---

[15] 'For an international lawyer, this is a stunning case'. M. Koskenniemi, 'International Law: Constitutionalism, Managerialism and the Ethos of Legal Education' (2007) *European Journal of Legal Studies* 1.

[16] J. Klabbers, *Treaty Conflict and the European Union* (Cambridge: Cambridge University Press, 2009) 148.

[17] M. Prost, *The Concept of Unity in Public International Law* (Oxford: Hart, 2012) 42–43.

[18] B. de Witte, 'A Selfish Court? The Court of Justice and the Design of International Dispute Settlement beyond the European Union' in M. Cremona & A. Thies (eds), *The European Court of Justice and External Relations Law* (Oxford: Hart, 2014) 41: 'If two Member States occasionally bring a dispute before an international tribunal instead of bringing an infringement action under the TFEU, where the subject matter of the dispute is only partly within the scope of EU law, and where the international tribunal has specialist knowledge of the subject, does this really form a threat to the autonomy of the EU legal order?'

[19] '[T]he Court analysed matters primarily, if not solely, through the prism of Community law'. S. Boelaert-Suominen, 'The European Community, the European Court of Justice and the Law of the Sea' (2008) 23 *The International Journal of Marine and Coastal Law* 643–713.

[20] *MOX Plant* (n9) para. 123.

ECHR with respect to a dispute involving EU law would violate Article 344 TFEU.[21] The ability to bring such a dispute to the ECtHR 'goes against the very nature of EU law'.[22]

Advocate General Kokott in *Opinion 2/13* also identified the possibility of inter-state cases as a potential violation of Article 344 TFEU. However, AG Kokott pointed out that such a problem can be fully addressed via the EU's own institutional framework, especially through the use of infringement proceedings against the offending Member State, as was the case in *Mox Plant*.[23] There would be no need, however, to include any express mechanism in the agreement itself that provided a rule of inadmissibility of inter-state cases between EU Member States. Such a mechanism to preserve the CJEU's judicial monopoly does not exist in other agreements to which the EU and the Member States are party. As AG Kokott points out:

> if the aim in the present case is to lay down an express rule on the inadmissibility of inter-State cases before the ECtHR and on the precedence of Article 344 TFEU as a prerequisite for the compatibility of the proposed accession agreement with EU primary law, this would implicitly mean that numerous international agreements which the EU has signed in the past are vitiated by a defect, because no such clauses are included in them.[24]

However, in *Opinion 2/13* the Full Court found that the draft Accession Agreement would only be compatible with Article 344 TFEU if it were to contain 'the express exclusion of the ECtHR's jurisdiction under ... over disputes between Member States or between Member States and the EU in relation to the application of the ECHR within the scope *ratione materiae* of EU law'.[25] Here the CJEU is not preventing a Member State from bringing a case against another Member State, as in *Mox Plant*. Rather, it requires an international agreement be amended to accommodate the specificities of EU law. This expansive reading Article 344 TFEU goes beyond the original aims and purpose of the provision. It has the practical effect of limiting the EU's ability to take part in international dispute settlement mechanisms. It is

---

[21] *Opinion 2/13*, EU:C:2014:2454, para. 208.

[22] *Opinion 2/13*, EU:C:2014:2454, para. 212.

[23] *Opinion 2/13*, View of AG Kokott, EU:C:2014:247, para. 118: 'In my view, the possibility of conducting infringement proceedings (Articles 258 TFEU to 260 TFEU) against Member States that bring their disputes concerning EU law before international courts other than the Court of Justice of the EU, with the added possibility that interim measures may be prescribed within those proceedings if necessary (Article 279 TFEU), is sufficient to safeguard the practical effectiveness of Article 344 TFEU'.

[24] View of AG Kokott, EU:C:2014:247, para. 117.

[25] *Opinion 2/13*, EU:C:2014:2454, para. 213.

another example of an internal issue (EU autonomy) being externalized at the international level.[26] In some instances, such as bilateral agreements between the EU and a third state, the Union may be able to include such safeguards. However, in multilateral settings, such as the ECHR context, other contracting parties may be more reluctant to allow specialized rules to accommodate the EU and Member States.

5.2.2 *Autonomy of the EU Legal Order*

The principle of autonomy has been an overarching concept that has regulated how the EU engages with international dispute settlement. The principle of autonomy has been subject to quite some academic debate in recent years, particularly since *Opinion 2/13*. In that case, the CJEU found that the draft Accession Agreement that was designed to allow the EU to accede to the European Convention on Human Rights would violate the autonomy of the EU legal order. Yet it should be recalled that the principle of autonomy has a much longer history, and has been applied in many areas of EU law that are not related to dispute settlement. The principle of autonomy has become an overarching constitutional principle of EU law, one that differs from other principles, such as direct effect and primacy.[27] While much of the academic focus has been on the application of this principle to the context of international dispute settlement, especially after cases such as *Opinion 2/13* (ECHR Accession) or *Opinion 1/17* (CETA), it should be recalled that the principle of autonomy has been applied and given expression in many other contexts.

At first, the 'autonomy' of the EU legal order was established vis-à-vis the legal orders of the EU Member States. If the EU Member States could dismiss the application of EU law on the grounds that it conflicted with their domestic

---

[26] T. Locke, 'The Future of the European Union's Accession to the European Convention on Human Rights after Opinion 2/13: Is It Still Possible and Is It Still Desirable?' (2015) 11 *European Constitutional Law Review* 239, 255: 'This stance again reveals the Court of Justice's lack of trust in the EU's own legal order. The consequence of this is that the EU is becoming an even more awkward partner on the international plane. Requiring the protection of the autonomy of EU law in a watertight manner requires an externalisation of internally resolvable issues, which is new and worrying because it makes the EU a difficult partner to deal with'.

[27] J.-W. van Rossem, 'The Autonomy of EU Law: More is Less?' in R. A. Wessel & S. Blockmans (eds), *Between Autonomy and Dependence: The EU Legal Order under the Influence of International Organisations* (T. M. C. Asser Press/Springer Verlag, 2013) 13–46 13, 18: 'In any event, the bottom line of this argument is that autonomy is not exactly in the same league as, say, primacy, fundamental rights protection or judicial review, but forms the premise upon which such fundamental principles of EU law are built'. See J. Odermatt, 'The Principle of Autonomy: An Adolescent Disease of EU External Relations Law?' in M. Cremona (ed), *Structural Principles in EU External Relations Law* (Oxford: Hart, 2018) 291–316.

legal systems or national legislation, this could have the effect of undermining the EU legal order and its autonomy. In *Costa*, the Court refers to EU law as 'an independent source of law'[28] and makes a clear link between the 'new legal order' narrative and the concept of autonomy. This concept of internal autonomy – the idea that the EU is not only a new legal order, but also distinct from its Member States – was instrumental in developing the EU legal order.

As the EU developed greater external competences, and increased its interaction with external actors, questions arose regarding the EU's relationship with third states and other organizations and the effects that this might have on EU law. A new 'threat'[29] emerged: that EU law could be undermined, not only by conflicting national legislation, but also by international law. The principle of autonomy became a way to regulate this relationship. The CJEU turned to external autonomy, the idea that the integrity of EU law and the EU legal order should not be undermined by the international action of the Union or the Member States. This principle is not only related to 'conflict' between the international and EU legal orders. International law may not always recognize the separate actorness of the EU, in the sense that it may view the Union as merely a reflection of the collective will of the EU Member States, or may treat EU law as simply an international law regime, with all that means in terms of hierarchy of norms and rules of treaty conflict. Preserving external autonomy became a way to ensure that the EU was not dealt with as just another international organization.

Autonomy is not a concept that is limited to the EU legal order, but also discussed in the context of international organizations. As the International Court of Justice stated in *Legality of Nuclear Weapons*, one of the purposes of treaties establishing international organizations 'is to create new subjects of law endowed with a certain autonomy'.[30] The autonomy of international organizations is often presented as a positive development in international law, one that strengthens the effectiveness of international law.[31] The

---

[28] Judgment in *Costa* v. *E.N.E.L*, 6/64, EU:C:1964:66.

[29] M. Parish, 'International Courts and the European Legal Order' (2012) 23 *European Journal of International Law* 141, 142: 'A new threat has recently emerged to the consistent application of EU law, namely interpretation of EU law by the ever growing range of international tribunals that sit outside the domestic legal order of any particular state'.

[30] *Legality of the Use by a State of Nuclear Weapons in Armed Conflict* (Advisory Opinion) [1996] ICJ Rep 66, 75.

[31] '[I]t cannot be excluded that autonomy has been seized upon by international legal scholars as a political banner under which one could demonstrate support for the role of international institutions – seen as a necessarily positive development – as opposed to the sovereign prerogatives of states, seen as harmful to the general interest'. J. D'Aspremont, 'The Multifaceted Concept of Autonomy of International Organizations: A Challenge to International Relations Theory?' in R. Collins & N. D. White (eds), *International Organizations and the Idea of Autonomy* (London: Routledge, 2011) 77.

development of greater institutional autonomy addresses a certain defect in the international legal order, that is, the fact that state interests and geopolitics can prevent an international organization from fully exercising its functions and realizing its objectives.[32] This development of an autonomous legal order is thus often viewed as a form of institutional maturity. In an international legal order which is characterized as decentralized, state-centric and lacking enforcement mechanisms, the development of international institutions possessing a greater degree of autonomy can be viewed as a positive development. There is thus nothing particularly novel in describing the EU legal order as an autonomous one. What is more remarkable is that EU autonomy is applied in relation to third states and other actors.

The CJEU summarized its position on what the principle of autonomy requires in *Opinion 1/00*[33] on the establishment of a European Common Aviation Area. In a passage that has been recalled a number of times since, the Court states that the preservation of autonomy of the Union legal order entails two requirements:

> [. . .] first, that the essential character of the powers of the Community and its institutions as conceived in the Treaty remain unaltered. . . . Second, it requires that the procedures for ensuring uniform interpretation of the rules of the ECAA Agreement and for resolving disputes will not have the effect of binding the Community and its institutions, in the exercise of their internal powers, to a particular interpretation of the rules of Community law referred to in that agreement.[34]

The first condition relates to the preservation of the 'essential character' of the powers of the Union and its institutions. The second seeks to ensure that an outside dispute settlement body would not have the power to interpret EU law if it is to have a binding effect on the Union. This presents what was understood as a narrow understanding of autonomy. This narrow conception of autonomy is focused primarily on preserving the exclusive powers of the Court to interpret the Treaties and EU law.[35] De Witte, for instance, summarizing the Court's position in these cases, states that 'the theme of the autonomy of

---

[32] '[T]he lack of institutional autonomy in international law is seen as the fundamental stumbling block in the way of realizing an international rule of law' R. Collins & N. D. White, 'Introduction and Overview' in R. Collins & N. D. White (eds), *International Organizations and the Idea of Autonomy* (London: Routledge, 2011) 23.

[33] *Opinion 1/00*, EU:C:2002:231.

[34] *Opinion 1/00*, EU:C:2002:231, para. 12.

[35] Locke (n26) 243: 'A narrow conception of autonomy, such as this, is appropriate as it serves the legitimate purpose of protecting the integrity of the EU law while retaining the EU's capacity as an external actor'.

the Community legal order is mentioned recurrently, and relates essentially to the preservation of the Court's own exclusive power to interpret Community law'.[36] Yet the principle of autonomy is not only developed for the sake of the CJEU; recent case law also shows that it is to preserve the 'essential character' of the EU legal order.[37] What constitutes the 'essential characteristics' remains an open and debated question. It also shows a move towards what has been described as a 'nebulous'[38] understanding of autonomy, in which it can be difficult to predict what is required in order to safeguard the 'essential characteristics' of the EU and its legal order.

5.2.3 *Opinion 2/13*

In *Opinion 2/13*, the CJEU ruled that the agreement designed to allow the EU to become a contracting party to the European Convention on Human Rights was 'liable adversely to affect the specific characteristics of EU law and its autonomy'.[39] The Opinion led to some quite strong criticism from academics.[40] The Opinion is relevant here because it is an example of how the CJEU found that the institutional innovations – requested by the Union and Member States – that were added to the draft Accession Agreement were still found to violate EU autonomy. The first of these institutional innovations was the 'co-respondent mechanism'. This was a procedure that would have

---

[36] B. de Witte, 'European Union Law: How Autonomous is its Legal Order?' (2010) 65 *Zeitschrift für öffentliches Recht* 141, 150.

[37] C. Contartese argues, 'it would be reductive to narrow down the case law on autonomy to a sort of fortress behind which the ECJ defends itself from all other international jurisdictions'. ' The Autonomy of the EU Legal Order in the ECJ's External Relations Case Law: From the "Essential" to the "Specific Characteristics" of the Union and Back' (2017) 54 *Common Market Law Review* 1627, 1669.

[38] Contartese (n37) 'Notwithstanding the abundant literature, the meaning of the term autonomy still appears 'nebulous'', 1627; P. Koutrakos, 'The Autonomy of EU Law and International Investment Arbitration' (2019) 88 *Nordic Journal of International Law* 1, 49 'its scope has been somewhat nebulous, its limits ill-defined and its function intrinsically linked to furthering the powers of the Court of Justice'.

[39] *Opinion 2/13*, EU:C:2014:2454.

[40] Some examples of early reactions to the Opinion include: S. Peers, 'The CJEU and the EU's accession to the ECHR: a clear and present danger to human rights protection', 18 December 2014, EU Law Analysis, http://eulawanalysis.blogspot.co.uk/2014/12/the-cjeu-and-eus-accession-to-echr.html; W. Michl, 'Thou shalt have no other courts before me', Verfassungsblog, 23 December 2014, www.verfassungsblog.de/en/thou-shalt-no-courts/; A. Buyse, 'CJEU Rules: Draft Agreement on EU Accession to ECHR Incompatible with EU Law', ECHR Blog, 20 December 2014, http://echrblog.blogspot.co.uk/2014/12/cjeu-rules-draft-agreement-on-eu.html. See J. Odermatt, 'A Giant Step Backwards? Opinion 2/13 on the EU's Accession to the European Convention on Human Rights' (2015) 47 *New York University Journal of International Law & Politics* 783.

been introduced to the ECtHR system allow the EU and a Member State to be included as 'co-respondents' in certain circumstances. This procedure is discussed in more detail in relation to the issue of international responsibility in Chapter 5. The CJEU found that this procedure would still require the ECtHR to assess rules of EU law concerning the division of powers between the EU and the Member States, and thus to make an assessment of EU law and 'risk adversely affecting the division of powers between the EU and its member states'.[41]

The second institutional innovation in the draft Accession Agreement was the 'prior involvement mechanism', a procedure that would allow the CJEU to carry out internal review before a case is heard in Strasbourg. This procedure was included to take into account the concerns of the Presidents of the two Courts in their Joint Communication.[42] Presidents Costa and Skouris specifically demanded that a procedure be put in place that would allow the CJEU to undertake internal review before a case goes to the ECtHR. Under this procedure, the ECtHR would be called upon to decide whether the CJEU has already ruled previously on the same question of law. Merely by granting the ECtHR the power to assess this question, the CJEU found, the ECtHR would be called upon to interpret the EU Treaties and the case law of the CJEU.

Opinion 2/13 demonstrates how certain innovations included in international dispute settlement may still not be sufficient to satisfy the requirements of the CJEU. It also highlights how one should be cautious about applying the principle of autonomy with a 'checklist approach'. According to this approach, an envisaged agreement must include 'sufficient safeguards'[43] to meet the CJEU's growing list of conditions. Hillion and Wessel, for example, provide a 'list of requirements' for the EU to participate in international dispute settlement, developed by examining past cases.[44] The checklist approach seems to overlook the fact that the 'essential requirements' of the EU legal order, while including a certain core, will depend on the specific circumstances and the design of the dispute settlement system. It is for this reason that the CJEU's jurisprudence has been criticized for being inconsistent, even contradictory.

---

[41] *Opinion 2/13*, EU:C:2014:2454, para. 231.
[42] Joint Communication from Presidents Costa and Skouris, CCBE (24 January 2011), www .ccbe.eu/fileadmin/user_upload/document/Roundtable_2011_Luxembourg/Joint_communic ation_from_Presidents_Costa_and_Skouris_EN.pdf.
[43] A. Rosas, 'The EU and International Dispute Settlement' (2016) 1 *Europe and the World: A Law Review* 1, 12.
[44] Hillion & Wessel (n3) 29–30.

Yet it is now clear that the CJEU does not apply such a checklist, but analyses whether the 'essential requirements' of the EU legal order would be jeopardized in respect of the particular agreement and set of circumstances. This reflects the fact that autonomy is a foundational constitutional *principle*, which is given expression and legal effect in different legal contexts. This means that dispute settlement in the context of investment-related disputes in a bilateral agreement (such as CETA discussed later) has different implications, and therefore different requirements, to that of joining a human rights treaty with a standing court (such as the ECtHR). One problem with this approach, however, is that it will not be clear to the EU's treaty partners – or to the Union negotiators – what the principle of autonomy requires in any given set of circumstances. It also means that the CJEU is open to the criticism that it applies the principle of autonomy to block agreements that it does not like.

The Court's focus is almost entirely on the negative dimension of autonomy, that is, ensuring that the EU legal order is insulated from external threats. Yet there is also a positive dimension of autonomy, which involves the EU's ability to act effectively and as a distinct actor on the international stage. The focus on the negative dimension has an effect on the EU's ability to act and engage other acts on the international stage. It does not present the EU as a mature legal entity, but as somewhat fragile – the international legal order must be adapted in order to preserve the integrity of the EU legal order.

Participation in international dispute settlement by the EU is also a way to ensure that the Union observes its own international obligations. External compliance and monitoring mechanisms are now a key feature of international human rights protection.[45] This would be especially important in the ECHR context, since there is currently no external mechanism to monitor the EU's compliance with human rights norms. The co-existence of different international and regional courts is now part of the international law landscape; it would be better to find ways for the CJEU to co-exist with other international courts. The EU legal order possesses the internal rules and procedures to address these concerns, without having to provide a thorough ex ante review of every agreement including dispute settlement provisions. Parish summarizes the position of the international law perspective:

> The Court of Justice should learn to be more relaxed about other international tribunals adjudicating on EU law. International courts are a growth industry, and it is inevitable that investment treaty law, international trade law, and a host of other areas of international law that

---

[45] See T. Ahmed, 'The Opposition of the CJEU to the ECHR as a Mechanism of International Human Rights Law' (2017) 4 *Journal of International and Comparative Law* 331.

international courts have mandates to apply overlap with the ever-expanding ambit of EU law.[46]

The issue, then, is not whether autonomy should be preserved, but what is the best way to do it. Rather than place trust in the EU's internal legal order, the approach of the CJEU has been to require the external order to adapt to the EU.

5.3 THE EU IN INTERNATIONAL DISPUTE SETTLEMENT BODIES

The 'internal' legal issues, such as the principle of autonomy, give rise to external legal issues when the EU seeks to design, establish and participate in international dispute settlement bodies. This section examines some examples of instances where the EU or Member States have been involved in international dispute settlement where EU law issues have arisen. The first, and most obvious, instance is when the EU appears and participates in disputes before international bodies. This can be as a party bringing proceedings (alone or together with one or more Member States), as a respondent or as third party (intervening party, amicus curiae). The second, and less apparent, instance is when EU Member States participate in dispute settlement bodies without the EU, but where issues related to the Union or Union law arise. This issue has become more prominent in the case of investment disputes involving EU Member States, usually under a bilateral investment treaty, where issues of EU law may arise.

5.3.1 *International Court of Justice*

The International Court of Justice (ICJ) is the principal judicial organ of the United Nations, and plays a significant role in resolving international legal disputes and the progressive development of international law. The EU cannot appear as a litigant before the ICJ, as the ICJ statute sets out that 'only states may be parties in cases before the Court'.[47] European states once appeared much more often on the ICJ's docket, and some of the ICJ's landmark judgments involved disputes between European states.[48] Today, there are fewer disputes between EU states, and their Union membership has arguably contributed to

---

[46]   Parish (n29) 141

[47]   Article 34(1) ICJ Statute.

[48]   E.g. *Case concerning the Barcelona Traction, Light and Power Co Ltd* (*Belgium* v. *Spain*) Second Phase (Judgment) (ICJ Reports 1970) 3; *Monetary Gold Removed from Rome in 1943* (*Italy* v. *France, United Kingdom of Great Britain and Northern Ireland and United States of America*) (Judgment) (ICJ Reports 1954) 19; *North Sea Continental Shelf* (*Federal Republic of Germany* v. *Denmark and Federal Republic of Germany* v. *Netherlands*) Merits (Judgment) (ICJ Reports 1969) 4.

this. As EU Member States are prohibited from bringing disputes involving EU law before an international court they may only bring cases to The Hague where there is no EU law dimension. For instance, in the dispute between Italy and Germany in *Jurisdictional Immunities*, Germany made a declaration stating that the dispute did not involve an EU law dimension.[49] When Belgium instituted proceedings against Switzerland in *Jurisdiction and Enforcement of Judgments in Civil and Commercial Matters*, Belgium declared that the European Court of Justice 'is without jurisdiction in the area'.[50] Although Belgium discontinued proceedings in this case, Hoffmeister argues that any judgment delivered by the ICJ 'would have dealt with a matter which had become a matter of Union law under the revised 2007 Lugano Convention' since the CJEU had found that it is exclusively competent in the field covered by the Lugano Convention.[51]

There is a possibility that the EU could appear before the ICJ in some circumstances. First, Article 43(2) of the ICJ's Rules of Court, allows a 'public international organization' to furnish the Court with information in contentious cases that involve a construction of a treaty to which the organization is party.[52] Similarly, Article 66(2) of the Rules of the Court could allow the Union to provide information in the context of advisory proceedings. The Union has not made use of this possibility.

Were an EU Member State to institute proceedings before the ICJ against another Member State in a dispute relating to EU law, the European Commission would almost certainly bring infringement proceedings against that Member State.[53] However, as the *Mox Plant* case demonstrates, it is not

---

49   ICJ Press Release 2008/44 of 23 December 2008, 2. Germany asserts that, although the present case is between two Member States of the European Union, the Court of Justice of the European Communities in Luxembourg has no jurisdiction to entertain it, since the dispute is not governed by any of the jurisdictional clauses in the treaties on European integration. It adds that outside of that 'specific framework' the Member States 'continue to live with one another under the regime of general international law'.)

50   ICJ Press Release 2009/36 of 22 December 2009, 2.

51   Hoffmeister (n4) 85.

52   Article 43(2) ICJ Rules of Court: 'Whenever the construction of a convention to which a public international organization is a party may be in question in a case before the Court, the Court shall consider whether the Registrar shall so notify the public international organization concerned. Every public international organization notified by the Registrar may submit its observations on the particular provisions of the convention the construction of which is in question in the case'.

53   See F. G. Jacobs, 'Member States or the European Union before the International Court of Justice' in I. Govaere, E. Lannon, P. Van Elsuwege & S. Adam (eds), *The European Union in the World: Essays in Honour of Marc Maresceau* (Leiden: Martinus Nijhoff, 2013) 245. Jacobs adds that in these instances, there would not only a breach of EU law, 'but also of international law, inasmuch as the TFEU, as a Treaty concluded between the European Union's 27 Member States, is an instrument of public international law', 255.

always clear whether a dispute concerns 'the interpretation or application of the Treaties'. The CJEU's broad reading of Article 344 TFEU would prevent EU Member States from utilizing the ICJ even if the dispute only incidentally touched upon issues of EU law, or where there was a possibility that the ICJ would interpret EU law. Such a broad reading, however, is not required to preserve the autonomy of the EU legal order, and would have the disadvantage of preventing EU Member States (who are also parties to the ICJ Statute) from making use of the world court.

The CJEU recognizes the importance of the ICJ and has on many occasions cited judgments when dealing with issues of public international law.[54] The CJEU does consider the ICJ as a hierarchically superior court, however, but as occupying separate legal spheres. The CJEU mostly uses ICJ judgments approvingly when dealing with issues of customary international law. The reverse is not the case, however. The ICJ has not discussed CJEU judgments or EU law in a substantive manner.

5.3.2 WTO

The EU is a founding member of the World Trade Organization (WTO), and is also active in that organization's dispute settlement body. Rosas describes the WTO's dispute settlement mechanism as 'by far the most important system of compulsory binding third-party settlement in which the EU participates'.[55] In the WTO context, it is the EU that has taken the lead in dispute settlement, including complaints against EU Member States. At the WTO, the EU is treated close to that of a 'state-like entity'[56], and EU law as domestic law. The EU's participation in the WTO dispute settlement is discussed in more detail in Chapter 6, in relation to international responsibility.

The EU's involvement in WTO dispute settlement has given rise to legal issues within the EU legal order, regarding issues such as the competence to take part in the agreement,[57] and the effect of recommendations or rulings of

---

[54] See, J. Odermatt, 'The International Court of Justice and the Court of Justice of the European Union: Between Fragmentation and Universality of International Law' in A. Skordas (ed), *Research Handbook on the International Court of Justice* (Cheltenham: Edward Elgar, 2021).

[55] Rosas (1143) 3.

[56] C. Binder and J. A. Hofbauer, 'The Perception of the EU Legal Order in International Law: An In and Outside View' (2017) *European Yearbook of International Economic Law* 139, 167.

[57] In *Opinion 1/94*, EU:C:1994:384, the Court was asked whether the European Community was exclusively competent to conclude the 1994 WTO Agreement. See J. Bourgeois, 'The EC in the WTO and Advisory Opinion 1/94: An Echternach Procession' (1995) 32 *Common Market Law Review* 763.

the Dispute Settlement Body (DSB).[58] However, unlike in other dispute settlement systems, these 'internal' legal issues have, for the most part, not caused problems in the 'external' environment. The WTO DSB is not called upon, for example, to deal with issues regarding the balance of competences in the EU legal order.[59]

The WTO DSB is an example of a dispute settlement mechanism that involves both the EU and the EU Member States. The WTO website shows that the EU has been a complainant in 104 cases, respondent in 84 cases, and a third party in 208 cases.[60] Even in instances where an EU Member State is addressed as a respondent, the EU will be involved in proceedings. This can be explained by the fact that the WTO DSB is concerned with trade disputes, and thus a field of exclusive EU competence. The WTO stands out as one of the few instances where the EU has acted as a 'full participant' in a dispute settlement mechanism in its own right.

The EU's involvement in the WTO DSB never gave rise to serious questions regarding EU autonomy. As with the ECHR system, the WTO DSB would allow a dispute between two EU Member States in their capacity as WTO members. Whereas the 'very possibility' of an EU Member State using such a procedure was found to violate Article 344 TFEU in the context of the ECHR accession,[61] there is no similar autonomy issue in the WTO context. One reason for this may be that such a possibility can be remedied through the EU's internal mechanisms.[62] In her View in *Opinion 2/13*, AG Kokott appears to allude to agreements such as the WTO agreement, which do not explicitly forbid inter-state applications by EU Member States: 'this would implicitly mean that numerous international agreements which the EU has signed in the past are vitiated by a defect, because no such clauses are included in them'.[63] In reality, it is highly unlikely that an EU Member State would institute proceedings before another Member State at the WTO, and such a step

---

[58]   See in general G. de Búrca & J. Scott (eds), *The EU and the WTO: Legal and Constitutional Issues* (Oxford: Hart, 2001); P. J. Kuijper & F. Hoffmeister, 'WTO Influence on EU Law: Too Close for Comfort?' in R. A. Wessel & S. Blockmans (eds) (n27) 131–58. A. Rosas, 'Implementation and Enforcement of WTO Dispute Settlement Findings: An EU Perspective' (2001) 4 *Journal of International Economic Law* 129.

[59]   Binder & Hofbauer (n56) describe the WTO DSB as one of the 'few instances where the EU is viewed as an entity with *sui generis* characteristics', 170.

[60]   World Trade Organization, 'Disputes by Member', www.wto.org/english/tratop_e/dispu_e/d ispu_by_country_e.htm.

[61]   *Opinion 2/13*, para. 208.

[62]   See View of AG Kokott, EU:C:2014:247, para. 118.

[63]   View of AG Kokott, EU:C:2014:247, para. 117.

would give rise to infringement proceedings against that Member State. In 2014, Denmark requested consultations with the European Union relating to a dispute over Atlanto-Scandian herring and Northeast Atlantic mackerel; however this was initiated on behalf of the Faroe Islands, which is not part of the EU and not a WTO member in its own right.[64]

The WTO dispute settlement system stands out in a number of respects. It is based on an agreement to which the EU is a party in its own right; it deals with an area of exclusive competence; and the 'actorness' of the EU has been accepted by non-EU states.

5.3.3 Investment Disputes

Issues of EU law, and questions relating to the nature of the EU, have also arisen in the context of investor-state dispute settlement (ISDS). ISDS mechanisms are found in numerous bilateral international agreements (BITs) concluded by the EU Member States. The EU has also included dispute settlement mechanisms in its new generation trade agreements, and the EU is a party to the Energy Charter Treaty. Since 2009, the Union has exclusive competence in the field of direct foreign investment, but not in the field of non-direct foreign investment ('portfolio' investments).[65] Arbitral tribunals established by these agreements exist on the plane of international law; they are not part of the legal order of the EU or the domestic system of EU Member States. This has led to questions about how they co-exist with the EU legal order and the CJEU.

The ISDS system itself has come under fire in recent years, with critics raising concerns regarding its impact on state sovereignty, as well as transparency and legitimacy issues.[66] The EU has been a strong proponent of establishing a Multilateral Investment Court (MIC) system that would replace ad hoc arbitration with a permanent investment court. It is important to take into account the political environment in which these cases arise. While the disputes appear to be rather technical in nature, they also show us something about the approaches of the CJEU and investment tribunals. The CJEU has

---

[64] Request for the Establishment of a Panel by Denmark in Respect of the Faroe Islands, European Union – Measures on Atlanto-Scandian Herring, 10 January 2014, WT/DS469/2.

[65] TFEU (Article 207) according to Article 3(1) TFEU, the Union has exclusive competence. See Opinion 2/15, 16 May 2017, EU:C:2017:376, para. 238: 'It follows that the European Union does not have exclusive competence to conclude an international agreement with the Republic of Singapore in so far as it relates to the protection of non-direct foreign investments'.

[66] See S. D. Franck, 'The Legitimacy Crisis in Investment Treaty Arbitration: Privatizing Public International Law through Inconsistent Decisions' (2005) 73 *Fordham Law Review* 1521.

shown no interest in finding ways to preserve the co-existence of investment tribunals and the CJEU. Similarly, investment tribunals have been reluctant to accept arguments based on the primacy of EU law. This section will not provide a comprehensive overview on the ever-expanding jurisprudence from the CJEU and from various arbitral tribunals, where these issues have arisen.[67]

5.3.3.1 EU Member State BITS: *Achmea*

A question that arose in relation to investment disputes was the existence of bilateral investment treaties concluded by the EU Member States. This includes both between EU Member States ('intra-EU BITS') and between an EU Member State and a non-EU country ('extra-EU BITS'). Intra-EU BITs were concluded by states before they became members of the European Union. After joining the EU, these agreements remained in force, and were not explicitly terminated upon accession (Section 3.4.3). The Commission developed a novel argument that these agreements had been 'terminated' through EU accession; however, that argument has not been accepted by arbitral tribunals. As discussed in Chapter 3, the automatic termination argument has been rejected by arbitral tribunals.[68] In 2020, the EU Member States agreed upon a plurilateral treaty for the termination of intra-EU BITs.[69] This agreement implements the CJEU's finding in *Achmea*, in which the Court found that arbitration clauses 'such as' the one in the BIT between the Netherlands and the Slovak Republic were incompatible with EU law.[70]

5.3.3.2 Dispute Settlement in EU Agreements – *Opinion 1/17*

In *Opinion 1/17*,[71] the CJEU examined whether the investor-State dispute settlement system established by the Comprehensive Economic Agreement

---

[67] See, e.g., A. Dimopoulos, *EU Foreign Investment Law* (Oxford: Oxford University Press, 2011); J. A. Bischoff, 'Just a Little BIT of "Mixity"? The EU's Role in the Field of International Investment Protection Law' (2011) 48 *Common Market Law Review* 1527; S. Gáspár-Szilágyi & M. Usynin, 'The Uneasy Relationship between Intra-EU Investment Tribunals and the Court of Justice's Achmea Judgment' (2019) 4 *European Investment Law and Arbitration Review* 29, 35.

[68] See Section 3.4.3 on prior treaties of EU Member States.

[69] Agreement for the termination of bilateral investment treaties between the EU Member States, 5 May 2020, https://ec.europa.eu/info/publication/200505-bilateral-investment-treaties-agreement_en.

[70] Judgment in *Slovak Republic* v. *Achmea BV*, Case C-284/16, EU:C:2018:158, para. 60: 'Articles 267 and 344 TFEU must be interpreted as precluding a provision in an international agreement concluded between Member States, such as Article 8 of the BIT'.

[71] *Opinion 1/17*, EU:C:2019:341.

between Canada and the EU (CETA)[72] was compatible with EU law. In the light of its previous case law, especially the *Achmea* judgment regarding intra-EU BITs, there was some speculation as to whether the CJEU would find the dispute settlement chapters in CETA to be incompatible with EU law.[73] Concerns regarding the merits of CETA were also raised by Belgian regional parliaments, and Belgium requested an Opinion pursuant to Article 218(11) TFEU.

The CJEU found that such a system was in principle compatible with EU law. The essential question was whether a tribunal established under the agreement would have the power to interpret and apply provisions of EU law. In contrast to the situation in *Achmea*,[74] where the agreement applied between EU Member States (intra-EU BIT), CETA established a dispute settlement system that would apply between the EU and a third state. The Court emphasized that the principle of autonomy requires the examination of two issues: The first was whether the CETA tribunal would have the power to interpret or apply EU rules. The second was whether the tribunal had the power to issue awards that would prevent the EU institutions from operating in accordance with the EU constitutional framework.

As in other autonomy cases, the CJEU first looked at whether the agreement (CETA) would affect the exclusive jurisdiction of the CJEU to give the definitive interpretation of EU law. The fact that the CETA Tribunal would stand outside the EU judicial system did not mean necessarily that EU autonomy would be affected.[75] This is because jurisdiction of the CETA Tribunal is confined to the interpretation and application of the relevant CETA provisions, in accordance with the principles and rules of international law applicable between the parties.[76] CETA expressly states that its bodies do not have jurisdiction 'to determine the legality of a measure, alleged to constitute a breach of this Agreement, under the domestic law of a Party'.[77] These provisions are designed to ensure that the Tribunal would not have the power to interpret or apply EU law.[78] The CJEU also examined certain other 'autonomy safeguards'. For instance, in determining whether a measure

---

[72] Comprehensive Economic and Trade Agreement (CETA) between Canada, of the one part, and the European Union and its Member States, of the other part, OJ [2017] L 11/23.

[73] Rosas (n43) 20 'It remains to be seen whether these safeguards are sufficient'.

[74] *Achmea* (n70).

[75] *Opinion 1/17* (n71).

[76] *Id.*, para. 122.

[77] Article 8.31.2 CETA (n72).

[78] *Opinion 1/17* (n71) paras 122, 133.

violates the agreement, the tribunal may only consider domestic law as a 'matter of fact' following the prevailing interpretation given by domestic courts. Domestic courts are not bound by the meaning given to their domestic law by the tribunal.[79] The CJEU held that this would prevent a situation whereby the tribunal would be interpreting EU law.

On the second issue, the Court examined the effect of awards issued by the CETA Tribunal, and whether they would prevent the EU institutions from operating in accordance with the EU constitutional framework. The Court examined whether the CETA Tribunal would have an adverse impact on the Union's right to define the level of protection of public interests under EU law – especially in the context of examining a defence put forward by the Union in response to a breach of the substantive protections under CETA.[80] The Court conceded that the principle of autonomy precluded the conclusion of an agreement:

> found capable of having the consequence that the Union – or a Member State in the course of implementing EU law – has to amend or withdraw legislation because of an assessment made by a tribunal standing outside the EU judicial system of the level of protection of a public interest established, in accordance with the EU constitutional framework, by the EU institutions.[81]

The Court was satisfied that CETA provides sufficient safeguards in this respect. It contains various clauses expressly confirming that the CETA tribunal does not have jurisdiction to declare incompatible with CETA the level of protection of a public interest established under EU law as well as guaranteeing the right to regulate in the public interest.[82]

Opinion 1/17 is not a groundbreaking judgment, and the CJEU applies its previous case law emphasizing that EU law 'stems from an independent source of law'.[83] The Opinion does show how the CJEU's application of the principle of autonomy is highly context specific. Whether a certain dispute settlement system undermines EU autonomy will depend on the type of relationship that will be established, and whether it may jeopardize the 'essential characteristics' of the EU legal order. The drafters went to great lengths to address this by including design elements to safeguard EU autonomy. Moreover, that EU law would be treated as a matter of fact, means that

---

[79]   *Id.*, paras 130–131.
[80]   *Id.*, paras 137, 149, 150.
[81]   *Id.*, para. 150.
[82]   *Id.*, paras 130–131.
[83]   *Id.*, para. 109.

the exclusive prerogative of the CJEU to provide binding interpretations of EU law is not threatened.[84]

Although they would not be binding on the Member States, the CETA Tribunal may still make incidental interpretations of EU law. Even if the CETA Tribunal is bound to follow the CJEU's interpretation of EU law, such an interpretation may simply not yet exist since investors can bring claims on the basis of recently enacted legislation which may have not yet been interpreted by domestic courts.[85] The possibility of the Tribunals interpreting EU law has not been removed entirely. Contrast this with *Opinion 2/13* and in *Achmea* where even hypothetical interference with the EU legal order gave rise to autonomy issues.

Furthermore, the fact that the CETA tribunal, in contrast to the one in *Achmea*, can only take into account EU law as a matter of fact means that the exclusive prerogative of the CJEU to provide binding interpretations of EU law is not threatened, thereby minimizing concerns regarding the potential impact of the agreement on the principle of autonomy.

The fact that CETA is an agreement between the EU (and its Member States) and Canada means that the concerns raised in relation to intra-EU BITs are not applicable. As the Court noted in its judgment, the principle of mutual trust is not applicable in the relationship between the EU and Canada, and thus, CETA cannot adversely affect the principle in question.[86] Furthermore, the fact that the CETA tribunal, in contrast to the one in *Achmea*, can only take into account EU law as a matter of fact means that the exclusive prerogative of the CJEU to provide binding interpretations of EU law is not threatened, thereby minimizing concerns regarding the potential impact of the agreement on the principle of autonomy.[87] *Opinion 1/17* reflects the idea that autonomy is a mechanism for ensuring that the EU and its institutions are not bound by a particular interpretation of EU law stemming from a body that stands outside the EU judicial system. It is not merely a mechanism for ensuring the judicial monopoly of the CJEU. The political context of the judgment should again be emphasized. A finding that CETA was incompatible with EU autonomy would have been severe blow to the EU's efforts to modernize and promote a system of investment protection.

---

[84]　*Id.*, para. 131.
[85]　M. Gatti, 'Opinion 1/17 in Light of Achmea: Chronicle of an Opinion Foretold?' (2019) 4 *European Papers* 1, 9–10.
[86]　*Opinion 1/17*, paras 128–129.
[87]　*Opinion 1/17*, para. 131.

5.3.3.3 EU Law Arguments before Investment Tribunals

Arbitral tribunals have on occasion been called upon to address arguments related to EU law and the nature of the EU legal order. Such arguments may be put forward by the parties themselves, or by the European Commission acting as intervening party or *amicus curiae*. Essentially, 'EU law' arguments present the EU as a distinctive legal order, which should be taken into account by the tribunal. The reaction to such arguments has been mixed. Existing on the plane of international law, and tasked with resolving disputes arising in the context of an investment treaty, arbitral tribunals appear reluctant to accept the arguments put forward, especially where they would lead to lack of jurisdiction for the tribunal. Moreover, there is a fine line between the EU Commission presenting the current state of EU law in a neutral manner, and pushing forward a certain interpretation of EU law. EU law arguments go further than presenting the EU legal order as a unique legal order, but also rest on the primacy of that legal order.

5.3.3.4 Challenges to Jurisdiction: Intra EU

The European Commission argued that EU law precludes investor-state arbitration between EU Member States, stating that it is 'contrary to Articles 267 and 344 of the TFEU and the fundamental principles of autonomy' as well as the decision in *Achmea*.[88] Arguments related to intra-EU disputes have arisen in the context of the Energy Charter Treaty, in cases such as *Foresight v. Spain*.[89] The Tribunal interprets Article 26 of the Energy Charter Treaty, which sets out the jurisdiction of the tribunals, in accordance with its 'ordinary meaning', and according to treaty interpretation in Article 31 VCLT. The Tribunal here is tasked to determine its jurisdiction in accordance with the requirements of the ECT, and not Union law. The intra-EU law argument was also rejected in *Eiser* v. *Spain*:

---

[88] The Commission argues: 'EU law precludes investor-State arbitration for intra-EU disputes. Such arbitration is contrary to Articles 267 and 344 of the TFEU and the fundamental principles of autonomy, full effectiveness, and mutual trust, which constitute the cornerstones of the EU legal order, as the Court of Justice confirmed in the judgment in *Slovak Republic v. Achmea B. V. . . .* ', *Foresight Luxembourg Solar 1 S.A.R.L.* v. *Kingdom of* Spain, Case 1:19-cv-03171-ER, Brief of the European Commission on Behalf of the European Union as Amicus Curiae, 5 March 2019, at 2.

[89] 'The Tribunal is not persuaded by the Respondent's submissions on the "primacy" of EU law. [...] The Tribunal must determine its jurisdiction exclusively in accordance with the jurisdictional requirements of the ECT'. *Foresight Luxembourg Solar 1 S.A.R.L., et al.* v. *Kingdom of Spain*, SCC Case No. 2015/150, Final Award, 14 November 2018, para. 218.

The Tribunal's jurisdiction is derived from the express terms of the ECT, a binding treaty under international law. The Tribunal is not an institution of the European legal order, and it is not subject to the requirements of this legal order.[90]

Unlike some other agreements concluded by the Union, the ECT does not include a 'disconnection clause' that prevents the application of the treaty in the relations between EU members.[91] The starting point for the Tribunal is the ECT and international law on treaty interpretation.[92] The starting point of the EU and the Commission is the primacy of EU law.

EU law arguments have also arisen in the context of determining the applicable law to be applied by the Tribunal. The applicable law is determined by the treaty itself, and often includes, in addition to that treaty, public international law and the law of the disputing state. Where does EU law fit? Should it be considered as part of the domestic law of the state, as part of public international law, or something else? There does not appear to be a consistent answer to this question. For example, Article 26(6) ECT sets out that disputes are to be decided by reference to the treaty and 'applicable rules and principles of international law'. The question of whether this includes EU law was addressed in *Greentech* v. *Italy*:

> In the context of the arbitral jurisdiction created by the ECT, reference to "international law" cannot be stretched to include EU law, absent doing violence to the text which would be impermissible under the Vienna Convention on the Law of Treaties ... The Tribunal has not been called upon to apply EU law, since Claimants asserted breaches of the ECT and international law, but not of EU law.[93]

Another response has been to refer to the 'dual nature' of EU law, existing as both a part of domestic and international law. In *Electrabel*, the Tribunal stated that EU law has a 'multiple nature' and it 'is a sui generis legal order, presenting different facets depending on the perspective from where it is analysed'.[94] In the

---

90   *Eiser Infrastructure Limited and Energía Solar Luxembourg S.A.R.L.* v. *Kingdom of Spain*, ICSID Case No. ARB/13/36, Final Award, para. 199.

91   On disconnection clauses, see Section 3.3.3.

92   *PL Holdings S.A.R.L.* v. *Republic of Poland*, SCC Case No. V 2014/163, Partial Award, 28 June 2017, para. 300; 'An easy answer to the challenge would be that this Tribunal determines its jurisdiction solely on the basis of the instrument that purports to found its jurisdiction and not on the norms of an entirely different legal order'.

93   *Greentech Energy Systems A/S, et al* v. *Italian Republic*, SCC Case No. V 2015/095, Final Award, 23 December 2018, para. 397.

94   *Electrabel SA* v. *The Republic of Hungary* (ICSID Case No. ARB/07/19), Decision on Jurisdiction, Applicable Law and Liability (2012), 4.117. See the discussion on the multiple nature of EU law in Chapter 1.

context of that dispute, the Tribunal found EU law to be part of international law, partially due to the fact that it is based on international treaties.[95] In other instances, EU law has been treated as domestic law.[96]

Another EU law argument relates to the potential unenforceability of awards, based on the fact that they contradict with EU law. For example, the Commission has argued that some awards constitute illegal state aid under EU law. The argument has also been put forward in respect of the *Achmea* judgment. The Tribunal in *Marfin* v. *Cyprus* dealt with this argument by finding that the issue of enforceability is an issue for the domestic courts, and not a limitation on jurisdiction.[97] Gáspár-Szilágyi and Usynin argue that the non-enforcement of awards has not been a relevant factor in other fields of dispute settlement, giving examples such as the South China Sea case and the Arctic Sunrise case, where the likely non-enforcement of an award did not result in a finding of lack of jurisdiction.[98] This is consistent with the fact that arbitral tribunals are constituted under, and operate within international law; they are not courts within the EU legal order and are not bound by CJEU judgments. This is true, but tribunals do not exist in a legal vacuum, but alongside other dispute settlement bodies and domestic courts. Koutrakos is critical of the way that arbitral tribunals show a 'distinct lack of engagement with the practical realities' of the conflict between EU law and international investment law.[99]

These cases bring the 'EU law approach' and 'international law approach' into sharp focus. Arbitral tribunals have mostly approached EU law issues from the international law perspective. This is understandable, given that arbitral tribunals are established by international treaty, and are primarily concerned with settling a dispute within that legal framework. One may criticize them for failing to understand EU law, or for not engaging with practical realities, but at the same time, the arguments of the EU/parties are

---

[95] *Id.*, 4.120. Given the debate about the nature of EU law, the Tribunal's reading that 'EU law is international law' is accurate but overly simplifies the issue.

[96] See *AES Summit Generation Limited and AES-Tisza Erömü Kft* v. *The Republic of Hungary*, ICSID Case No. ARB/07/22, Award, 23 September 2010, 7.6.6. 'Regarding the Community competition law regime, it has a dual nature: on the one hand, it is an international law regime, on the other hand, once introduced in the national legal orders, it is part of these legal orders'.

[97] *Marfin Investment Group* v. *The Republic of Cyprus*, Case No. ARB/13/27, Award, 26 July 2018, para. 596: 'It will be up to the courts at the enforcement stage to draw the necessary consequences from the Achmea judgment and their national laws with respect to the enforceability of this Award'.

[98] Gáspár-Szilágyi & Usynin (n67) 46.

[99] P. Koutrakos, 'The Relevance of EU Law for Arbitral Tribunals: (Not) Managing the Lingering Tension' (2016) 17 *Journal of World Investment & Trade* 873, 881.

often put forward in blunt terms.[100] Some techniques have been suggested to avoid clashes. This includes tribunals taking more care to understand the EU law issues at play (comity) or applying EU law as one of the relevant sources of international law (systemic integration). Whereas other dispute settlement bodies have been more open to accepting the relevance of EU law arguments, such as in the WTO context, in the context of investment arbitration there seems to be greater reluctance. Academic analysis of EU arguments in invest tribunals confirms this approach. Binder and Hofbauer find that investment tribunals have 'not recognized any primacy/supremacy stemming from the EU legal order'.[101] Gáspár-Szilágyi and Usynin demonstrate how arbitral tribunals have rejected arguments based on *Achmea*, mostly on procedural grounds.[102]

5.4 CONCLUSION

The CJEU is responsible for the interpretation of EU law, and disputes regarding EU law, whereas international judicial bodies are responsible for the application of international law, usually with respect to a specific treaty. On the face of it, these bodies operate in separate spheres. However, the co-existence of the CJEU and other forms of international dispute settlement bodies has shown different ways for these legal orders to interact. In the case of the ICJ, the inter-state nature of dispute settlement has meant that the EU does not appear as a litigant. Article 344 TFEU has also meant that EU Member States are to utilize the ICJ and inter-state proceedings only in cases where no EU law element exists. In the WTO context, the EU acts a single actor, and its arguments that it should be equated with a domestic legal order have mostly been accepted. In the case of the ECHR, the Strasbourg Court has mostly sought to resolve tensions. The process of the EU's accession to the ECHR also shows the extent to which the EU legal order now requires specialized rules to

---

[100] 'Certain matters, especially those concerning the role of the ECJ in the interpretation of the EU Treaties and the EU legal system are not open for negotiation in international contexts'. E. Paasivirta, 'European Union and Dispute Settlement: Managing Proliferation and Fragmentation' in M. Cremona, A. Thies & R. A. Wessel (eds), *The European Union and International Dispute Settlement* (Oxford: Hart, 2017) 53.

[101] C. Binder and J.A. Hofbauer, 'The Perception of the EU Legal Order in International Law: An In- and Outside View' (2017) *European Yearbook of International Economic Law* 139, 199.

[102] Gáspár-Szilágyi & Usynin (n67) 52: 'the Court of Justice's *Achmea* ruling in essence questions the very existence of such tribunals; a regional court, deriving its jurisdiction from another set of international treaties, is telling another international tribunal (even if just ad hoc) that their very existence under a different set of international treaties is precluded by the former set of treaties'.

be included in international agreements to allow EU participation. There has been more tension in the field of investment disputes. In the field of extra-EU disputes, the CJEU has found that such dispute settlement bodies are compatible with EU law, as long as they include certain safeguards, such as ensuring that no tribunal could interpret provisions of EU law. Where the EU or EU Member States have put forward arguments that are based on the primacy of EU law, however, arbitral tribunals have, on the whole, not shown a high degree of deference to the CJEU and EU law, focusing on the tribunals' founding instruments and on public international law.

In the field of international dispute settlement the EU has requested its internal law, especially the autonomy of the EU legal order, to be addressed at the international level. This has been met with mixed responses. In the context of the ECHR, the EU was afforded specialized treatment, based on the fact that the EU would become the ECHR's first non-state contracting party. This approach may give rise to future problems. For instance, in the negotiations on the future relationship between the EU and the UK, the role of the Court of Justice was a point of contention. In the context of dispute settlement, parties will be reluctant to afford the EU special treatment.

6

International Responsibility

6.1 INTRODUCTION

This chapter explores another pillar of public international law: responsibility for internationally wrongful acts. In doing so, it examines how rules of international responsibility, especially those regarding the responsibility of international organizations, have been influenced by the unique nature of the EU and the EU legal order. The chapter begins by discussing and framing the debate about the responsibility of international organizations (Section 6.3). It briefly discusses some of the unique features of the EU legal order that may require the law of responsibility to be 'adapted' in the EU context. Section 6.4 turns to the Articles on the Responsibility of International Organizations[1] (ARIO) developed by the International Law Commission (ILC). It focuses on the methodological and conceptual hurdles facing the ILC, and explores how it sought to take into account the unique nature of the EU when developing the draft articles. It then deals with the text of the draft articles, and discusses how they may be applied to the EU context. It critically analyses whether the articles sufficiently take into account the diversity of international organizations, which, unlike states, cannot be considered to be sovereign entities, nor legally equal. The chapter applies a similar methodology as the other chapters, combining references to academic debate and legal sources, drawing upon the work of the ILC and the Special Rapporteur. It seeks to understand, using the ILC's draft articles as a lens, how the EU has influenced the development of international law in the field of international responsibility.

---

[1] Draft Articles on the Responsibility of International Organizations with Commentaries, in Report of the International Law Commission, sixty-third session, 26 April–3 June, 4 July–12 August 2011, UN Doc. A/66/10, at 52; GAOR, sixty-sixth session, Supplement No. 10 (2011) ('ARIO').

The topic of international responsibility is possibly the international law issue where EU lawyers and international lawyers talk past one another the most. The limited literature focusing on the EU and international responsibility has been written primarily from an 'EU perspective'.[2] This literature tends to use the starting point of the unique nature of the EU legal order, discussing the specific issues that arise in relation to the EU such as shared competences and mixed agreements. While it is important to discuss these internal legal issues regarding the EU, this line of literature almost exclusively deals with these internal aspects, without much reflection on the wider international law concepts. Like much of the literature focusing on the EU in international law generally, there is discussion about why the EU is unique, but little critical discussion about how and why these unique features are relevant for the law of international responsibility.

From the public international law perspective, there has been far less focus on the EU as such. International law literature tends to examine the EU among other international organizations. This tends to downplay the unique legal characteristics of the EU. While focusing on the European Union and its special characteristics, it also takes into account the need for public international law to develop general rules aimed at universal application. The aim is to assess the ILC's success or otherwise in balancing two competing goals: (1) creating a residual framework of general rules that are applicable to a diverse body of organizations and (2) accommodating the 'principle of specialty' in international organizations. Can the ARIO provide a general and universally applicable framework for the responsibility of IOs that still takes into account sufficiently the unique characteristics of organizations such as the EU?

The debate surrounding the EU and international responsibility also provides further insight into how the EU is viewed from a public international law

---

[2] P.-J. Kuijper & E. Paasivirta, 'EU International Responsibility and its Attribution: From the Inside Looking Out' in M. Evans & P. Koutrakos (eds), *The International Responsibility of the European Union: European and International Perspectives* (Oxford: Hart, 2013) 35; E. Paasivirta & P.-J. Kuijper, 'Does One Size Fit All? The European Community and the Responsibility of International Organizations' (2005) 36 *Netherlands Yearbook of International Law* 169; M. Björklund, 'Responsibility in the EC for Mixed Agreements – Should Non-Member Parties Care? (2001) 70 *Nordic Journal of International Law* 373; E. Neframi, 'International Responsibility of the European Community and of the Member States under Mixed Agreements' in E. Cannizzaro (ed), *The European Union as an Actor in International Relations* (The Hague: Kluwer, 2002) 193. C. Tomuschat, 'The International Responsibility of the European Union' in E. Cannizzaro (ed), *The European Union as an Actor in International Relations* (The Hague: Kluwer, 2002) 177; F. Hoffmeister, 'Litigating against the European Union and Its Member States – Who Responds under the ILC's Draft Articles on International Responsibility of International Organizations?' (2010) 21 *European Journal of International Law* 723.

perspective. The way in which the ILC and the Special Rapporteur approached a number of legal issues helps demonstrate how the EU is viewed in international law more generally. The EU was highly vocal during the development of the draft articles and sought to influence every stage of the process. However, the EU was not successful in shaping the outcome in an active manner, through its public statements and comments. The EU has influenced the law of responsibility in a more passive manner: through its existence as a unique international actor, and its body of legal practice, the Union influenced the draft articles in an indirect manner.

This chapter focuses on the 'external' responsibility of the EU and the Member States, and therefore does not examine the issue of responsibility of EU Member States for violations of EU law or of the EU Treaties. A well-developed system of responsibility exists within the EU legal order, which has established a complete and exhaustive set of procedures and remedies to deal with breaches by the EU Member States. Breaches of the EU Treaties, or of EU law, by EU Member States are therefore not governed by the general system of international responsibility. As discussed in Chapter 2, although it could be argued that the law of international responsibility still exists as a 'fallback',[3] the EU has developed, for all practical purposes, its own legal order regarding responsibility.[4]

The EU Treaties themselves say little about the responsibility of the EU at the international level. While the Treaties state that the EU has legal personality, and allow the EU to assume international legal obligations, nothing in the Treaties deals with the consequences of a breach of these international obligations. Moreover, the case law of the Court of Justice of the EU has little to say about the EU's international responsibility. When the Court determines that an EU act is not in accordance with the EU's international obligations, it is concerned with the validity of the act within the EU legal order, leaving aside for the most part issues of international responsibility.[5] The Treaties and the case law of the CJEU may shed light on certain issues, but on the whole do not play a large role in determining the rules of responsibility at the international level. Nonetheless it has been argued that the EU's internal legal

---

[3] B. Simma & D. Pulkowski, 'Of Planets and the Universe: Self-contained Regimes in International Law' (2006) 17(3) *European Journal of International Law* 483, 516–517.

[4] For discussion on whether the EU should be considered a 'self-contained regime', see the discussion in Section 1.3.3.

[5] 'In the event of non-performance of the Agreement by the Commission, therefore, the Community could incur liability at international level. ... That being so, the question is whether the Commission was competent under Community law to conclude such an agreement'. Judgment in *France v. Commission*, C-327/91, EU:C:1994:305, para. 25–26.

order can and should play a role in developing international legal rules on international organizations.

6.2 RESPONSIBILITY OF INTERNATIONAL ORGANIZATIONS IN INTERNATIONAL LAW

Any legal system requires consequences for breaches of an obligation and certain limits on the exercise of public power. The law of responsibility was initially developed regarding the exercise of power by states, the primary actors in international law. It is understandable, then, that the ILC's early work focused on the issue of state responsibility. Yet it became increasingly clear that this responsibility regime was incomplete without a similar set of rules pertaining to international organizations. The growing importance of international organizations in international relations as well as the increasing capacity of these organizations to breach international obligations, including international human rights, meant that the issue of responsibility of international organizations became the focus of attention in legal circles. While international lawyers have discussed the topic of responsibility of international organizations for decades, it has recently received a great deal of attention in academic debate. There are several reasons for this renewed focus on the responsibility of international organizations.

First, as international organizations further develop powers, they are increasingly capable of taking decisions that have far-reaching effects, including on the enjoyment of rights of individuals. The growing capacity of the acts and omissions of international organizations to have consequences for the enjoyment of rights of third parties gave rise to questions about the 'accountability' of international organizations.[6] The concept of accountability is broader than responsibility, and includes legal, political, administrative, financial and democratic dimensions. At its heart, it seeks to ensure that international organizations, like other bodies with the potential to affect the rights of others, are held to account for their actions. International responsibility,

---

[6] The International Law Association's 2004 Report on the accountability of international organizations states that 'Accountability of IO-s is a multifaceted phenomenon. The form under which accountability will eventually arise will be determined by the particular circumstances surrounding the acts or omissions of an IO, its member States or third parties. These forms may be legal, political, administrative or financial. A combination of the four forms provides the best chances of achieving the necessary degree of accountability'. International Law Association, Berlin Conference (2004) Final Report, Accountability of International Organizations 5. See I. F. Dekker, 'Accountability of International Organizations: An Evolving Concept?' in J. Wouters, E. Brems, S. Smis & P. Schmitt (eds), *Accountability for Human Rights Violations by International Organizations* (Antwerp: Intersentia, 2010) 21–36.

however, focuses on the more narrow issue: ensuring that international actors incur legal consequences from a breach of their obligations.

The renewed attention on the responsibility of international organizations was therefore linked to the perceived 'impunity gap', whereby IOs were seen as not being able to be held to account for their actions at the international level. The concern was also linked to events at the international level that involved international organizations, such as human rights abuses committed in the context of UN peacekeeping operations.[7] In the context of the EU, the increasing powers and competences of the Union, as well as its increased involvement at the international level, also gave rise to questions regarding its international responsibility. In fields such as trade, for example, the international responsibility of the EU has been recognized. Regarding the EU's responsibility for human rights violations, or for acts committed as part of its CFSP, the law of international responsibility, and the way it applies to the EU, remains a controversial subject.

The second reason for the renewed attention on the responsibility of international organizations has been the work on this subject by the International Law Commission. In 2000, the ILC decided that the topic 'Responsibility of international organizations' should be included in its long term programme of work, and in 2001 the UN General Assembly formally requested the ILC to begin work on the topic.[8] The ILC took up this project at the time when its Articles on State Responsibility (ASR) were nearing completion.[9] The topic of responsibility of international organizations was viewed as being a 'necessary counterpart' to this work, as it would logically flow

---

[7] See V. L. Kent, 'Peacekeepers as Perpetrators of Abuse: Examining the UN's Plans to Eliminate and Address Cases of Sexual Exploitation and Abuse in Peacekeeping Operations' (2005) 14(2) *African Security Review* 85–92; U. Häussler, 'Human Rights Accountability of International Organizations in the Lead of International Peace Missions' in J. Wouters, E. Brems, S. Smis & P. Schmitt (eds), *Accountability for Human Rights Violations by International Organizations* (Antwerp: Intersentia, 2010) 215; F. Mégret & F. Hoffmann, '"The UN as a Human Rights Violator?" Some Reflections on the United Nations Changing Human Rights Responsibilities' (2003) 25 *Human Rights Quarterly* 314.

[8] UNGA, Report of the International Law Commission on the work of its fifty-second session, UN Doc. A/Res/55/152, para. 8: '*Requests* the International Law Commission, taking into account paragraph 259 of its report, to begin its work on the topic "Responsibility of international organizations" and to give further consideration to the remaining topics to be included in its long-term programme of work, having due regard to comments made by Governments'.

[9] Draft articles on Responsibility of States for Internationally Wrongful Acts, with commentaries, adopted by the International Law Commission at its fifty-third session, Rep. of the International Law Commission on the work of its fifty-third session, 23 April–1 June and 2 July–10 August 2001, A/56/10, reproduced in Yearbook of the International Law Commission 2001, vol. II(2) (hereinafter 'ASR').

on from and complement its work on state responsibility.[10] Throughout the period during which the Special Rapporteur and the ILC focused on this issue, academic debate turned towards the numerous legal issues that arose from this topic, including academic discussion from EU lawyers who were interested in how the ILC would approach the EU and its unique legal order.

6.3 THE EU AND THE ARIO

In developing the rules on the responsibility of international organizations, the ILC had to address a number of conceptual issues. One of the main issues relates to the diversity of international organizations. States are sovereign and legally equal entities, and it is theoretically possible to establish legal rules that are applicable to all of them, irrespective of their power, size and internal legal order. International organizations, on the other hand, are not sovereign entities, and display a remarkable diversity in their legal structures and the extent to which they exercise autonomous powers. Given this diversity, there would be a far greater challenge in developing rules suitable for general application. Another related issue was that some international organizations (not only the EU) may be viewed as 'unique' or 'sui generis', for which rules of general application would have little or no practical value. The argument of the EU was that the ILC's draft rules should be capable of taking into account the unique nature of the EU and its legal order. This section first examines how the ILC sought to deal with the issue of the diversity of IOs generally. It then examines the claims that the EU should be considered 'unique' for the purposes of international responsibility and the draft articles. It finally examines the way in which the EU sought to influence the development of the draft articles through information provided to the ILC, comments made on the various drafts as well as positions made by the EU Member States at the Sixth Committee of the United Nations General Assembly.

6.3.1 *The Diversity of International Organizations*

In addition to universal international organizations such as the United Nations, the international landscape also includes a variety of regional organizations, international financial institutions, collective security organizations, as well as specialized organizations in the field of trade, science, space, the

---

[10] Report of the International Law Commission on the work of its fifty-second session, 1 May–9 June and 10 July–18 August 2000, Official Records of the General Assembly, Fifty-fifth session, Supplement No.10. UN Doc. A/55/10, 135.

environment and a myriad other issues. Not only do these organizations differ in the nature of issues dealt with, they also differ in their membership, legal structure and internal machinery. Given this diversity, would it be possible to develop rules of general application that could apply to this wide variety of IOs? Special Rapporteur Gaja noted this issue in his final report:

> There are very significant differences among international organizations with regard to their powers and functions, size of membership, relations between the organization and its members, procedures for deliberation, structure and facilities, as well as the primary rules including treaty obligations by which they are bound. Because of this diversity and its implications, the draft articles where appropriate give weight to the specific character of the organization (...).[11]

Throughout the process, the question of how to give 'appropriate weight' to the specific characteristics of IOs remained a key question. The issue of diversity was brought up by international organizations themselves in the comments they submitted to the ILC. The Secretariat of the United Nations, for example, pointed to the need to take into account the 'specificities of the various international organizations'.[12] The strongest supporter of this argument was the European Union, which argued from the outset that the draft articles must take into account the unique nature of the EU, specifically its role as a regional economic integration organization (REIO).[13] The European Commission consistently questioned the appropriateness of developing general rules intended to apply to all IOs:

> The European Commission expresses some concerns as to the feasibility of subsuming all international organizations under the terms of this one draft in the light of the highly diverse nature of international organizations, of which the European Community is itself an example.[14]

How, then, could this conceptual hurdle be addressed? The ILC had several options regarding how to approach the issue of the diversity of international organizations.

The first option would have been to narrow its focus to a limited range of IOs. For instance, it could have focused on the types of IOs for which the topic

---

[11]　ARIO (n1) Commentary 3, para. 7.
[12]　G. Gaja, Special Rapporteur, International Law Commission, Eighth Report on Responsibility of International Organizations, 14 March 2011, UN Doc. A/CN.4/640, 5 ('Eighth Report').
[13]　See Paasivirta & Kuijper (n2).
[14]　International Law Commission, sixtieth session Geneva, 5 May – 6 June and 7 July– 8 August 2007, Responsibility of International Organizations, Comments and Observations Received from International Organizations, 4.

of responsibility had brought attention and criticism. It could have narrowed its definition of 'international organization' to include only intergovernmental and universal organizations such as the United Nations. This would have reflected one of the key rationales behind developing rules of responsibility for IOs, that is, responsibility arising from the conduct of peacekeeping and peace enforcement operations.[15] Indeed, an early draft included a definition of an IO that required it to carry out 'government' (state-like) functions:

> For the purposes of the present draft articles, the term 'international organ-ization' refers to an organization which includes States among its members insofar it exercises in its own capacity certain governmental functions.[16]

For an IO to incur responsibility, it was argued, an IO must not only possess international legal personality, it must also be capable of 'acting' in some way with a certain degree of autonomy from its members:

> For an organization to be held as potentially responsible it should not only have legal personality and thus some obligations of its own under international law. What is required is also that in the exercise of the relevant functions the organization may be considered as a separate entity from its members and that thus the exercise of these functions may be attributed to the organization itself.[17]

It is for this reason that earlier drafts of the definition of an international organization included references to the exercise of 'governmental functions' of an IO. This would have had the benefit of limiting the application of the draft articles to the very IOs that had the capacity to affect rights and obligations through their acts and omissions, leaving aside those IOs that are merely forums for cooperation and decision-making. This of course leads to its own set of difficulties, including the question of what 'governmental functions'

---

[15] Pellet noted that that 'many specific problems arise in this regard and they should become increasingly numerous in view of the resumption of the operational activities of international organizations and, in particular, activities by the United Nations to maintain international peace and security'. Report of the International Law Commission on the work of its fifty-second session, 1 May–9 June and 10 July–18 August 2000, Official Records of the General Assembly, Fifty-fifth session, Supplement No.10, 135. Hafner notes that '[a] further reason for a need for the codification of responsibility of international organisations seems to be the call for growing accountability of international organisations conducting military-like operations such as peacekeeping operations': G. Hafner, 'Is the Topic of Responsibility of International Organizations Ripe for Codification? Some Critical Remarks' in U. Fastenrath, R. Geiger, D.-E. Khan, A. Paulus, S. von Schorlemer & C. Vedder (eds), *From Bilateralism to Community Interest: Essays in Honour of Judge Bruno Simma* (Oxford: Oxford University Press, 2011) 700.

[16] G. Gaja, Special Rapporteur, International Law Commission, First Report on Responsibility of International Organizations, 26 March 2003, UN Doc. A/CN.4/532 ('First Report'), 115.

[17] Gaja, First Report (n16) 113.

actually entails with regard to IOs. The idea of limiting the draft articles to such a narrow range of IOs was rejected early on by the ILC. Instead, the ILC decided to adopt a broad definition capable of capturing a large range of organizations:

> 'international organization' means an organization established by a treaty or other instrument governed by international law and possessing its own international legal personality. International organizations may include as members, in addition to States, other entities.[18]

This definition includes all international organizations enjoying legal personality, not just 'intergovernmental organizations'.[19] It includes bodies that have non-states as members as well as bodies that might be established upon a basis other than a treaty. The ILC's definition is deliberately broad and designed to capture the great variety of international bodies that exist.[20] The European Union clearly falls within these criteria since it was established by a treaty and possesses its own legal personality.[21]

A second option would have been to develop a different set of rules that would apply for different types of organizations. Such an approach was considered at an early stage in the ILC's work:

> The definition of international organizations [...] comprises entities of a quite different nature. Membership, functions, ways of deliberating and means at their disposal vary so much that with regard to responsibility it may be unreasonable to look for general rules applying for all intergovernmental organizations, especially with regard to the issue of responsibility into which States may incur for activities of the organization of which they are members. It may be necessary to devise specific rules for different categories of international organizations.[22]

This proposal was also rejected. Instead, the ILC decided to adopt rules aimed at general application, irrespective of the category to which organizations belong. Blokker argued in favour of general rules in this way:

> [W]hile it is true that there is a great variety of international organizations, it may be questioned why this should imply that there should be a great variety

[18]   Article 2(a) ARIO (n1).
[19]   Article 2(a) ARIO (n1).
[20]   See J. Wouters & J. Odermatt, 'Are All International Organizations Created Equal?' (2012) 9 *International Organizations Law Review* 7–14.
[21]   Article 47, Treaty on European Union ('TEU'). On the EU's legal personality, see section 7.2 below.
[22]   Report of the International Law Commission on the work of its fifty-fourth session, 29 April– 7 June and 22 July–16 August 2002, Official Records of the General Assembly, Fifty-fourth session, Supplement No. 10 (A/57/10), para. 470.

of responsibility rules for these organizations and why there could not be one set of rules[23]

One argument in favour of this approach was that, in the same way that the draft articles on state responsibility apply to all states, irrespective of their size, power or economic development, rules on responsibility of international organizations should not differ depending on the difference between IOs. The difference between international organizations, in terms of their institutional set up and autonomy, is legally relevant, however. States remain legally equal entities in the eyes of international law. As Pellet notes, '[s]tates can be big or small, wealthy or poor, but they are supposedly equal'.[24] International organizations, on the other hand, 'are neither sovereign nor equal; all their powers are strictly at the service of their member states'.[25] International organizations, while they may enjoy international legal personality, vary widely in their institutional design, their powers, their decision-making processes and the relationship between the organization and its members. States enjoy general competence, and possess full rights and responsibilities under international law. International organizations, on the other hand are governed by the 'principle of speciaty' and 'are invested by the states which created them with powers, the limits of which are a function of the common interest whose promotion those states entrust them'.[26] One of the criticisms of the draft articles is that they failed to sufficiently take into account the principle of specialty.[27]

The constitutive instrument of an IO cannot always be deemed to be a purely 'internal' instrument, likened to the constitutional order of a state. Whereas the internal legal order of a state is for the most part irrelevant for the purposes of international responsibility, the same cannot be said of the instrument establishing an IO, which is both an international legal instrument and

---

[23] N. M. Blokker, 'Preparing Articles on Responsibility of International Organizations: Does the International Law Commission Take International Organizations Seriously? A Mid-Term Review' in J. Klabbers & A. Wallendahl (eds), *Research Handbook on the Law of International Organizations* (Cheltenham: Edward Elgar, 2011) 335.

[24] A. Pellet, 'International Organizations Are Definitely Not States. Cursory Remarks on the ILC Article son the Responsibility of International Organizaitons' in M. Ragazzi (ed), *Responsibility of International Organizations: Essays in Memory of Ian Brownlie* (Leiden: Martinus Nijhoff, 2013) 41, 49.

[25] P. Reuter, Sixth Report on the Question of Treaties Concluded between States and International Organizations or between Two or More International Organizations, (1977) II Yearbook of the International Law Commission, para. 6.

[26] Legality of the Use by a State of Nuclear Weapons in Armed Conflict (Advisory Opinion) [1996] ICJ Rep 66, 78–79, para. 25.

[27] See Pellet (n24) 46.

an internal 'constitutional' one. International organizations are heterogeneous legal entities, and it may be appropriate to develop rules applicable to different types of organizations. One can understand the ILC's reluctance to develop specific rules for certain types of organization. Like the articles on state responsibility, the ARIO were intended to be secondary rules of general application. In this way they would parallel the ASR, which apply to all states. Crawford stresses, 'the underlying concepts of state responsibility—attribution, breach, excuses, and consequences—are general in character'.[28] The idea of developing different rules for different types of organizations is not only conceptually inelegant; it goes against the very aim of creating rules of general character.

Another problem with trying to 'categorise' international organizations is more practical. Such an approach would have invited a much more difficult question of how to define different types of international organizations, a topic with which international law scholars have had difficulty. How the ILC would have categorized different international organizations is uncertain. The term 'regional economic integration organization' that is often employed in international practice does not really capture the complexity of the EU legal order and the wide variety of roles it now plays. Indeed, almost every international organization could genuinely argue that in some way its legal setup sets it apart from other IOs: 'surely, it will not do to have an identical regime for entities as disparate as the World Bank, the EU, and say, the European Forest Institute; hence to the extent that organisations welcome a general responsibility regime, they nonetheless feel that their situation is different'.[29]

The ILC embarked on the ambitious goal of developing such a general regime. Most of the criticism of the ARIO stems from the argument that the ILC failed to give due regard to the diversity of IOs and to take into account these differences. The most vocal critic in this regard was the European Union. Shortly before adoption of the ARIO in 2011 the European Commission commented:

> for now the European Union remains unconvinced that the draft articles and the commentaries thereto adequately reflect the diversity of international organizations. Several draft articles appear either inadequate or even inapplicable to regional integration organizations such as the European

---

[28] J. Crawford, 'State Responsibility' Rüdiger Wolfrum (ed)in Max Planck Encyclopedia of Public International Law, (online edn). http://opil.ouplaw.com/home/EPIL

[29] J. Klabbers, 'Self-control: International Organizations and the Quest for Accountability' in M. Evans & P. Koutrakos (eds), *The International Responsibility of the European Union: European and International Perspectives* (Oxford: Hart, 2013) 76.

Union, even when account is taken of some of the nuances now set out in the commentaries. [...]

In view of these comments the European Commission considers that the International Law Commission should give further thought as to whether the draft articles and the commentaries, as they stand now, are apt for adoption by the Commission on second reading or whether further discussion and work is needed.[30]

What, exactly, are the unique features of the EU and the EU legal order that should have been taken into account? Even if the EU is considered to be a 'new legal order', what significance, if any, should this have in determining the international responsibility of the EU and the Member States?

6.3.2 *The Unique Nature of the EU Legal Order*

International organizations are bound by agreements to which they are party and certain rules of customary international law.[31] International organizations may also incur responsibility for breaches of those obligations under international law. There is nothing controversial about the idea that an IO may commit an internationally wrongful act for which it incurs international responsibility. Complex questions arise, however, due to the nature of international organizations, which are made up of states, which also possess international legal personality and have their own international legal obligations. Many of these issues are complicated further in the context of the EU as a composite legal order comprising of Member States that retain their legal personality.

Kuijper and Paasivirta point to an important paradox that underlies the EU's role in the international legal order. On the one hand, the EU is the IO that is 'the most independent from its Member States'.[32] The EU has a distinct legal personality, and exercises a great deal of autonomy in wide range of fields. Yet the EU is also an international organization that is closely intertwined with the legal systems of its Member States. While the EU has its own

---

[30]   Comments of the European Commission, Comments and Observations Received from International Organizations, 14 February 2011, Doc. A.CN.4/637, 8.

[31]   Interpretation of the Agreement of 25 March 1951 between the WHO and Egypt, (Advisory Opinion) (1980) ICJ Rep 73, 89–90.

[32]   Kuijper & Paasivirta (n2) 38. 'The EU, therefore, is the victim of a paradox in international relations. It seeks to act as a strong and unified actor towards the outside world in international relations and that is what it is supposed to do according to its latest charter, the Treaty of Lisbon. However, because of its basic structure, it is highly dependent on its Member States for carrying out its policies and implementing its laws, including in the field of international relations'.

organs, in most cases it is the EU Member States that are implementing and enforcing EU law.[33] The EU is both independent from, and dependent on, its Member States. Many of the arguments made in the literature and put forward by the EU regarding the unique nature of the EU legal order, stem from this underlying paradox.

The first feature that is discussed in relation to the EU and international responsibility is the nature of competences in the EU legal order. This refers to the 'horizontal' relationship between the EU and the Member States. The issue of competences is of course not unique to the EU context. Other IOs must grapple with the distribution of powers between the IO and its members. IOs may only exercise powers and competences that have been assigned to them by their members. It was argued, however, that the nature of competences is much more complex in the EU legal order. Competences are not divided neatly into spheres of EU or Member State competence; in many cases the EU Member States will retain competences in a field despite the EU exercising considerable legislative powers in that field. Moreover, unlike most other organizations, there are significant fields where the EU exercises exclusive competence.

In this regard, one may question to what extent the issue of EU competences should be regarded as a purely internal issue. The EU takes the position that the balance of competences is a matter that is only relevant within the EU legal sphere. The CJEU has made clear that no entity other than the Court may answer questions about the extent of the competences of the EU and the Member States. However, the EU has developed a long-standing practice of entering into mixed agreements whereby both the EU and the Member States enter into international obligations concurrently. With this practice has come the phenomenon of declarations of competences. As argued in Chapter 5, this has the consequence of 'externalizing' the issue of competence. For the EU's treaty partners, for example, the issue of who is responsible for implementing an obligation under an international agreement cannot be considered a purely internal issue; it may have consequences for determining the extent of international responsibility of the EU and the Member States. The extent to which competences, including declarations of competence made by the EU, should be relevant in determining responsibility, was one of the key topics in the debate.

The second main issue relates to the 'vertical' relationship between the EU and the Member States. Like other IOs and other corporate legal entities, the EU is only capable of acting through its own organs and agents. In most cases,

---

[33] Kuijper & Paasivirta (n2) 41–42.

EU law is implemented, not by authorities of the Union, but by the authorities of the EU Member States. The EU Member States therefore play a 'dual-role'. The EU is a separate and distinct legal entity under international law, but it is highly reliant on the authorities of Member States to give effect to its law. Most of the EU's international obligations, even in areas where it exercises exclusive competence, will be carried out by the EU Member States. The EU does not have its own border police, customs officials, or other law enforcement agencies. In the EU context this is referred to as 'executive federalism'.[34]

> Executive federalism implies that the EU has no layer of federal bureaucracy to speak of, and that directly applicable legislation, such as the sanctions regulation in the Bosphorus case, automatically becomes part of the law of the land of the Member States and is implemented and applied by Member State authorities.[35]

In these instances, the body in question that is 'acting' is the EU Member State, but it is doing so pursuant to EU law. How does one conceive of this relationship between the EU and the Member State? Is the Member State considered to be an 'agent or organ' of the EU? Should the EU Member State be held responsible for acts that are carried out when implementing binding EU law? This 'vertical' relationship between the EU and the Member States is the second argument put forward in favour of 'special' rules in relation to the EU. It particularly influences the arguments of the EU for the development of a special rule of attribution in order to cover these particular circumstances.

Another issue that is often stressed is the way in which the EU plays a role as an actor in its own right on the international plane. Rather than being a forum for cooperation between the members of the organization, the EU has its own identity as an actor in international law. While other IOs have external relations and diplomatic relations, the EU does so in a more 'state-like' manner; it is not so much that the EU has a separate identity on the international plane, but that this identity is closer to that of a state in fields where it operates. The EU's role as an international actor means that the way in which the EU incurs responsibility at the international level is also quite different to those 'classic' international organizations. The types of agreements to which the EU enters typically include obligations that would apply to states, such as

---

[34] See R. Schütze, 'From Rome to Lisbon: "Executive Federalism" in the (new) European Union' (2010) 47 *Common Market Law Review* 1385.

[35] P.-J. Kuijper, 'International Responsibility for EU Mixed Agreements' in C. Hillion & P. Koutrakos (eds), *Mixed Agreements Revisited: The EU and its Member States in the World* (Oxford: Hart, 2010) 213–214.

in the field of trade or human rights. This may also have consequences for the law of responsibility.

A further issue that sets the EU apart from other IOs is the nature of EU law. The EU legal order differs from that of other IOs in that it represents a well-developed mechanism of enforcement against the EU Member States. The European Commission may bring infringement proceedings against those states that fail to implement EU law and the CJEU exercises judicial review of EU acts. This level of judicial review and enforcement of EU law, it was argued, also sets the EU apart from many other international organizations. Furthermore, much of EU legislation comes in the form of Directives, which are binding upon the Member States, yet they nevertheless give the Member State a degree of discretion on how that result should be achieved. It is not always immediately evident what degree of discretion a Member State has when implementing Union law. Literature on the EU and international responsibility tends to emphasize these unique features, stressing that the EU is a sui generis body in international law.

To what extent are these features relevant for the purposes of developing rules of international responsibility? It is one thing to point to features that make the EU legal order unique; it is another thing to argue that these unique features require specific rules of responsibility at the international level. The EU argued that the unique features of its legal order justified specific rules that took into account the nature of the EU and/or 'regional integration organizations'.

6.4 ILC'S DRAFT ARTICLES ON RESPONSIBILITY OF INTERNATIONAL ORGANIZATIONS AND THEIR APPLICATION TO THE EUROPEAN UNION

6.4.1 *ILC Methodology*

It should be acknowledged from the outset that there was a great deal of disagreement about the methodology employed by the ILC in developing the ARIO. In many ways, it followed its previous methodology when codifying international treaty law (see Chapter 2). Having developed a set of rules applicable to states, the ILC used this as a basis for developing rules applicable to international organizations. Just as the 1969 VCLT was used as a logical starting point in developing the 1986 VCLT-IO, the ILC's Articles on State Responsibility were used as a starting point in developing rules on the responsibility of international organizations. This approach has some benefits but also some major drawbacks. The benefit is that it allows a conceptual parallel between the two sets of rules, arguably strengthening the coherence of the law of international responsibility. It also helps address certain issues where there is yet insufficient or undeveloped state practice. This approach was also useful from a practical perspective – using the ASR as a starting point, the Special Rapporteur and the ILC could identify parallel rules that exist in the context of international organizations and adapt them accordingly.

Yet the ILC's methodology has also been sharply criticized. It is based on a 'top-down' approach based on the ASR, rather than on a 'bottom-up' study based on international practice. Such an approach may have been warranted in the field of treaty law, where concepts relating to the application and interpretation of treaties could be 'adapted' to the practice of IOs. In the context of the law of responsibility, however, there are sufficient differences between states and IOs to warrant substantially different sets of rules. Moreover, the ILC's approach allows the inclusion of certain rules in the ARIO, not because they are necessarily based in international practice, but because they are a parallel to the provision in the ASR. While this may have the benefit of plugging holes in the ARIO, it also means that certain rules are included without allowing sufficient international practice to have developed.

This lack of practice regarding international organizations was another challenge facing the ILC. In contrast to the field of state responsibility,[36] the ILC had little practice upon which to base its articles, a fact that was acknowledged by the ILC itself: '[o]ne of the main difficulties in elaborating rules concerning the responsibility of international organizations is due to the limited availability of pertinent practice'.[37] Much of the criticism of the ARIO stems from the fact that the ILC undertook a project to codify an area of law before international practice had matured. Having two parallel bodies of rules is conceptually appealing, but it is based on an assumption that international organizations can be treated more or less in a similar manner to states for the purposes of international responsibility. The response to the Draft Articles indicates otherwise. While they have been adopted by the General Assembly, they are far from being universally recognized as reflecting

---

[36] There was a tendency in the literature to assert that the rules on responsibility of IOs were 'underdeveloped' or 'embryonic'. This assumes that in time more concrete rules regarding responsibility of IOs could have been fleshed out. See I. Dekker, 'Making Sense of Accountability in International Institutional Law: An Analysis of the Final Report of the ILA Committee on Accountability of International Organisations from a Conceptual Legal Perspective' (2006) 36 *Netherlands Yearbook of International Law* 83, 84: 'The general international legal system governing the activities of international organisations is still in a kind of embryonic phase, at least in comparison with the existing body of rules of international law for states'.

[37] ARIO (n1) Commentary 2, para. 5.

customary international law. Moreover, many international organizations, the very bodies that should make use of these articles, remain highly critical of them. Importantly for this study, the European Union has also been highly critical of the ILC's work, arguing that the ARIO fails to take into account sufficiently the unique nature of the EU and its legal order.

6.4.2 *The EU's Contribution to the Draft Articles*

In developing the draft articles, international organizations were given the opportunity to provide their comments and opinions on drafts as well as to provide examples of relevant practice from their organization. The EU set out to influence the development of the draft articles from the very beginning. The EU recognized that it would be one of the organizations on which the draft articles would potentially have most impact.[38] The EU welcomed the ILC's project, but closely followed developments and was highly critical of its work.

Taking the lead in this regard was the Legal Service of the European Commission. The comments on earlier drafts reflect this, where comments are made under the title 'European Commission' rather than European Union/Community. Most of this process took place before the coming into force of the Lisbon Treaty, and therefore during a period where there was an institutional duality between the European Union and Community. Many of the comments made by the European Commission reflect its position in the Community, rather than the Union. There is relatively little discussion, for example, of responsibility regarding areas such as the Common Foreign and Security Policy (CFSP) or military issues.[39] EU Member States generally supported the EU position, and also represented the EU in the United Nations Sixth Committee, where the Union was able to voice its concerns over certain aspects of the drafts. There were concerns that, while the ILC invited comments from IOs, these comments were not sufficiently taken into

---

[38] Upon the adoption of the articles, it stated that '[t]he European Union is the international organisation which is potentially most impacted by international law rules of responsibility of organisations given its large scale participation in international treaties and activities'. Statement on behalf of the European Union by L. Gussetti, Director, Principal Legal Adviser, European Commission, at the UN General Assembly 6th Committee (Legal), 66th Session: Report of the International Law Commission on the Work of Its Sixty-Third Session on Responsibility of International Organizations, 24 October 2011, New York, http://eu-un.europa.eu/articles/en/article_11568_en.htm.

[39] Comments and Observations Received from International Organizations, 25 June 2004, UN Doc. A/CN.4/545, 25 June 2004, 27: 'The European Community does not take a position on question (c) as it does not relate to Community law' referring to the question of 'Attribution of the conduct of peacekeeping forces to the United Nations or to contributing States'.

account. Only a relatively small number of IOs gave comments from the hundreds of IOs that exist. For a project intended for application to international organizations, the ILC's methodology remained largely state-oriented.

From the outset, the EU sought to set itself apart from the 'classical' model of international organization.[40] This was based on two main features. The first relates to the nature of the EU as a unique international organization[41]:

> the EC is not only a forum for its Member States to settle or organize their mutual relations, but it is also an actor in its own right on the international scene. The EC is a party to many international agreements with third parties within its areas of competence. Quite often the EC concludes such agreements together with its Member States, each in accordance with its own competencies. In that case the specificity of the EC lies in the fact that the EC and the Member States each assume international responsibility with respect to their own competencies. The EC is also involved in international litigation, in particular in the context of the WTO.[42]

The European Commission repeatedly highlighted the fact that the EU is a party to a multitude of international agreements in its areas of competence, and is involved in international litigation regarding these legal commitments. The second argument is based on the unique nature of the EU legal order:

> the EC is regulated by a legal order of its own, establishing a common market and organizing the legal relations between its members, their enterprises and individuals. Legislation enacted under the EC Treaty forms part of the national law of the Member States and thus is implemented by Member States' authorities and Courts. In that sense, the EC goes well beyond the normal parameters of classical international organizations as we know them.

---

[40] 'Comments and Observations received from International Organizations', Yearbook of the International Law Commission, Documents of the Fifty-Sixth Session (2004) 28: 'Unlike classical intergovernmental organizations, the EC constitutes a legal order of its own, with comprehensive legislative and treaty-making powers, deriving from transfer of competence from the member States to the Community level'.

[41] Permeating the European Commission's comments is the idea of the EU as 'a rather specific international organization: "The European Commission attaches great importance to the work of the International Law Commission, but necessarily looks at it from the perspective of a rather specific international organization." 'Comments and Observations received from International Organizations', Yearbook of the International Law Commission, Documents of the Fifty-Eighth Session (2006) 127.

[42] Statement on behalf of the European Union, Professor G. Nesi, Legal Adviser of the Permanent Mission of Italy to the United Nations. Sixth Committee, Report of the International Law Commission Chapter IV, Responsibility of International Organizations Item 152, New York, 27 October (2003), http://eu-un.europa.eu/articles/en/article_2940_en.htm.

It is important that the ILC draft articles should fully reflect the institutional and legal diversity of structures that the community of states has already established.[43]

It highlights that EU law is closely woven into the national law of the Member States, and is implemented by the Member States' authorities and courts.[44] The Commission also submitted, along with other IOs, examples from EU practice and case-law. The Commission was not 'neutral' in this process – it selected practice and jurisprudence that would bolster its argument that special rules of attribution were needed. The EU had a particular interest in shaping the development of international law in this field.

One important argument put forward by the Commission was that a special rule of attribution had emerged in the EU context and as such should be reflected in the ARIO. It argued that:

> The special situation of the European Union and other potentially similar organizations could be accommodated in the DARIO articles by special rules of attribution of conduct, so that the actions of organs of member states could be attributed to the organization, by special rules of responsibility, so that responsibility could be attributed to the organization, even if organs of member states were the prime actors of a breach of an obligation borne by the organization, or by a special exception or saving clause for organizations such as the European Community.[45]

Paasivirta and Kuijper put forward a special provision to apply in cases where the Member States act as de facto organs of the EU:

> Without prejudice to article 4, in the case of a REIO the conduct of its member states and their authorities shall be considered as an act of the REIO under international law to the extent that such conduct falls within the competencies of the REIO as determined by the rules of that REIO.[46]

It was unlikely that the ILC, a body representing international legal experts from across the globe, would include a clause in the ARIO that specifically mentions the European Union. As seen from international treaty practice (see

---

[43] *Id.*

[44] International Law Commission, Sixty-third session, Geneva, 26 April–3 June and 4 July–12 August 2011, Responsibility of International Organizations, 7. 'unlike traditional inter national organizations, the European Union acts and implements its international obligations to a large extent through its member States and their authorities, and not necessarily through "organs" or "agents" of its own'.

[45] Observations of Mr Kuijper (Observer for the European Commission), Sixth Committee, Summary Record of its 21st Meeting, 18 November 2004, UN Doc. A/C.6/59/SR.21, para. 18.

[46] See Paasivirta & Kuijper (n2) 216.

Chapter 3) non-EU states are highly reluctant to agree to the inclusion of clauses that mention the EU, preferring terms such as 'Regional Economic Integration Organization'.[47] The EU favoured the inclusion of a similar 'REIO' clause that would take into account the nature of organizations, such as the EU, that are more 'state-like' in nature.

The European Commission therefore stressed a number of unique elements of the EU legal order that it believed to be relevant for the purposes of international responsibility. According to the EU's comments on various drafts of the ARIO, these comments for the most part did not influence the final text. Is such criticism really warranted? Even if the ILC did not develop specific rules for the EU or other REIOs, this does not mean that it failed to develop rules that are flexible and adaptable enough to take into account bodies such as the EU. This was exactly the approach the ILC sought to take. The following sections turn to the question of how the ILC aimed to provide the ARIO with provisions that were capable of such flexibility. Whereas the ARIO have been criticized for not taking into account the diversity of IOs, they have also been criticized for providing too much 'flexibility', watering down what could have been a more robust responsibility regime. The criticism of the ARIO tends to reflect a similar criticism levelled against the ILC's work on the law of treaties: that it failed to take into account the characteristics of supranational international organizations.[48]

6.4.3 *Attribution*

One of the most complex questions regarding responsibility of IOs, especially in the EU context, is the question of attribution. As discussed earlier, it will often not be clear exactly who has committed an internationally wrongful act, the IO or a member or members. This is especially the case in instances where the IO does not act through its own organs.[49] The issue of attribution is often discussed regarding the question of peacekeeping. When states put their troops and personnel at the disposal of an international organization,

---

[47] 'Comments and Observations' (n40) 28 : 'It may also be noted that concepts such as "regional economic integration organization" have emerged in the drafting of multilateral treaties, which seem to reflect some of these special features'.

[48] J.-M. Cortés Martín, 'European Exceptionalism in International Law? The European Union and the System of International Responsibility' in M. Ragazzi (ed), *The Responsibility of International Organizations: Essays in Memory of Sir Ian Brownlie* (Leiden: Martinus Nijhoff, 2013) 189, 192.

[49] J. Klabbers, *International Law* (Cambridge: Cambridge University Press, 2013) 135. As Klabbers explains, 'attribution is problematic, largely because organizations do not have their own troops or officials'.

questions arise regarding whether violations of international law should be regarded as acts of the state, of the organization, or both. Much of the international law literature in this field has therefore focused on the complex issue of attribution in the context of UN peacekeeping operations.

Article 4 of the ARIO sets out that there is an internationally wrongful act of an international organization 'when conduct consisting of an action or omission (a) is attributable to that organization under international law'.[50] Attribution makes up the first element of an internationally wrongful act of an IO. This corresponds with Article 2 ASR, setting out attribution as the first element of an internationally wrongful act of a state under international law.[51] Since the element of attribution is a key element of state responsibility, it was used as a basis in developing principles of responsibility of international organizations.[52] Regarding state responsibility, attribution is concerned with determining whether conduct can be characterized an 'act of the State'.[53] This idea that there must not only be a breach of an obligation, but a link between the action and the wrongdoer is a relatively simple one. Yet this concept becomes more complex when applied to legal persons such as states and international organizations who are only capable of acting through their own organs, representatives and agents. In the context of international organizations, especially the EU, it will often be difficult to discern when an act should properly be regarded as act of the organization.

6.4.4 *Attribution in the EU Context*

The question of attribution was therefore a particularly important one for the EU. In most cases, the EU 'acts' through its Member States, who are responsible for implementing Union law and it will often be difficult to determine who has 'committed' a certain act. As discussed earlier, this is complicated mostly by the nature of competences in the EU legal order and the specific method of executive federalism in which the EU carries out its legal

---

[50]   Article 4 ARIO (n1).
[51]   Article 2 ASR (n9).
[52]   See ILC Commentary on ARIO (n1): 'As in the case of States, the attribution of conduct to an international organization is one of the two essential elements for an internationally wrongful act to occur'.
[53]   L. Condorelli & C. Kress, 'The Rules of Attribution: General Considerations' in J. Crawford, A. Pellet & S. Olleson (eds), *The Law of International Responsibility* (Oxford: Oxford University Press, 2010) 221. 'the legal operation having as its function to establish whether given conduct of a physical person, whether consisting of a positive action or an omission, is to be characterized, from the point of view of international law, as an "act of the State" (or the act of any entity possessing international legal personality)'.

obligations. While the body that is 'acting' may be the Member State, the 'normative control' lies with the organization. It is for this reason that the EU was particularly concerned with ensuring that rules on attribution took into account the specific nature of the EU legal order, including a special rule of attribution based on the specific nature of the EU. This is based on the argument that, when the Member State is implementing EU law, the EU is exercising normative control over the state, and therefore this should be considered conduct of the organization for the purposes of international responsibility. The EU argued that practice had developed allowing attribution to international organizations of the acts of the organization's Member States.[54] Much of the practice discussed by the Special Rapporteur and cited in the literature focuses on the EU in two fields of international dispute settlement: the World Trade Organization and the European Court of Human Rights.

6.4.4.1 WTO Practice

As an international dispute settlement mechanism that has expounded on the issue of attribution, the practice of World Trade Organization (WTO) can shed some light on issues in the EU context. Examples from WTO practice were cited by the EU, and EU lawyers in support of a special rule of attribution in relation to the EU, supporting the idea that the EU Member States may act as de facto organs of the EU when implementing EU law. The EU, which is a WTO member alongside the Member States, has been found to be internationally responsible for acts that were committed by the authorities of the Member States. There is nothing in the WTO Agreement or in EU law that would shed light on the issue of responsibility for breaches of WTO law. There is also no declaration of competence in the context of the WTO. However, it is widely accepted that the EU has exclusive competence in the field of trade and is the main actor, having functionally replaced the EU Member States in most fields concerning WTO commitments.

The case law of the WTO has also been discussed as demonstrating a special rule of attribution having been developed, an oft-cited example being *LAN Equipment*.[55] In this case, the EU was 'ready to assume the entire international responsibility for all measures in the area of tariff concessions, whether the

---

[54] 'Comments and Observations by Governments and International Organizations', International Law Commission, Documents of the fifty-seventh session, A/CN.4/556, 12 May 2005, 32.

[55] European Communities – Customs Classifications of Certain Computer Equipment (adopted 22 June 1998) WT/DS63, 67, 68.

measure complained about has been taken at the [EU] level or at the level of Member States'.[56] One of the questions related to responsibility for certain tariff treatment that found its origin in EU law, but was applied by the customs authorities of the EU Member States. From the EU perspective, the Union would be the responsible party since it set the tariff and it has exclusive competence in the field. This was the position argued by the European Commission. In this case, the Member States act without discretion in implementing a law developed at the EU level.

When the ILC discussed this case, it saw this as an example of the EU having assumed responsibility for an act of the EU Member State.[57] It has been pointed out, however, that the Commission had argued in favour of the opposite approach, that the Member States were in fact acting as organs of the EU.[58] There are other instances where it has been accepted that the EU Member States can be considered as organs of the EU for the purposes of responsibility in the field of trade. In *Selected Customs Matters* the panel concluded that:

> the authorities in the Member States – including customs authorities desig-nated for that purpose by the Member States and independent bodies, such as a judicial authority or an equivalent specialized body – act as organs of the European Communities when they review and correct administrative actions taken pursuant to EC customs law.[59]

In *EC Trademarks* the panel:

> accepted the European Communities' explanation of what amounts to its *sui generis* domestic constitutional arrangements that Community laws are gen-erally not executed through authorities at Community level but rather through recourse to the authorities of its member States, which in such a situation, act 'as de facto as organs of the Community, for which the

---

[56]   Oral pleading of the European Commission to the Panel 'European Communities – Customs Classification Of Certain Computer Equipment', 12 of June 1997, para. 6.

[57]   ARIO (n1) Commentary to Article 9.

[58]   As Delgado-Casteleiro and Larik argue, '[t]he EU was not arguing that it wanted to be held responsible regardless of what the rules of attribution stated; indeed it argued that the rule of attribution in those cases involving organs of its Member States functionally acting as EU organs means that their conduct should be attributed to the EU and not the Member States'. A. Delgado Casteleiro & J. Larik, 'The "Odd Couple" The Responsibility of the EU at the WTO' in M. Evans & P. Koutrakos (eds), *The International Responsibility of the European Union: European and International Perspectives* (Oxford: Hart, 2013) 233, 243. See P.-J. Kuijper, 'Attribution – Responsibility – Remedy Some Comments on the EU in Different International Regimes', Amsterdam Law School Research Paper No. 2014-23, 10.

[59]   EC- Selected Customs Matters, Panel Report WT/DS315/R, para. 7.553.

Community would be responsible under WTO law and international law in general.[60]

In the WTO context, a rule emerged whereby the EU Member States will be deemed as organs of the EU when implementing EU law in a field of exclusive competence and as such, responsibility for a breach under international law can be attributed to the EU.[61] While there are numerous references made to WTO law in this debate, it is a very specific example. For the most part, the EU Member States, all of whom are WTO members, have allowed themselves to be represented by the Union in the dispute settlement system, a practice that has been accepted by the other WTO members. It is also a field where the EU has exclusive competence, and where Member States play little role. Kuijper also points out that another relevant issue is that the EU would be the party responsible for putting an end to any possible breach – since the EU Member State itself would not be able to rectify the breach alone, this would require modification of EU legislation.[62] WTO practice, while important in discussing how the EU's responsibility is dealt with in international dispute settlement, is nevertheless a 'highly peculiar'[63] case study. It is influenced by the nature of the WTO and the Dispute Settlement Understanding,[64] as well as the exclusive nature of EU competence in the field of trade.

It is also in the field of trade and in the WTO context where the EU participates as an 'international actor' in its own right, rather than a form of cooperation between the Member States. Moreover, it is a field where the EU acts as a 'single actor' with little participation by the Member States.[65] The non-involvement of the Member States may be due to both legal and political reasons. Upon assessing EU practice at the WTO, Eeckhout concludes that the Union 'is eager to take up responsibility'[66] at the WTO. The EU has an interest in establishing itself as an actor in this field – by arguing that it is the

---

[60]   Protection of Trademarks and Geographical Indications for Agricultural Products and Foodstuffs (*United States* v. *European Communities*), 20 April 2005, WTO Panel, WT/DS174/R, para. 7.725.

[61]   Cortés Martín (n48) 194: 'If a member State's authority is functionally an EU organ, technically any breach committed by it will be attributed to the EU'.

[62]   Kuijper (n58) 11: 'In the background the fact that it was the EU that would have to modify the legislation or to enforce it more stringently must have played a role'.

[63]   Delgado Casteleiro & Larik (n58) 233.

[64]   The particular nature of the WTO system is described in Delgado Casteleiro & Larik (n58) 248–254.

[65]   P. Eeckhout, 'The EU and its Member States in the WTO – Issues of Responsibility' in L. Bartels & F. Ortino (eds), *Regional Trade Agreements and the WTO Legal System* (Oxford: Oxford University Press, 2006) 449, 450.

[66]   Eeckhout (n65) 456.

EU and not the Member States that should be found responsible, the EU is helping to establish its presence as an international actor in its own right. D'Aspremont argues, for instance, that

> There is a general tendency for the EU – like the United Nations – to 'generously' claim responsibility for actions pertaining to its areas of competence in a way that may lead one to think that the EU construes responsibility with autonomous identity and independence on the international plane.[67]

For these reasons, the WTO context should not be seen as indicative of how the question of attribution is dealt with generally. As will be discussed later, while the ILC and the Special Rapporteur discussed WTO practice, it did not find that this justified a special rule of attribution regarding the EU.

6.4.4.2 ECHR Practice

The ILC's discussion on the topic of IO responsibility in connection with the act of a state makes extensive use of the case law of the European Court of Human Rights and European Commission of Human Rights, especially cases that deal with EU/EC law. Whereas in the WTO context the EU Member States can be seen as acting as EU organs when implementing EU law, a different approach has emerged in the ECHR context. It represents a very different type of dispute settlement body: the EU is not a party to the Convention; the Convention is not confined to a particular field of EU competence; and it involves the rights of individuals. The ECtHR's jurisprudence should be understood in the light of this. Since the EU is not a contracting party, an applicant who alleges a human rights violation stemming from an EU act will have to bring their case against the EU Member State implementing EU law. As a human rights court responsible for ensuring that the rights in the Convention are fulfilled, the ECtHR seeks to ensure that a party may be held responsible. The ECtHR's jurisprudence can be understood in the light of it wanting to avoid gaps in legal protection that would leave a victim without a remedy. In these circumstances, the ECtHR may be more willing to attribute the action to the Member State, rather than to the Union.[68] The Court has underlined the fact that a Contracting Party's

---

[67] J. d'Aspremont, 'A European Law of International Responsibility? The Articles on the Responsibility of International Organizations and the European Union' in V. Kosta, N. Skoutaris & V. Tzevelekos (eds), *The EU Accession to the ECHR* (Oxford: Hart, 2014) 75, 76.

[68] See Kuijper (n35) 211. Hoffmeister (n2) 735: 'Whereas attribution of Member States' conduct to the Union would lead to the undesired result that the case would have to be declared inadmissible, attribution to the Member State affirms the jurisdiction of the Court'.

membership in an international organization does not absolve it from its duties under the Convention.

The Court's case law relating to the EU mainly relates to two types of situations. The first is the situation in *Matthews*, where the Court held that an EU Member State could be responsible for a breach of the Convention even where that was brought about by EU law.[69] The Member State was sued for violations that took place at the level of EU primary law. The ECtHR held that nothing prevents a state from transferring powers to an international organization such as the EU; however, the obligation to protect those rights is still incumbent on the Contracting Party. The ECtHR stated that '[t]he Convention does not exclude the transfer of competences to international organizations provided that Convention rights continue to be "secured"'.[70]

The second line of case law relates to Member State action involving the implementation of secondary EU law, as occurred in *Bosphorus*.[71] This involved an EU Member State, Ireland, implementing a binding Community regulation. In this instance, Ireland impounded an aircraft in order to implement Community law, which itself sought to implement a resolution of the United Nations Security Council. The action under review was committed by Ireland, and therefore fell within the ECtHR's jurisdiction. However, in implementing EU law, Ireland had little discretion. The ECtHR held:

> a Contracting Party is responsible under Article 1 of the Convention for all acts and omissions of its organs regardless of whether the act or omission in question was a consequence of domestic law or of the necessity to comply with international legal obligations.[72]

A Contracting Party cannot absolve itself of its obligations by transferring competences to an international organization.[73] However, Ireland did not incur responsibility in this case, since the rights at issue were protected by the EU 'in a manner which can be considered at least equivalent to that for which the Convention provides'.[74] This has come to be known as the 'equivalent protection test'. The ECtHR will not find a breach of human rights obligations in these instances unless there is a manifest deficiency in

---

[69] *Matthews v. United Kingdom* (ECtHR) Reports 1999-I 251.

[70] *Id.*, 265.

[71] *Bosphorus Hava Yollari Turizm ve Ticaret Anonim Şirketi v. Ireland*, App. No. 45036/98, 2005-VI Eur. Ct. H.R. 107.

[72] *Id.*, 153.

[73] *Id.*, 154.

[74] *Id.*, 158.

protection. The ECtHR has acknowledged that the EU legal order provides equivalent protection to the ECHR system.[75]

The ECtHR has since applied the *Bosphorus* judgment in a variety of circumstances relating to international organizations, not only the EU. In applying *Bosphorus*, the Court will examine two key issues. First, it will examine whether there is state action in connection with the act of an IO, which would give the Court jurisdiction in the case. The *Bosphorus* presumption would not apply in situations where there is only action by the EU, without action by a Member State. It will then examine the extent to which the IO involved provides equivalent human rights protection to the ECHR system. Ryngaert points out that in recent case law, the Court has focused more on the second question, with less attention being paid to the question of state action. He also argues that there is a trend to avoid the application of *Bosphorus* in recent cases, 'either by the Court discerning no relevant State action, or by identifying State *discretion*'.[76] This leads to a line of somewhat messy case law stemming from the application of *Bosphorus*. Ryngaert argues that this stems from 'the ECtHR's unease with reviewing the action of IOs, legal subjects which have, so far, not become ECHR contracting parties'.[77] Indeed, one of the reasons it was decided that the EU should accede to the ECHR is the need to fill the 'gap' in legal protection that exists from the EU not being a party to the Convention.

Special Rapporteur Gaja paid quite some attention to the jurisprudence of the ECtHR.[78] In examining the question of a special rule of attribution, he took into account the findings in *Bosphorus* discussed earlier.[79] The Special Rapporteur found that this practice indicated that no rule had developed whereby a Member State's action implementing binding acts of an IO (where there is no discretion) should be attributed to the organization.[80]

---

[75] *Id.*, 161 'the Court finds that the protection of fundamental rights by Community law can be considered to be, and to have been at the relevant time, "equivalent" … to that of the Convention system'.

[76] C. Ryngaert, 'Oscillating between Embracing and Avoiding Bosphorus: The European Court of Human Rights on Member State Responsibility for Acts of International Organisations and the Case of the EU' (2014) 39(2) *European Law Review* 176, 191.

[77] Ryngaert (n76) 191.

[78] See Seventh Report on the Responsibility of International Organizations by G. Gaja, Special Rapporteur, 61st Session of the International Law Commission, 27 May 2009, A/CN.4/610 ('Seventh Report'), para. 33.

[79] *Bosphorus* (n71).

[80] Arguing that *Bosphorus* and other judicial decisions 'clearly do not lend support to the proposal of considering that conduct implementing an act of an international organization should be attributed to that organization' See Seventh Report (n78) para. 33.

While the ECtHR seeks to ensure that a remedy is available to victims, its jurisprudence is also shaped by the fact that it takes into account the autonomy and distinct legal personality of the EU. The presumption of equivalent protection developed in *Bosphorus* can be seen as a manifestation of this. The ECtHR leaves open the possibility for responsibility of the Union, but in each case finds that the EU has ensured protection equivalent to that of the ECHR system. On the one hand, the Court seeks to respect the separate and distinct legal personality of an international organization – it will not find a Member State to be responsible for an act of an IO simply due to its membership. On the other hand, the Court seeks to prevent the situation whereby an ECHR contracting party could avoid its obligations by transferring powers to an international organization.

Questions regarding EU responsibility in the ECHR context were also discussed during debates about the EU's accession to the ECHR. Although the CJEU's negative Opinion on the draft Accession Agreement set back the process on EU accession to the ECHR, the discussions regarding EU responsibility are particularly illuminating. An important innovation in the draft Accession Agreement was the introduction of a 'co-respondent procedure'. This procedure was introduced in order to comply with Protocol 8, which states that the Accession Agreement should contain provisions for 'the mechanisms necessary to ensure that proceedings by non-Member States and individual applications are correctly addressed to Member States and/or the Union as appropriate'.[81] One of the questions before the Strasbourg Court upon accession will be who should be a respondent in a given case: the EU, the Member States or both? The co-respondent mechanism would allow the EU and the Member States to appear as 'co-respondents' before the Court (Section 5.2.3). This means that the Court will not be engaged on the question of who the proper respondent should be, a topic that would likely invite the ECtHR to examine EU law and issues relating to competences, thereby violating the 'autonomy' of the EU legal order. The Explanatory Report states that the co-respondent mechanism was necessary in order 'to accommodate the specific situation of the EU as a non-State entity with an autonomous legal system that is becoming a Party to the Convention alongside its own member States'.[82] Under this model, it remains the prerogative of the applicant to

---

[81] Article 1(b), Protocol (No. 8) relating to Article 6(2) of the Treaty on European Union on the accession of the Union to the European Convention on the Protection of Human Rights and Fundamental Freedoms, OJ C 326, 26 October 2012, 273.

[82] Council of Europe, Final Report to the CDDH, Appendix V, Draft explanatory report to the Agreement on the Accession of the European Union to the Convention for the Protection of Human Rights and Fundamental Freedoms ('Draft Explanatory Report') (2013) para. 38.

choose the party against whom to bring proceedings. However, the co-respondent procedure allows another party (either the EU or an EU Member State or Member States) to be added as a co-respondent in certain instances. A co-respondent is not an intervening party, but a full party to a case,[83] and judgments would be equally binding on both the respondent and co-respondent. While it was generally agreed that a co-respondent mechanism was the best way to ensure cases are addressed to the appropriate party, there was disagreement regarding how such a procedure should function in practice.[84]

The Accession Agreement set out two situations where the co-respondent mechanism would apply. The first scenario allows the EU to be added as a co-respondent in cases where an application has been brought against one or more EU Member States, and the allegation against the Member State 'calls into question the compatibility with the Convention rights at issue of a provision of European Union law, including decisions taken under the TEU and under the TFEU, notably where that violation could have been avoided only by disregarding an obligation under European Union law'.[85] This was designed to cover *Bosphorus* situations, where the alleged violation of the Convention rights stems from a Member State implementing binding EU law. In these cases, the violation may be found in an act of an EU Member State, but the breach can only be rectified at the EU level. The second scenario allowed EU Member States to become co-respondents where an allegation against the EU 'calls into question the compatibility with the [Convention] rights at issue ... of a provision of the [TEU], the [TFEU] or any other provision having the same legal value pursuant to those instruments, notably where that violation could have been avoided only by disregarding an obligation under those instruments'.[86] In such cases, it is not the EU that would be capable of rectifying such a violation, since the TEU and TFEU can only be amended by the Member States.

As a co-respondent is a full party to the case, the judgment of the Strasbourg Court would apply to both respondents.[87] Under this format, there would be joint responsibility between the EU and the Member State for the violation of the Convention, and it would be up to the respondent and co-respondent to

---

[83]   Article 3(1), Council of Europe, Final Report to the CDDH, Appendix I, Draft revised agreement on the accession of the European Union to the Convention for the Protection of Human Rights and Fundamental Freedoms ('EU-ECHR Agreement') (2013).

[84]   X. Groussot, T. Lock & L. Pech, 'EU Accession to the European Convention on Human Rights: A Legal Assessment of the Draft Accession Agreement of 14th October 2011' (2011) 18 *Robert Schuman Foundation Policy Paper* 7.

[85]   Article 3(2) EU-ECHR Accession Agreement (n83).

[86]   Article 3(3) EU-ECHR Accession Agreement (n83).

[87]   Article 3(1) EU-ECHR Accession Agreement (n83).

decide how to repair any violation. The Accession Agreement addressed the issue of responsibility in cases where a co-respondent is involved. Article 3(7) stated that:

> If the violation in respect of which a High Contracting Party is a co-respondent to the proceedings is established, the respondent and the co-respondent shall be jointly responsible for that violation, unless the Court, on the basis of the reasons given by the respondent and the co-respondent, and having sought the views of the applicant, decides that only one of them be held responsible.[88]

This means that in cases where the EU or Member States appear as respondent and co-respondent, there will be a presumption in favour of joint responsibility, but this presumption can be rebutted if the Strasbourg Court decides to find only one party to be responsible. The co-respondent procedure was designed so that the Strasbourg Court would not have to wade into delicate questions regarding the apportionment of responsibility between the EU Member States and the European Union, which will often touch upon the issue of competences in the EU legal order.

Although the co-respondent mechanism was designed to respect the autonomy of the EU legal order, the CJEU referred to it as one of the reasons why the *draft accession* agreement violated the autonomy of the EU and EU law.[89] In the Court found that this procedure would still require the ECtHR to assess rules of EU *Opinion 2/13* law concerning the division of powers between the EU and the Member States, thereby violating the autonomy of the EU legal order.[90] It has been argued that the inclusion of the co-respondent mechanism illustrates the fact that, in the ECHR context, rules of attribution are still anything but clear.[91] Although it points to the complexity of the issue in the EU context, it was mainly designed to ensure the autonomy of the EU, and to guarantee that the ECtHR would not delve into issues regarding EU competences.

---

[88] Article 3(7) EU-ECHR Accession Agreement (n83).

[89] *Opinion 2/13*, EU:C:2014:2454.

[90] *Opinion 2/13*, EU:C:2014:2454, para. 230–231: 'A decision on the apportionment as between the EU and its Member States of responsibility for an act or omission constituting a violation of the ECHR established by the ECtHR is also one that is based on an assessment of the rules of EU law governing the division of powers between the EU and its Member States and the attributability of that act or omission. Accordingly, to permit the ECtHR to adopt such a decision would also risk adversely affecting the division of powers between the EU and its Member States' (Section 5.2.3).

[91] Cortés Martín (n48)198: 'If the responsibility of the EU, where member states act in the execution of EU law, were clear, it would not have been necessary to establish this co-defendant mechanism in the accession agreement to the convention'.

Article 1(4) of the Accession Agreement set out:

> For the purposes of the Convention, of the Protocols thereto and of this Agreement, an act, measure or omission of organs of a member State of the European Union or of persons acting on its behalf shall be attributed to that State, even if such act, measure or omission occurs when the State implements the law of the European Union, including decisions taken under the Treaty on the European Union (hereinafter referred to as 'the TEU') and under the Treaty on the Functioning of the European Union (hereinafter referred to as the 'TFEU').[92]

This means that an act of an EU Member State will be attributed to that state, even when implementing Union law. In cases where the EU and a Member State or Member States appear as a respondent and co-respondent, there is a presumption in favour of joint responsibility.[93] In a comment on the Accession Agreement, Gaja was critical of the solution devised by the negotiators.[94] Rather than including an assumption in favour of joint responsibility between the EU and the Member State, Gaja was in favour of allowing the ECtHR to determine which party was responsible.

The jurisprudence of the ECHR shows quite a different trend from that of the WTO context.[95] In the context of the WTO, conduct of the EU and of the Member States could be attributed to the Union. In contrast, the ECtHR will not attribute conduct of a Member State to the EU when implementing binding EU law. The difference in outcomes may be explained in part by the different contexts in which responsibility is addressed. In the ECHR context, where the EU is not a party, the Court is concerned with ensuring that a remedy is available to individuals. At the WTO, the EU is an active player that is keen to argue in favour of Union responsibility. Another issue could be the fact that the ECHR predates the EU. The ECtHR is at pains to ensure that a Contracting Party cannot rely on their EU (or other organization) membership to avoid their existing human rights obligations. The EU predates the WTO Agreement and was a negotiating party in the Uruguay Round. In this way, there may be less anxiety about the EU Member States avoiding their WTO commitments through EU membership.

---

[92] Article 1(4) EU-ECHR Accession Agreement (n83).
[93] Draft Explanatory Report (n82) 7.
[94] G. Gaja, 'The "Co-Respondent Mechanisms" According to the Draft Agreement for the accession of the EU to the ECHR' in V. Kosta, N. Skoutaris & V. Tzevelekos (eds), *The EU Accession to the ECHR* (Oxford: Hart, 2014) 341.
[95] Cortés Martín (n48) 195.

6.4.4.3 Models of Attribution

International practice does not firmly point to the development of a special rule of attribution that applies in the EU context. The ILC acknowledged that such a rule does not appear to have yet developed.[96] The academic literature points to a number of different models of attribution that have emerged in practice.

The first approach has been described as the 'organic model'.[97] This is the classic manner by which an international organization would incur responsibility, that is, by acting via its own organs implementing its own law. In the context of the EU, there are a number of fields where the Union acts via its own organs. It has at its disposal a number of institutions, bodies, offices and agencies that manage and carry out Union law and Union policies in fields as diverse as competition law, agriculture, aid and development. The ARIO give a prominent role to the organic model. The obvious challenge with the organic model is that it can only capture a certain amount of EU action. In most cases, the EU is not acting through its 'own' organs, but carries out conduct through its Member States.

The second approach to attribution is described as the 'competence model'.[98] Under this approach to attribution, international responsibility broadly corresponds to competence. Rather than attributing conduct to the actor involved in the breach of an obligation, this would entail an inquiry into who, either the EU or the Member States, exercises competence in the field. This would mean, for example, that in an area of exclusive competence, the EU would be internationally responsible in the event of a breach, even if it were the EU Member State that had acted. This approach also runs into immediate difficulties in the EU context since competences are not neatly divided between the EU and the Member States, and most international agreements are concluded by the EU and the Member States alongside each other. This would mean that the 'declaration of competence' drafted by the EU and the Member States would come into play when determining issues of responsibility. One of the original rationales behind the declaration of competence was to help identify the appropriate party, either the EU or the Member State(s), who could be held responsible in event of breach of an obligation. It has been argued that these declarations should be considered to be purely informative and 'should not be assimilated to treaty provisions'.[99] As

---

[96] See Seventh Report (n78) 12–13.
[97] Kuijper & Paasivirta (n2) 49.
[98] Kuijper & Paasivirta (n2) 54.
[99] Kuijper & Paasivirta (n2) 57.

argued in Section 3.3.2, declarations of competence are made in connection to an obligation arising from a treaty, and are not only informative, but also legally relevant for the EU and its treaty partners.

Where responsibility is linked to competences, it invites third parties to examine the internal legal order of the EU. It expects that third parties are to have an understanding of complex issues of EU law and the internal division of competences.[100] It is not evident why an internal issue of competence should be relevant when determining an international law issue such as attribution of responsibility. Competence does not seem to be one of the criteria for attribution in the ARIO. As argued earlier, that a special rule had emerged was mostly based on WTO practice.[101] Kuijper and Paasivirta acknowledge that the competence model remains a 'novelty' in international law,[102] which has developed in the context of a different understanding of how international organizations function than that of the EU.

Another possibility is joint responsibility. Joint responsibility applies, for instance, under Annex IX, Article 6 of UNCLOS if parties fail to provide information on who is responsible for a specific matter. As discussed earlier, the draft agreement on the EU's accession to the ECHR also envisaged joint responsibility under the co-respondent mechanism.

6.4.4.4 Response of the ILC

The ILC did not find that a specialized rule of attribution had come into existence with regard to the EU, despite the arguments of the European Union and academic commentary in support of a specialized rule.[103] However, the door was left open for the development of specialized rules in other ways, such as through the *lex specialis* provision (Section 6.4.5.2).[104] International practice remains diverse, and is influenced by the context of the dispute settlement

---

[100] P. Eeckhout, *EU External Relations Law*, 2nd edn (Oxford: Oxford University Press, 2011) 264: 'The difficulty with that position is that it forces the EU's treaty partners to have expertise on complex matters of EU external competence, leading to the possibility that they may fear that such matters could be an obstacle to invoking the responsibility of the EU or its Member States under a mixed agreement'. P. M. Olson, 'Mixity from the Outside: The Perspective of a Treaty Partner' in C. Hillion & P. Koutrakos (eds), *Mixed Agreements Revisited: The EU and its Member States in the World* (Oxford: Hart, 2010) 331–348.

[101] Kuijper & Paasivirta (n2) 57.

[102] Kuijper & Paasivirta (n2) 67.

[103] G. Gaja, Special Rapporteur, International Law Commission, Second Report on Responsibility of International Organizations, 2 April 2004, UN Doc. A/CN.4/541, 5–8.

[104] D'Aspremont (n67) 78: 'Although falling short of an explicit acknowledgment of a rule of attribution of conduct, this solution does not bar the general rules of attribution from yielding to any specific rule pertaining to the relations between the EU and its MS'.

mechanism involved. Given this diversity, there was no 'common thread' pointing towards specific rules developing in the context of the EU.[105] It is likely that international law in this field will continue to develop as the EU takes part in more international dispute settlement mechanisms, in which 'tailor made solutions'[106] will be developed.

The discussion on the topic of attribution also highlights a point of divergence between the EU and international law perspectives. From an EU perspective, competence is very much the touchstone of international responsibility. The ARIO, however, is viewed as taking a 'power-oriented' approach[107] that gives less emphasis to normative control exercised by IOs. The tension between these two approaches is evident in the literature and the discussions in the ILC context.

6.4.4.5 Other Rules of Attribution

Chapter II ARIO sets out rules for the 'Attribution of conduct to an international organization'. This section briefly discusses these rules in light of the EU. As a starting point, the ARIO considers that the act of an organ or agent of international organization will be considered an act of that organization.[108] This general rule of attribution corresponds with Article 4 ASR, which states that the conduct of a state organ will be considered to be an act of that state.[109] Conduct is attributable to an international organization when the agent or organ is performing tasks assigned to it by the international organization. The term agent comprises both legal and natural persons. Conduct of an organ or agent is attributable to an international organization only when they act in

---

[105] Cortés Martín (n48) 192–193. Cortés Marín argues in this regard 'it is doubtful whether there is a common thread by way of international courts and tribunals dealing with the EU's international responsibility'.

[106] Paasivirta & Kuijper (n2) 203. 'International law issues have typically arisen gradually and they are being addressed on a case-by-case basis, often marked by tailor-made solutions . . .'

[107] 'In essence, the DARIO takes a power-oriented approach to responsibility and transplants it into the more delicately constructed world of competences – and it is unsurprising that there is no easy fit'. M. Evans & P. Okowa, 'Approaches to Responsibility in International Courts' in M. Evans & P. Koutrakos (eds), *The International Responsibility of the European Union: European and International Perspectives* (Oxford: Hart, 2013) 101, 103.

[108] Article 6 ARIO (n1). 'The conduct of an organ or agent of an international organization in the performance of functions of that organ or agent shall be considered an act of that organization under international law, whatever position the organ or agent holds in respect of the organization'.

[109] Article 4(1) ASR (n9): 'The conduct of any State organ shall be considered an act of that State under international law, whether the organ exercises legislative, executive, judicial or any other functions, whatever position it holds in the organization of the State, and whatever its character as an organ of the central Government or of a territorial unit of the State'.

performance of those functions, not, for instance, when they act in their private or other capacity. In determining the functions of organs and agents, the 'rules of the organization' will be taken into account, although these are not the only criteria. Since in the EU context the Member States are often responsible for implementing acts of the organization, it was considered whether the organs of the Member States could be considered those of the EU under this article. However, the Special Rapporteur rejected the idea that the Member State organs could be regarded as those of the IO in those circumstances.

The EU, like any international organization, is only capable of acting through its organs.[110] As discussed earlier, in many cases the EU will be acting through its Member States, who play a dual role in relation in the implementation of EU law. Academic opinion was mixed on whether the EU Member States can be viewed as 'organs' of the EU. At first sight, this may seem logical. In these circumstances, the Member States' authorities are the actual hands that implement decisions of the EU. However, Kuijper and Paasivirta acknowledge that in international law 'the actual degree of control of the Community institutions over Member State organs is generally considered too weak'.[111] One reason for this is that when implementing EU law, Member States have a certain margin of discretion. The EU exercises what is considered normative or legal control, but this cannot be considered 'effective control' for the purposes of the ARIO.

Article 7 ARIO – 'at the Disposal of' another IO

Article 7 deals with the situation where state organs or agents of an international organization are placed 'at the disposal of' another international organization.[112] In this situation, the conduct will be considered to be the conduct of the latter organization for the purposes of international law 'if

---

[110] See S. Talmon, 'Responsibility of International Organizations: Does the European Community Require Special Treatment?' in M. Ragazzi (ed), *International Responsibility Today: Essays in Memory of Oscar Schachter* (Leiden: Martinus Nijhoff, 2005) 405, 410, Talmon refers to the finding of the Permanent Court of International Justice (PCIJ) in *German Settlers in Poland*, Advisory Opinion, 1923, that 'States can act only by and through their agents and representatives'

[111] P.-J. Kuijper & E. Paasivirta, 'Further Exploring International Responsibility: The European Community and the ILC's Project on Responsibility of International Organizations' (2004) 1 *International Organizations Law Review* 111, 126.

[112] Article 7 ARIO (n1). 'The conduct of an organ of a State or an organ or agent of an international organization that is placed at the disposal of another international organization shall be considered under international law an act of the latter organization if the organization exercises effective control over that conduct'.

the organization exercises effective control over that conduct'.[113] This article applies to the situation, for example, when a state puts its military forces at the disposal of the UN for peacekeeping operations. It creates a link between the IO and the state or other IO through the notion of 'effective control'. The element of control is to be assessed on a case-by-case basis examining the facts of each case. It is clear from the academic discussion and the commentary to this article that it was developed mainly with military and peacekeeping situations in mind. It may be difficult to envisage situations outside of this context where an IO exercises 'effective control' over the state or IO organ. It would be quite a stretch to argue that where an EU Member State is implementing EU law, the Union is exercising 'effective control' over the Member State. However, it has been argued that the Union 'borrows' the Member State authorities, for example, to implement WTO obligations.[114] While the EU could be seen as exercising 'effective control' over state organs in this way, this also seems to be a stretch. Kuijper and Paasivirta point out that the idea that the EU Member State authorities are put at the disposal of the EU 'grates at the ears of the average Community lawyer'.[115] 'Normative control' exercised by the EU is of a different level and character of control than that envisaged in Article 7 of the ARIO.

Article 9

Whereas the above-mentioned rules of attribution are based on objective elements, Article 9 introduces a rule whereby conduct may be attributable to an IO where it adopts the conduct in question as its own. This is based on a similarly worded provision in the ASR.[116] The provision in the ASR is meant to deal with cases where the state acknowledges the conduct of private entities as its own.[117] Whereas Article 11 of the ASR is based on state practice involving the adoption of conduct by the state, there is far less practice of an international organization adopting acts in a similar manner. The ILC took into account practice of the EU, such as the pleadings made before a WTO Panel in *European Communities – Customs Classification of Certain Computer Equipment*.[118] Here the EC was ready to assume *responsibility* for the measures, but was not adopting the conduct

---

[113] Article 7 ARIO (n1).
[114] E. Steinberger, 'The WTO Treaty as a Mixed Agreement: Problems with EC's and the EC Member States' Membership of the WTO' (2006) 17(4) *European Journal of International Law* 837, 851.
[115] Kuijper & Paasivirta (n111) 127.
[116] Article 11 ASR (n9) 'Conduct acknowledged and adopted by a State as its own'.
[117] ASR (n9) Commentary to Article 11.
[118] ARIO Commentary (n1) 30.

as its own. Article 9 seems to provide a counterpart to Article 11 of the ASR, and is not founded on relevant practice of international organizations.

6.4.5 *Specialized Rules*

Since the ILC decided not to adopt special rules of attribution regarding the EU or REIOs, the question remained regarding whether the ARIO could deal with the pressing challenge of the diversity of IOs in another way. The ILC's proposed solution was to include clauses that would allow the diversity of organizations to be taken into account. For example, it made a number of references to the 'rules of the organization' in several parts of the draft articles, which allow the internal legal order of the organization to be considered. It also included a '*lex specialis*' rule that could also to take into account the diversity of IOs. This gave rise to a new string of criticism: that these rules allowed IOs to 'contract out' of general rules of responsibility through reference to their 'internal' legal orders.

6.4.5.1 'Rules of the Organization'

The first method by which the ILC sought to take into account the diversity of international organizations is through multiple references to the 'rules of the organization' throughout the ARIO. Article 2 of the ARIO defines 'Rules of the organization' for the purposes of the articles as follows:

> 'rules of the organization' means, in particular, the constituent instruments, decisions, resolutions and other acts of the international organization adopted in accordance with those instruments, and established practice of the organization[119]

This definition closely resembles the term used in the VCLT-IO[120] and the Vienna Convention on Succession of States in Respect of Treaties.[121] The

---

[119]   Article 2 ARIO (n1).
[120]   Article 2(1)(j), Vienna Convention on the Law of Treaties between States and International Organizations or between International Organizations (21 March 1986) 25 ILM 543 (1986), not yet in force ('VCLT-IO'): '"rules of the organization" means, in particular, the constituent instruments, decisions and resolutions adopted in accordance with them, and established practice of the organization'. Article 5, Article 7, Article 27, Article 36, Article 46, all mention the 'rules of the organization'.
[121]   Article 5, Vienna Convention on Succession of States in Respect of Treaties (23 August 1978) 1946 UNTS 3, entered into force 6 November 1996: 'The present Convention applies to any treaty which is the constituent instrument of an international organization and to any treaty adopted within an international organization without prejudice to any relevant rules of the organization'.

definition includes the constituent instruments of the organization, the decisions and resolutions adopted in accordance with those instruments, as well as the 'established practice' of the organization. The ARIO adds to this 'other acts' alongside decisions and resolutions. In the context of the EU, this means that not only the constituent EU Treaties should be viewed as 'rules of the organization', but also the body of legislative and other acts that it adopts. The EU had argued that the definition of 'rules of the organization' should also include references to the general principles of law of the organization and the case law of the organization's court.[122] These comments reflect the importance of the CJEU and its jurisprudence in EU law. This is not an issue that has been clarified in the Commentary, however. Given the fact that the CJEU plays such an instrumental role in determining the balance of competences between the EU and the Member States, as well as other issues that may be important in determining issues of responsibility, the jurisprudence of the Court should also be included as comprising the 'established practice' of the EU for these purposes.

6.4.5.2 References to 'Rules of the Organization'

The term 'rules of the organization' is used throughout the ARIO, although it is clear from the context that the term is not always used for the same purpose. In some cases, its use suggests that the rules of the organization are to be viewed as 'internal rules' analogous to the domestic law of a state. In other parts, the rules of the organization are understood as having an international legal character, having the status of international legal instruments. This shows how the constituent treaties of an IO, including the EU Treaties, have a dual character: depending on the circumstances, they can be viewed as either an international legal instrument or an internal constitutional instrument.

Article 5 ARIO sets out that '[t]he characterization of an act of an international organization as internationally wrongful is governed by international law'. This means that, for the purposes of determining whether an act of an international organization is internationally wrongful, the question must be answered with reference to *international law*, not the internal law of the organization. This article is based on Article 3 of the ASR, which sets out that '[t]he characterization of an act of a State as internationally wrongful is governed by international law. Such characterization is not affected by the

---

[122] Statement on Behalf of the European Union by Dr J. G. Lammers, Legal Adviser, MFA, Item 144: Report of the International Law Commission on the work of its fifty-sixth session. Responsibility of International Organizations. Sixth Committee, 59th Session of the UN General Assembly (New York).

characterization of the same act as lawful by internal law'.[123] This means that the internal law of a state cannot be used to justify the breach of an international obligation by that state. The ARIO does away with the second sentence of article 3 ASR, which refers to the states' internal law. The ILC recognizes the difficulty in transferring this approach in the ASR to the context of international organizations. This difficulty arises from the hybrid nature of the rules of international organizations as belonging to both international and internal law. This is because

> the rules of an international organization cannot be sharply differentiated from international law. At least the constituent instrument of the international organization is a treaty or another instrument governed by international law; other rules of the organization may be viewed as part of international law.[124]

The ILC recognizes that the rules of the organization cannot be viewed as purely the 'internal law' of that organization, but also as forming part of international law. The 'rules of the organization' cannot therefore be compared with the 'internal law' of a state in all situations. The ILC was mindful of not simply replacing the term 'internal law' in the ASR with the term 'rules of the organization' throughout the ARIO.

The 'rules of the organization' are also referred to in Article 64 on *lex specialis* (Section 6.4.5.2). In defining what constitutes 'special rules of international law' for the purposes of this provision, the ARIO states that they 'may be contained in the *rules of the organization* applicable to the relations between an international organization and its members'.[125] This provision explicitly states that the 'rules of the organization' should be considered as belonging to the realm of international law rather than the internal order of the IO.

In other parts, the rules of the organization are understood as 'internal rules'. For instance, Article 6 ARIO deals with the attribution of conduct. Paragraph 2 allows the 'rules of the organization' to be taken into account 'in the determination of the functions of its organs and agents'.[126] Article 6 reflects the position of the European Commission, which was of the opinion that a general rule on attribution of conduct should include a reference to the rules of the organization. The 'rules of the organization' are also referred to in Article 32 ARIO, which sets out that an organization may not rely on its

---

[123] Article 3 ASR (n9).
[124] ARIO (n1) Commentary to Article 5.
[125] Article 64 ARIO (n1). Emphasis added.
[126] Article 6 ARIO (n1).

internal rules as justification for failure to comply with its international obligations. This rule is the international organization counterpart to the rule that states may not invoke internal rules to justify non-compliance with their international obligations. This rule is also found in Article 27(2) of the VCLT-IO.[127] This is because the rules of the organization apply in the relations between the organization and its members, and cannot be invoked in relation to third states. Again, the 'rules of the organization' are viewed as belonging to the internal law of the IO, analogous with the internal law of a state, which cannot be relied upon to justify non-compliance with international obligations.

Article 45 ARIO regarding the admissibility of claims indirectly refers to the 'rules of the organization'. The article parallels Article 44 of the ASR, setting out the need to exhaust local remedies. The ILC's commentary accompanying this article specifically refers to EU practice in this regard. It discusses an instance whereby the Director-General of the Legal Service of the European Commission made a statement on behalf of the Union before the Council of the International Civil Aviation Organization. In this instance EU Member States argued that claims by the United States regarding EC legislation on aircraft were inadmissible since domestic remedies had not been exhausted, both in the legal systems of the Member States, and at the level of the EU via the European Court of Justice.[128] The ILC concludes from this practice 'whether a claim is addressed to the EU Member States or the responsibility of the European Union is invoked, exhaustion of remedies existing within the European Union would be required'.[129] While Article 45 does not explicitly mention the rules of the organization, its inclusion in the ARIO 'helps safeguard the jurisdictional system of the Union by accepting that exhaustion of "local remedies" may have to take place within the organization'.[130]

The way in which the 'rules of the organization' are used throughout the ARIO show that they have a somewhat indeterminate status. Depending on the provision of the ARIO in question, the 'rules of the organization' may be viewed as having an international legal significance for the law of responsibility, or may be viewed as analogous with the internal legal order of a state. The ILC decided not to take a firm position on the legal status of the 'rules of the organization'. The ILC's indeterminate position on this issue reflects the indeterminate nature of the rules of the organization in the context of IOs – they can be considered as

---

[127] Article 27(2) VCLT-IO (n120): 'An international organization party to a treaty may not invoke the rules of the organization as justification for its failure to perform the treaty'.

[128] ARIO (n1) Commentary to Article 45, 73.

[129] ARIO (n1) Commentary to Article 45, 73.

[130] Kuijper & Paasivirta (n2) 47.

both internal law and as international law, depending on the particular rule. This touches upon one of the issues discussed throughout this study, that is, the idea that the EU Treaties cannot be viewed as solely 'internal' law of the IO, of no international legal relevance.

The ILC was criticized for not taking a clear-cut approach to this issue. There has been academic discussion about how the rules of the organization should be characterized. According to the one view, the rules of the organization are purely internal as they deal with questions on how the IO regulates its own legal order. Another view sees the rules of the organization as belonging to the realm of international law, since they are normally based on a treaty or international legal instrument and therefore can be regarded as 'specialized' international law. A third view sees the constituent treaty of an organization transform in status: at the point of its creation the constituent instrument of an international organization moves from being an international legal instrument to being an internal constitutional instrument that applies only between the organization and its members and between its members.[131]

The ILC acknowledges in its commentary that there is disagreement regarding the legal nature of the rules of the organization:

> Many consider that the rules of treaty-based organizations are part of international law. Some authors have held that, although international organizations are established by treaties or other instruments governed by international law, the internal law of the organization, once it has come into existence, does not form part of international law.[132]

Some international lawyers dispute the characterization of the rules of the organization as belonging to the realm of international law. D'Aspremont, for example, is critical of the approach taken by the ILC:

> The ILC decided not to take a 'clear-cut' position on the nature of [the rules of the organization] as either international law or internal law of the organization, which leaves the scope of application of the ARIO severely indeterminate. As a result, some provisions of the ARIO could be construed as to endow the rules of the organizations with an international character – in contradiction which their intrinsically internal nature –, paving the way for the exact opposite effects from those envisaged by the Commission.[133]

---

[131] C. Ahlborn, 'The Rules of International Organizations and the Law of International Responsibility' (2011) 8 *International Organizations Law Review* 397, 398.

[132] ARIO (n1) Commentary to Article 10, 32.

[133] J. d'Aspremont, 'The Articles on the Responsibility of International Organizations: Magnifying the Fissures in the Law of International Responsibility' (2012) 9 *International Organizations Law Review* 15, 26.

Ahlborn is also critical of the fact that the ILC decided not to take decisive view on the nature of the rules of the organization for the purposes of responsibility,[134] arguing that the constituent instruments of organizations should be viewed as 'contracts between states at the moment of the creation of an international organization' but from that moment, they then operate as constitutions during the life of the organization.[135] The secondary law of an IO, moreover, should not be characterized as having an international legal character.[136]

The problem arises from a much wider debate within public international law about the character of the constituent instrument of an international organization.[137] In many parts of the ARIO the term 'rules of the organization' has simply replaced the term 'internal law' that was used in the ASR. Yet it would not have been appropriate for the ILC to have simply replaced 'internal law' with 'rules of the organization' in all cases. This is because there is a key difference between states and international organizations in this regard. In relation to states, internal law is generally not relevant when determining issues of responsibility, except, for instance, when determining who can be considered an 'organ' of the state.[138] For international organizations, the constituent instrument is not a purely internal 'constitutional' instrument, but becomes relevant in resolving certain questions regarding responsibility.

Although the ILC has been criticized for not giving a clear view on the status of the rules of the organization, it would have been difficult for the ILC to seek to resolve this issue, especially when it remains a highly debated topic in public international law.[139] It reflects the fact that there may be circumstances where, despite the IO's internal law being of a constitutional character, it is nonetheless relevant in determining issues of responsibility. For instance, the rules of the organization will be taken into account when determining whether *lex specialis* exists under Article 64. It flows from the 'dual nature' of the IO's constituent instrument: it is both a treaty instrument between the Member States, governed by international law, but it also establishes a new

---

[134]   Ahlborn (n131) 398.
[135]   Ahlborn (n131) 403.
[136]   Ahlborn (n131) 417.
[137]   C. Brölmann, *The Institutional Veil in Public International Law: International Organisations and the Law of Treaties* (Oxford: Hart, 2007) 144.
[138]   Article 4(2) ASR (n9).
[139]   K. Schmalenbach, 'Article 5. Treaties Constituting International Organizations and Treaties Adopted' in O. Dörr & K. Schmalenbach (eds), *Vienna Convention on the Law of Treaties: A Commentary* (Heidelberg: Springer, 2012) 91–92. 'The constituent instruments' Janus face is the starting point of the controversy between the so called "traditionalists" and "constitutionalists". Whereas the former school of thought stresses the contractual nature of constituent instruments, the latter emphasizes their self-contained and evolutionary nature'.

legal person with rights and duties on the international plane, and regulates the internal order of this new body.

The paradox regarding the 'rules of the organization' is even more complex regarding the EU. As discussed in Chapter 1, the EU has argued that it has become an autonomous constitutional legal order. Many EU lawyers would reject the notion that the EU Treaties and EU law and practice are a part of international law. At the same time, it is the EU that has argued that its internal legal order, and the unique characteristics, should be taken into account for the purposes of international responsibility. Kuijper and Paasivirta point out that for the EU the 'rules of the organization' are 'more extensive and complicated in the EU than in any other international organization'.[140] Yet they are critical of the utility of the referring to the 'rules of the organization' in the EU context:

> most of the articles on the rules of the organisation in the draft articles, though important for the Union, in particular for the integrity of it[s] juris-dictional system, do not really deal with the big structural questions which are important if the Union is going to be able to fit somehow into the rules on responsibility of the ILC.[141]

Another criticism is that categorizing the 'rules of the organization' as being international in character goes against the idea of the EU as an autonomous legal order. EU law is no longer seen (if it ever was) as simply as sub-branch of international law, but as a developed legal order in its own right.[142] The Commentary also acknowledges that there may be a 'special case' regarding organizations that have a high degree of integration, such as the European Union. In this regard, the ILC refers to the CJEU's case law, particularly *Costa v. E.N.E.L.*,[143] which set out that the EU treaties have created a new legal order. The ILC does not expand on this, however.

6.4.5.3 Lex Specialis

In addition to the references to the 'rules of the organization' in the ARIO, the ILC also included a *lex specialis* rule that would allow, under certain circumstances, the application of 'special rules of international law':

[140] Kuijper & Paasivirta (n2) 37.
[141] Kuijper & Paasivirta (n2) 47.
[142] Schmalenbach (n139) 92–93. 'There is a vivid and still undecided academic debate on the legal nature of the constituent instruments of the European Union; that is, whether they have discarded their original character as inter-State agreements governed by the international law of treaties'.
[143] Judgment in *Costa* v. *E.N.E.L*, 6/64, EU:C:1964:66.

These articles do not apply where and to the extent that the conditions for the existence of an internationally wrongful act or the content or implementation of the international responsibility of an international organization, or a State in connection with the conduct of an international organization, are governed by special rules of international law. Such special rules of international law may be contained in the rules of the organization applicable to the relations between an international organization and its members.[144]

Article 64 ARIO finds its counterpart in Article 55 ASR, which sets out that:

These articles do not apply where and to the extent that the conditions for the existence of an internationally wrongful act or the content or implementation of the international responsibility of a State are governed by special rules of international law.[145]

The *lex specialis* provisions in the ASR and ARIO give effect to the notion that normative priority is to be given to more specialized rules.[146] It also recognizes the residual nature of rules of responsibility. Under the ASR, states may derogate from these general rules of responsibility in their mutual relations. Similarly, the relationship between international organizations, or between states and international organizations, may be governed by special rules of international law. What is more controversial however is that in the ARIO, special rules of international law may be based on the rules of the organization. This gives rise to the question of whether the internal legal order of the EU should be considered 'special rules of international law' for the purposes of these draft articles.

While the ILC decided against specialized rules for the EU or for REIOs it did eventually adopt a *lex specialis* principle in Article 64 ARIO. In the commentary to Article 64, the ILC specifically refers to the practice of the European Union in this regard:

it may be useful to refer to one issue which has given rise in practice to a variety of opinions concerning the possible existence of a special rule: that of the attribution to the European Community (now European Union) of conduct of States members of the Community when they implement binding acts of the Community.[147]

---

[144] Article 64 ARIO (n1).
[145] Article 55 ASR (n9).
[146] 'Fragmentation of International Law: Difficulties arising from the Diversification and Expansion of International Law', Report of the Study Group of the International Law Commission finalized by Martti Koskenniemi, 13 April 2006, UN Doc. A/CN.4/L.682, 1–256 and 18 July 2006, UN Doc. A/CN.4/L.702, para. 64.
[147] ARIO (n1) Commentary to Article 64, 100.

It is clear that the *lex specialis* rule was added partly with the EU in mind. In addition to the references to the 'rules of the organization' it can be viewed as another way in which the ILC sought to take into account the specific circumstances of an international organization, without having to design specific rules for that body. Like the 'rules of the organization', the inclusion of the principle of *lex specialis* has also given rise to a line of academic commentary and criticism. D'Aspremont argues that Article 64, while not a panacea, 'allows (theoretically) the emergence of special rules of international responsibility in relation to REIOs like the EU, especially when it comes to attribution of conduct'.[148] However, he argues against the existence of special rules of responsibility regarding the EU because 'the rules of the organization pertaining to its relation with its Member States are of an internal nature and therefore cannot constitute special rules for the sake of article 64'.[149] The argument is that specialized rules can only take precedence over general rules when they are of the same status. D'Aspremont concludes, therefore, 'the rules of the EU about the distribution of competences cannot be considered to have the same status as the rules of attribution of the general regime of international responsibility and can accordingly not be considered "special"'.[150] They are of an internal nature, and cannot be seen as constituting *lex specialis* for the purposes of the general responsibility regime. Rather, specialized rules have emerged in the practice of international courts and dispute settlement mechanisms. Ahlborn similarly argues that the 'internal rules' of an international organization cannot be regarded as *lex specialis*,[151] arguing that that the term *'lex specialis'* when referring to the internal rules of the organization, is misleading,[152] preferring the term 'self-contained' or 'sectoral' regimes.

The inclusion of the *lex specialis* rule demonstrates a certain influence the EU was able to exercise over the drafting of the articles. The EU asserted that '[g]iven the very diverse nature of international organizations it is clear that there is a need for a *lex specialis* provision'.[153] There is disagreement over the

---

[148]   D'Aspremont (n67) 8.
[149]   D'Aspremont (n67) 8.
[150]   D'Aspremont (n67) 9.
[151]   Ahlborn (n131).
[152]   Ahlborn (n131) 438: 'Considering the internal nature of the rules of the organization, however, it is submitted that the contractual term *lex specialis* is misleading if applied to the internal legal orders of international organizations'.
[153]   Statement on behalf of the European Community by Mr Patrick Hetsch, Director, European Commission Legal Service, at the 64th Session of the United Nations General Assembly 6th Committee on Agenda Item 81, 27 October 2009, New York: Report of the International Law Commission on the Work of its 61st Session, Responsibility of International Organizations.

extent to which such a provision will be applicable to the EU context. The real thrust of the criticism comes, not from the inclusion of the *lex specialis* rule, but by the indication that 'rules of the organization' can be considered *lex specialis*. It has been suggested that this could allow international organizations such as the EU to 'contract out' of the general regime of international responsibility by reference to rules that are 'internal' to that organization.[154] The rules of an IO, it is argued, are to be considered as only applicable to the legal order of that IO, and should not be opposable to parties that are not members of that organization. The inclusion of the internal rules of the IO as *lex specialis* reflects the fact that that the rules of the organization are not entirely 'internal'; they are still to be regarded as 'specialized' international law. One must keep in mind that the *lex specialis* rule does not allow the internal rules of the organization to 'displace' the general regime in all circumstances. IOs, just like states, cannot invoke their internal law as a justification for breaching their international obligations. The academic commentary on the provision demonstrates that the extent of the *lex specialis* provision remains unclear. The ARIO leaves many of these conceptual questions unaddressed and the precise contours of the *lex specialis* rule will be fleshed out in future practice.

One of the main criticisms of allowing specialized rules of IOs to be taken into account for the purposes of international responsibility is that, in many cases, they would essentially subject third states to the internal rules of an international organization. This would mean that a non-contracting party would be subject to legal rules to which they have not given their consent. The rules of an organization, according to this argument, only have legal effect *within* that organization, and between the contacting parties who have consented to those rules. This argument is based on the legal principle *res inter alios acta, aliis nec nocet nec prodest* ('a thing done between others does not harm or benefit others') that is recognized in international law. Simply put, EU law is the internal law of the organization, which can only be given effect within that legal system. It cannot, therefore, be relied upon in determining issues regarding third states, particularly on an issue as important as the EU's international responsibility. The ILC's study on fragmentation of international law discusses the issue of the EU's complex legal order, including the issue of competences and mixed agreements, stating that '[i]t has of course

---

[154] 'On its face the [ARIO] *lex specialis* provision might lead to an enclave of "untouchable" international organizations to which the [ARIO] could not be applied' N. Gal-Or, 'Responsibility of the WTO for Breach of an International Obligation under the Draft Articles on Responsibility of International Organizations' (2012) 50 *The Canadian Yearbook of International Law* 197.

been stressed on the part of the EU that none of this will have any effect on the rights of third States – and indeed, no such effect could ensue from legal developments that from the perspective of the latter are strictly *inter alios acta*.[155]

One complication in this regard is that it is difficult to separate rules as being 'internal' or 'international'. For instance, in many cases before international dispute settlement bodies, such as the WTO, the adjudicating body will take into account the internal legal order of the EU. For example, Hoffmeister argues that, in international litigation involving the EU, the internal rules of the EU regarding competences are 'of primordial importance for both the third state or applicant in question and the Union and its Member States alike'.[156] Here we see the development of specialized rules develop through the EU's interaction with the wider international legal order.

Despite the criticism of the inclusion of the *lex specialis* rule, it may be defended for a number of reasons. It allows for a conceptual coherence between the ARIO and ASR. It reflects the idea that the rules are of a general and residual character, and allows the development of more specific rules. Indeed, one of the criticisms of the ARIO was that it was developed before sufficient practice had emerged. The *lex specialis* rule allows for the development of specialized rules of responsibility, but recognizes a fallback to a general system of responsibility.[157] It allows for the possibility of special rules to develop in the EU context (and in other IOs) without the ARIO having to include such rules (via a REIO clause) in the articles themselves.

6.5 CONCLUSION

The process of developing draft articles on the responsibility of international organizations provides another example of how the EU is viewed from a public international law perspective. It demonstrates the divergence, discussed in Chapter 1, between the EU law view, emphasizing the unique nature of the EU, and international law view, which tends to favour abstract rules of general application. The purpose of this chapter was not to analyse in

---

[155] ILC (n146) para. 219.
[156] Hoffmeister (n2) 745
[157] V.-J. Proulx, 'An Uneasy Transition? Linkages Between the Law of State Responsibility and the Law Governing the Responsibility of International Organizations' in M. Ragazzi (ed), *Responsibility of International Organizations: Essays in Memory of Ian Brownlie* (Leiden: Martinus Nijhoff, 2013) 109, 117. *Lex specialis* 'provides for the application of specialized norms of attribution regulating the conduct of the EU (and other similar organizations) when its member States implement its binding decisions, primarily through a *renvoi* to the relevant "rules of the organization"'.

depth the provisions of the ARIO and its possible application to the EU context. It sought to highlight, using the ILC's project on responsibility, the 'EU' and 'international law' views of responsibility and the extent to which the ILC was capable of reconciling these approaches.

EU lawyers tend to be critical of the ARIO, arguing that they fail to take into account the unique nature of the EU. This is an example of how arguments in favour of 'EU exceptionalism' in international law are often met with scepticism and caution from non-EU states. Rather than outright rejection of the EU position, the Special Rapporteur sought to taken into account the diversity of international organizations in other ways, such as the rules of the organization and the inclusion of a *lex specialis* rule. One can understand the reluctance of the ILC to include 'EU-specific' language in draft articles that are intended to have a broad and universal coverage. The ILC resisted calls to attach greater importance to the diversity of international organizations, leaning towards rules capable of a universal application.

While the ILC had to be mindful of ensuring that the ARIO were flexible enough to take into account the diversity of international organizations, it had to ensure they were also rigid enough to ensure a consistent and harmonized approach in the law of responsibility. The ILC considered, for example, limiting the ARIO to only a narrow category of IO, or developing different sets of rules for different categories of IOs. Instead, it sought to develop rules aimed at universal application with a high enough level of abstraction to apply to the wide variety of international organizations that exist. While this may be criticized for failing to take into account the specific types of IOs that exist, it was the correct approach. The ARIO should be seen as a flexible set of principles of a residual character rather than as a strict set of rules to be applied immediately in every circumstance.

The story of the development of the ARIO again demonstrates the difficulties of applying 'state-centric' rules to the context of international organizations.[158] It has parallels to the story of the ILC's codification of the law of treaties or its study on customary international law (Section 2.1.1). On the one hand, the ILC sought to retain the coherence of the system of treaty law, using the VCLT as the logical starting point in developing rules applicable regarding international organizations. In the context of international responsibility, the challenge is far greater. Many of the criticisms of the ARIO – failing to give due regard to the diversity of IOs; an over-reliance on

---

[158] Kuijper & Paasivirta (n2) 65. 'The state-centred structures of international law make it difficult to capture the EU realities of implementation, not by its own organs but by the authorities of the Member States'.

the previous codification project; lack of sufficient practice – were also made regarding the ILC's project on the law of treaties relating to international organizations. Similarly, the ARIO retains sufficient flexibility for tailor-made solutions to be developed regarding the EU. While the EU and academics may question the utility of the ARIO, it is likely to be used as a framework on which such solutions are built. For example, the EU may seek to use the *lex specialis* rule to include specific terms regarding responsibility of the EU in its international agreements. It has done so, for example, in UNCLOS and in the (now rejected) draft accession agreement to the ECHR. When entering into future international agreements, the EU should include provisions that set out how issues of responsibility are to be addressed. Such an approach does not imply a rejection of the ARIO; it simply means that the EU and its treaty partners should clarify more clearly *ex ante* issues regarding the responsibility of the EU and the Member States.

More broadly, the ARIO can be seen as a rejection of the position put forward by the EU and several academic commentators that there is a fundamental difference between regional economic integration organizations (REIOs) and 'traditional' organizations. Kuijper and Paasivirta for example argued that the REIO is recognized in international law as a different category of international organization.[159] The Special Rapporteur and the ILC rejected this argument early on. As has been discussed throughout the Chapter, the ILC insisted on rules that recognized the unitary nature of the rules of responsibility, reflecting the idea that

> The rules on the International Responsibility of States and the Responsibility of International Organizations form a single, unitary system. International law subjects all breaches of any rule of international law, irrespective of the origin and contents of these rules, to a relatively uniform set of secondary principles.[160]

This experience demonstrates that the arguments made by the EU about it being a 'new legal order' gain little traction in international legal forums such as the ILC.

Lastly, it should be added that the ARIO is influenced, in part, by the nature of the 'problem' it sought to address. The problems associated with the

---

[159]   Paasivirta & Kuijper (n2) 212: '[i]f there is recognition that REIOs carry out their obligations by means different from other international organizations, and do it in a manner that is closely connected with their member state authorities, should that not also be recognised in the rules of their international responsibility?'

[160]   A. Nollkaemper, 'Constitutionalization and the Unity of the Law of International Responsibility' (2009) 16 *Indiana Journal of Global Studies* 540, 552.

responsibility of IOs related to issues such as violations committed in the context of peacekeeping, or other similar breaches of international law where there appeared to be a failure to ensure responsibility for IOs. While the issue of responsibility in the EU context is no doubt an important one for international law, it is by no means the most pressing issue in the responsibility debate. To date, there has been no 'crisis of responsibility' where a party alleging a breach of international law by the EU or a Member State has been left without legal redress. While the ARIO apply to the EU, they are likely to have more practical effect in situations outside the EU context.

7

Concluding Remarks

When the European Communities were first established they were a form of 'legal experiment',[1] in which international law was used as the building blocks of a new type of international organization. Discussions about the European Union from an international law perspective often looked at how the EU could be a model for the functioning of the international legal order. Cassese, for example, put EU law forward as a model for the international system, especially the way in which EU law can have supremacy over inconsistent national law.[2] Slaughter and Burke-White[3] argued that the 'European way of doing law' could be a model for the rest of the world and for international law generally.[4] Alter describes how the transformation of the EU's supranational legal order 'showed the world that combining domestic enforcement with international legal oversight contributes to making international law more effective'.[5] The internalization of EU law into the law of the domestic legal

---

[1] 'The European Communities were set up, in the 1950s, as ingenious experiments of international law, combining some of the innovative tools experimented earlier on for other international organizations, but doing so in an unprecedented way and, certainly in the case of the EEC, within a broad scope of activity that was unheard of'. B. de Witte, 'European Union Law: How Autonomous is its Legal Order?' (2010) 65 *Zeitschrift für öffentliches Recht* 141, 142, 144.

[2] A. Cassese, 'Towards a Moderate Monism: Could International Rules Eventually Acquire the Force to Invalidate Inconsistent National Laws?' in A. Cassese (ed), *Realizing Utopia: The Future of International Law* (Oxford: Oxford University Press, 2012) 187.

[3] A. Slaughter & W. W. Burke-White, 'The Future of International Law Is Domestic (or, The European Way of Law)' (2006) 47 *Harvard International Law Journal* 327.

[4] Slaughter & Burke-White (n3) 352. 'the European way of law uses international law to transform and buttress domestic political institutions, it is a model for how international law can function, and in our view, will and must function to address twenty-first century international challenges'.

[5] K. J. Alter, 'The Global Spread of European Style International Courts' (2012) 35 *West European Politics* 135.

system was also viewed as a method that could be applied to the integration of international law.[6] In discussions on international constitutionalism, 'the EU has been taken as a model of international constitutional development'.[7] These debates have shown how the EU 'generally exercises a positive influence on the development and strengthening of international law'.[8] The argument is that the EU does this both through its 'rule-based approach' to global co-operation, but also through simply 'being there' as a model for regional and political integration.[9] Alvarez concludes that 'the European example is now most often cited by international lawyers not by way of contrasting public international law regimes but by way of suggesting the probable or desired trajectory of some of the more specialized international law regimes'.[10] The EU has been discussed as a model in terms of how international law could address individuals,[11] or even international law's democratic deficit.[12]

Discussions today about the European Union from a public international law perspective do not present the Union in such a positive light. They are more likely to focus on the EU's resistance to international law. The CJEU's resistance towards the system of investment arbitration and to the European Convention on Human Rights, have been put forward as such examples. Much of this has focused on the role of courts, and on instances of 'clashes' between legal orders. Focusing on clashes that take place in courts only provides one part of the picture, and tends to overstate the nature of the problem.

Moving beyond courts, one views how the EU has interacted with international law in other areas, such as when concluding international agreements (Chapter 3) or within international organizations (Chapter 4). The picture presented in this book has not been one of discord and disagreement,

---

[6] This method of internalization, it is argued, can help increase compliance with international law. See A. Burley (Slaughter) & W. Mattlie, 'Europe before the Court: A Political Theory of Legal Integration' (1993) 47 *International Organization* 1, 41.

[7] M. Weller, 'The Struggle for an International Constitutional Order' in D. Armstrong (ed), *Routledge Handbook of International Law* (London: Routledge, 2009) 179, 181.

[8] C. Timmermans, 'The EU and Public International Law' (1999) 4 *European Foreign Affairs Review* 181, 193.

[9] Timmermans (n8) 194.

[10] J. E. Alvarez, *International Organizations as Law-Makers* (Oxford: Oxford University Press, 2006) 468.

[11] See J. Klabbers, 'The European Union in the Law of International Organizations: Misfit or Model?' in R. A. Wessel & J. Odermatt (eds), *Research Handbook on the European Union and International Organizations* (Cheltenham: Edward Elgar, 2019) 25–41.

[12] See A. von Bogdandy, 'The European Lesson for International Democracy: The Significance of Articles 9–12 EU Treaty for International Organizations' (2012) 23 *European Journal of International Law* 315, 317.

but has shown the ways that international law has accommodated or adapted the European Union's activity at the international level. It has shown how the international legal order, while state-centric, has been flexible enough to accommodate composite legal actors like the European Union. This is not to say that legal questions about the European Union do not arise. But they can be addressed largely within the international legal order.

Throughout the study, different approaches to legal questions, from the law of treaties to issues of international responsibility, can be explained by these fundamentally different views of the EU's place within the international legal order. Chapter 1 identified and explained these diverging views. The later chapters showed how these different conceptualizations are not confined to academic debates, but also have practical consequences. In international treaty negotiations, in discussions before the UN Sixth Committee and the International Law Commission, in international organizations and international dispute settlement bodies, we see the relevance of these different understandings. Of course, these debates are shaped not only by legal disagreements, but also by power and interests. The EU seeks to assert its role as an independent actor, and in many cases, third states seek to downplay its independent identity. Disagreements relating to the nature and relevance of EU law before investment tribunals, or the CJEU's jurisprudence regarding EU autonomy, are also explained by the political disagreements about the role of investment tribunals.

The goal of this research has not been to find ways to overcome these diverging views or to find a 'unifying theory' that can explain the EU's position and role in the international legal order. Neither is it concerned with finding the 'correct' approach or single answer to these questions. The aim has been to show, using examples from the EU's international practice, how these diverging views have played out, and their consequences. Before international dispute settlement bodies or in international organizations, for example, the 'EU law view' remains contested. It is hoped that this helps to bridge the divide between EU law and international law scholars, both of whom may discuss the same issues but from vastly different perspectives. If international law scholarship fails to consider the special features of the EU and its internal dynamics, it risks losing its relevance to EU law scholars, who may dismiss it as misguided and uninformed. The Union should no longer be viewed as a 'black box', the internal workings of which should remain a mystery to those outside the EU. Conversely, examining the EU in isolation, without a broader understanding of its place in the international legal order, also contributes to the EU's isolation.

In debates about the EU's place in the international legal order, there appear to be two sources of disagreement. The first relates to the relevance of the EU's internal law. The second relates to the extent to which the EU is considered as an independent actor.

7.1 THE RELEVANCE OF EU LAW

One question that pervades these debates is whether, and to what extent, the EU's internal law is relevant when determining issues about how international law applies to the EU. From the perspective of international law, the starting point is that the EU Treaties and EU law are only relevant to the EU and its Member States, and cannot affect third parties – EU law is *res inter alios acta*. This fits with the idea in international law that the internal legal order of its subjects is largely irrelevant for determining the application of international law. For instance, in order to understand the United States' approach to international law, one should also understand the US Constitution and its law related to the incorporation and application of international law in its domestic system.[13] However, that state cannot rely on its internal law to justify a breach of its international obligations. By analogy, one could argue that the EU's internal legal order, and issues such as competences, can help explain the EU's behaviour, but is irrelevant when seeking to understand how international law applies to the Union. This is also the approach taken by the EU institutions. The EU legal order is not only irrelevant to third parties, but also something that needs to be protected from international law.

In which circumstances might the EU's internal rules be relevant? The preceding chapters gave numerous examples of instances where the EU or its negotiating partners pointed to specific aspects of the EU's internal law in order to justify special rules. The inclusion of a 'declaration of competences' clause in EU agreements, for example, is justified by the nature of competences in the EU legal order, which are not neatly divided and clear to third parties. When discussing issues of international responsibility, the EU's particular practice of 'executive federalism' was put forward as a rationale for developing specific rules of responsibility to apply with respect to the EU. This touches upon a broader issue in the law of international organizations, where the 'law of the organization' can be conceived as being both the internal constitutional law or the organization, or as belonging to international law. In certain circumstances, these internal issues become externalized, such as when the EU concludes

---

[13] A. Aust, *Handbook of International Law*, 2nd edn (Cambridge: Cambridge University Press, 2010) 430. 'Just as a basic knowledge of the complexities of the US Constitution or the UN Charter, and how each actually works, is necessary for anyone concerned with international relations, so an understanding of the Union and its laws and procedures is just as important'.

agreements with 'EU-specific' clauses. Before international tribunals, the European Commission has requested that EU law be taken into account, including case-law of the CJEU, when determining issues of jurisdiction and applicable law. The EU often requests this special treatment based on the peculiarities of its legal system. This internal law becomes legally relevant because the EU and third states *have agreed* that they are relevant. A more complex question is whether this always requires the consent of third parties. Could certain aspects of the EU legal order be objectively relevant? EU-specific clauses, for example, tend to be presented as ad hoc solutions to address a certain issue arising from EU law. It has been argued (see Chapter 2) that over time, such tailor-made solutions can transform into objective rules. Chapter 2 discussed how the EU's practice could contribute to the formation of customary international law that applies in relation to states and international organizations. This has been framed as practice as 'European exceptionalism', or as a threat to the unity of international law. This is understandable, since international law appears to provide rules applicable equally to all subjects irrespective of power. The EU's practice can also be viewed as contributing to the formation of rules and principles applicable in the relations between the Union and other states and organizations. Even if the EU's internal law is not always legally relevant to third states, any country or organization dealing with the Union should understand the complexities of Union law and its foreign relations powers.[14] The problems that have arisen for third states in relation to mixed agreements is an example.[15]

Internal law has less relevance when it is framed in terms of autonomy and primacy. I have argued that these principles are important for the EU legal order internally, and have played a key part of the EU maturing as a constitutional polity. However, when the EU has presented arguments based on the autonomy of EU law, they appear to have been given less weight. There is no requirement under international law for third states to recognize EU autonomy. However, when third states and organizations wish to enter into agreements with the EU, they may be asked to include provisions designed to safeguard EU autonomy, especially regarding the interpretation

---

[14] M. Fitzmaurice & O. Elias, *Contemporary Issues in the Law of Treaties* (Utrecht: Eleven International, 2005) 107. 'The external role of the EU as a legal entity vis-à-vis other States in the treaty-making process … is conditioned by its extremely complicated internal law. The lack of proper understanding of all the intricacies of the system have led to many misunderstandings and a sense of insecurity from non-Member States'.

[15] See, e.g., J. Odermatt, 'Facultative Mixity in the International Legal Order: Tolerating European Exceptionalism?' in M. Chamon & I. Govaere (eds), *EU External Relations Post-Lisbon: The Law and Practice of Facultative Mixity* (Brill, 2020) 291–316.

of EU law. When the EU seeks to assert the relevance of EU autonomy to its external relations, however, it is likely to encounter more resistance. This could be because such arguments appear to go further than recognizing a unique feature of the EU legal order, but also require 'special treatment' for the EU and its legal order.

7.2 LEGAL PERSONALITY OF THE EU

Another point of disagreement has been the extent to which the EU can be viewed as a separate and distinct actor in international law. As discussed in Chapter 1, there are diverging views about the nature of the EU in this regard. It is sometimes viewed as an independent actor in its own right, and sometimes viewed as a collective vehicle of its Member States. This can be seen, for example, in discussions about the EU's potential contribution to the formation of customary international law, where the EU was largely framed as an expression of the collective will of its members, rather than an international actor as such. This question is also legally relevant when the EU concludes international agreements alongside its Member States, or when issues relating to responsibility are addressed.

Article 47 TEU sets out that '[t]he Union shall have legal personality'. First, it sets out the Union as a separate and distinct legal person from the EU Member States. As a legal person, the EU is capable, for example, of entering into contracts or acquiring property.[16] This does not mean, however, that the EU necessarily has international legal personality. As De Baere points out, '[w]hether an entity possesses international legal personality is a conclusion that must be drawn within international law'.[17] As discussed earlier, the EU Treaties are *res inter alios acta* to third parties. International legal personality stems not only from Article 47 TEU but also from international law. In *Reparation for Injuries Suffered in the Services of the United Nations* the ICJ held that 'the Organisation is an international person ... it is a subject of international law and capable of possessing international rights and duties, and that it has capacity to maintain its rights by bringing international claims'.[18] First,

---

[16] Article 335 TFEU.
[17] G. De Baere, *Constitutional Principles of EU External Relations* (Oxford: Oxford University Press, 2008)144.
[18] *Reparation for Injuries Suffered in the Service of the United* Nations (Advisory Opinion) [1949] ICJ Rep 174, 179. See F. Hoffmeister, 'The Contribution of EU Practice to International Law in Developments in EU External Relations Law' in M. Cremona (ed), *Developments in EU External Relations Law* (Oxford: Oxford University Press, 2008) 42. P. Gautier, 'The Reparation for Injuries Case Revisited: The Personality of the European Union' (2000) 4 *Max Planck Yearbook of United Nations Law* 331–361.

the entity should have a separate legal identity. The second criterion is that the organization has the capacity to enter into international relations with other states. These two criteria are now fulfilled in the context of the EU.[19] An international legal person may, for example, conclude international treaties, join international organizations, take part in international dispute settlement mechanisms, and enter into diplomatic relations with other states and organizations.[20] The EU regularly does all these things, and its international legal personality is now widely accepted.[21]

However, the EU's status as an independent actor in international law is not always fully accepted externally. The examples from international organizations (see Chapter 4) demonstrate how the EU often struggles to convince states that it is more than a collection of its Member States, but a distinct legal actor. There is another paradox pervading the EU's international action: it is both an independent legal actor with distinct legal personality, but at the same time composed of sovereign states. It is both independent from, and dependent upon the Member States.

The sources of tension are not always due to legal disagreements. Both the multilateral system and the European Union are facing considerable challenges.

[19]   J.-C. Piris, *The Lisbon Treaty: A Legal and Political Analysis* (Cambridge: Cambridge University Press, 2010) 86–87: 'As for the former second pillar, the EU as such had already concluded many international agreements, thus demonstrating that it had already an implied legal personality'. A. Dashwood, 'External Relations Provisions of the Amsterdam Treaty' in D. O'Keeffe & P. Twomey (eds), *Legal Issues of the Amsterdam Treaty* (Oxford: Hart, 1999) 220: 'In the view of the writer, applying the criteria enunciated by the International Court of Justice in the *Reparation for Injuries* case, there are solid grounds for regarding the European Union as being already possessed of international legal personality ... ' A. Dashwood, 'Editorial Comments' (2001) 38 *Common Market Law Review* 825: 'The Member States of the EU have thus taken the step of acknowledging that, for some purposes at least, the Union is capable of functioning as an independent subject of the international legal order – in other words, that in enjoys legal personality – and that it has capacity to enter into binding international agreements'. See the discussion in J. Klabbers, 'Presumptive Personality: The European Union in International Law' in M. Koskenniemi (ed), *International Law Aspects of the European Union* (The Hague: Kluwer Law International, 1998) 231–253.

[20]   R. A. Wessel, 'Revisiting the International Legal Status of the EU' (2000) 5 *European Foreign Affairs Review* 507, 511: 'It is the capacities of the entity that ultimately reveal the "independent" position of a legal person. Thus, international legal persons may have a capacity to bring international claims, they may have international procedural capacity (for instance to start a procedure before an international court), to try making capacity, the right to establish diplomatic relations or the right to recognize other subjects of international law'.

[21]   See P. de Schoutheete & S. Andoura, 'The Legal Personality of the European Union' (2007) 60(1) *Studia Diplomatica* 7: 'There is little doubt that the European Union has implicitly acquired an international legal personality'. P. Eeckhout, *EU External Relations Law*, 2nd edn (Oxford: Oxford University Press, 2011) 3: 'Whether the EU ... had international legal personality was a matter of debate for some time, but the Treaty of Lisbon ended that debate by providing, in Art 47 TEU for such overall legal personality'.

Many of the global challenges discussed in international law debates are the same as those discussed in European Union politics – climate change; challenges associated with a digital economy; migration and refugee movements; security and nuclear non-proliferation – are issues that are addressed by the EU and in multilateral forums. In many cases, the approach favoured by the Union may cause tensions with other states or within international organizations. The EU remains a self-interested actor; it is established for the interests of its Member States and citizens. In its action on the international scene, the Union must not only respect the principles of the United Nations Charter and international law, but must also 'safeguard [the Union's] values, fundamental interests, security, independence and integrity'.[22] There is a thus a tension between these goals – the EU is a professed supporter of international law and multilateralism, but also pursues its aims and objectives in a 'realist' manner. The EU will continue to actively influence international legal developments and pursue its interests. In doing so, the EU has also shaped international law in a more foundational manner.

---

[22] Article 21(2)(a) TEU.

Index

Achmea case, 187–188, 189–190, 193–194
AES Summit Generation Limited and AES-Tisza Erömü Kft v The Republic of Hungary, **193**
Afghanistan, 105–106
AFSJ (Area of Freedom, Security and Justice), 95
Ahlborn, C., 237, 240
AIDCP (Agreement on the International Dolphin Conservation Programme), 71
Air Transport Association of America and Others v Secretary of State for Energy and Climate Change, **4**, 34, 134
Alvarez, J. E., 247
Amtenbrink, F., 5, 167
Anklagemindigheden v Poulsen and Diva Navigation, **103**
application of international law within the EU legal order, debates around, 1
Arctic Council, 146
ARIO (Articles on Responsibility of International Organizations), 39, 196
  criticisms, 206
  definition of 'international organization', 40
  development of rules on international responsibility, 201–210
  state centric approach, 39
  see also responsibility for internationally wrongful acts.
Article 3(5) TEU, 4, 138
Article 344 TFEU, 173, 176, 184–185, 194
Article 47 TEU, 251
Article 50 ECHR, 154

Article 50 TEU, 52, 92
Article 52 TEU, 89
ASEAN (Association of Southeast Asian Nations), 72, 73
AU (African Union), 72, 73, 143
Aust, A., 62
autonomy
  CJEU's focus on preserving, 31
  comparison with universal regime of the UN, 174
  ECHR and, 179–182
  ECtHR jurisprudence and, 223
  EU principle of, 238, 250–251
  EU's claims of and anxieties about fragmentation of international law, 14
  international dispute settlement and the principle of, 176–182, 188–190, 195
  international law as threat to integrity and of EU legal order, 2–3
  inter-state disputes and potential for violation, 174
  investor-state arbitration and, 191
  of IOs, 177–178, 201, 203–205
  'new legal order' model and, 19–20, 29
  pluralist vision vs constitutionalist vision of 'autonomous' regimes, 30–31
  safeguarding autonomy of EU legal order, 112–115, 129, 170, 171–173, 188–189, 225
  third States and, 177–178

Barroso-Ashton-Strategy, 160, 163, 166
Bartels, L., 93, **103**
BCBS (Basel Committee on Banking Supervision), 132

Belgium, 92, 183, 188
Belilos v Switzerland, 110
Besson, S., 56
Bogiatzi, 113
Borrell, Josep, 140
Bosphorus Hava Yollari Turizm ve Ticaret
    Anonim Şirketi v Ireland, 221
Boyle, A., 92
Bretton Woods institutions, 156
Brexit
    Court of Justice of the EU and, 195
    EU-specific clauses of treaties and, 93–94
    judicial practice in customary international
        law and, 52
    management of, 60
    revocation question, 52
    succession of obligations, 125
Brita v Hauptzollamt Hamburg Hafen, 34,
    64

Canada, 105
Cannizzaro, E., 3
CARICOM (Caribbean Community), 73, 143
cases
    AES Summit Generation Limited and AES-
        Tisza Erömü Kft v The Republic of
        Hungary, 193
    Air Transport Association of America and
        Others v Secretary of State for
        Energy and Climate Change,
        34, 134
    Anklagemindigheden v Poulsen and Diva
        Navigation, 103
    Belilos v Switzerland, 110
    Bogiatzi, 113
    Bosphorus Hava Yollari Turizm ve Ticaret
        Anonim Şirketi v Ireland, 221
    Brita v Hauptzollamt Hamburg Hafen, 64
    Case concerning the Barcelona Traction,
        Light and Power Co Ltd (Belgium
        v Spain), 182
    Commission v Austria, 112
    Commission v Council, 10
    Commission v Finland, 112
    Commission v Greece, 166
    Commission v Ireland, 172
    Commission v Luxembourg, 51
    Commission v Sweden, 112
    Commune de Mesquer, 166
    Costa v ENEL, 51, 177, 238
    Eastern Sugar BV v Czech Republic, 113

Eiser Infrastructure Limited and Energía
    Solar Luxembourg S.A.R.L.
    v Kingdom of Spain, 191
Electrabel SA v The Republic of Hungary,
    28, 192
Eureko BV v The Slovak Republic, 114
European American Investment Bank AG
    (EURAM) v Slovak Republic, 173
Foresight Luxembourg Solar 1 S.A.R.L. et al.
    v Kingdom of Spain, 191
France v Commission, 117, **198**
Germany v Council, **133**
Greentech v Italy, 192
Hansen v Hauptzolamt Flensburg, 96
International Fruit Company and Others
    v Produktschap voor Groenten en
    Fruit, **125, 152**
Intertanko and Others, 166
Ireland v United Kingdom (MOX Plant
    case), 173–175, 183
Kadi and Al Barakaat International
    Foundation v Council and
    Commission, 22–23, 27, 28, 56, **112**
    see also Kadi cases
Legality of the Use by a State of Nuclear
    Weapons in Armed Conflict, 177
Marfin Investment Group v The Republic of
    Cyprus, 193
Matthews v United Kingdom, **221**
Monetary Gold Removed from Rome in 1943
    (Italy v France, United Kingdom of
    Great Britain and Northern
    Ireland and United States of
    America), **182**
North Sea Continental Shelf (Federal
    Republic of Germany v Denmark
    and Federal Republic of Germany
    v Netherlands), **89, 182**
Opel Austria v Council, **100**
Opinion 1/17, 171, 176, 187–190
Opinion 2/13, 10, 175–176, 179–182, 190, 225
Parliament v Council, 51
PL Holdings S.A.R.L.
    v Republic of Poland, 192
R. & V. Haegeman v Belgian State, 103
Racke v Hauptzollamt Mainz, 64
Reparation for Injuries Suffered in the
    Services of the United Nations, 251
Rupert Joseph Binder v Czech Republic, 113
Slovak Republic v Achmea BV, 187–188,
    189–190, 193–194

cases (cont.)
  Walz v Clickair SA, **34**, 51
  Wightman, 52
Cassese, A., 246
Catalonia, 92
CETA (Comprehensive Economic and Trade
    Agreement), 104–105, 188, 189, 190
  investor-State dispute settlement system,
    187–190
CFSP (Common Foreign and Security
    Policy), 4, 68, 96, 97, 140, 200,
    212
CJEU (Court of Justice of the EU)
  application of VCLT provisions, 64, 129
  Brexit and, 195
  customary international law and, 34–35, 46,
    50–56
  focus on autonomy of EU legal order, 31
  human rights jurisprudence, 55
  international dispute settlement bodies and,
    169–171
  international responsibility and, 198
  interpretation of Member States'
    obligations, 112
  judicial monopoly over the interpretation of
    EU law, 172–173, 194, 208
  Kadi judgment, 22–23
    see also Kadi cases.
  'new legal order' and, 10–12, 29
  resistance to international law, 247
  succession and, 125
  see also EU law.
clashes between legal orders, 2, 25, 27, 31,
    166–167, 194, 247
  techniques for avoidance of, 194
COJUR (Council Working Group on Public
    International Law), 43
Commission v Austria, 112
Commission v Council, 10
Commission v Finland, 112
Commission v Greece, 166
Commission v Ireland, 172
Commission v Luxembourg, 51
Commission v Luxembourg & Belgium, 16
Commission v Sweden, 112
common agricultural policy, 147
Common Foreign and Security Policy, *see*
    CFSP.
Commune de Mesquer, 166
Comprehensive Economic and Trade
    Agreement, *see* CETA.

Convention for the Strengthening of the Inter-
    American Tropical Tuna
    Commission, 71
Convention on the Rights of Persons with
    Disabilities, RIO clause, 71
Costa v ENEL, 51, 177, 238
COTIF (Convention Concerning
    International Carriage by Rail), 71
Cotonou Agreement, 94
Council of Europe, 67, 70, 82–83, 88, 110, 138,
    145, 154, 158, 160
Court of Justice of the EU, *see* CJEU.
Crawford, J., 92, 206
Cremona, M., 104
customary international law, 33–58
  CJEU's application of principles, 34, 50–53
  debate around the EU's contribution to
    development, 33–34
  EU's role in formation and identification, 48
  ILC's approach, 36–41
  judicial practice, 48–55
    Brexit and, 52
    identification duties, 53–55
    impact of international courts, 50
    role of national courts, 49–50
    role of the CJEU, 50–53
  organization practice, 41–48
    contributions 'as such', 44, 57–58
    IOs as catalysts of State practice, 43–44
    States acting through IOs, 42–43
  regional custom, 55–56
  role of international organizations, 57–58
  Special Rapporteur's Fourth Report, 38
  state-centric approach, 37–38
  VCLT-IO stipulations, 46
Czech Republic, 113

d'Aspremont, J., 236, 240
declarations of competence
  EU-specific clauses, 75, 81–82, 249
  third States and, 78–79, 82
  UNCLOS requirements, 80, 81
  under international law, 81–82
Denmark, 91, 95, 186
descriptication, UN Convention, 108
diplomacy
  diplomatic and consular law, 4, 49
  diplomatic correspondence, 49
  diplomatic influence of the EU, 26
  diplomatic law as self-contained regime, 15
  EU's diplomatic practice, 34

EU's UNGA upgrade saga and, 162–163
role of in EU membership and
    participation, 167
role of treaties in diplomatic life, 59, 140
strategic focus of EU's diplomatic
    attention, 161
diversity of IOs, 39, 41, 196, 201, 206, 207,
    232, 243
domestic law, 74, 116, 184, 188–189, 192–193,
    221, 233
Draft Conclusions on Identification of
    Customary International Law
    (ILC, 2018), 34–35

Eastern Sugar BV v Czech Republic, 113
EBRD (European Bank for Reconstruction
    and Development), 146, 155
ECHR (European Convention on Human
    Rights)
    additional protocols, 127
    autonomy and, 179–182
    EU accession, 141
    EU participation clause, 70
    funding, 154
    inter-state disputes and, 174–176, 181, 185,
        194–195
    judges, 159–160
    relationship to other treaties, 88
    rights of the EU to make reservations, 110
    state centric language, 74
    territorial application, 95–96
    voting model, 157–158
EC-Russian Federation Partnership and
    Cooperation Agreement, 90
ECSC (European Coal and Steel
    Community), 122
ECtHR (European Court of Human Rights)
    autonomy and, 223
    funding issues, 154
    international dispute settlement and,
        180–181, 194
    international responsibility and, 220–226
    interpretation and application of Additional
        Protocols, 127
    inter-state cases and, 175
    potential for complex legal questions on
        application of jurisdiction and
        territory to the EU, 96
    privileges and immunities granted to
        participants and judges, 88
Eeckhout, P., 142

EIB (European Investment Bank), 155
Eiser Infrastructure Limited and Energía Solar
    Luxembourg S.A.R.L. v Kingdom
    of Spain, 191
Electrabel SA v The Republic of Hungary,
    28, 192
EMSA (European Maritime Safety
    Agency), 164
Energy Charter Treaty, 88, 90, 186, 191
ERTA doctrine, 139
Estonia, 140
EU law
    as model for the international system, 246
    CJEU's monopoly over the interpretation of,
        172–173, 194, 208
    comparison with international law, 246–249
    conception of as separate discipline, 23–24
    internal law, 63, 68, 81–82, 117, 118, 195, 241,
        249–250
    internal/external dichotomy, 29–30
    international dispute settlement bodies and,
        172–182
    international organizations and, 137–142
    relevance of, 249–251
    see also CJEU (Court of Justice of the EU)
EU legal order
    CJEU's focus on preserving autonomy of, 31
    international law as threat to integrity and
        autonomy of, 2–3
    international responsibility and, 207–210
    relationship with international law, 1–2, 4,
        7
    safeguarding autonomy of, 112–115, 129, 170,
        171–173, 188–189, 225
    treaties and, 66–69
Eureko BV v The Slovak Republic, 114
EUROCONTROL (European Organization
    for the Safety of Air
    Navigation), 146
European American Investment Bank AG
    (EURAM) v Slovak Republic, 173
European Commission, role in negotiation of
    treaties, 97–98
European Common Aviation Area, 178
European Community (EC),
    establishment, 246
European Convention for the Protection of
    Human Rights and Fundamental
    Freedoms, 55, *see also* ECHR
    (European Convention on
    Human Rights)

European Convention on Human Rights, 70,
see ECHR (European Convention
on Human Rights).
European exceptionalism, 6, 13, 19, 243, 250
European External Action Service, 134
European Investment Bank (EIB), 155
European Space Agency, 141
European Union (EU)
as 'creature of international law', 1, 9, 12, 14
difference between other international
organizations and, 19
legal personality, 251–253
legal relationship with third states, 13
place in the world, 27
potential contribution to the formation of
custom, 44–46
struggle for acceptance as distinct legal
actor, 20
European Union in international law
divergent views
explaining, 22–27
academic and professional
specialization, 23–25
interests and values, 26–27
state-centrism, 25
overcoming
acceptance of EU's multiple nature,
28–30
integration of EU into international
legal order, 31
external views, 14–22
classic intergovernmental organization,
19–20
models of the EU, 20–22
Regional Economic Integration
Organization, 18
self-contained regime, 18, 29
internal view
EU law perspective, 10–14
legal conflicts, 27
sui generis description, 10, 14, 18, 28, 50, 75,
192, 201, 210, 218
European Union in International Law,
The (Klabbers), 1
Europeanization of international law
scholarship on, 1
Wouters et al's description, 1
EU-specific treaty clauses
Brexit and, 93–94
declaration of competence clause, 75,
81–82, 249

declarations of competence under
international law, 81–82
disconnection clause, 82–87, 129
participation clause, 69–75
relationship to other treaties, 88
territorial application, 89–96
accession of a new Member State, 90
change in status of territory, 91–92
defining, 94–96
withdrawal of a Member State, 93–94
value of, 130
evolution of EU's treaty practice, treaties, EU
legal order and &W, 66–69

FAO (Food and Agriculture Organization), 147
candidates for positions, 159
EU's membership status, 151–152
Faroe Islands, 186
financial crisis (2008/9), 133, 149
Flanders, 92
Foresight v Spain, 191
fragmentation of international law, 15, 17,
84, 241
France, 91
France v Commission, 117, **198**
FSB (Financial Stability Board), 132–133,
139, 167

G20 (Group of 20), 139, 167
G7 (Group of 7), 167
Gaja, G., 202
Gardiner, R., 29
Gáspár-Szilágyi, S., 193
Germany, 90, 92, 183
Germany v Council, **133**
Greenland, 91
Greentech v Italy, 192

Hague Conference on Private International
Law, 146, 154
Hansen v Hauptzollamt Flensburg, 96
Hillion, C., 180
Hoffmeister, F., 5, 183
human rights, 5, 7, 26–27, 68, 110
active treaty partnerships, 60
CJEU and, 55–56
competence issues and, 157
'essential clauses', 119
treaty terminology, 74
see also ECHR (European Convention on
Human Rights); ECtHR

(European Court of Human Rights)
Hungary v Slovakia, **34**

ICAO (International Civil Aviation Organization), 134, 145, 235
ICCAT (International Convention for the Conservation of Atlantic Tunas), 72
ICJ (International Court of Justice)
CJEU's recognition of importance, 184
customary international law and, **50**, 52, 55–56
Legality of Nuclear Weapons case, 177
Reparation for Injuries Suffered in the Services of the United Nations, 251
role in CJEU's reasoning, 54
role in international dispute settlement, 182–184, 194
succession of IOs, 121
ILC (International Law Commission), 8
approach to customary international law, 36–41
dichotomy between States and IOs, 47
discussion of disconnection causes, 84–85
Draft Articles on Responsibility of International Organizations, 210–242
see also ARIO (Articles on Responsibility of Internat)
fragmentation of international law, 84, 241
provisional application of treaties, work on, 105
reference to *Costa v ENEL*, 51
'state-centric' approach, 65
succession rules, 121
transfer of competences analysis, 46
work on responsibility of IOs, 200–201
IMF (International Monetary Fund), 149
voting system, 156
IMO (International Maritime Organization), 134, 145
EU upgrade saga, 164–166
'impunity gap', international organizations, 200
independence movements, law of treaties and, 92
international courts
examples of, 50
impact on judicial practice of customary international law, 50

status of the CJEU, 50
International Criminal Court, 5, 50
international dispute settlement, 169–195
bodies
EU participation
investment disputes
Member State BITS (*Achmea*, 187–188
EU law related to, 172–182
Article 344 TFEU, 176
principle of autonomy, 176–179
EU participation, 182–194
International Court of Justice, 182–184
investment disputes, 186–194
see also investment disputes.
World Trade Organization, 184–186
EU participation, 186–194
EU's influence, 171
EU's promotion of, 169–171
human rights context, 174–176, 181, 185, 194–195
MOX Plant case, 173–175, 183
recent increase in forms of, 169
responsible bodies, 194
International Fruit Company and Others v Produktschap voor Groenten en Fruit, **125**, **152**
international law
changing landscape, 169
comparison with EU law, 246–249
customary. *see* customary international law
debates around application of within the EU legal order, 1
declarations of competence under, 81–82
EU as 'creature of', 1, 9, 12, 14
European Union in, *see* European Union in international law.
Europeanization of, 1
EU's resistance to, 247
examples of EU influence, 5
fragmentation of, 15, 17, 84, 241
sovereign state as foundation of, 26
state-centrism and, 25
see also state-centrism.
threat to integrity and autonomy of EU legal order, 2–3
US approach, 249
International Law Commission, *see* ILC.
International Maritime Organization, *see* IMO.
International Monetary Fund, *see* IMF.

international organizations (IOs), 131–168
  challenges facing the EU, 142–145
    legal obstacles, 144–145
    state-centrism, 74, 142–144, 243
  contributions to customary international
    law, 44–48, 57–58
  definitions, 40–41, 132, 203–205
  development of rules on international
    responsibility, 201–210
  diversity of, 39, 41, 196, 201–207, 232, 243
  EU engagement with as clash between two
    types of legal orders, 166–167
  EU law and, 137–142
    CJEU jurisprudence, 140–141
    EU Treaties, 137–141
      representation, 140–141
      right to join IOs, 139
    issues not in EU treaties, 141–142
  EU's participation, 131
    candidates for positions, 158–160
    funding, 153–155
    membership, 145–153
      full membership, 146–147
      observer status, 148–149
      parallel membership, 150–153
      status less than observer, 149–150
      treaty regimes, 147
    voting, 155–158
      'bloc voting' concerns, 155, 156, 157–158
  examples of, 132
  existing studies on the EU's presence in,
    135–136
  ILC's draft articles on responsibility of,
    210–242
  'impunity gap', 200
  influence on EU legislation, 133
  intergovernmental bodies, 132
  law of international organizations, 52, 249
  ordinary vs organizations exercising State
    functions, 68
  participation in the work of the UNGA,
    42–43
  reasons for participation, 133–135
  role in State practice of customary
    international law, 43–44
  State conduct of customary international
    law through, 42–43
  upgrading the EU's role, 160–166
    UN and UN system, 161–166
      International Maritime Organization
        (IMO), 164–166
      UNGA saga, 161–163
    ways in which the 'EU' acts in, 135
Intertanko and Others, 166
investment disputes, 186–194
  cases, 191
  EU agreements (CETA) 7, 187–190
  intra-EU challenges to jurisdiction,
    191, 194
  Member State BITS (*Achmea*), 187–188,
    189–190, 193–194
  tribunals, 191
IOSCO (International Organization of
        Securities Commissions), 132
Ireland, 95, 173
Ireland v United Kingdom (MOX Plant case),
        173–175, 183
IRENA (International Renewable Energy
        Agency), 156
ISDS (investor-state dispute settlement), 186
ISPS Code (International Ship and Port
        Facility Security Code), 164
Italy, 183
ITLOS (International Tribunal for the Law of
        the Sea), 154, 158

Jacqué, J.-P., 96

Kadi cases
  academic debate, 22–23
  clash of values and, 27
  duality of the EU and, 28
  integrity of EU law and, **112**
  right to property and, 56
Klabbers, J., 1, 27, 62, 112, 174
Kochenov, D., 5
Konstadinides, T., 57
Koskenniemi, M., 28
Kuijper, P-J., 80, 120, 207, 214
Kyoto Protocol, 5, 76

law of the sea, 47, 49, 174, *see also* UNCLOS
        (UN Convention on the Law of
        the Sea)
law of treaties, *see under treaties*.
legal actors, 39
legal orders, clashes between, 2, 25, 27, 31,
        166–167, 194, 247
legal personality
  EU, 93, 125, 144, 198, 204, 207, 223, 251–253
  IOs, 40, 44, 132, 203–204, 205, 223
  merger and, 123

states, 207

Legality of the Use by a State of Nuclear Weapons in Armed Conflict, 177

lex specialis, 15, 31, 228, 232, 234, 237–244
  international responsibility and, 238–242
  UNCLOS and, 244

Ličková, M., 23, 84–85

Lisbon Treaty, 122–123
  EU membership of the FAO and, 151
  EU membership of the IMO and, 165
  EU participation in IOs, 137, 142
  EU's UNGA upgrade and, 161–162
  objective for EU's status in the world, 160

Lowe, V., 143

Lugano Convention, 183

Marfin Investment Group v The Republic of Cyprus, 193

Marrakesh treaty, opinion of AG Wahl, 103

Matthews v United Kingdom, **221**

McMahon, F., 20

mixed agreements
  accession of new Member States and, 90
  CJEU case law and, 51
  declarations of competence and, 75–81, 111, 208
  EU's long-standing practice, 208
  fragmentation of international law and, 241
  international responsibility and, 197
  legal problems of 'mixity', 150–151
  limits of EU and Member States' powers, 99–100
  provisional application and, 103–108
  reservations to treaties and, 111
  third states and, 250
  validity of treaties and, 117
  withdrawal of a Member State and, 94

mixity, 131, 136, 139, 150

Monetary Gold Removed from Rome in 1943 (Italy v France, United Kingdom of Great Britain and Northern Ireland and United States of America), 182

MOX Plant case, 173, 175, 183

multilateralism, EU Treaties as demonstration of commitment to, 137–141

Murphy, S.D., 47

Myers, P., 122, 124

Namibia, 121

national courts, role of in judicial practice of customary international law, 49–50

Netherlands, 91

'new legal order'
  autonomy and, 19–20, 29, 177
  CJEU and, 10–12, 29
  comparison with 'self-contained regime', 15, 18
  conceptual starting point, 24
  created by EU treaties, 238
  international responsibility and, 207
  skepticism of international lawyers, 13–14

Nobel Peace Prize, 27

North Sea Continental Shelf (Federal Republic of Germany v Denmark and Federal Republic of Germany v Netherlands), **89**, 182

OECD (Organization for Economic Co-operation and Development), 121, 138, 145, 148

Opel Austria v Council, **100**

Opinion 1/17, 171, 176, 187–190

Opinion 2/13, **10**, 175–176, 179–182, 190, 225
  view of the Advocate General, 175, 185

Orakhelashvili, A., 19

OSCE (Organization for Security and Co-operation in Europe), 138

overseas territories, law of treaties and, 91

Paasivirta, E., 80, 207, 214

Parish, M., 181

Parliament v Council, 51

Pellet, A., 205

pi, 185

PL Holdings S.A.R.L. v Republic of Poland, **192**

Portugal, 91

Prost, M., 174

Pulkowski, D., 16

R. & V. Haegeman v Belgian State, **103**

Racke, 64

Racke v Hauptzollamt Mainz, 64

REIOs (regional economic integration organization), 18, 69, 70, 71, 72, 75, 144, 156, 202, 206, 214, 240, 244

Reparation for Injuries Suffered in the Services of the United Nations, 251

Repasi, R., 167

res inter alios acta, 63, 241, 249, 251

responsibility for internationally wrongful acts, 196–245
  development of the rules, 201–210

responsibility for internationally (cont.)
  diversity of organizations, 39, 201–207
  EU legal order and, 207–210
  EU's system, 198
  focus of literature, 197
  ILC's Draft Articles
    attribution, 215–216
      ECHR practice, 220–226
      EU context, 216–232
      ILC response, 228–229
      models of, 227–228
      other rules, 229–232
      WTO practice, 217–220
    criticisms, 205–206, 211, 215, 232, 236, 243
    EU's contribution, 212–215
    methodology, 210–212
    specialized rules, 232–242
      lex specialis rule, 238–242
      'rules of the organization', 232–238
  ILC's work, 200–201
  IOs in international law, 199–201
  underlying concepts, 206
*Restatement (Third) of Foreign Relations Law
    of the United States*, 42
Reuter, P., 62, 68, 89, 126
RIOs (regional integration organizations), 18,
    51, 70, 74, 206, 210
Rosas, A., 184
Rupert Joseph Binder v Czech Republic, 113
Russia, 90

Schütze, R., 13, 25
Scotland, 92
self-contained regime, EU as, 18, 29
Simma, B., 16
Slovak Republic v Achmea BV, 187–188,
    189–190, 193–194
Solas Convention (International Convention
    for the Safety of Life at Sea), 164
South Sudan, 90
sovereign state, as foundation of international
    law, 26
Spain, 91–92
state-centrism
  customary international law and, 37–38
  ECHR, 74
  ILC, 65
  international law and, 25
  IOs and, 74, 142–144, 243
  RIO/REIO participation and, 74
  UN, 143

Strasbourg Court, *see* ECtHR (European
    Court of Human Rights).
succession, 57, 61, 93, 120, 121, 122, 123, 124,
    125, 129
sui generis, 10, 14, 18, 28, 50, 75, 192, 201, 210, 218
Suse, A., 107
Syrian Arab Republic, 119

Talmon, S., 78, 81
TFEU (Treaty on the Functioning of the
    European Union)
  capacity to join IOs, 139, 141–142
  change in status of territories, 91–92
  conflict clause, 113
  consent to be bound, 102
  economic and monetary union, 149
  international dispute settlement, 176,
    184–185, 191, 194
  international responsibility and, 226
  prior treaties of Member States, 112
  provisional application of an agreement, 103
  representation in IOs, 140
  reservations, 109
  scope for suspension, 17
  signature on an agreement, 100
  suspension of international agreements, 118
  territorial scope of EU Treaties, 89–90
third States
  acceptance of need to enter agreements
    with, 66
  conflict clauses and, 113
  declarations of competence and, 78–79, 82
  disconnection clauses and, 84
  dispute settlement system, 188
  EU's legal relationship with, 13
  instruments of ratification, acceptance or
    approval and, 103, 104
  principle of autonomy and, 177–178
  provisional application of treaties and, 104
  rules of organizations and, 235, 241
  status after withdrawal from the EU, 93–94
  territorial application clauses and, 96
  transfer of personality and, 123
Tomka, P., 74
treaties
  applicable law regulating treaties to which
    the EU is a party, 63–66
  doubts around the continued relevance
    of, 59
  EU legal order and, 66–69
    evolution of EU's treaty practice, 66–69

EU treaty practice
  as demonstration of commitment to
    multilateralism, 137–141
  comparison of bilateral and multilateral
    treaties, 67
  constant change, 67–68, 69
  types of treaty entered into, 68
EU-specific clauses, 69–96, 130, 250
  see also EU-specific treaty clauses.
law of treaties, 59–130
  application of principles of customary
    international law, 34
  application to EU practice, 97–128
    additional protocols and other
      instruments, 127–128
    conclusion of agreements
      consent to be bound, 101–102
      effect of ratification, 108
      entry into force, 102–103
      negotiation, 97–100
      provisional application, 103–108
      signature, 100–101
    prior treaties of Member States, 111–115
    reservations, 108–111
    succession of treaties, 127
      from organizations to Member States,
        125–127
      IOs, 121–122
      one organization to another, 122–124
    suspension, 118–120
    termination, 118, 119–120
    validity of treaties, 115–118
  availability as subsidiary fall-back
    position, 17
  debates around ILC's work, 47, 61, 215, 244
  dichotomy between states and IOs, 128
  disconnection causes and, 85
  international responsibility and, 37
  participation of non-state entities in
    treaties, 62
  withdrawal of a Member State and, 52
  see also VCLT (Vienna Convention on
    the Law of Treaties).
  role of for the EU, 59–62
  VCLT on what comprises a treaty, 81

Ukraine, 59, 107
UN (United Nations)
  importance to the EU, 138
  state-centrism, 143
  upgrading the EU's role, 161–166

UN Charter, 138
UN Convention against Corruption, 71, 147
UN Convention on the Rights of Persons with
  Disabilities, 74, 76, 147
UN Framework Convention on Climate
  Change, 147
UN Security Council, 138, 140, 149, 156,
  221
UNCLOS (UN Convention on the Law of
  the Sea)
  declaration of competence requirements,
    80, 81
  dispute settlement provisions, 173
  EU participation, 68
  EU's use of *lex specialis* rule, 244
  International Tribunal (ITLOS), 154, 158
  openness to signature by international
    organizations, 70
  relationship to other treaties, 88
  voting rights, 156
UNGA (UN General Assembly)
  acceptance of the EU as a distinct legal
    actor, 20
  EU upgrade saga, 161–163
  EU's membership status, 149
  participation of IOs, 42–43
United Kingdom (UK)
  MOX *Plant* case, 173–175, 183
  withdrawal from the EU, *see* Brexit.
United States, 42, 137, 235
  approach to international law, 249
Usynin, M., 193

VCLT (Vienna Convention on the Law of
  Treaties)
  as applicable law regulating treaties to which
    the EU is a party, 64–65
  ILC's work, 61
  on capability of state representatives,
    98–100
  on *inter se* agreements, 86
  on the meaning of a treaty, 81
  relevance to the EU, 128
  state applicability, 64
VCLT-IO, 61
  applicability to treaties to which the EU is
    a party, 64–66
  customary international law and, 46–47
  entry into force of a treaty, 102
  flexibility provisions, 101
  manifest violation, definition, 116

VCLT-IO (cont.)
  prohibition on use of internal rules to justify
      non-compliance, 235
  relevance to the EU, 128
  reservations, 111
  scope, 66
  treaty making powers of IOs, 99
Verwey, D., 79, 128
voting, 144, 148, 150, 155–157, 158, 167

Waldock, Humphrey, 125
Walz v Clickair SA, **34**, 51
WCO (World Customs Organization), 146
Wessel, R. A., 126, 180
Western European Union, *see* WEU.
WEU (Western European Union), 124

Wightman, 52
Wood, Michael, 35
World Bank, 156
Wouters, J., 1, 107
WTO (World Trade Organization)
  as example of self-contained regime, 15
  budget contributions of members, 153
  Dispute Settlement Body, 159
  EU's membership status, 145
  international dispute settlement
      mechanism, 184–186
  UK's post-Brexit status, 93–94
  voting rights, 157

Yanukovych, Viktor, 59
Yugoslavia, 90

www.ingramcontent.com/pod-product-compliance
Ingram Content Group UK Ltd.
Pitfield, Milton Keynes, MK11 3LW, UK
UKHW020454010325
455719UK00016B/574